W9-AOS-737

Property of
FAMILY OF FAITH
LIBRARY

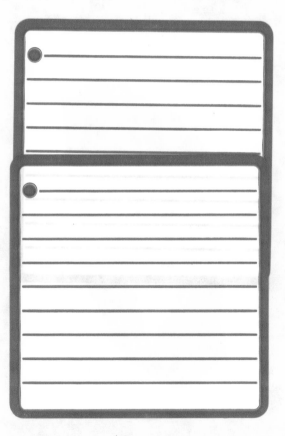

MANAGEMENT

Readings toward a General Theory

edited by William B. Wolf

University of Southern California

Wadsworth Publishing Company, Inc.

Belmont, California

To my wife

Second printing, April 1965

© 1964 by Wadsworth Publishing Company, Inc., Belmont, California. All rights reserved. No part of this book may be reproduced in any form, by mimeograph or any other means, without permission in writing from the publisher.

L.C. Cat. Card No.: 64–18695
Printed in the United States of America

CONTENTS

Family of Faith Library

Property of
FAMILY OF FAITH
LIBRARY

v

FOREWORD

This book was first undertaken in 1961. It has gone through a number of revisions, and I have done considerable soul-searching to establish what, if anything, would be its contribution. What you find here is the result of this effort. It has grown out of field tests with graduate students, discussions with colleagues, and serious analysis.

In essence, it consists of (1) readings that have had a significant effect upon my own intellectual development, and will, I believe, have similar impact on other students of administration; (2) articles that—when read alongside each other—illustrate an underlying philosophy: namely, that each organization tends to develop its own character, and that successful management usually involves making accommodations to adjust for the uniqueness of that individual character.

The student of management, then, must develop an awareness of both the common features and the unique features of organizations. Moreover, the teacher who develops or aspires to develop managers must either explicitly or implicitly provide a framework for the diagnosis of functioning organizations. As a result, the manager will be better able to see his role in the system, will have a perspective for seeing the areas of inherent conflict, and will be better able to adjust management techniques to the needs of his specific organization. At present, the bulk of management literature focuses upon the common aspects of organizations and virtually neglects the differences. But there are numerous signs that conditions are changing, and it is my hope that this book will help accelerate the rate of change.

I am convinced that the "correct" theory of management or principles of management must be developed along the lines of providing a useful framework or method of diagnosing organizations in terms of their specific needs. What I see as the evolving theory of management is primarily a methodology for viewing the functioning of complex organizations. Only in this way will the theory be sufficiently inclusive to encompass the multitude of variables involved in determining the how, what, why, where, when, and who of managing in a specific organizational setting.

In a sense, the theory of management which I see evolving is going through a metamorphosis similar to that which has occurred in the United States with respect to the theory of unionism. Until shortly after World War II, American labor economists were concerned primarily with local theories of unionism—conducting numerous debates, for example, on the validity of Selig Perlman's theory of unions. However, as labor economists broadened their observations to unions in other countries of the world, they began to focus upon unionism as it is related to industrial-relations systems. As a result, unionism and union practices became explainable in terms of cultural, political, social, and economic forces.

In a similar manner, the theory of management must develop. That is, management and organizations must be studied in terms of political, social, cultural, technological, and economic factors. It is the interaction of such factors that provides understanding of the modus operandi of managing in different organizational settings.

The general ideas underlying this book can probably be presented best in terms of the organization of the materials. The book is divided into three parts: Common Aspects of Organization, Differential Aspects of Organization, and An Approach to the Theory of Management.

Part One consists of three chapters. The first chapter deals primarily with the manager concept and what is to be expected from an adequate "theory of management." The main goals of the chapter are to remove some of the semantic confusion that is associated with the subject, and to dispel some of the false beliefs about theory as it applies to management.

Chapter 2 presents a number of perspectives for viewing organizations. The first selection, a simple description of the growth and development of a business firm, provides an introduction to much of what follows; experiments with both graduate and undergraduate students has proved that it is a useful device for introducing the subject. The next selection describes Max Weber's model of bureaucracy. Although Weber's model is primarily mechanistic, it is an excellent frame of reference for obtaining insights into some of the common features of organizations.

The third selection is a classic article by Philip Selznick, "Foundations of the Theory of Organization." It presents Selznick's conceptualization of the organization as an "adaptive social system" and introduces many useful concepts for the study of such systems. The next reading is Herbert Blumer's description of social movements. Blumer's article provides a framework for understanding much of the activity encountered in the large organization. In fact, his discussion of areas such as esprit de corps, formulation of ideology, and development of operating tactics suggests important guides to managerial action.

The fifth selection in Chapter 2 is taken from Herbert Simon's classic book *Administrative Behavior*. It provides an additional perspective for viewing the organization—namely, as a decision-making and decision-implementing system. His concern is with the process of decision making and the allocation of the decision-making function. In his analysis he sees the rationality of organization decisions as being the central concern of administrative theory. Thus, his approach leads to a consideration of free will, values, and the related forces which influence and control the decisions made within organizations.

The balance of Chapter 2 consists of readings that focus on general processes in organizations. The first of these is an article on leadership by Chester I. Barnard, an outstanding practitioner and theorist, whose thinking influenced many of the authors included in this collection: e.g., Herbert Simon, Philip Selznick, Melville Dalton, Robert Tannenbaum. This selection provides a thorough and practical analysis of leadership, and introduces a number of Barnard's ideas about organizations. It clears away much of the fiction that surrounds the subject of leadership and brings into focus the nature of leadership, its functions, and other relevant aspects of the topic.

The next selection is a general description of the communication process as it occurs in organizations. It provides a way of thinking about organizations that helps one understand the difficulty of maintaining coordination and control.

The final selection in Chapter 2, "Bureaupathology," is a chapter from *Modern Organization Theory* by Victor Thompson. "Bureaupathology" is a word coined by Thompson to describe organizational behavior "which is functional for less than the system as a whole." Whether or not such behavior is pathological is a moot point. It is encountered in almost all large organizations and thus can be considered as "normal," even though it may not directly contribute to the organization's effectiveness. Thus, in large organizations one is apt to encounter routinization, strong attachment to subgoals, impersonality, categorization, resistance to change, unwillingness to exercise initiative, and an exaggerated dependence upon regulations and quantitative standards. In this selection Thompson not only describes many of these tendencies; he also explains why they appear.

In summary, the selections in Chapter 2 present a number of complementary ways of viewing organizations in general. In contrast, the readings in Chapter 3 are much more concrete and tangible accounts of the dynamics of organizations. Thus, these selections put "meat and viscera" upon the skeleton of organization as it is developed in Chapter 2.

The first selection in Chapter 3, "Banana Time," by Donald Roy, is a very readable account of the behavior of a small work group. It illustrates the manner in which one group of workers functioned within a relatively large organization. In so doing, it illustrates Selznick's general observations about the behavior of workers in satisfying their personal needs and about the dynamics of informal organization. Similarly, the selection by Melville Dalton analyzes a case study of the conflict between line and staff departments in three industrial plants. The selection by Pfiffner and Sherwood illustrates the role of power and politics in the functioning organization. The selection by Edward Gross deals with a research study of the manner in which primary groups may reinforce formal bureaucracy. Finally, "Observation of a Business Decision," by Richard Cyert, Herbert Simon, and Donald Trow, describes a firm's decision on the use of electronic data processing.

Part Two, "Differential Aspects of Organization and Management," stresses aspects that are unique to specific organizations. It draws together a number of case studies and research reports which illustrate the differences in organizations. Moreover, it highlights the impact of a number of strategic forces as they interact to give each organization its unique character.

Part Three of the book, "An Approach to the Theory of Management," summarizes and integrates many of the ideas presented in the preceding sections. Its goal is to provide what may be thought of as a rudimentary theory of management.

In assembling a book of readings, the editor is always caught in the dilemma of winnowing through a vast body of literature and selecting the best. The selections included here are generally from the fields of sociology, social psychology, anthropology, and political science. However, some are taken from the more applied areas such as public administration and business administration.

This collection is designed primarily as a supplementary book of readings for courses in management or administration. It is not specifically limited to any one kind of administration, such as business administration or public administration. Rather, it is designed to provide general knowledge of administration and to suggest the kind of reasoning which underlies a general theory of management or administration. Thus, it will prove useful for courses in business administration, public administration, hospital administration, educational administration, and the like.

In compiling this book I have received stimulation and suggestions from numerous colleagues. In particular, I should like to thank Fred Massarik, University of California at Los Angeles; Jack London, University of California at Berkeley; and Dean Joseph McGuire, University of Kansas. In addition, I am deeply indebted to Daniel Coleman and the numerous other graduate students at the University of Southern California who have reviewed parts of these materials and offered helpful suggestions.

William B. Wolf

PART 1

COMMON ASPECTS OF ORGANIZATIONS

CHAPTER *1*

INTRODUCTION

For many years men have studied the "art" of managing. More recently there has been a growing intensity in the search for "the theory of management." Despite the general interest in this goal, there is considerable confusion as to what such a theory should do and what management actually is. In the words of Harold Koontz, there is a "management theory jungle." This book represents a direct attack upon that jungle. Hence, at the outset it is essential to explain what we expect from a theory of management, and what is encompassed by "the concept of the manager."

Management is usually related to "getting things done" and to "being practical." Among men of affairs there is a tendency to shy away from theory and to differentiate between theory and practice. In fact, a common cliché in the business world is "That is all right in theory, but not in practice." In all likelihood the manager's suspicion of theory is well founded. He expects guides to solve specific problems, and instead he is presented with principles that often are simply ambiguous or mutually contradictory proverbs.

Despite these criticisms, it does appear useful and meaningful to seek a general theory of management. However, we must at the outset recognize the limits of theory in the social sciences: a social-science theory is merely an abstraction from reality; it is never perfectly descriptive of total reality. It is simply a device for bringing together a multitude of facts so that one may comprehend them all at once. In so doing, it provides a framework for studying, predicting, and controlling the phenomena involved. Moreover, we need to recognize that theory, and the understanding that comes with it, does not necessarily build skill. An understanding of the theory of management does not necessarily make a man an excellent manager, any more than an understanding of the theory of internal-combustion engines would guarantee to make a man a skilled engineer. True, theory and the understanding that comes with it should help to develop skills. But theory without intensive experience can seldom develop skill.

The benefit derived from a theory of management can be recognized when we consider the alternatives available to the teacher and his students. If management is to be taught, the subject must have either an explicit or implicit theoretical base. As the distinguished French industrialist Henri Fayol once pointed out, "Without theory no teaching is possible."[1] Thus, we need a theory of management. Such a theory has to be "good"; that is, it should abstract from complex reality and help us organize our thinking and facilitate learning. It should give students a perspective, so that they will no longer be trapped by the complexity of the subject. The criticism that "they can't see the forest for the trees" will no longer apply. A good theory of management should not only help one see the forest and the trees; it should provide useful paths through the forest.

Beyond this, we need a theory of management that will be a guide to action. Such a theory is far from a realization; in fact, the quest for *the* theory of management may never be satisfied, any more than psychologists have established *the* theory of personality. However, we may begin by developing a framework that is useful in explaining managerial behavior, and which with considerable research and refinement may eventually be used as a guide to action.

---

[1] Henri Fayol, *General and Industrial Management* (London: Sir Isaac Pitman & Sons, Ltd., 1949), pp. 14–15.

THE MANAGER CONCEPT: A RATIONAL SYNTHESIS

*Robert Tannenbaum**

In order to treat a subject scientifically, we need a precise definition of the key words involved. What, then, do we mean by "management," and what does the concept of the manager encompass? A review of the literature points to a startling diversity of terms and definitions. It appears that each writer develops his own nomenclature. Fortunately for our purpose, Robert Tannenbaum of the University of California at Los Angeles has made a critical review of a large segment of the management literature and has synthesized the concept of the manager. In the process, he has reduced or eliminated much of the ambiguity surrounding the concept of the manager. Moreover, he alerts us to the kind of confusion which we are apt to encounter as we expand our readings about management.

The selection presented here consists of Tannenbaum's classification of the functions of managers. In the first part of his article (which is not included here) Tannenbaum has summarized the formulations of authorities such as E. F. L. Brech (*The Nature and Significance of Management*), Marshall Edward Dimock (*The Executive in Action*), and Chester I. Barnard (*The Functions of the Executive*).

On the basis of his analysis, Tannenbaum concludes: "It is possible to classify into five groups the various functions discussed by the writers."

Our reading starts with these five groups. It then proceeds to Tannenbaum's synthesis of the manager concept.

. . . It is possible to classify into five groups the various functions discussed by the writers. Each group is characterized by the fact that (a) the functions of which it is comprised are the same or similar but are assigned different names or (b) that the functions are different but are closely related or (c) that they overlap in content.

In the first group are "organization," "lay out the broad lines of administrative structure," and "develop and maintain a system of communication which jointly involves a scheme of organization and an executive personnel." In the second group are "initiation and approval of decisions," "planning," "formulate and define the purposes, objectives, ends, of the organization," "formulation and determination of policy," and "direction." In the third group are the terms "control," "supervision," and "appraisal." In the fourth group are "inspiration," "motivation," "leadership," and "promote the securing of personal services." And in the fifth

* Reprinted from *The Journal of Business*, 22, No. 4 (October 1949), 232–241, by permission of the University of Chicago Press. Copyright 1949 by The University of Chicago.

group are "trusteeship" and "representation." Finally, it should be noted that "co-ordination" appears as a function in many of the quotations.

This grouping of the functions of managers as presented by various writers provides a convenient basis for the development of a synthesis of the manager concept which is attempted in the following section.

THE FUNCTIONS OF MANAGERS: A SYNTHESIS

The functions of managers may now be listed and discussed in detail. No claim to complete originality is made for this presentation. It represents, for the most part, an effort logically to combine selected ideas of many writers into a meaningful and useful functional definition of the manager.

No special brief is held for the terminology chosen or for the particular grouping of activities used. The terms and groupings to be found in the presentation are those which seem to be most appropriate and useful to this study and which, in most instances, closely conform to general usage. Wherever exception is taken to earlier formulations or wherever new terminology or ideas are presented, such exceptions or novelties will be specifically indicated.

In speaking of the functions of managers, it is not intended to imply that each manager in an enterprise performs all the functions. Such is seldom, if ever, the case. Managers, like nonmanagers, are specialists. They typically specialize in specific functions or a specific function. The functions of managers are those performed exclusively by managers as a group.

It is the thesis of the present discussion that all managerial activities are included in three functions: organization, direction, and control. These are derived from the groupings presented at the conclusion of the preceding section and will now be discussed.

Organization

The term "organization" implies an arrangement in which all units are so related to each other that they may work as a whole, each unit having its proper task to perform;[1] and "to organize" means "to arrange or constitute in interdependent parts, each having a special function, act, office, or relation with respect to the whole."[2] These statements include two basic concepts, namely, units or parts each having its proper or special task to perform and an arrangement involving an interdependence or relationship between the units or parts. The managerial function of organization involves these two concepts. Managers must determine the degree and type of specialization to be effectuated within the enterprise and they must determine the relationships that are to exist among the specialized units.[3]

---

[1] Cf. "Order," *Webster's Dictionary of Synonyms* (Springfield, Mass.: G. & C. Merriam Co., 1942).

[2] "Organize," *Webster's New International Dictionary* (2d ed.; Springfield, Mass.: G. & C. Merriam Co., 1924).

[3] Organization as a managerial function has been defined variously by different writers. Some of the definitions include the two concepts presented above. Some in-

With respect to the degree and type of specialization, it should be recalled that one of the characteristics of the individuals, groups, and complexes comprising an enterprise is that they each contribute specialized services to the group or complex of which they are a part. The determination of these specializations involves analysis first and then synthesis.

The function of organization begins with the objective of the enterprise, i.e., with the good or service to be produced. It must be determined by analysis what services of individuals will be necessary to produce the good or service in question. This determination entails questions relating to both degree and type. How specialized should be the services to be contributed by each individual occupying a position, and what should be the type of these services? Both of these questions must be answered.[4] When they are, the process of synthesis can begin. First, the individuals contributing specialized services must be combined into groups. The nature of these groups is similarly determined by the degree and type of group specialization desired. Next, groups are combined into complexes and these into superior complexes, and so on until the supreme complex is achieved; and always the degree and type of specialization are the determinants of the nature of each of these units.[5]

The services contributed by the managers who comprise the managerial superstructure are also specialized, as has previously been indicated; and the determination of the degree and type of the specialization of these

clude only one, while others include concepts which the present writer would not include as a part of the function of organization. Some examples of these definitions follow: "Organization: the structure of (1) the responsibilities and duties by means of which the activities of the enterprise are distributed among the (executive and supervisory) personnel employed in its service; (2) the formal inter-relations established among the personnel by virtue of such duties" (Brech, *op. cit.*, p. 41). "The act of defining the responsibilities of the members of an enterprise and the relations between them" (Alvin Brown, *Organization* [New York: Hibbert Printing Co., 1945], p. 269; Brown defines "responsibility" as "the prescribed endeavor of an individual" [*ibid.*, p. 270]). "Organisation ... may be defined very simply as—'determining what activities are necessary to any purpose (or "plan") and arranging them in groups which may be assigned to individuals'" (L. Urwick, *The Elements of Administration* [New York: Harper & Bros., 1943], p. 36). "Organization ... refers to the means ordinarily employed by management in the analysis of activities involved in operation of the business enterprise and in the synthesis of these into a coordinated whole" (Mitchell, *op. cit.*, p. 70). "It [organization] means the authority relationships between the personnel employed in the enterprise, ..." and "organizing is the process of determining the kind and extent of the specialization to be employed in performing tasks" (Lewis C. Sorrell, *Transportation, Production and Marketing* [Chicago: Traffic Service Corp.; reprinted from *Traffic World*, issues of 1930 and 1931], p. 75).

[4] Ideally, these questions should be answered in the abstract, i.e., without reference to specific individuals and the services they are capable of supplying. Practically, it is often impossible to do this, both because no individual may be available capable of contributing the desired services and because adaptations must be made with reference to the services present members of the enterprise are capable of contributing. See Brown, *op. cit.*, pp. 9 f. The important point here is that emphasis should be on the positions in the enterprise structure rather than on specific individuals.

[5] In the literature on organization, the question of the type of group and complex specialization is frequently discussed under the heading of departmentation. The three most frequently mentioned types of specialization are territorial, commodity, and functional. For example, see Petersen and Plowman, *op. cit.*, chaps. viii and ix; and Sorrell, *op. cit.*, pp. 74–79.

services must be made by managers. Certain aspects of this determination lead to a consideration of the second concept involved in the managerial function of organization, namely, the determination of the relationships that are to exist among the specialized units in an enterprise.

The relationships established among the managers of an enterprise determine the relationships among the groups and complexes which they head. So it is upon the former relationships that attention must be focused. The managerial relationships are always expressed in terms of authority and responsibility, and they are established by delegation. Therefore, each of these three concepts must first be defined.

Authority is the right to command or to act.[6] Thus, a person having authority has the right not only to act himself but also to expect action of others. But what is the source of this right? In practice, authority appears to originate at the top of a structural hierarchy—under private enterprise, with the owners—and to flow from owners to their representatives, the managers, and from superior managers to their subordinates.[7] Hereafter in this presentation, authority, when viewed in this customary manner, will be referred to as formal authority.[8]

Responsibility involves being subject to another who may exact redress in case of default. Responsibility is answerability or accountability. One is typically responsible to another for the performance of tasks assigned to him by the latter.[9]

Delegation is the act of investing with formal authority to act for another. "Delegation always means the conferring of authority, and can never mean anything else."[10] A delegation of formal authority must always include a definition of the limits within which that authority may be exercised.

As has been indicated, the fountainhead of all formal authority in a private enterprise is the owners—in a corporation, the stockholders. The latter typically retain some formal authority but delegate most of it to their elected representatives, the board of directors.[11] The board, in turn, becomes responsible to the stockholders for exercising the delegated formal authority within the specified limits.[12] The board retains some formal authority and delegates the balance to the manager who heads the supreme complex. The delegation establishes the specialization for this manager, and

---

[6] Cf. Urwick, *op. cit.*, p. 42; Brown, *op. cit.*, p. 267; and Petersen and Plowman, *op. cit.*, pp. 62–69.

[7] See Mitchell, *op. cit.*, p. 77.

[8] In the second article in this series occasion will be taken to examine adequately the source of the ability to exercise effective authority.

[9] Cf. Urwick, *op. cit.*, p. 41; Petersen and Plowman, *op*, *cit.*, p. 69.

[10] Mooney and Reiley, *op. cit.*, p. 17. Cf. Brown, *op. cit.*, p. 268; Dimock, *op. cit.*, p. 174; Petersen and Plowman, *op. cit.*, p. 66.

[11] For example, the stockholders typically reserve to themselves the right markedly to change the character of the business or to abandon it and to make changes in the capital structure.

[12] The relationship indicated between the stockholders and the board is the one imposed by law and generally assumed in theory. But in the modern, large-scale corporation, in which there is often a significant separation between ownership and management (including the board), the relationship is often quite tenuous. See A. A. Berle and G. C. Means, *The Modern Corporation and Private Property* (New York:

he becomes responsible to the board within the limits of the delegation. This process continues downward through the managers of superior and subordinate complexes to the managers of groups. The latter delegate to the individuals comprising their groups formal authority to perform designated tasks, and the individuals become responsible for such performance. *These individuals are never delegated formal authority to command, nor are they able to delegate authority to others.*[13]

A manager who delegates formal authority to subordinates does not thereby escape responsibility to his superior for the exercise of the formal authority which the latter delegated to him. He is able to assume that responsibility by holding his own subordinates responsible for the formal authority which he has delegated to them.[14]

The formal authority which is delegated to subordinates may itself be specialized into the authority to prescribe and the authority to enforce. The former is authority to indicate how designated activities shall be performed, the latter is authority to see that the activities are performed;[15] some managers exercise both types of authority, others, only one type. Formal authority may also be centralized or decentralized. The more centralized the authority, the more it has been reserved for execution by managers at the higher levels in the managerial superstructure; the more decentralized the authority, the more it has been delegated to the managers at the lower levels in the managerial superstructure.[16]

The process of delegation establishes definite relationships between managers and therefore between the specialized groups and complexes which they head. These relationships are those of superior and subordinate. A subordinate is always responsible to a superior for the accomplishment of that for which he has been delegated formal authority. Formal authority is delegated downward through the managerial hierarchy; responsibility extends upward through the same hierarchy. The superior-subordinate interconnections are the channels of formal communication, both downward and upward, within an enterprise; and the managers are themselves the centers of communication.[17]

Direction

Once managers have determined the degree and type of specialization to be effectuated within the enterprise and the relationships that are to ex-

---

Macmillan Co., 1932); Marshall E. Dimock and Howard K. Hyde, *Bureaucracy and Trusteeship in Large Corporations* (Temporary National Economic Committee Monograph No. 11 [Washington, D.C.: U.S. Government Printing Office, 1940]); Gordon, *op. cit.*, chaps. ii and iii.

[13] See Mooney and Reiley, *op. cit.*, pp. 17 f. Cf. Urwick, *op. cit.*, pp. 47 and 64.

[14] Cf. Mooney and Reiley, *op. cit.*, p. 17: "The one to whom authority is delegated becomes responsible to the superior for doing the job, but the superior remains responsible for getting the job done." Cf. also Dimock, *op. cit.*, p. 177: "The executive is accountable to his superior for all the responsibility vested in him, but ... he may delegate a portion of it to a subordinate on the assumption that he never completely divests himself of it and that the subordinate is merely doing a job for him."

[15] See Mitchell, *op. cit.*, pp. 83–86.

[16] See Sorrell, *op. cit.*, pp. 82–84; Petersen and Plowman, *op. cit.*, pp. 282 ff.

[17] Cf. Barnard, *op. cit.*, pp. 217–19.

ist among the specialized units, they have provided themselves with a mechanism for the attainment of purpose.[18] They must next employ the mechanism. The first function of managers involving such employment is the function of direction. Direction is the use of formal authority in order to guide subordinates.[19] Direction involves the devising of the purposes of action and the methods or procedures to be followed in achieving them. The decisions to be made in connection with direction must answer the questions "what?" "how?" "when?" and "where?"

The devising of the purposes of action provides the "what-content" of direction. It has already been seen that the individuals comprising groups, the groups comprising complexes, and the subordinate complexes comprising superior complexes must in each case have an enterprise purpose, end, or objective. In addition, each individual, manager and non-manager, has a purpose to achieve in his own activity. Managers must formulate these purposes for their subordinates and order them put into effect.

The devising of purposes begins with the broad purpose or purposes of the enterprise. These are then translated into subpurposes for the superior complexes comprising the supreme complex. The subpurposes are further subdivided for the subordinate complexes, and so on down the structural hierarchy until each individual has his own purpose. These translations or subdivisions are made successively by managers, starting with those at the top of the hierarchy of the managerial superstructure (typically the board of directors) and moving down to those who head groups. As Holden, Fish, and Smith have said:

> First, there is the broad general objective for the company as a whole. . . . It is usually established by the board of directors, through approval of the objective proposed either by general management or originated by the board itself. . . .
>
> It is not enough to establish the general objective. As a matter of fact, that concerns mostly the first and second zones of management. To be really successful the co-operation of every person in the organization is needed. The general objective must therefore be translated into terms of each and every department. For example, the sales department's objective may be to sell a given volume at a price, and with a certain expense; that of the manufacturing department may be to produce the quantity and quality desired, at a given time and cost. These departmental objectives may in turn be broken down to divisions, locations, and individuals. The final test is to have every single person with his own particular objective, all being co-ordinated to produce successive cumulative results leading to the general objective for the company as a whole.[20]

The devising of methods or procedures to be followed in achieving

---

[18] Cf. Sheldon, *The Philosophy of Management*, p. 32.

[19] Cf. Petersen and Plowman, *op. cit.*, p. 171. No available term is adequate for the proper designation of this function. The term "direction" seems to be the most appropriate, although in usage "to direct" is often synonymous with "to conduct, manage, or control."

[20] *Op. cit.*, pp. 203 f. Cf. Barnard, *op. cit.*, pp. 192, 206, and 231 f.

purposes provides the "how-," "when-," and "where-content" of direction. Here, again, the broad and general decisions are made by managers at the top of the managerial hierarchy, and these decisions are made ever more specific by successive subordinates down through that hierarchy.

Directive decisions, once made, serve as a basis for the guidance of action. The vast majority of directive decisions are made to guide subordinates in actions which are repeated frequently. Relatively few such decisions are made to guide actions which are performed but once. In the case of any action frequently repeated, a tremendous burden would be placed on managers if a duplicate decision had to be made each time the action were to be repeated. To avoid this unnecessary duplication in decision-making, managers have developed numerous devices or tools to be used in providing guidance for repetitive action.[21] In practice these devices are variously referred to as "budgets," "policies," "procedures," "practices," "methods," "rules," "regulations," "routines," "schedules," "instructions," "specifications," "designs," etc.[22] The importance of these devices to managers cannot be overly stressed. Because they obviate the necessity for redeciding questions, they release for other purposes much valuable time which otherwise would have to be devoted to such redecision. These devices are also used by managers as criteria of action, since each of them implies a standard of performance to be attained. Serving as a guide to action and a criterion of action are simply two aspects of the same thing.

Control

The second function of managers involving the employment of the mechanism for the attainment of purpose (the organization) is the function of control. Control is the use of formal authority to assure, to the extent possible, the attainment of the purposes of action by the methods or procedures which have been devised. The execution of this function involves the selection and training of individuals, the provision of incentives, and the exercise of supervision.[23]

One aspect of the function of organization previously discussed is the determination by managers of the degree and type of specialization to be effectuated within an enterprise. In part, this determination results in

[21] Some of these devices are also used in providing guidance for nonrepetitive action.

[22] Some of these terms are by no means mutually exclusive from the point of view of definition. Furthermore, in practice they are often used to refer to different things. There is a crying need for standardized terminology here. The term "policy" provides an excellent example of this need. It has been used in so many ways that it is necessary for each user to define the term in order for it to have any precise meaning in the context in which it is used by him. See Chester I. Barnard, "Comments on the Job of an Executive," *Harvard Business Review*, XVIII, No. 3 (spring, 1940), 296.

[23] These components of the function of control (selection and training, incentives, and supervision) may appear at first glance to be unrelated activities. They do, to some extent, involve different managerial techniques. However, each is essential to the attainment of purpose by the methods or procedures which have been devised and is therefore logically classified under the function of control as defined.

specifications of the types of services which will be required of individuals. Managers must next match these specifications with individuals—managers and nonmanagers—able to contribute the desired types of services. Such individuals may be found either within or without the enterprise. If they are found, they may be selected to fill positions calling for the types of services they are able to contribute. If such individuals are not found, then other individuals, either from within or without the enterprise, with the capacity for contributing the desired services must be selected and then trained until their capacity becomes ability.

The task of matching individuals with specifications is not an easy one. An individual's ability to contribute the desired types of services is often closely related to such intangible personal factors as his character, personality, temperament, and the like; and when individuals work together in co-operative groups, these factors are important determinants of interpersonal compatibility. Since no completely adequate measures of these factors have as yet been devised, the selection of individuals requires the exercise of judgment on the part of the manager making the selection.

Now, each manager is responsible to his superior for the accomplishment of assigned tasks; and since the ability of a manager to meet such responsibility depends in part on the quality of his subordinates, and since the determination of that quality is based to a greater or less extent on the exercise of judgment, he must be able to select his own subordinates. In no other way can he reasonably be held for their performance.[24] The selection of subordinates is particularly crucial from the point of view of control when those subordinates are themselves managers.[25] This is true because the intangible personal factors play such an important role in their work.[26]

By selecting subordinates and training them when necessary, managers try to provide themselves with individuals able to contribute the types of services necessary for the attainment of purpose. Any single manager can reasonably be held responsible for such attainment only if he has been the one whose judgment has determined the ability of his subordinates.[27]

It is not enough that individuals be found who are able (or who can be trained to be able) to contribute desired services to the enterprise. They must also be willing to do so. Ability must be supplemented by strong motivation. Unlike the flow of services from a machine, that from an individual is subject to considerable variation in intensity through time

---

[24] Cf. Petersen and Plowman, *op. cit.*, p. 68.

[25] In this connection, Gordon reports: "In the writer's conversations with top executives, the latter have uniformly stressed the importance of the wise choice of chief subordinates as a significant element in effective business leadership" (*op. cit.*, p. 108).

[26] See Barnard, *The Functions of the Executive*, pp. 220–23.

[27] Many writers view selection as being a phase of the function of organization. To these writers, organization includes both structural and staffing considerations. A good case can be made for this point of view. I prefer, however, to include selection within the function of control. To me, the right to select subordinates—particularly managerial subordinates—is so essential to an assurance of the attainment of purpose that selection seems most properly classifiable as a phase of the managerial function of control.

depending upon the motivation of the individual; thus it becomes necessary not only to make individuals willing to contribute desired services but to regulate as far as possible the intensity of the flow of the services. Incentives must be provided for these purposes.

An incentive as here viewed is any device which is offered to induce an individual—manager or nonmanager—to contribute services at a desired intensity to an enterprise. The inducements which may be offered to motivate an individual are numerous. They include various material things; opportunities for distinction, prestige, personal power, and the like; desirable physical conditions of work; pride of workmanship, sense of adequacy; feelings of altruism, loyalty, etc.; social compatibility; customary working conditions and conformity to habitual practices and attitudes; opportunity for the feeling of participation in the course of events; solidarity or satisfaction of the gregarious instinct; and coercion.[28] The proper use of incentives by a manager is a method by which he may secure and regulate the service contributions of subordinates that are so essential to the attainment of the purpose for which he is responsible.

Individuals who are able and adequately motivated to contribute services may still, for many reasons, execute commands imperfectly. It will be recalled that directive decisions are often expressed in terms of criteria of action or standards of performance. The observation of performance, the comparison of it with the predetermined criteria or standards, and the taking of remedial steps where called for are essential if the purposes of action are to be attained by the methods or procedures which have been devised. These entail the exercise of supervision.[29] Supervision involves overseeing, inspection, the use of accounting and statistical devices, the use of reports, etc., for the purpose of determining the facts of performance; and it involves appraisal or evaluation for the purpose of comparing performance with standards. It is important to recognize that

[28] I have adapted this listing from Barnard, *The Functions of the Executive*, chap. xi. This chapter, titled "The Economy of Incentives," contains the best discussion of incentives which I have as yet encountered. See also *ibid.*, pp. 83–86 and 227–31.

[29] Many writers use the word "control" to stand for that which I designate by "supervision." Others follow the practice I do. Still others use the words "appraisal" or "evaluation." Here, as before, no available word is completely satisfactory to connote all that one would desire. The weakness of "supervision" is that it often implies work carried on by those near the bottom of the managerial hierarchy. Regardless of the word used, the ideas behind the words are usually similar; e.g., Brech: " 'Continuous control and supervision of the activities of the organisation' is nothing else than the obverse of planning. It is the task of seeing that the plans laid down are being currently and effectively carried out, or establishing good reasons for failures and departures" (*op. cit.*, p. 16). Fayol: "Control . . . he [Fayol] regarded as an aspect of Administration. He defined it as, 'Seeing that everything is being carried out in accordance with the plan which has been adopted, the orders which have been given, and the principles which have been laid down' " (Urwick, *op. cit.*, p. 105). Copeland: "After a plan is in operation, the executive has the task of checking up to learn whether it is being carried out in accordance with the policy formulated to meet the conditions and with the sequence and timing decided upon. This follow-through is the essence of executive control" (Melvin T. Copeland, "The Job of an Executive," *Harvard Business Review*, XVIII, No. 2 [winter, 1940], 158). For a use of "supervision" see Sorrell, *op. cit.*, p. 81. For a use of "evaluation" see Mitchell, *op. cit.*, p. 99. For uses of "appraisal" see Holden, Fish, and Smith, *op. cit.*, pp. 8 f., 15, 20 f., 77 f.

supervision is exercised not only by the managers of groups but by all managers who have subordinates, including the manager of the supreme complex and the board of directors.

The Managerial Technique of Command

Command is a managerial technique used in connection with the execution of all the functions of managers. A command is an order from a superior to a subordinate to do something. Through command, organizational, directive, and control decisions can be translated into action. Command, therefore, is (along with decision-making) probably one of the most important and pervasive of the managerial techniques.

Additional "Functions" Considered

In the classification of functions based on the formulations of other writers presented at the end of the preceding section, "trusteeship" and "representation" comprised the fifth group of functions. In the writer's opinion, the so-called "function of representation" is not one of those functions performed exclusively by managers, nor can it serve as a basis for differentiating managers from nonmanagers.

It is often pointed out that managers must represent the enterprise, or some portion thereof, in dealings with such external units as stockholders, consumers, suppliers of goods used by the enterprise, organized labor, competitors (either individually or in trade associations), government units, the general public, etc. Managers speak and act for the units they manage. They often enter into contracts with an external unit, acting as an agent of the enterprise of which they are a member. All of this is true, but it is also true, at times, of nonmanagers as well. The act of representation on the part of a nonmanager is never sufficient in practice to give him the status of a manager.

In this connection, it is important to note that all the services contributed by certain individuals to an enterprise are not necessarily managerial in character. Managers often reserve to themselves some nonmanagerial work to perform which they consider too important to delegate to someone else.[30] Much representation work performed by managers is of this character.

It was also noted at the end of the preceding section that many writers consider co-ordination to be a function of managers. Again the writer disagrees with such a point of view. Co-ordination and its relationship to management has earlier been discussed, and more will be said of this concept in the section to follow.

MANAGERS AND NONMANAGERS DIFFERENTIATED

At the outset of this article, it was indicated that primary concern would be with differentiating managerial services from nonmanagerial services and that this could best be accomplished by isolating those func-

[30] See Barnard, *The Functions of the Executive*, pp. 6 and 215 f.; and Sorrell, *op. cit.*, p. 80.

tions performed exclusively by managers. Such isolation has been attempted. Now the separate threads of this article can be drawn together and combined into meaningful conclusions.

It is the thesis of this study that managers are those who use formal authority to organize, direct, or control responsible subordinates (and therefore, indirectly, the groups or complexes which they may head) in order that all service contributions be co-ordinated in the attainment of an enterprise purpose.

Managers always stand in a relationship of formal authority over subordinates who, in turn, are responsible to their superior. Managers use formal authority in order to execute the functions of managers—organization, direction, and control. The objective of the execution of the functions is the co-ordination of service contributions in the attainment of an enterprise purpose. *An individual is not a manager, does not manage, unless he has and uses formal authority to organize, direct, or control responsible subordinates.*[31] *Unless he conforms to this specification, he is a nonmanager.*

It has previously been observed that when specialized services are being contributed toward the attainment of an enterprise purpose, co-ordination is essential. This co-ordination is supplied by managers through their execution of the functions of managers. As has been indicated, many writers consider co-ordination to be a function of managers. Co-ordination is not properly a function; it is something to be achieved. And it is achieved by adequate organization, direction, and control. *The services of managers (involving organization, direction, and control) are necessary to co-ordinate the specialized service-contributions of the units which they head in the attainment of an enterprise purpose. The services of managers are needed for no other reason.*[32]

From what has been said it can be seen that managers can be differentiated from nonmanagers.[33] Managers always have subordinates; nonmanagers never do. Nonmanagers may organize, direct, or control (in a sense) themselves or the material objects with which they work, but they never organize, direct, or control responsible subordinates.[34] Furthermore,

[31] In business enterprises individuals may be called managers who do not fit this specification. From our point of view, they are managers in name only. In determining who is a manager, one must look to functions performed and not to titles.

[32] Cf. Barnard, *The Functions of the Executive*, pp. 215–17.

[33] This statement is contrary to the opinion of some other writers. For example, Brown says: "*Management* has been very widely used in the literature of business to denote both the act of management and those who manage. As so used, it represents the concept of an upper tier of endeavor which can never be exactly defined. Because it cannot be defined, this treatise has concluded that, however useful the notion may be in treating of administration in general, it does not help in understanding organization. Those who 'manage' have responsibilities which differ from other responsibilities only in scope. Their acts are acts of administration differing only in scope from any act of administration. The authority which they exercise differs only in like manner. Indeed, the distinction between management and labor is a highly artificial one which probably has not helped our social economy" (*op. cit.*, p. 104, n. 1).

[34] Mary Parker Follett erred on this point: "Should planning that is done incidentally as it were be called managing? Is not responsibility always a part of manag-

it is important to see that managers as well as nonmanagers may be managed. All managers, except the one (or ones) who heads the supreme complex, are managed by their superiors. They, in turn, manage their subordinates. The crucial distinction to be made is between managers and nonmanagers—not between managers and the managed.[35]

One final point needs emphasis. The services of all individuals are essential if the purpose of the enterprise is to be attained. The distinction between managers and nonmanagers is based on differences in the types of specialized services contributed by the two groups and on no other criterion.

---

ing? Should anyone, strictly speaking, be said to manage unless he both plans and takes some responsibility for that planning? I should say that when men are allowed to use their own judgment in regard to the manner of executing orders, *and accept the responsibility involved in that,* they are managing" (Metcalf and Urwick [eds.], *op. cit.,* p. 88). See also *ibid.,* pp. 84 f., for similar statements.

[35] Many writers err on this point. For example, Petersen and Plowman refer to "that group of persons, who, by reason of rank or position, issues orders and is thereby distinguished from another group who puts them into effect" (*op. cit.,* p 39). Cf. Neil W. Chamberlain, *The Union Challenge to Management Control* (New York: Harper & Bros., 1948), p. 165.

2

THE GENERAL NATURE OF ORGANIZATIONS

According to our definition, "management" always occurs in the context of an organization. Without an organization, there can be no management. Thus, a prerequisite for the study of management is an understanding of the general nature of organizations. This chapter provides essential background material by presenting the general frameworks of outstanding organizational theorists.

THE NATURE OF ORGANIZATIONS
*William B. Wolf**

There are a number of ways of viewing organizations. Probably the easiest way to present some of them is to start with a relatively simple but complete description of one organization, and then to proceed to more sophisticated treatments of the subject. Accordingly, this reading has been selected to provide orientation and perspective by describing the growth and development of a fictional business organization.

THE GAITED ROCKING HORSE COMPANY

What is the general nature of an organization?[1] How can it be visualized as a functioning entity? Probably the easiest way to answer these and related questions is first to describe the growth and development of a specific enterprise. What follows is a concrete description. It is fictional but in a sense it is very real, for it represents a synthesis of observations made in approximately 100 different firms.

An Organization's Dynamics

Let us suppose that you decide to start a business. You want to be in business for yourself. Furthermore, let's suppose you decide to manufacture wooden rocking horses in your garage. You study production costs and sales prices, and discover that you can produce at a significant price advantage over other manufacturers. Hence, you withdraw $1,000 from your savings account, and buy some wood and some simple woodworking tools. Presto! You are in business.

As you attempt to merchandise your horses, you discover that it takes more than a price advantage to sell your product. You need something unique and distinctive. In studying this problem you get a sudden inspiration: Why not put a special gear arrangement in the horse so that it will change its rocking gait when spurred on by the rider? You design and produce a prototype of a gaited rocking horse.

The new product design proves worthwhile, sales pick up, and soon you have to hire five men to assist you. You know these men well—their capabilities, their aims and ambitions, and their family backgrounds. You have few problems in training them. All you have to do is demonstrate

* *The Management of Personnel* (Belmont, Calif.: Wadsworth Publishing Co., Inc., 1961), pp. 9–25. © 1961 by Wadsworth Publishing Company, Inc.

[1] The word *organization* has a variety of meanings. As used here it refers to the cooperative system brought about by organizing, directing, and controlling people, tools, and techniques. In this sense an organization is the *whole* or the *Gestalt* resulting from the interaction of its parts upon each other as well as upon it as a whole. Thus, what we define as an organization is analogous to a *field* as that term is used in physics.

what is wanted. Since you are working on the job alongside the men, there are few problems of communication. Furthermore, since you have worked on all the jobs yourself, you know the relative efficiency of each man. If a man consistently turns in low production, you fire him.

Rapid growth of business. Let us suppose that a chain of retail stores has been induced to carry the gaited rocking horse. Sales volume increases tremendously, and you move to a larger building. Your work force increases to 75 employees. At this stage, you can't find enough hours in the day to handle your business. You are on the road servicing customers and pushing the line. In addition, you are trying to schedule production, purchase materials, engineer changes, and handle personnel relations.

Furthermore, although you are making more money than you had ever expected, you find yourself extremely hard pressed for cash. Why? Because you are not paid in advance for your sales, and you must pay your workers and supplier promptly on receipt of their services. For the present, most of your money is tied up in work in process or horses that have already been shipped out. In order to conserve working capital you initiate a drive. You put pressure on the workers to increase their rates of output, and you attempt to get suppliers to carry you for 60 to 90 days. However, letting accounts-payable liabilities accumulate is so costly that you are forced to abandon the idea. You discover that most suppliers offer a 2 per cent discount for accounts paid within ten days. If you don't take advantage of such discounts, you are actually paying so high an interest rate that borrowing at any reasonable rate of interest would be better.

In order to maintain control of your operations, you hire an assistant to take over some of the responsibilities for production. He tackles his job eagerly. He points out that you have never set up a cost-control system, that you need a formal inspection system, that a production-control unit should be set up, and that layout and production methods should be re-engineered. You tend to resent your new assistant's suggestions, but you know he is right. Your organization has "grown like Topsy." You have been so busy with the major problems that you just couldn't take care of everything.

In short, the business is suffering from a bad case of growing pains. You find yourself in the paradoxical situation of being pressed for more and more capital the faster your business grows—and the business is continuing to grow. The gaited rocking horse has become increasingly popular, and orders are pouring in from all over the country. The more business you do, the more desperate is your need for working capital.

You go to your local banker to arrange for a commercial loan at around 6 per cent interest. He is sympathetic and understanding, but he still steadfastly refuses to offer more than a three-month loan. He points out that your bank balance has always been close to zero and that, although your future looks promising, he has numerous other independent businessmen with just as bright prospects. Statistics show that a large number of them are destined to fail. As a banker he cannot risk his depositors' funds. It is quite obvious that a three-month loan would be of little help. You won't have any more cash in three months than you have now.

Establishment of corporation. Your banker suggests that you might solve your capital problem by taking in a partner or by incorporating and selling stock. The possibility of taking in your wife's brother as a partner seems worth considering. He is willing to put up $36,000 in cash for one-third interest in the business. In addition, he is willing and able to take over the responsibilities of the production manager. This would lighten your work load.

As you weigh the idea, however, certain disadvantages become apparent to you. Each partner is liable without limit for all debts contracted by the partnership; thus, each partner's personal fortune may be in jeopardy if the business fails. Furthermore, each partner has rather broad powers to act as an agent to commit the whole partnership. Another disadvantage is that the partnership can be dissolved when either partner finds the existing arrangement unsatisfactory. Unless the partners agree to the sale of a share of the partnership, dissolution would involve liquidation of the assets of the partnership.

Thus, although the formation of a partnership with your brother-in-law might solve your capital problem, you see in it certain disadvantages that tend to discourage such an arrangement. Besides, you really aren't certain that you can get along with your brother-in-law anyway. Therefore, you decide to form a corporation; and for a small fee you have your lawyer draw up the necessary papers of incorporation.

You decide to issue 20,000 shares of stock. At first you consider selling 10,000 shares to outside interests. You go to a local investment-banking firm—they merchandise securities. Like any merchant, they get their profit from the difference between their buying price and their selling price. In your case they attempt to drive a hard bargain. They offer you $10 a share and plan to resell at $13.50 per share. Because of your newness and small size they feel that the marketing of your stock may be costly. Rather than sell your stock through this medium, you decide to maintain a *closed corporation*. You raise capital by selling stock to select friends and relatives. Your efforts prove successful, and the immediate need for working capital is mitigated.

Changes in organization. Let us see what has been happening to your manufacturing plant in the meantime. The original garage shop has grown. You now have a single-story concrete block building, previously owned by a furniture company that had gone bankrupt in the 1958 recession. The urgent need for space and the costliness of available alternatives made the purchase of the plant too good a bargain to pass up. In addition, the down payment was small, and the difference between the down payment and the purchase price was secured by a mortgage loan on the property.

Your assistant is running the plant. He is gallantly attempting to cut costs and maintain production. The shortage of working capital has cast its shadow over the entire manufacturing operation. Where possible, units are manufactured after orders are received. Few items are carried in inventory. Even repair parts are manufactured to order. Raw materials are purchased on a hand-to-mouth basis. Considerable flexibility is maintained in the manufacturing process. Most of all, the machines used are general-purpose woodworking equipment. When the Christmas rush begins, most of the cutting and turning of wood is subcontracted, so that the plant's major activities are assembling, painting, and packaging.

Some interesting changes in the organization of the plant have occurred. Finding it necessary to divide your organization, you have set up a sales division and a manufacturing division. Under manufacturing there is a plant service unit that handles shipping, receiving, storage, and internal transportation; a plant engineering and maintenance unit; a purchasing unit; the production departments; and an office unit that handles internal accounting controls and services such as stenography, duplicating, filing, mailing, control of records and reports, processing of accounts payable and accounts receivable. Each of these units has its respective supervisors.

The procedure for getting things done has changed. In the past you were the only supervisor. You had daily contact with your employees. You established policies, assigned jobs, and followed up to ensure control, direction, and coordination. Now you find yourself dealing with a more complicated organization. Each unit seems to have developed interests within itself; yet, unless all parts of your organization function together as a coordinated whole, you are in trouble. For example, the purchasing agent slipped up in the buying of gear mechanisms; consequently, shipments were held up for two weeks while a local machine shop tooled up and ran the required part. Not only was capital tied up for a long period, but you were forced to bear the cost of idle personnel and idle equipment. For reasons you don't fully understand, the plant never seems to run smoothly. Machinery breaks down, workers quit, defective parts are manufactured, and there is grumbling and dissatisfaction on the part of personnel. You put pressure on the foremen but they claim they are helpless.

What's more, you are suddenly shocked by the fact that your workers have petitioned for a National Labor Relations Board (NLRB) election to certify an industrial union as their bargaining agent. You talk to some of the old-timers to ascertain the extent to which the union represents the workers. Some of them say they think that 30 to 40 per cent of the men have signed with the union; one tells you that at least 90 per cent have signed. When you ask why the men would take this action, you get nothing but vague statements.

At first the fact that a union is making progress in representing your workers seems a personal affront. You have always tried to deal fairly with the workers, and to look after their interests where possible. When Bob Graham was laid up in an auto accident, you personally covered his hospital bills. Then there was the time that Bill Smith's wife was seriously ill; you loaned Smith $500 to help him through the crisis. At Christmas time you give each employee a turkey and hold a gala party. Your wages are comparable to those for similar work in the area. You are hurt by the lack of gratitude. If the boys had only come in and told you what was bothering them, you would have tried to settle the problem. Instead they turned to an outsider—a union organizer. Or perhaps, you think, the boys have been sold a bill of goods by the union.

Whatever the reasons for the union's presence, you must face up to the fact that it is there. According to the law, it is an "unfair labor practice" for you to interfere with the organization of the union. You may, however, express your opinion on the issue as long as it doesn't interfere with the freedom of choice of your workers. A check of the existing labor law indicates that once the union is certified as bargaining agent, you must bargain with it in good faith. "Good faith" is a nebulous concept. The interpretations of the NLRB indicate that it involves a willingness to discuss matters related to wages, employment, and working conditions, plus a willingness to put your agreements into writing.

The union wins the representation election by a substantial majority. It demands higher wages, increased vacation pay, an insurance plan, paid holidays, and a seniority system to cover transfers, layoffs, promotions, and rehiring. The union paper directs its attack at you. You're accused of stalling in negotiation, of trying to bribe, confuse, and mislead. From here on, it seems as though you can't do anything correctly. If you offer concessions you are denounced for trickery; if you get tough and fight back you only seem to prove the union's accusations. Your assistant and one of the foremen suggest that the "air should be cleared"; the union must know that the company means business. They decide to fire one of the shop stewards for violating shop rules. It is an open and shut case, since the man was caught in the act and there were numerous witnesses. However, within fifteen minutes the entire department is shut down and there is a good chance that the entire plant will be struck. The situation is saved only by your allowing the man to return to work pending arbitration of the case.

You recognize that you are spending more and more time plugging gaps. In the meantime, the efficiency of the plant continues to drop, and production only limps along. You should be concentrating on sales and market expansion, and you aren't getting anywhere. You need help—but where can you find it?

Changes in leadership. At this point, one of the nation's largest manufacturers of toys approaches you about buying the company. They are willing to pay $100,000 in cash and to give you 10,000 shares of stock in their company. This means that your proceeds from the sale will be taxed at the capital-gains rate. You will have a handsome sum of cash! The offer is too good to pass up. You sell.

What happens to the Gaited Rocking Horse Company? Its nature changes. Before, it was a one-plant company; and you, as the owner and president, were known to all in the firm. Now it is just a relatively small part of a larger firm. The manufacturing plant is one of twenty. Furthermore, the man running the Gaited Rocking Horse business is one of the executives from the purchasing company. Your former employees don't like him. He is from New York City and somehow he is informally dubbed the "city slicker." In checking to find out why the new boss is disliked, you run into a confusing array of statements: "He snoops around the plant"; "He isn't interested in anything but costs"; "He is trying to make a name for himself"; and so forth.

When you try to get facts to support these remarks, you see that to a considerable extent the new boss is a victim of his environment; that is, he is operating under a number of pressures and is subjected to a body of controls that limit his freedom to act. His supervisors have told him that production costs can and should be reduced; therefore, one of his immediate goals is to cut costs. However, he really doesn't understand the social organization of your firm. Thus, in his efforts to achieve his goal he ignores long-standing traditions and upsets established patterns of getting things done.

The workers are suspicious of the new boss. They don't know him, and rumors begin to spread about his lack of sincerity in dealing with the men in the plant. Many of the old-timers begin to worry about "what the boss expects." Their anxiety is heightened when they see that he is not doing some of the things you used to do when you ran the company. Thus, when the new boss fails to hold the Tuesday-morning supervisors' meetings that you had always held, the supervisors begin to wonder. They had come to expect the top man to consult with them on the more important details of the business. Now that this isn't being done, their pride is hurt and they are concerned about the shape of things to come.

Since the supervisors don't know where they stand, they attempt to feel out the new man. They tend to analyze his every action, and frequently they attach deep meaning to his slightest activity. Furthermore, they try to avoid exposing any details of their operations that may be misinterpreted, or otherwise jeopardizing their own positions. All of this goes on below the surface, and tangible evidence of its existence is slight. However, the new boss senses an atmosphere of "tacit resistance" in his organization. He realizes that he doesn't know enough about the details of the plant, and he finds that he doesn't get essential information from his subordinates. Yet he can't discipline the men without more tangible evidence of insubordination. What can he do?

In this case he does several things. First, he asks for a number of written reports on production schedules, output per day, scrap, and so forth. These reports contain much of the information that he has found difficult to get through informal means. Moreover, if a foreman fails to fill out such reports, it becomes a tangible case of insubordination and supplies grounds for disciplinary action.

Of course, the foremen don't like this. They complain that they spend most of their time as clerks; they don't have a chance to be supervisors; the reports are apt to be misleading; and so forth. What really bothers them is that the increased reliance on formal reports and rules and regulations has resulted in more of an impersonal bureaucracy. The foreman has lost his discretion in handling daily incidents. Moreover, his reports provide data that can be misleading. For example, in one department both of the skilled assemblers were absent on the same day. The foreman thought it was better to build up a backlog of work in process rather than try to break in green hands on the assembly job. Naturally, the production report showed that not one unit was assembled that day. Two days later the foreman received a note to the effect that daily output had dropped significantly and the situation should be corrected. There was no chance to explain.[2]

Technical Aspects of the Plant

This is a good place to become more objective about the Gaited Rocking Horse business. In order to understand what has been happening and why certain problems exist, let us assume that a group of students is being taken on a tour of the plant. They would be amazed at the intricacies involved in producing a simple product such as the gaited horse. The tour would start at the receiving docks, proceed through the production departments, and finally end up in the shipping department. If the students were given the de luxe tour, they would probably be awed by the amount of paper work that is essential to coordinated manufacturing: sales forecasts, purchase orders, inventory records, operation sheets, inspection reports, production schedules, parts lists, receiving reports, invoices, accounts-payable records, and so forth. The better students might leave with a fairly good understanding of the technical aspects of the manufacturing process: machines, routing, clerical records, division of labor, and the like. However, they probably would not understand another, equally important aspect of the plant—namely, its social organization.

Social Aspects of the Plant

Everyone is to some extent aware of the social organization of a plant, but few understand its dynamics. For example, during their tour the students would probably notice that in certain sections of the plant the workers were talking and joking in a relaxed manner. In other areas they might notice a certain tenseness—everyone pretending to be busy. In any event, they would observe some interactions among the people.

Supervisory hierarchy. The students would probably recognize the structure of the company's supervisory hierarchy: the president at the top; next in rank, the production manager; then the foremen; and at the bottom, the workers. In the study of personnel management, it is particularly important to understand that, to a large extent, a person's position in this hierarchy determines his behavior, his relationships with others, and his point of view about events occurring in the plant.

Plant mores. In addition to this formal social structure, there is a dynamic and complex pattern of relations which the people in the organization have worked out for themselves. Common interests, feelings of kinship, and mutuality of respect grow out of the interactions of the workers. Over a period of time there develop in the plant certain mores and patterns of behavior. These in effect constitute the plant's own society. The society of the plant reflects the broader society in which we live, but at the same

---

[2] This description represents incidents that tend to occur in many organizations. Unfortunately, the full impact of mergers and changes in leadership has not, to this writer's knowledge, received much attention. One excellent descriptive study has been made, however, by Alvin W. Gouldner in his book *Patterns of Industrial Bureaucracy* (Glencoe, Ill.: The Free Press, 1954).

time it has its unique features. The workers have developed special patterns of interaction.

Impact of the boss. If the students observed closely the actions of the men in the plant, they would probably notice also that the image of the president of the company is reflected throughout the organization—in the attitudes of the men, their hobbies, and their personalities. This pattern is more than an accident. Almost every organization tends to be the shadow of one man or several men. In this company, the president tends to be a dominating force because he selects key people. Moreover, he passes on promotions, demotions, and transfers. Thus, the key persons in the organization depend upon the president's approval for their success and advancement. They are under economic and social pressure to adjust to his tastes.

Status systems. While touring the plant, the students would probably also notice signs of status systems. As in every society, the plant's society includes a number of symbols, representing an individual's rank, duties, rights, privileges, and obligations in the organization. Many symbols of status stem directly from the supervisory hierarchy. For example, the titles of jobs indicate the status of the men holding them: the president outranks the plant manager, the plant manager outranks the foremen, the foremen outrank the workers. Moreover, within each job group numerous symbols of status exist. Many of these symbols are obvious; others are subtle. Thus, at the foreman level the students might notice the following symbols of status: size and location of the office, nature of the work supervised, number of people supervised, and so forth. At the worker level, symbols of status include the clothes worn, the position of a desk or workbench, the machine operated, and the like.

Some of the more inquisitive students might question the significance of these status systems. Why not abolish the symbols of status? How do they contribute to efficient production?

One reason for the existence of status systems should be obvious. The first step in creating an organization is to establish the nucleus of a status system: a formal organization, with an established supervisory hierarchy, is set up. Such a hierarchy is essential. Unless the supervisor-subordinate relationships are clearly set forth, confusion and chaos will reign. Everyone might give orders and no one would follow them.

In addition to meeting the needs of the organization, status systems serve to satisfy the needs of individuals. Each individual tends to consider himself as the center of the universe. He has personal motivations for developing and securing his position in the social environment of the plant. The needs of individuals vary; one man's feast may be another's famine. But common to most is the psychological satisfaction of being respected and accepted by the work group. A conflicting need, which also is manifested in varying degrees, is the need to excel. Systems of status provide the emoluments that satisfy such needs. Superiority, acceptance, and importance are identified through the status systems. For example, Bill Black is one of the senior workers in the Gaited Rocking Horse Company. He has worked hard and exhibited an ability to get jobs done. Among the status symbols that he has acquired—although he has not been promoted to foreman rank—are use of the company car, and job assignments outside the plant to investigate suppliers. He has also a special work area in the northeast corner of the building. He is frequently asked to work with product development on making prototype models. He calls all the foremen by their first names. He has a special parking place in the company parking lot. He is called upon to help remedy bottlenecks in the production line. Many of the workers seek his advice on problems connected with the work.

Thus, status systems are needed to help ensure coordination of the activities of the various parts of the enterprise (although, in some instances, they may have the opposite effect).[3] Furthermore, symbols of status serve as part of the systems of reward and punishment that are used to motivate individuals within the organization.

Summary

The Gaited Rocking Horse case is an oversimplification. However, it provides a feel for some of the aspects of a business firm. Probably most important, it illustrates the dynamic nature of an organization—its tendency to grow and develop. In a sense, one can perceive different stages of growth—that is, there appear to be periods of infancy, adolescence, and maturity in the life of a relatively permanent organization. However, there is no set timetable for predicting when a specific organization will develop to a certain stage.

Furthermore, a functioning organization is a social system. The nature of this system is determined by numerous causal forces operating inside and outside the organization. For instance, working capital can be a crucial factor in governing the manner in which a business firm operates, as can other variables such as size or the division of labor. These and related factors will be discussed subsequently. Moreover, in the discussion to follow, the Gaited Rocking Horse Company will be used as a point of reference for illustrating other aspects of organizations.

COMMON FEATURES OF ORGANIZATIONS

Almost all relatively permanent organizations have a number of features in common—certain general similarities involving objectives, structure, and functions. What follows is a brief discussion of these common features.

Objectives

An organization is more than a group or a crowd of people. For an organization to exist, there must be a central goal or goals. Thus, all organizations consist of a number of persons brought together to participate in a common effort. In the Gaited Rocking Horse Company, the primary goal of the group is the production of rocking horses at a profit.

[3] Cf. Chester I. Barnard, "Functions and Pathology of Status Systems in Formal Organizations," in *Organization and Management* (Cambridge, Mass.: Harvard University Press, 1948), pp. 207–244.

Structure

A second feature common to almost all organizations is the fact that they have a structure with formal and informal aspects. To visualize the nature of this structure, one should first note that organizations are composed of men and physical and social factors which combined form a co-operative system. These cooperative systems may vary in complexity and size. Usually they consist of a number of groups existing within a larger group. Thus, the Gaited Rocking Horse Company itself is divided into a number of subgroups. Each such group is in itself an organization. For example, the purchasing department is an organization of five people; at the same time, as part of the manufacturing division, it is a part of a larger organization. The point to be emphasized is that most organizations are not isolated, independent units. Instead, they are intimately bound or entwined through cause-and-effect relationships with the broader scope of events and happenings.

Often the interrelationships within an organization are highlighted by the process of specialization and division of labor. Almost all large organizations apply the concept that certain groups or individuals should have specialized functions. Thus, in the Gaited Rocking Horse Company there developed a specialized division dealing with sales and another division dealing with manufacturing. Within the manufacturing division there is further specialization in the processes performed: some departments cut and prepare wood, others assemble gear boxes, and so forth.

Formal structure. Closely related to specialization and division of labor is the fact that almost all organizations have a formal structure; i.e., an explicitly stated arrangement of men and machines. In the main, this arrangement is consciously planned. The purpose of the formal structure is to ensure the orderly and efficient functioning of the organization. Frequently this structure appears on paper as an *organization chart*, which delineates the primary areas of authority and responsibility by showing who reports to whom and what tasks fall under each position. In many organizations the organization chart is supplemented by detailed written descriptions of the jobs.

The need for a formal organization can be readily appreciated by reviewing the experience of the Gaited Rocking Horse Company. As the business grew, it became humanly impossible for one man to carry the burden of managing. It was necessary to divide the work. Thus, at one time the Gaited Rocking Horse Company had the following organization. At the top were the president and the chairman of the board of directors. The work of the company was carried on by two divisions reporting directly to the president—the manufacturing division and the sales division. Under the manufacturing division were a number of departments—personnel, purchasing, engineering, accounting, woodworking, drilling, painting, assembling, and plant services. Under the sales division were sales managers covering different types of distribution—e.g., department-store sales, hardware sales, specialty-house sales, and foreign sales.

This brings into focus one particularly important characteristic of formal organizations: that is, the relationships between the departments may be established in a variety of different ways. Some of the departments are known as *line departments*—the departments that are engaged in transforming raw materials into the finished product. In the Gaited Rocking Horse Company, the line departments are referred to as the "manufacturing departments" (the departments responsible for such tasks as sawing, drilling, assembling, and painting horses). In line departments, channels of communication are formally established so that information flows from one level of supervision to the next. For example, in the line organization the president may decide that production for the next month should be doubled. He tells his decision to the vice-president in charge of manufacturing, who in turn tells it to the foremen, who in turn tell it to their leadmen, who pass it on to the workers. The orders literally pass down the line of authority.

A second type of department is the *staff department*. Staff departments are in a sense supplementary to the main functions of a business (i.e., the manufacture and distribution of a product). For example, a personnel department was established in the Gaited Rocking Horse Company when it became too large for one man to do his own hiring. This department is primarily an advisory staff department. It advises line supervisors about ways of dealing with personnel problems, and it performs a number of services for the line such as recruiting, screening, and indoctrinating new employees. Frequently, it may provide numerous other services: organizing social activities for the employees, publishing the plant newspaper, supervising the first-aid station, and so forth. In short, the personnel department has no power to give orders to line supervisors—it simply suggests, advises, educates, and performs helpful services.

Another type of staff department that was established in the Gaited Rocking Horse Company is the inspection department. This department was set up to minimize antagonism between line departments, which were always squabbling as to who was responsible for defective parts. The inspection department was set up as a scapegoat and a control department. Its job is simply to inspect and to inform all concerned parties of the number and causes of rejections. The department has no authority over line departments.

With respect to staff departments, it is helpful to distinguish between *advice* and *service*. Services are concerned with activities that are needed directly by the line. They involve more than advice. Advice can be taken or ignored, whereas services frequently have to be maintained if the line is to function. Examples of services are scheduling production, repairing machines, and shipping finished goods.

The difference between line and staff departments is frequently difficult to establish. In a general sense, one can think of line departments as those that are directly concerned with getting the work out. Thus, in a restaurant the line organization deals with the flow of work from the kitchen to the customer. In a retail store it is usually considered to be the selling activities. In contrast, staff departments are auxiliary to the line organization. They simply advise, educate, inspect, or render service; they do not give orders to the line, nor do they have direct authority or responsibility over the line.

Informal structure. Almost all organizations also contain informal groups and procedures that are not specified or consciously established in the formal arrangement of jobs and men. These informal organizations[4] develop spontaneously as the people in the organization interact (i.e., associate) with one another. Although these relationships and codes of conduct are not as readily perceived as the formal organization, they are also of significance.

If one looked closely at any department of the Gaited Rocking Horse Company, he would be certain to perceive an informal structure. It develops in every persistent group. For example, in the assembly department a number of such relationships and behavior patterns have evolved. The assembly department is the one that "puts the horse together." Into it flow a mass of semiprocessed parts—rockers, gears, bodies for horses, legs, tails, heads, screws, bolts, and other parts that will make up the complete gaited rocking horse. The organization of the work in this department is, in certain respects, unique. Under an arrangement called a *unit system*, the department is organized into a number of three-man teams. Each team assembles a complete unit. It does all the work involved in assembling horses. In the busy season there are between eight and ten teams working. During the slack period the number of teams is reduced.

What type of informal organization exists in the assembly department? Within each team of assemblers, one can perceive some interesting relationships. First of all, *each group seems to have its own leader.* The leader has been selected informally by the workers. (Management considers all assemblers to be of the same rank and pays them equally.) Frequently, but not always, the team leader is one of the older men who has had long service with the company. The reasons for a group's choice of leader are too complex to cover in detail here. However, a feeling for what happens may be obtained by looking closely at one unit.

An analysis of Team A reveals that Gene Neuman is its leader. Gene is older and has greater seniority than the other two men in the group. Furthermore, he is an officer in the local union and is extremely active in civic affairs. Next in rank in the team is Dave Johnson. Dave is slightly younger than Gene, and he started to work six months after Gene. Gene and Dave are close friends. They ride together to and from work, they live in the same community, their wives and children are close friends, and they have numerous social contacts with each other. The third man on this team is Max Polotnick. Max works hard and contributes his share to the team's output. He gets along with Gene and Dave, but a lack of common interests and a difference in cultural backgrounds tend to limit

---

[4] The term "informal organization" is apt to be misleading. It is used here because it is accepted by most writers on the subject. The reader, however, should be warned that it is meaningless to think of an operating organization as having two distinct and separate structures (i.e., a formal and an informal). Actually the formal and informal structures are intimately related—and knowledge of the one is relatively useless unless it is studied in relation to the other and in relation to the whole of which they are part.

his discussions with them to matters that develop on the job. Max is a Polish refugee. Most of his ties are with a small group living in the Polish section of town.

In short, a number of factors contribute to the relationships between the men on any one team. Some of the more obvious factors are age, seniority, ability, ethnic background, off-the-job activities, and education.

If the department as a whole is studied, the workers' tendencies to rank the various teams will be noticed. Some teams are considered better than others. Thus, the workers look forward to being on Team A or B but not Team C. However, it is difficult to use the teams alone as a basis for understanding the social organization of the department; for numerous overlapping cliques and friendship groups exist among members of different teams. The role and relative rank of each worker tend to depend upon the setting in which his behavior occurs. As different combinations of men are brought together under differing pressures, their behavior changes.

Other aspects of the informal organization of the assembly department are perceived in the manner in which the men talk and what they talk about. Where relationships are impersonal, the men's language tends to be restrained. Where ties are close, there is surprising frankness and forcefulness of expression. For example, one of the workers failed to shut off a machine as he had been instructed by his leadman. The leadman yelled, "What the hell's wrong?" The worker replied, "Take it easy, buddy." In contrast, when Winsor, the foreman, felt ready to blow his top, he stated that he usually "cooled off by taking a walk." After he was more in control of himself, he "would reason it out with the men."

Another interesting feature of the informal aspect of the organization is the picturesque speech used by the men to describe their work environment. Terms have been coined to suit the jobs: the gear mechanism is the "jump box"; the big boss is "Smilie"; the rush season is the "stampede." Thus, in shoptalk one might hear: "Last November Smilie blew a gasket. The stampede was on and we didn't have a jump box in the shop."

One way to illustrate informal aspects of the department is to follow the experience encountered by a person taking a job—for instance, as an assembler in the Gaited Rocking Horse Company. The new man will immediately learn that mastery of the technical skills is only a small part of his job. He also has to learn the language of the shop, the informal status system, the ways of doing things, and the code of acceptable conduct. The first few days will be a feeling-out period. His fellow workers will be sizing him up and educating him to the facts of life—"the ropes"—in the department. Probably one thing that will be impressed upon him is that he shouldn't "kill the job." He shouldn't produce too much. Later on, he will recognize that there is a tacit agreement among the workers as to what constitutes a "fair day's work." Anybody violating this level of productivity is condemned as a *rate buster*.[5]

[5] For an interesting descriptive report on *rate busters*, see Orvis Collins, Melville Dalton, and Donald Roy, "Restriction of Output and Social Cleavage in Industry," *Applied Anthropology*, 5, No 3 (Summer 1946), 1–14; Melville Dalton, "The Industrial Rate Buster: A Characterization," *Applied Anthropology*, 7, No. 1 (Winter

Also during this "feeling-out period," the "gang" will probably put the new employee to the test. Frequently work groups have an initiation ceremony that rivals the hazing in college fraternities. For example, the new man may be asked to find a left-handed monkey wrench. If he doesn't bite on that, a dozen other practical jokes may be devised to impress him with his lack of knowledge and to reveal his attitudes. Before he is one of the group, he will have to learn to observe the mores (the customs) of the shop. This code of behavior generally includes the following dicta:

> You should screen or otherwise censor the things you tell your supervisor so as to protect your fellow workers; that is, in shoptalk, you shouldn't be a "squealer."
>
> You shouldn't be a "rate buster."
>
> You should assume a role consistent with the job you hold. This means that you should dress like your fellow workers—not like the supervisors; you should associate with workers at your level in the plant's hierarchy—not supervisors; you should use the group's jargon; and so forth.
>
> You should learn to recognize and respect the symbols of status within the plant.

Functions

In all organizations the same managerial functions are performed.[6] These functions have been described in a variety of terms. Perhaps confusion can be avoided by again referring to the Gaited Rocking Horse Company. By looking back at the development of the company, we can isolate the essential functions of management.

Organizing. At the outset, you (as the originator of the company) decided what was to be done and how it was to be done. You decided to manufacture rocking horses in your garage, with the help of a few men. In making these decisions, you were performing the function of organizing. Organizing consists of deciding what is to be done and how it is to be done.[7]

1948), 5–18; William F. Whyte, *Money and Motivation* (New York: Harper & Brothers, 1955). Whyte's book contains much of the Collins, Roy, and Dalton materials as well as a theoretical analysis of the "Problems of Human Organization."

[6] These functions have been described by a number of writers. Unfortunately, each author tends to coin his own terminology; however, a careful reading usually reveals that the same general functions are described. For an excellent summary of the literature, see Robert Tannenbaum, "The Manager Concept: A Rational Synthesis," *The Journal of Business*, 22, No. 4 (Oct. 1949), 225–241; see also Herbert A. Simon, *Administrative Behavior*, 2nd ed. (New York: Macmillan Co., 1957), p. 96; Luther Gulick and Lyndall Urwick, eds., *Papers on the Science of Administration* (New York: Institute of Public Administration, 1937), pp. 3–45; Mary Cushing and Howard Niles, *Middle Management*, rev. ed. (New York: Harper & Brothers, 1949), p. 15; Oliver Sheldon, *The Philosophy of Management* (Englewood Cliffs, N.J.: Prentice-Hall, Inc., 1923), pp. 31–33; Robert Aaron Gordon, *Business of Leadership in the Large Corporation* (Washington, D.C.: Brookings Institution, 1945), p. 5.

[7] One function of management that appears to be gaining increased attention is that of *search* (i.e., finding and identifying existing and potential problems). In

Directing. Once the work was organized, you had to direct the individuals in the organization as to what was expected of them. In assigning tasks and otherwise directing the men, you performed a second function of management; i.e., directing.

Control. In addition to organizing and directing, you had to ensure that the work proceeded according to plan. This involved a third function of management—the function of control. Control involves budgeting; the recruiting, selecting, training, and motivating of workers; and the use of other devices for appraising performance.

Coordination. To the three above-mentioned functions of management should be added the function of coordination. This function is difficult to isolate because it is included in all of the other functions. However, its importance and its pervasiveness warrant treating it as a separate function. In essence, coordination consists of bringing together the various parts of the company so that a smoothly operating cooperative system exists.[8]

Summary

In the foregoing discussion, we have considered some of the features common to almost all organizations. The following points were emphasized:

1. Every organization is composed of groups within groups, which constitute the whole organization.

2. Organizations have formal structures indicating the hierarchy of jobs and the tasks that are performed in each position. Within the formal structure are different types of departments (i.e., line and staff). The line is responsible for the accomplishment of the principal purpose of the organization. The staff advises, educates, inspects, and performs specialized services.

3. The organization is only vaguely described by its formal structure. To develop an understanding of the organization as a functioning unit, one needs to consider numerous other aspects of its environment. One of these is the informal structuring that develops through group-sanctioned behavior, and the intricacies of human interaction that occur.

4. Common functions performed by management in all organizations include organizing, directing, control, and coordination.

---

this book, search is considered as a part of organizing. However, recent trends in organization theory may justify treating it as a separate function. This is especially true of recent developments based upon information theory, game theory, and cybernetics. For example, see James G. March and Herbert A. Simon, *Organizations* (New York: John Wiley & Sons, Inc., 1958).

[8] Cf. James D. Mooney and Alan C. Reiley, *The Principles of Organization* (New York: Harper & Brothers, 1939), p. 5; Henry C. Metcalf and L. Urwick, eds., *Dynamic Administration* (New York: Harper & Brothers, 1940), p. 71.

MAX WEBER ON BUREAUCRACY
*Reinhard Bendix**

One of the most important general statements on formal organization is that of the German scholar Max Weber. His model of bureaucracy has been used as a reference point in many studies, and as such it provides us with an approach for visualizing essential characteristics of large-scale organizations.

Where the rule of law prevails, a bureaucratic organization is governed by the following principles:

(1) Official business is conducted on a continuous basis.

(2) It is conducted in accordance with stipulated rules in an administrative agency characterized by three interrelated attributes: (a) the duty of each official to do certain types of work is delimited in terms of impersonal criteria; (b) the official is given the authority necessary to carry out his assigned functions; (c) the means of compulsion at his disposal are strictly limited, and the conditions under which their employment is legitimate are clearly defined.

(3) Every official's responsibilities and authority are part of a hierarchy of authority. Higher offices are assigned the duty of supervision; lower offices, the right of appeal. However, the extent of supervision and the conditions of legitimate appeal may vary.

(4) Officials and other administrative employees do not own the resources necessary for the performance of their assigned functions but they are accountable for their use of these resources. Official business and private affairs, official revenue and private income are strictly separated.

(5) Offices cannot be appropriated by their incumbents in the sense of private property that can be sold and inherited. (This does not preclude various rights such as pension claims, regulated conditions of discipline and dismissal, etc., but such rights serve, in principle at least, as incentives for the better performance of duties. They are not property rights.)

(6) Official business is conducted on the basis of written documents.[1] Without (1) the continuity of official business, (2) the delimitation of authority through stipulated rules, (3) the supervision of its exercise, (4) and (5) the separation of office and incumbent, and (6) the documentary basis of official business, there cannot be a system of legal domination in which the exercise of authority consists in the implementation of enacted norms.

---

* From *Max Weber: An Intellectual Portrait* by Reinhard Bendix (New York: Doubleday & Co., Inc., 1960), pp. 418–425. Copyright © 1960 by Reinhard Bendix. Reprinted by permission of Doubleday and Company, Inc.

[1] *Theory*, pp. 330–32.

This specification of the "apparatus" under legal domination can be contrasted to the system of administration under patrimonial rule. First, whether or not the patrimonial ruler and his officials conduct administrative business is usually a matter of discretion; normally they do so only when they are paid for their troubles. Second, a patrimonial ruler resists the delimitation of his authority by the stipulation of rules. He may observe traditional or customary limitations, but these are unwritten; indeed, tradition endorses the principled arbitrariness of the ruler. Third, this combination of tradition and arbitrariness is reflected in the delegation and supervision of authority. Within the limits of sacred tradition the ruler decides whether or not to delegate authority, and his entirely personal recruitment of "officials" makes the supervision of their work a matter of personal preference and loyalty. Fourth and fifth, all administrative "offices" under patrimonial rule are a part of the ruler's personal household and private property; his "officials" are personal servants, and the costs of administration are met out of his treasury. Sixth, official business is transacted in personal encounter and by oral communication, not on the basis of impersonal documents.[2]

Under legal domination the occupational position and personal orientation of officials is bound to be affected by the contrasting administrative organization. Where the implementation of enacted rules is emphasized, the employment of the official is also governed by rules; and, once hired, the official obeys impersonal rules, not the will of his lord and master. Obedience to rules and the conduct of official business by means of written documents require technical qualifications that are more or less absent from administrative work done as a personal service or an avocation. Under legal domination the implementation of rules must be regular as well as regulated, or else the rule of law would be applied only intermittently; also, to be continuous, administrative work must be a full-time occupation. Finally, where each office involves regulated duties and authorizations, these must be independent from the person of the incumbent. Consequently, his compensation cannot be derived from the revenue of the office, nor can he be permitted to appropriate either the perquisites of office or the office itself. The typical bureaucratic alternative is to reward the official by monthly allowances in money or in kind, and to ensure the quality and continuity of his service by offering him the opportunity of a lifetime career, usually with pension provisions upon retirement.[3]

Under legal domination, therefore, the bureaucratic official's position is characterized by the following attributes:

(1) He is personally free and appointed to his position on the basis of contract.

2 These conditions apply also under feudalism in a modified form, but there is no need to specify these modifications. See p. 360 ff. above, for the contrast between patrimonialism and feudalism.

3 Weber repeatedly discussed the differences between bureaucratic and patrimonial administration, which have been restated briefly in the preceding two paragraphs. However, he did not distinguish the administrative consequences that result from the type of supreme authority and the characteristics of the officialdom that emerge from these consequences. Cf. *Theory*, pp. 342–45, and *WuG*, Vol. II, pp. 679, 737–38, 752.

(2) He exercises the authority delegated to him in accordance with impersonal rules, and his loyalty is enlisted on behalf of the faithful execution of his official duties.

(3) His appointment and job placement are dependent upon his technical qualifications.

(4) His administrative work is his full-time occupation.

(5) His work is rewarded by a regular salary and by prospects of regular advancement in a lifetime career.

With these characteristics of administrative organization under legal domination before us, we may now turn to the most important attributes and consequences of bureaucracy in the modern world.

According to Weber, such an organization is technically superior to all other forms of administration, much as machine production is superior to nonmechanical methods. In precision, speed, lack of equivocation, knowledge of the documentary record, continuity, sense of discretion; uniformity of operation, system of subordination, and reduction of frictions, bureaucracy surpasses honorific and avocational forms of administration.[4] This is a long list of advantages, but they are relative. Weber emphasized that bureaucracy also produces obstacles when a decision must be adapted to an individual case. This reservation is noteworthy as a concomitant of the attribute that is central to his conception of bureaucracy: the idea of calculability. This is a logical consequence of the rule of law. In an administration governed by rules, decisions must be predictable if the rules are known. Weber expressed this notion by the exaggerated simile of the "modern judge [who] is a vending machine into which the pleadings are inserted together with the fee and which then disgorges the judgment together with its reasons mechanically derived from the Code."[5]

> [The calculability of decision-making] and with it its appropriateness for capitalism ... [is] the more fully realized the more bureaucracy "depersonalizes" itself, i.e., the more completely it succeeds in achieving the exclusion of love, hatred, and every purely personal, especially irrational and incalculable, feeling from the execution of official tasks. In the place of the old-type ruler who is moved by sympathy, favor, grace, and gratitude, modern culture requires for its sustaining external apparatus the emotionally detached, and hence rigorously "professional," expert.[6]

Thus, contrary to many interpretations, Weber did not maintain that bureaucratic organizations operate as efficiently as "slot machines." He said rather that such organizations operate more efficiently than alternative systems of administration and that they increase their efficiency to the extent that they "depersonalize" the execution of official tasks.

In this connection it is interesting to consider Weber's answer to critics of Prussian bureaucracy who questioned the ideal of administrative impersonality. These critics pointed out that the rules governing administrative practice merely provide outside boundaries for the "creative"

---

[4] The translation of this passage in *Essays*, p. 214, makes Weber's statement more absolute than it is. Cf. *Law*, p. 349, for a more accurate translation.

[5] *Ibid.*, p. 354.

[6] *Law*, p. 351.

activity of the official. Therefore, rules have primarily a negative effect; they do not directly and positively determine the official's action. Weber suspected this approach of being a romantic smoke screen for the harsh realities of Prussian government. To him the discretionary activity of the modern bureaucratic official differed from the discretion and personally motivated favors characteristic of prebureaucratic forms of administration. "Behind every act of purely bureaucratic administration there stands a system of rationally discussable 'grounds,' i.e., either a subsumption under norms or calculation of means and ends."[7] In a modern bureaucracy even discretionary acts imply the supremacy of impersonal ends; personal favors and arbitrariness cannot be openly avowed. To be sure, this "canonization of the abstractly impersonal" is fused with the endeavor of individual officials to preserve and enhance their power. But in modern bureaucracy this universal endeavor requires an appeal to impersonal ends.[8] The technical superiority of bureaucratic administration therefore depends on its orientation toward impersonal rules that enhance the uniform reliability and hence the calculability of its operation.

A second attribute of modern bureaucracy is its "concentration of the means of administration." By using the same terminology as Marx, Weber wanted to emphasize that this process of concentration had occurred not only in the economy but also in government, the army, political parties, universities, and indeed in most large-scale organizations. As the size of such organizations increases, the resources necessary to run them are taken out of the hands of autonomous individuals and groups and placed under the control of a ruling minority, in part because such resources exceed the financial capacity of individuals.[9] Thus the craftsman was expropriated as merchant enterprises came to own the tools of production; the feudal vassal was expropriated as a public official when governments came to monopolize the administration of public affairs; the private scholar was expropriated as the universities built up their own laboratories and libraries upon which the scholar came to depend. The means of production, of administration, and of scholarship all were integral parts of the individual household at one time, but became separated as the process of concentration advanced. As a result, modern bureaucratic administration is distinguished by the separation of business from the family household, of public office from its incumbent, and of research facilities from the individual scholar.

A third attribute of modern bureaucracy is its leveling effect on social and economic differences. This effect is seen most easily if bureaucratic and nonbureaucratic methods of administration are contrasted:

[7] *Ibid.*, p. 355.

[8] The passage referred to in this paragraph may be found in different translations in *Essays*, pp. 219–20, and *Law*, pp. 354–55.

[9] This is, of course, related to the increasing complexity of functions performed by governments and other organizations as their size increases. Cf. the earlier reference to this process in Chapter XI, pp. 380–81. Weber's emphasis on the parallelism of this process in all types of large-scale organization is contained in his lecture on socialism. Cf. *GAzSuS*, pp. 489–99. See also *Essays*, pp. 221–24, and *GPS*, p. 140.

Every nonbureaucratic administration of a large social structure [such as patrimonial government] depends upon the fact that those who outrank others in social, economic, or honorific terms are associated in one way or another with the performance of administrative functions. This usually means that the incumbent is rewarded for his assumption of administrative duties by the economic exploitation of his position, which he may also use for purposes of social prestige.[10]

The development of bureaucracy does away with such plutocratic privileges, replacing unpaid, avocational administration by notables with paid, full-time administration by professionals, regardless of their social and economic position. Also, it rejects the "decision-making from case to case" that is typical of nonbureaucratic forms of administration. Authority is exercised in accordance with rules, and everyone subject to that authority is legally equal.[11] Connected with these leveling tendencies is a major change in the system of education. Administration by notables usually is administration by amateurs; bureaucracy usually is administration by experts. Equal eligibility for administrative appointments means in fact equal eligibility of all who meet the stipulated educational requirements. Educational diplomas have replaced privilege as the basis of administrative recruitment, just as scientific education and technical expertise have replaced the cultivation of the mind through classical literature and the cultivation of manners through competitive games among social equals. The expert, not the cultivated man, is the educational ideal of a bureaucratic age.[12]

Fourth and finally, a fully developed bureaucracy implements a system of authority relationships that is practically indestructible. Whereas the notable does administrative work on an avocational and honorific basis, the bureaucrat's economic sustenance and entire social existence are identified with the "apparatus." He shares the interests of his administrative colleagues in the continued functioning of the machine in which they are so many specialized cogs. The population ruled by a bureaucracy cannot, on the other hand, dispense with it or replace it with something else. Short of chaos, public affairs depend today upon the expert training, functional specialization, and coordination of a bureaucratic administration with its uninterrupted performance of the manifold tasks that are regularly assigned to the modern state. Weber emphasized that the bureaucratic form of administration is both permanent and indispensable, contrary to the arguments of anarchists and socialists who believe that administration can be

---

[10] *WuG*, Vol. II, p. 666. This same passage is translated more literally in *Essays*, p. 224.

[11] Weber noted that this leveling effect of bureaucratization has many equivocal results, but I defer consideration of this point to pp. 430–31 below and to Chapter XIV.

[12] *Essays*, pp. 240–43. Note especially Weber's statement that the struggle between the ideal of the expert and the older ideal of the educated or cultivated man is at the basis of all present discussions of the educational system. This is as true in the age of man-made earth satellites as it was before World War I when Weber wrote. Cf. also the earlier discussion of feudal and patrimonial education, pp. 363–64, and the contrast between an autonomous and a university-trained legal profession, pp. 406–11.

done away with in an ideal society or that it can be used to implement a freer and more equitable social order. In Weber's view bureaucracy is here to stay, and any future social order promises only to be more oppressive than the capitalist society of today.

FOUNDATIONS OF THE THEORY OF ORGANIZATION
*Philip Selznick**

Weber's bureaucracy is a starting place for developing an awareness of the nature of organizations. But it is only a starting place. In the Selznick reading we have a broader discussion. It starts with an analysis of the essential features of organizations, and builds a number of concepts for understanding the functioning organization. In so doing, it gives a useful framework for viewing many of the modern-day studies of organization.

Trades unions, governments, business corporations, political parties, and the like are formal structures in the sense that they represent rationally ordered instruments for the achievement of stated goals. "Organization," we are told, "is the arrangement of personnel for facilitating the accomplishment of some agreed purpose through the allocation of functions and responsibilities."[1] Or, defined more generally, formal organization is "a system of consciously coordinated activities or forces of two or more persons."[2] Viewed in this light, formal organization is the structural expression of rational action. The mobilization of technical and managerial skills requires a pattern of coordination, a systematic ordering of positions and duties which defines a chain of command and makes possible the administrative integration of specialized functions. In this context *delegation* is the primordial organizational act, a precarious venture which requires the continuous elaboration of formal mechanisms of coordination and control. The security of all participants, and of the system as a whole, generates a persistent pressure for the institutionalization of relationships, which are thus removed from the uncertainties of individual fealty or sentiment. Moreover, it is necessary for the relations within the structure to be determined in such a way that individuals will be interchangeable and the organization will thus be free of dependence upon

* From *American Sociological Review*, 13 (February 1948), 25–35. Reprinted by permission.

[1] John M. Gaus, "A Theory of Organization in Public Administration," in *The Frontiers of Public Administration* (Chicago: University of Chicago Press, 1936), p. 66.

[2] Chester I. Barnard, *The Functions of the Executive* (Cambridge: Harvard University Press, 1938), p. 73.

personal qualities.[3] In this way, the formal structure becomes subject to calculable manipulation, an instrument of rational action.

But as we inspect these formal structures we begin to see that they never succeed in conquering the non-rational dimensions of organizational behavior. The latter remain at once indispensable to the continued existence of the system of coordination and at the same time the source of friction, dilemma, doubt, and ruin. This fundamental paradox arises from the fact that rational action systems are inescapably imbedded in an institutional matrix, in two significant senses: (1) the action system—or the formal structure of delegation and control which is its organizational expression—is itself only an aspect of a concrete social structure made up of individuals who may interact as *wholes*, not simply in terms of their formal roles within the system; (2) the formal system, and the social structure within which it finds concrete existence, are alike subject to the pressure of an institutional environment to which some over-all adjustment must be made. The formal administrative design can never adequately or fully reflect the concrete organization to which it refers, for the obvious reason that no abstract plan or pattern can—or may, if it is to be useful—exhaustively describe an empirical totality. At the same time, that which is not included in the abstract design (as reflected, for example, in a staff-and-line organization chart) is vitally relevant to the maintenance and development of the formal system itself.

Organization may be viewed from two standpoints which are analytically distinct but which are empirically united in a context of reciprocal consequences. On the one hand, any concrete organizational system is an *economy;* at the same time, it is an *adaptive social structure.* Considered as an economy, organization is a system of relationships which define the availability of scarce resources and which may be manipulated in terms of efficiency and effectiveness. It is the economic aspect of organization which commands the attention of management technicians and, for the most part, students of public as well as private administration.[4] Such problems as the span of executive control, the role of staff or auxiliary agencies, the relation of headquarters to field offices, and the relative merits of single or multiple executive boards are typical concerns of the science of administration. The coordinative scalar, and functional principles, as elements of the theory of organization, are products of the attempt to explicate the most general features of organization as a "technical problem" or, in our terms, as an economy.

Organization as an economy is, however, necessarily conditioned by the organic states of the concrete structure, outside of the systematics of delegation and control. This becomes especially evident as the attention of

[3] Cf. Talcott Parsons' generalization (after Max Weber) of the "law of the increasing rationality of action systems," in *The Structure of Social Action* (New York: McGraw-Hill, 1937), p. 752.

[4] See Luther Gulick and Lydall Urwick (editors), *Papers on the Science of Administration* (New York: Institute of Public Administration, Columbia University, 1937); Lydall Urwick, *The Elements of Administration* (New York, Harper, 1943); James D. Mooney and Alan C. Reiley, *The Principles of Organization* (New York: Harper, 1939); H. S. Dennison, *Organization Engineering* (New York: McGraw-Hill, 1931).

leadership is directed toward such problems as the legitimacy of authority and the dynamics of persuasion. It is recognized implicitly in action and explicitly in the work of a number of students that the possibility of manipulating the system of coordination depends on the extent to which that system is operating within an environment of effective inducement to individual participants and of conditions in which the stability of authority is assured. This is in a sense the fundamental thesis of Barnard's remarkable study, *The Functions of the Executive.* It is also the underlying hypothesis which makes it possible for Urwick to suggest that "proper" or formal channels in fact function to "confirm and record" decisions arrived at by more personal means.[5] We meet it again in the concept of administration as a process of education, in which the winning of consent and support is conceived to be a basic function of leadership.[6] In short, it is recognized that control and consent cannot be divorced even within formally authoritarian structures.

The indivisibility of control and consent makes it necessary to view formal organizations as *cooperative* systems, widening the frame of reference of those concerned with the manipulation of organizational resources. At the point of action, of executive decision, the economic aspect of organization provides inadequate tools for control over the concrete structure. This idea may be readily grasped if attention is directed to the role of the individual within the organizational economy. From the standpoint of organization as a formal system, persons are viewed functionally, in respect to their *roles*, as participants in assigned segments of the cooperative system. But in fact individuals have a propensity to resist depersonalization, to spill over the boundaries of their segmentary roles, to participate as *wholes*. The formal systems (at an extreme, the disposition of "rifles" at a military perimeter) cannot take account of the deviations thus introduced, and consequently break down as instruments of control when relied upon alone. The whole individual raises new problems for the organization, partly because of the needs of his own personality, partly because he brings with him a set of established habits as well, perhaps, as commitments to special groups outside of the organization.

Unfortunately for the adequacy of formal systems of coordination, the needs of individuals do not permit a single-minded attention to the stated goals of the system within which they have been assigned. The hazard inherent in the act of delegation derives essentially from this fact. Delegation is an organizational act, having to do with formal assignments of functions and powers. Theoretically, these assignments are made to roles or official positions, not to individuals as such. In fact, however, delegation necessarily involves concrete individuals who have interests and goals which do not always coincide with the goals of the formal system. As a consequence, individual personalities may offer resistance to the demands made upon them by the official conditions of delegation. These resistances

---

[5] Urwick, *The Elements of Administration, op. cit.,* p. 47.

[6] See Gaus, *op. cit.* Studies of the problem of morale are instances of the same orientation, having received considerable impetus in recent years from the work of the Harvard Business School group.

are not accounted for within the categories of coordination and delegation, so that when they occur they must be considered as unpredictable and
accidental. Observations of this type of situation within formal structures
are sufficiently commonplace. A familiar example is that of delegation to a
subordinate who is also required to train his own replacement. The subordinate may resist this demand in order to maintain unique access to the
"mysteries" of the job, and thus insure his indispensability to the organization.

In large organizations, deviations from the formal system tend to
become institutionalized, so that "unwritten laws" and informal associations are established. Institutionalization removes such deviations from
the realm of personality differences, transforming them into a persistent
structural aspect of formal organizations.[7] These institutionalized rules
and modes of informal cooperation are normally attempts by participants
in the formal organization to control the group relations which form the
environment of organizational decisions. The informal patterns (such as
cliques) arise spontaneously, are based on personal relationships, and are
usually directed to the control of some specific situation. They may be
generated anywhere within a hierarchy, often with deleterious consequences for the formal goals of the organization, but they may also function to widen the available resources of executive control and thus contribute to rather than hinder the achievement of the stated objectives of
the organization. The deviations tend to force a shift away from the purely
formal system as the effective determinant of behavior to (1) a condition
in which informal patterns buttress the formal, as through the manipulation of sentiment within the organization in favor of established authority;
or (2) a condition wherein the informal controls effect a consistent modification of formal goals, as in the case of some bureaucratic patterns.[8] This
trend will eventually result in the formalization of erstwhile informal activities, with the cycle of deviation and transformation beginning again
on a new level.

The relevance of informal structures to organizational analysis un-
derlines the significance of conceiving of formal organizations as cooperative systems. When the totality of interacting groups and individuals becomes the object of inquiry, the latter is not restricted by formal, legal, or
procedural dimensions. The *state of the system* emerges as a significant
point of analysis, as when an internal situation charged with conflict qualifies and informs actions ostensibly determined by formal relations and objectives. A proper understanding of the organizational process must make
it possible to interpret changes in the formal system—new appointments or
rules or reorganizations—in their relation to the informal and unavowed

---

[7] The creation of informal structures within various types of organizations has
received explicit recognition in recent years. See F. J. Roethlisberger and W. J.
Dickson, *Management and the Worker* (Cambridge: Harvard University Press,
1941), p. 524; also Barnard, *op. cit.*, chap. ix; and Wilbert E. Moore, *Industrial Relations and the Social Order* (New York: Macmillan, 1946), chap. xv.

[8] For an analysis of the latter in these terms, see Philip Selznick, "An Approach to a Theory of Bureaucracy," *American Sociological Review*, Vol. VIII,
No. 1 (February, 1943).

ties of friendship, class loyalty, power cliques, or external commitment. This is what it means "to know the score."

The fact that the involvement of individuals as whole personalities tends to limit the adequacy of formal systems of coordination does not mean that organizational characteristics are those of individuals. The organic, emergent character of the formal organization considered as a cooperative system must be recognized. This means that the *organization* reaches decisions, takes action, and makes adjustments. Such a view raises the question of the relation between organizations and persons. The significance of theoretical emphasis upon the cooperative *system* as such is derived from the insight that certain actions and consequences are enjoined independently of the personality of the individuals involved. Thus, if reference is made to the "organization-paradox" —the tension created by the inhibitory consequences of certain types of informal structures within organizations—this does not mean that individuals themselves are in quandaries. It is the nature of the interacting consequences of divergent interests within the organization which creates the condition, a result which may obtain independently of the consciousness or the qualities of the individual participants. Similarly, it seems useful to insist that there are qualities and needs of leader*ship*, having to do with position and role, which are persistent despite variations in the character or personality of individual leaders themselves.

Rational action systems are characteristic of both individuals and organizations. The conscious attempt to mobilize available internal resources (e.g., self-discipline) for the achievement of a stated goal—referred to here as an economy or a formal system—is one aspect of individual psychology. But the personality considered as a dynamic system of interacting wishes, compulsions, and restraints defines a system which is at once essential and yet potentially deleterious to what may be thought of as the "economy of learning" or to individual rational action. At the same time, the individual personality is an adaptive structure, and this, too, requires a broader frame of reference for analysis than the categories of rationality. On a different level, although analogously, we have pointed to the need to consider organizations as cooperative systems and adaptive structures in order to explain the context of and deviations from the formal systems of delegation and coordination.

To recognize the sociological relevance of formal structures is not, however, to have constructed a theory of organization. It is important to set the framework of analysis, and much is accomplished along this line when, for example, the nature of authority in formal organizations is reinterpreted to emphasize the factors of cohesion and persuasion as against legal or coercive sources.[9] This redefinition is logically the same as that which introduced the conception of the self as social. The latter helps make possible, but does not of itself fulfill, the requirements for a dynamic theory of personality. In the same way, the definition of authority as conditioned by sociological factors of sentiment and cohesion—or more gener-

[9] Robert Michels, "Authority," *Encyclopedia of the Social Sciences* (New York: Macmillan, 1931), pp. 319 ff.; also Barnard, *op. cit.*, chap. xii.

ally the definition of formal organizations as cooperative systems—only sets the stage, as an initial requirement, for the formulation of a theory of organization.

STRUCTURAL-FUNCTIONAL ANALYSIS

Cooperative systems are constituted of individuals interacting as wholes in relation to a formal system of coordination. The concrete structure is therefore a resultant of the reciprocal influences of the formal and informal aspects of organization. Furthermore, this structure is itself a totality, an adaptive "organism" reacting to influences upon it from an external environment. These considerations help to define the objects of inquiry; but to progress to a system of predicates *about* these objects it is necessary to set forth an analytical method which seems to be fruitful and significant. The method must have a relevance to empirical materials, which is to say, it must be more specific in its reference than discussions of the logic or methodology of social science.

The organon which may be suggested as peculiarly helpful in the analysis of adaptive structures has been referred to as "structural-functional analysis."[10] This method may be characterized in a sentence: *Structural-functional analysis relates contemporary and variable behavior to a presumptively stable system of needs and mechanisms.* This means that a given empirical system is deemed to have basic needs, essentially related to self-maintenance; the system develops repetitive means of self-defense; and day-to-day activity is interpreted in terms of the function served by that activity for the maintenance and defense of the system. Put thus generally, the approach is applicable on any level in which the determinate "states" of empirically isolable systems undergo self-impelled and repetitive transformations when impinged upon by external conditions. This self-impulsion suggests the relevance of the term "dynamic," which is often used in referring to physiological, psychological, or social systems to which this type of analysis has been applied.[11]

It is a postulate of the structural-functional approach that the basic need of all empirical systems is the maintenance of the integrity and continuity of the system itself. Of course, such a postulate is primarily useful in directing attention to a set of "derived imperatives" or needs which are

[10] For a presentation of this approach having a more general reference than the study of formal organizations, see Talcott Parsons, "The Present Position and Prospects of Systematic Theory in Sociology," in Georges Gurvitch and Wilbert E. Moore (ed.), *Twentieth Century Sociology* (New York: The Philosophical Library, 1945).

[11] "Structure" refers to both the relationships within the system (formal plus informal patterns in organization) and the set of needs and modes of satisfaction which characterize the given type of empirical system. As the utilization of this type of analysis proceeds, the concept of "need" will require further clarification. In particular, the imputation of a "stable set of needs" to organizational systems must not function as a new instinct theory. At the same time, we cannot avoid using these inductions as to generic needs, for they help us to stake out our area of inquiry. The author is indebted to Robert K. Merton, who has, in correspondence, raised some important objections to the use of the term "need" in this context.

sufficiently concrete to characterize the system at hand.[12] It is perhaps rash to attempt a catalogue of these imperatives for formal organizations, but some suggestive formulation is needed in the interests of setting forth the type of analysis under discussion. In formal organizations, the "maintenance of the system" as a generic need may be specified in terms of the following imperatives:

(1) *The security of the organization as a whole in relation to social forces in its environment.* This imperative requires continuous attention to the possibilities of encroachment and to the forestalling of threatened aggressions or deleterious (though perhaps unintended) consequences from the actions of others.

(2) *The stability of the lines of authority and communication.* One of the persistent reference-points of administrative decision is the weighing of consequences for the continued capacity of leadership to control and to have access to the personnel or ranks.

(3) *The stability of informal relations within the organization.* Ties of sentiment and self-interest are evolved as unacknowledged but effective mechanisms of adjustment of individuals and sub-groups to the conditions of life within the organization. These ties represent a cementing of relationships which sustains the formal authority in day-to-day operations and widens opportunities for effective communication.[13] Consequently, attempts to "upset" the informal structure, either frontally or as an indirect consequence of formal reorganization, will normally be met with considerable resistance.

(4) *The continuity of policy and of the sources of its determination.* For each level within the organization, and for the organization as a whole, it is necessary that there be a sense that action taken in the light of a given policy will not be placed in continuous jeopardy. Arbitrary or unpredictable changes in policy undermine the significance of (and therefore the attention to) day-to-day action by injecting a note of capriciousness. At the same time, the organization will seek stable roots (or firm statutory authority or popular mandate) so that a sense of the permanency and legitimacy of its acts will be achieved.

(5) *A homogeneity of outlook with respect to the meaning and role of the organization.* The minimization of disaffection requires a unity derived from a common understanding of what the character of the organization is meant to be. When this homogeneity breaks down, as in situations of internal conflict over basic issues, the continued existence of the organization is endangered. On the other hand, one of the signs of "healthy" organization is the ability to effectively orient new members and readily slough off those who cannot be adapted to the established outlook.

This catalogue of needs cannot be thought of as final, but it approximates the stable system generally characteristic of formal organiza-

---

[12] For "derived imperative" see Bronislaw Malinowski, *The Dynamics of Culture Change* (New Haven: Yale University Press, 1945), pp. 44 ff. For the use of "need" in place of "motive" see the same author's *A Scientific Theory of Culture* (Chapel Hill: University of North Carolina Press, 1944), pp. 89–90.

[13] They may also *destroy* those relationships, as noted above, but the need remains, generating one of the persistent dilemmas of leadership.

tions. These imperatives are derived, in the sense that they represent the conditions for survival or self-maintenance of cooperative systems of organized action. An inspection of these needs suggests that organizational survival is intimately connected with the struggle for relative prestige, both for the organization and for elements and individuals within it. It may therefore be useful to refer to a *prestige-survival motif* in organizational behavior as a short-hand way of relating behavior to needs, especially when the exact nature of the needs remains in doubt. However, it must be emphasized that prestige-survival in organizations does not derive simply from like motives in individuals. Loyalty and self-sacrifice may be individual expressions of organizational or group egotism and self-consciousness.

The concept of organizational need directs analysis to the *internal relevance* of organizational behavior. This is especially pertinent with respect to discretionary action undertaken by agents manifestly in pursuit of formal goals. The question then becomes one of relating the specific act of discretion to some presumptively stable organizational need. In other words, it is not simply action plainly oriented internally (such as in-service training) but also action presumably oriented externally which must be inspected for its relevance to internal conditions. This is of prime importance for the understanding of bureaucratic behavior, for it is of the essence of the latter that action formally undertaken for substantive goals be weighed and transformed in terms of its consequences for the position of the officialdom.

Formal organizations as cooperative systems on the one hand, and individual personalities on the other, involve structural-functional homologies, a point which may help to clarify the nature of this type of analysis. If we say that the individual has a stable set of needs, most generally the need for maintaining and defending the integrity of his personality or ego; that there are recognizable certain repetitive mechanisms which are utilized by the ego in its defense (rationalization, projection, regression, etc.); and that overt and variable behavior may be interpeted in terms of its relation to these needs and mechanisms—on the basis of this logic we may discern the typical pattern of structural-functional analysis as set forth above. In this sense, it is possible to speak of a "Freudian model" for organizational analysis. This does not mean that the substantive insights of individual psychology may be applied to organizations, as in vulgar extrapolations from the individual ego to whole nations or (by a no less vulgar inversion) from strikes to frustrated workers. It is the *logic*, the *type* of analysis which is pertinent.

This homology is also instructive in relation to the applicability of generalizations to concrete cases. The dynamic theory of personality states a set of possible predicates about the ego and its mechanisms of defense, which inform us concerning the propensities of individual personalities under certain general circumstances. But these predicates provide only tools for the analysis of particular individuals, and each concrete case must be examined to tell which operate and in what degree. They are not primarily organs of prediction. In the same way, the predicates within the theory of organization will provide tools for the analysis of particular cases. Each organization, like each personality, represents a resultant of complex forces, an empirical entity which no single relation or no simple formula can explain. The problem of analysis becomes that of selecting among the possible predicates set forth in the theory of organization those which illuminate our understanding of the materials at hand.

The setting of structural-functional analysis as applied to organizations requires some qualification, however. Let us entertain the suggestion that the interesting problem in social science is not so much why men act the way they do as why men in certain circumstances *must* act the way they do. This emphasis upon constraint, if accepted, releases us from an ubiquitous attention to behavior in general, and especially from any undue fixation upon statistics. On the other hand, it has what would seem to be the salutary consequence of focusing inquiry upon certain necessary relationships of the type "if ... then," for example: If the cultural level of the rank and file members of a formally democratic organization is below that necessary for participation in the formulation of policy, then there will be pressure upon the leaders to use the tools of demagogy.

Is such a statement universal in its applicability? Surely not in the sense that one can predict without remainder the nature of all or even most political groups in a democracy. Concrete behavior is a resultant, a complex vector, shaped by the operation of a number of such general constraints. But there is a test of general applicability: it is that of noting whether the relation made explicit must be *taken into account* in action. This criterion represents an empirical test of the significance of social science generalizations. If a theory is significant it will state a relation which will either (1) be taken into account as an element of achieving control; or (2) be ignored only at the risk of losing control and will evidence itself in a ramification of objective or unintended consequences.[14] It is a corollary of this principle of significance that investigation must search out the underlying factors in organizational action, which requires a kind of intensive analysis of the same order as psychoanalytic probing.

A frame of reference which invites attention to the constraints upon behavior will tend to highlight tensions and dilemmas, the characteristic paradoxes generated in the course of action. The dilemma may be said to be the handmaiden of structural-functional analysis, for it introduces the concept of *commitment* or *involvement* as fundamental to organizational analysis. A dilemma in human behavior is represented by an inescapable commitment which cannot be reconciled with the needs of the organism or the social system. There are many spurious dilemmas which have to do with verbal contradictions, but inherent dilemmas to which we refer are of a more profound sort, for they reflect the basic nature of the empirical system in question. An economic order committed to profit as its sustaining incentive may, in Marxist terms, sow the seed of its own

---

[14] See R. M. MacIver's discussion of the "dynamic assessment" which "brings the external world selectively into the subjective realm, conferring on it subjective significance for the ends of action." *Social Causation* (Boston: Ginn, 1942), chaps. 11, 12. The analysis of this assessment within the context of organized action yields the implicit knowledge which guides the choice among alternatives. See also Robert K. Merton, "The Unanticipated Consequences of Purposive Social Action," *American Sociological Review*, I, 6 (December, 1936).

destruction. Again, the anguish of man, torn between finitude and pride, is not a matter of arbitrary and replaceable assumptions but is a reflection of the psychological needs of the human organism, and is concretized in his commitment to the institutions which command his life; he is in the world and of it, inescapably involved in its goals and demands; at the same time, the needs of the spirit are compelling, proposing modes of salvation which have continuously disquieting consequences for worldly involvements. In still another context, the need of the human organism for affection and response necessitates a commitment to elements of the culture which can provide them; but the rule of the super-ego is uncertain since it cannot be completely reconciled with the need for libidinal satisfactions.

Applying this principle to organizations we may note that there is a general source of tension observable in the split between "the motion and the act." Plans and programs reflect the freedom of technical or ideal choice, but organized action cannot escape involvement, a commitment to personnel or institutions or procedures which effectively qualifies the initial plan. *Der Mensch denkt, Gott lenkt.* In organized action, this ultimate wisdom finds a temporal meaning in the recalcitrance of the tools of action. We are inescapably committed to the mediation of human structures which are at once indispensable to our goals and at the same time stand between them and ourselves. The selection of agents generates immediately a bifurcation of interest, expressed in new centers of need and power, placing effective constraints upon the arena of action, and resulting in tensions which are never completely resolved. This is part of what it means to say that there is a "logic" of action which impels us forward from one undesired position to another. Commitment to dynamic, self-activating tools is of the nature of organized action; at the same time, the need for continuity of authority, policy, and character is pressing, and requires an unceasing effort to master the instruments generated in the course of action. This generic tension is specified within the terms of each cooperative system. But for all we find a persistent relationship between *need* and *commitment* in which the latter not only qualifies the former but unites with it to produce a continuous state of tension. In this way, the notion of constraint (as reflected in tension or paradox) at once widens and more closely specifies the frame of reference for organizational analysis.

For Malinowski, the core of functionalism was contained in the view that a cultural fact must be analyzed in its setting. Moreover, he apparently conceived of his method as pertinent to the analysis of all aspects of cultural systems. But there is a more specific problem, one involving a principle of selection which serves to guide inquiry along significant lines. Freud conceived of the human organism as an adaptive structure, but he was not concerned with all human needs, nor with all phases of adaptation. For his system, he selected those needs whose expression is blocked in some way, so that such terms as repression, inhibition, and frustration became crucial. All conduct may be thought of as derived from need, and all adjustment represents the reduction of need. But not all needs are relevant to the systematics of dynamic psychology; and it is not adjustment as such but reaction to frustration which generates the characteristic modes of defensive behavior.

Organizational analysis, too, must find its selective principle; otherwise the indiscriminate attempts to relate activity functionally to needs will produce little in the way of significant theory. Such a principle might read as follows: *Our frame of reference is to select out those needs which cannot be fulfilled within approved avenues of expression and thus must have recourse to such adaptive mechanisms as ideology and to the manipulation of formal processes and structures in terms of informal goals.* This formulation has many difficulties, and is not presented as conclusive, but it suggests the kind of principle which is likely to separate the quick and the dead, the meaningful and the trite, in the study of cooperative systems in organized action.[15]

The frame of reference outlined here for the theory of organization may now be identified as involving the following major ideas: (1) the concept of organizations as cooperative systems, adaptive social structures, made up of interacting individuals, sub-groups, and informal plus formal relationships; (2) structural-functional analysis, which relates variable aspects of organization (such as goals) to stable needs and self-defensive mechanisms; (3) the concept of recalcitrance as a quality of the tools of social action, involving a break in the continuum of adjustment and defining an environment of constraint, commitment, and tension. This frame of reference is suggested as providing a specifiable *area of relations* within which predicates in the theory of organization will be sought, and at the same time setting forth principles of selection and relevance in our approach to the data of organization.

It will be noted that we have set forth this frame of reference within the over-all context of social action. The significance of events may be defined by their place and operational role in a means-end scheme. If functional analysis searches out the elements important for the maintenance of a given structure, and that structure is one of the materials to be manipulated in action, then that which is functional in respect to the structure is also functional in respect to the action system. This provides a ground for the significance of functionally derived theories. At the same time, relevance to control in action is the empirical test of their applicability or truth.

COOPTATION AS A MECHANISM OF ADJUSTMENT

The frame of reference stated above is in fact an amalgam of definition, resolution, and substantive theory. There is an element of *definition* in conceiving of formal organizations as cooperative systems, though of course the interaction of informal and formal patterns is a question of fact; in a sense, we are *resolving* to employ structural-functional analysis on the assumption that it will be fruitful to do so, though here, too, the specification of needs or derived imperatives is a matter for empirical inquiry; and

---

[15] This is not meant to deprecate the study of organizations as *economies* or formal systems. The latter represent an independent level, abstracted from organizational structures as cooperative or adaptive systems ("organisms").

our predication of recalcitrance as a quality of the tools of action is itself a *substantive theory*, perhaps fundamental to a general understanding of the nature of social action.

A theory of organization requires more than a general frame of reference, though the latter is indispensable to inform the approach of inquiry to any given set of materials. What is necessary is the construction of generalizations concerning transformations within and among cooperative systems. These generalizations represent, from the standpoint of particular cases, possible predicates which are relevant to the materials as we know them in general, but which are not necessarily controlling in all circumstances. A theory of transformations in organization would specify those states of the system which resulted typically in predictable, or at least understandable, changes in such aspects of organization as goals, leadership, doctrine, efficiency, effectiveness, and size. These empirical generalizations would be systematized as they were related to the stable needs of the cooperative system.

Changes in the characteristics of organizations may occur as a result of many different conditions, not always or necessarily related to the processes of organization as such. But the theory of organization must be selective, so that explanations of transformations will be sought within its own assumptions or frame of reference. Consider the question of size. Organizations may expand for many reasons—the availability of markets, legislative delegations, the swing of opinion—which may be accidental from the point of view of the organizational process. To explore changes in size (as of, say, a trades union) as related to changes in non-organizational conditions may be necessitated by the historical events to be described, but it will not of itself advance the frontiers of the theory of organization. However, if "the innate propensity of all organizations to expand" is asserted as a function of "the inherent instability of incentives"[16] then transformations have been stated within the terms of the theory of organization itself. It is likely that in many cases the generalization in question may represent only a minor aspect of the empirical changes, but these organizational relations must be made explicit if the theory is to receive development.

In a frame of reference which specifies needs and anticipates the formulation of a set of self-defensive responses or mechanisms, the latter appear to constitute one kind of empirical generalization or "possible predicate" within the general theory. The needs of organizations (whatever investigation may determine them to be) are posited as attributes of all organizations, but the responses to disequilibrium will be varied. The mechanisms used by the system in fulfillment of its needs will be repetitive and thus may be described as a specifiable set of assertions within the theory of organization, but any given organization may or may not have recourse to the characteristic modes of response. Certainly no given organization will employ all of the possible mechanisms which are theoretically available. When Barnard speaks of an "innate propensity of organization to expand" he is in fact formulating one of the general

[16] Barnard, *op. cit.*, pp. 158–9.

mechanisms, namely, expansion, which is a characteristic mode of response available to an organization under pressure from within. These responses necessarily involve a transformation (in this case, size) of some structural aspect of the organization.

Other examples of the self-defensive mechanisms available to organizations may derive primarily from the response of these organizations to the institutional environments in which they live. The tendency to construct ideologies, reflecting the need to come to terms with major social forces, is one such mechanism. Less well understood as a mechanism of organizational adjustment is what we may term *cooptation*. Some statement of the meaning of this concept may aid in clarifying the foregoing analysis.

Cooptation is the process of absorbing new elements into the leadership or policy-determining structure of an organization as a means of averting threats to its stability or existence. This is a defensive mechanism, formulated as one of a number of possible predicates available for the interpretation of organizational behavior. Cooptation tells us something about the process by which an institutional environment impinges itself upon an organization and effects changes in its leadership and policy. Formal authority may resort to cooptation under the following general conditions:

(1) When there exists a hiatus between consent and control, so that the legitimacy of the formal authority is called into question. The "indivisibility" of consent and control refers, of course, to an optimum situation. Where control lacks an adequate measure of consent, it may revert to coercive measures or attempt somehow to win the consent of the governed. One means of winning consent is to coopt elements into the leadership or organization, usually elements which in some way reflect the sentiment or possess the confidence of the relevant public or mass. As a result, it is expected that the new elements will lend respectability or legitimacy to the organs of control and thus reestablish the stability of formal authority. This process is widely used, and in many different contexts. It is met in colonial countries, where the organs of alien control reaffirm their legitimacy by coopting native leaders into the colonial administration. We find it in the phenomenon of "crisis-patriotism" wherein normally disfranchised groups are temporarily given representation in the councils of government in order to win their solidarity in a time of national stress. Cooptation is presently being considered by the United States Army in its study of proposals to give enlisted personnel representation in the court-martial machinery—a clearly adaptive response to stresses made explicit during the war, the lack of confidence in the administration of army justice. The "unity" parties of totalitarian states are another form of cooptation; company unions or some employee representation plans in industry are still another. In each of these cases, the response of formal authority (private or public, in a large organization or a small one) is an attempt to correct a state of imbalance by *formal* measures. It will be noted, moreover, that what is shared is the *responsibility* for power rather than power itself. These conditions define what we shall refer to as *formal cooptation*.

(2) Cooptation may be a response to the pressure of specific centers of power. This is not necessarily a matter of legitimacy or of a general and diffuse lack of confidence. These may be well established; and yet organized forces which are able to threaten the formal authority may effectively shape its structure and policy. The organization in respect to its institutional environment—or the leadership in respect to its ranks—must take these forces into account. As a consequence, the outside elements may be brought into the leadership or policy-determining structure, may be given a place as a recognition of and concession to the resources they can independently command. The representation of interests through administrative constituencies is a typical example of this process. Or, within an organization, individuals upon whom the group is dependent for funds or other resources may insist upon and receive a share in the determination of policy. This form of cooptation is typically expressed in informal terms, for the problem is not one of responding to a state of imbalance with respect to the "people as a whole" but rather one of meeting the pressure of specific individuals or interest-groups which are in a position to enforce demands. The latter are interested in the substance of power and not its forms. Moreover, an open acknowledgment of capitulation to specific interests may itself undermine the sense of legitimacy of the formal authority within the community. Consequently, there is a positive pressure to refrain from explicit recognition of the relationship established. This form of the cooptative mechanism, having to do with the sharing of power as a response to specific pressures, may be termed *informal cooptation*.

Cooptation reflects a state of tension between formal authority and social power. The former is embodied in a particular structure and leadership, but the latter has to do with subjective and objective factors which control the loyalties and potential manipulability of the community. Where the formal authority is an expression of social power, its stability is assured. On the other hand, when it becomes divorced from the sources of social power, its continued existence is threatened. This threat may arise from the sheer alienation of sentiment or from the fact that other leaderships have control over the sources of social power. Where a formal authority has been accustomed to the assumption that its constituents respond to it as individuals, there may be a rude awakening when organization of those constituents on a non-governmental basis creates nuclei of power which are able effectively to demand a sharing of power.[17]

[17] It is perhaps useful to restrict the concept of cooptation to formal organizations, but in fact it probably reflects a process characteristic of all group leaderships. This has received some recognition in the analysis of class structure, wherein the ruling class is interpreted as protecting its own stability by absorbing new elements. Thus Michels made the point that "an aristocracy cannot maintain an enduring stability by sealing itself off hermetically." See Robert Michels, *Umschichtungen in den herrschenden Klassen nach dem Kriege* (Stuttgart: Kohlhammer, 1934), p. 39; also Gaetano Mosca, *The Ruling Class* (New York: McGraw-Hill, 1939), p. 413 ff. The alliance or amalgamation of classes in the face of a common threat may be reflected in formal and informal cooptative responses among formal organizations sensitive to class pressures. In a forthcoming volume, *TVA and the Grass Roots*, the author has made extensive use of the concept of cooptation in analyzing some aspects of the organizational behavior of a government agency.

The significance of cooptation for organizational analysis is not simply that there is a change in or a broadening of leadership, and that this is an adaptive response, but also that *this change is consequential for the character and role of the organization*. Cooptation involves commitment, so that the groups to which adaptation has been made constrain the field of choice available to the organization or leadership in question. The character of the coopted elements will necessarily shape (inhibit or broaden) the modes of action available to the leadership which has won adaptation and security at the price of commitment. The concept of cooptation thus implicitly sets forth the major points of the frame of reference outlined above: it is an adaptive response of a cooperative system to a stable need, generating transformations which reflect constraints enforced by the recalcitrant tools of action.

SOCIAL MOVEMENTS
*Herbert Blumer**

A useful framework for understanding large, relatively permanent organizations is provided by Professor Blumer's discussion of the general features of social movements. Although one seldom thinks of hospitals, schools, businesses, and related organizations as social movements, they do encompass most of the features of such movements: division of labor, social rules, values, traditions. Moreover, a large part of the public-relations and human-relations activities of large organizations can be placed into perspective by the use of Blumer's model.

Social movements can be viewed as collective enterprises to establish a new order of life. They have their inception in a condition of unrest, and derive their motive power on one hand from dissatisfaction with the current form of life, and on the other hand, from wishes and hopes for a new scheme or system of living. The career of a social movement depicts the emergence of a new order of life. In its beginning, a social movement is amorphous, poorly organized, and without form; the collective behavior is on [a] primitive level . . . , and the mechanisms of interaction are the elementary, spontaneous mechanisms . . . As a social movement develops, it takes on the character of a society. It acquires organization and form, a body of customs and traditions, established leadership, an enduring division of labor, social rules, and social values—in short, a culture, a social organization, and a new scheme of life.

* From Alfred McClung Lee (ed.), *Principles of Sociology* (New York: Barnes & Noble, Inc., 1946), Chap. 22, pp. 199–211. Reprinted by permission.

Our treatment of social movements will deal with three kinds—general social movements, specific social movements, and expressive social movements.[1]

GENERAL SOCIAL MOVEMENTS

New Cultural Trends

By general social movements we have in mind movements such as the labor movement, the youth movement, the women's movement, and the peace movement. Their background is constituted by gradual and pervasive changes in the values of people—changes which can be called cultural drifts. Such cultural drifts stand for a general shifting in the ideas of people, particularly along the line of the conceptions which people have of themselves, and of their rights and privileges. Over a period of time many people may develop a new view of what they believe they are entitled to—a view largely made up of desires and hopes. It signifies the emergence of a new set of values, which influence people in the way in which they look upon their own lives. Examples of such cultural drifts in our own recent history are the increased value of health, the belief in free education, the extension of the franchise, the emancipation of women, the increasing regard for children, and the increasing prestige of science.

Indefinite Images and Behavior

The development of the new values which such cultural drifts bring forth involves some interesting psychological changes which provide the motivation for general social movements. They mean, in a general sense, that people have come to form new conceptions of themselves which do not conform to the actual positions which they occupy in their life. They acquire new dispositions and interests and, accordingly, become sensitized in new directions; and, conversely, they come to experience dissatisfaction where before they had none. These new images of themselves, which people begin to develop in response to cultural drifts, are vague and indefinite; and correspondingly, the behavior in response to such images is uncertain and without definite aim. It is this feature which provides a cue for the understanding of general social movements.

Characteristics of General Social Movements

General social movements take the form of groping and uncoordinated efforts. They have only a general direction, toward which they move in a slow, halting, yet persistent fashion. As movements they are unorganized, with neither established leadership nor recognized member-

---

[1] Attention is called, in passing, to spatial movements, such as nomadic movements, barbaric invasions, crusades, pilgrimages, colonization, and migrations. Such movements may be carried on as societies, as in the case of tribal migrations; as diverse peoples with a common goal, as in the case of the religious crusades of the Middle Ages; or as individuals with similar goals, as in most of the immigration into the United States. Mechanisms of their collective operation will be dealt with in the following discussion of social movements. In themselves, such movements are too complicated and diversified to be dealt with adequately here.

ship, and little guidance and control. Such a movement as the women's movement, which has the general and vague aim of the emancipation of women, suggests these features of a general social movement. The women's movement, like all general social movements, operates over a wide range— in the home, in marriage, in education, in industry, in politics, in travel— in each area of which it represents a search for an arrangement which will answer to the new idea of status being formed by women. Such a movement is episodic in its career, with very scattered manifestations of activity. It may show considerable enthusiasm at one point and reluctance and inertia at another; it may experience success in one area, and abortive effort in another. In general, it may be said that its progress is very uneven with setbacks, reverses, and frequent retreading of the same ground. At one time the impetus to the movement may come from people in one place, at another time in another place. On the whole the movement is likely to be carried on by many unknown and obscure people who struggle in different areas without their striving and achievements becoming generally known.

A general social movement usually is characterized by a literature, but the literature is as varied and ill-defined as is the movement itself. It is likely to be an expression of protest, with a general depiction of a kind of utopian existence. As such, it vaguely outlines a philosophy based on new values and self-conceptions. Such a literature is of great importance in spreading a message or view, however imprecise it may be, and so in implanting suggestions, awakening hopes, and arousing dissatisfactions. Similarly, the "leaders" of a general social movement play an important part—not in the sense of exercising directive control over the movement, but in the sense of being pace-makers. Such leaders are likely to be "voices in the wilderness," pioneers without any solid following, and frequently not very clear about their own goals. However, their example helps to develop sensitivities, arouse hopes, and break down resistances. From these traits one can easily realize that the general social movement develops primarily in an informal, inconspicuous, and largely subterranean fashion. Its media of interaction are primarily reading, conversations, talks, discussions, and the perception of examples. Its achievements and operations are likely to be made primarily in the realm of individual experience rather than by noticeable concerted action of groups. It seems evident that the general social movement is dominated to a large extent by the mechanisms of mass behavior, such as we have described in our treatment of the mass. Especially in their earlier stages, general social movements are likely to be merely an aggregation of individual lines of action based on individual decisions and selections. As is characteristic of the mass and of mass behavior, general social movements are rather formless in organization and inarticulate in expression.

The Basis for Specific Social Movements

Just as cultural drifts provide the background out of which emerge general social movements, so the general social movement constitutes the setting out of which develop specific social movements. Indeed, a specific social movement can be regarded as the crystallization of much of the motivation of dissatisfaction, hope, and desire awakened by the general social movement and the focusing of this motivation on some specific objective. A convenient illustration is the antislavery movement, which was, to a considerable degree, an individual expression of the widespread humanitarian movement of the nineteenth century. With this recognition of the relation between general and specific social movements, we can turn to a consideration of the latter.

SPECIFIC SOCIAL MOVEMENTS

Characteristics

The outstanding instances of this type of movement are reform movements and revolutionary movements. A specific social movement is one which has a well-defined objective or goal which it seeks to reach. In this effort it develops an organization and structure, making it essentially a society. It develops a recognized and accepted leadership and a definite membership characterized by a "we-consciousness." It forms a body of traditions, a guiding set of values, a philosophy, sets of rules, and a general body of expectations. Its members form allegiances and loyalties. Within it there develops a division of labor, particularly in the form of a social structure in which individuals occupy status positions. Thus, individuals develop personalities and conceptions of themselves, representing the individual counterpart of a social structure.

A social movement, of the specific sort, does not come into existence with such a structure and organization already established. Instead, its organization and its culture are developed in the course of its career. It is necessary to view social movements from this temporal and developmental perspective. In the beginning a social movement is loosely organized and characterized by impulsive behavior. It has no clear objective; its behavior and thinking are largely under the dominance of restlessness and collective excitement. As a social movement develops, however, its behavior, which was originally dispersed, tends to become organized, solidified, and persistent. It is possible to delineate stages roughly in the career of a social movement which represent this increasing organization. One scheme of four stages has been suggested by Dawson and Gettys.[2] These are the stage of social unrest, the stage of popular excitement, the stage of formalization, and the stage of institutionalization.

Stages of Development

In the first of these four stages people are restless, uneasy, and act in the random fashion that we have considered. They are susceptible to appeals and suggestions that tap their discontent, and hence, in this stage, the agitator is likely to play an important role. The random and erratic behavior is significant in sensitizing people to one another and so makes possible the focusing of their restlessness on certain objects. The stage of popular excitement is marked even more by milling, but it is not quite so

[2] C. A. Dawson and W. E. Gettys, *Introduction to Sociology* (rev. ed.; New York: Ronald Press Co., 1935, chap. 19).

random and aimless. More definite notions emerge as to the cause of their condition and as to what should be done in the way of social change. So there is a sharpening of objectives. In this stage the leader is likely to be a prophet or a reformer. In the stage of formalization the movement becomes more clearly organized with rules, policies, tactics, and discipline. Here the leader is likely to be in the nature of a statesman. In the institutional stage, the movement has crystallized into a fixed organization with a definite personnel and structure to carry into execution the purposes of the movement. Here the leader is likely to be an administrator. In considering the development of the specific social movement our interest is less in considering the stages through which it passes than in discussing the mechanisms and means through which such a movement is able to grow and become organized. It is convenient to group these mechanisms under five heads: (1) agitation, (2) development of *esprit de corps*, (3) development of morale, (4) the formation of an ideology, and (5) the development of operating tactics.

The Role of Agitation

Agitation is of primary importance in a social movement. It plays its most significant role in the beginning and early stages of a movement, although it may persist in minor form in the later portions of the life-cycle of the movement. As the term suggests, agitation operates to arouse people and so make them possible recruits for the movement. It is essentially a means of exciting people and of awakening within them new impulses and ideas which make them restless and dissatisfied. Consequently, it acts to loosen the hold on them of their previous attachments, and to break down their previous ways of thinking and acting. For a movement to begin and gain impetus, it is necessary for people to be jarred loose from their customary ways of thinking and believing, and to have aroused within them new impulses and wishes. This is what agitation seeks to do. To be successful, it must first gain the attention of people; second, it must excite them, and arouse feelings and impulses; and third, it must give some direction to these impulses and feelings through ideas, suggestions, criticisms, and promises.

Agitation operates in two kinds of situations. One is a situation marked by abuse, unfair discrimination, and injustice, but a situation wherein people take this mode of life for granted and do not raise questions about it. Thus, while the situation is potentially fraught with suffering and protest, the people are marked by inertia. Their views of their situation incline them to accept it; hence the function of the agitation is to lead them to challenge and question their own modes of living. It is in such a situation that agitation may create social unrest where none existed previously. The other situation is one wherein people are already aroused, restless, and discontented, but where they either are too timid to act or else do not know what to do. In this situation the function of agitation is not so much to implant the seeds of unrest, as to intensify, release, and direct the tensions which people already have.

Agitators seem to fall into two types corresponding roughly to these two situations. One type of agitator is an excitable, restless, and aggressive individual. His dynamic and energetic behavior attracts the attention of people to him; and the excitement and restlessness of his behavior tends to infect them. He is likely to act with dramatic gesture and to talk in terms of spectacular imagery. His appearance and behavior foster the contagion of unrest and excitement. This type of agitator is likely to be most success-ful in the situation where people are already disturbed and unsettled; in such a situation his own excited and energetic activity can easily arouse other people who are sensitized to such behavior and already disposed to excitability.

The second type of agitator is more calm, quiet, and dignified. He stirs people not by what he does, but what he says. He is likely to be a man sparing in his words, but capable of saying very caustic, incisive, and biting things—things which get "under the skin" of people and force them to view things in a new light. This type of agitator is more suited to the first of the social situations discussed—the situation where people endure hardships or discrimination without developing attitudes of resentment. In this situation, his function is to make people aware of their own position and of the inequalities, deficiencies, and injustices that seem to mark their lot. He leads them to raise questions about what they have previously taken for granted and to form new wishes, inclinations, and hopes.

The function of agitation, as stated above, is in part to dislodge and stir up people and so liberate them for movement in new directions. More specifically, it operates to change the conceptions which people have of themselves, and the notions which they have of their rights and dues. Such new conceptions, involving beliefs that one is justly entitled to privileges from which he is excluded, provide the dominant motive force for the social movement. Agitation, as the means of implanting these new concep-tions among people, becomes, in this way, of basic importance to the success of a social movement.

A brief remark relative to the tactics of agitation may be made here. It is sufficient to say that the tactics of agitation vary with the situation, the people, and the culture. A procedure which may be highly successful in one situation may turn out to be ludicrous in another situation. This suggests the problem of identifying different types of situations and cor-relating with each the appropriate form of agitation. Practically no study has been conducted on this problem. Here, one can merely state the truism that the agitator, to be successful, must sense the thoughts, interests, and values of his listeners.

The Development of Esprit de Corps

Agitation is merely the means of arousing the interest of people and thus getting them to participate in a movement. While it serves to recruit members, to give initial impetus, and to give some direction, by itself it could never organize or sustain a movement. Collective activities based on mere agitation would be sporadic, disconnected, and short-lived. Other mechanisms have to enter to give solidity and persistency to a social move-ment. One of these is the development of *esprit de corps*.

Esprit de corps might be thought of as the organizing of feelings on behalf of the movement. In itself, it is the sense which people have of belonging together and of being identified with one another in a common undertaking. Its basis is constituted by a condition of rapport. In developing feelings of intimacy and closeness, people have the sense of sharing a common experience and of forming a select group. In one another's presence they feel at ease and as comrades. Personal reserve breaks down and feelings of strangeness, difference, and alienation disappear. Under such conditions, relations tend to be of cooperation instead of personal competition. The behavior of one tends to facilitate the release of behavior on the part of others, instead of tending to inhibit or check that behavior; in this sense each person tends to inspire others. Such conditions of mutual sympathy and responsiveness obviously make for concerted behavior.

Esprit de corps is of importance to a social movement in other ways. Very significant is the fact that it serves to reinforce the new conception of himself that the individual has formed as a result of the movement and of his participation in it. His feeling of belonging with others, and they with him, yields him a sense of collective support. In this way his views of himself and of the aims of the movement are maintained and invigorated. It follows that the development of *esprit de corps* helps to foster an attachment of people to a movement. Each individual has his sentiments focused on, and intertwined with, the objectives of the movement. The resulting feeling of expansion which he experiences is in the direction of greater allegiance to the movement. It should be clear that *esprit de corps* is an important means of developing solidarity and so of giving solidity to a movement.

How is *esprit de corps* developed in a social movement? It would seem chiefly in three ways: the development of an in-group–out-group relation, the formation of informal fellowship association, and the participation in formal ceremonial behavior.

The in-group–out-group relation. The nature of the in-group–out-group relation should be familiar to the student. It exists when two groups come to identify each other as enemies. In such a situation each group regards itself as the upholder of virtue and develops among its members feelings of altruism, loyalty, and fidelity. The out-group is regarded as unscrupulous and vicious, and is felt to be attacking the values which the in-group holds dear. Before the out-group the members of the in-group not only feel that they are right and correct, but believe they have a common responsibility to defend and preserve their values.

The value of these in-group–out-group attitudes in developing solidarity in a social movement is quite clear. The belief on the part of its members that the movement is being opposed unjustly and unfairly by vicious and unscrupulous groups serves to rally the members around their aims and values. To have an enemy, in this sense, is very important for imparting solidarity to the movement. In addition, the "enemy" plays the important role of a scapegoat. It is advantageous to a movement to develop an enemy; this development is usually in itself spontaneous. Once made, it functions to establish *esprit de corps*.

Informal fellowship. *Esprit de corps* is formed also in a very significant way by the development of informal association on the basis of
fellowship. Where people can come together informally in this way, they
have the opportunity of coming to know one another as human beings instead of as institutional symbols. They are then in a much better position
to take one another's roles and, unwittingly, to share one another's experience. It seems that in such a relationship, people unconsciously import and
assimilate into themselves the gestures, attitudes, values, and philosophy of
life of one another. The net result is to develop a common sympathy and
sense of intimacy which contributes much to solidarity. Thus, we find in
social movements the emergence and use of many kinds of informal and
communal association. Singing, dancing, picnics, joking, having fun, and
friendly informal conversation are important devices of this sort in a social
movement. Through them, the individual gets a sense of status and a sense
of social acceptance and support, in place of prior loneliness and personal
alienation.

Ceremonial behavior. The third important way in which social movements develop *esprit de corps* is through the use of formal ceremonial behavior and of ritual. The value of mass meetings, rallies, parades, huge
demonstrations, and commemorative ceremonies has always been apparent
to those entrusted with the development of a social movement; the value is
one that comes from large assemblages, in the form of the sense of vast
support that is experienced by the participant. The psychology that is
involved here is the psychology of being on parade. The individual participant experiences the feeling of considerable personal expansion and
therefore has the sense of being somebody distinctly important. Since
this feeling of personal expansion comes to be identified with the movement as such, it makes for *esprit de corps.* Likewise, the paraphernalia of
ritual possessed by every movement serves to foster feelings of common
identity and sympathy. This paraphernalia consists of a set of sentimental
symbols, such as slogans, songs, cheers, poems, hymns, expressive gestures,
and uniforms. Every movement has some of these. Since they acquire
a sentimental significance symbolizing the common feelings about the
movement, their use serves as a constant reliving and re-enforcement of
these mutual feelings.

Esprit de corps may be regarded, then, as an organization of group
feeling and essentially as a form of group enthusiasm. It is what imparts
life to a movement. Yet just as agitation is inadequate for the development
of a movement, so is mere reliance on *esprit de corps* insufficient. A movement which depends entirely on *esprit de corps* is usually like a boom and
is likely to collapse in the face of a serious crisis. Since the allegiance which
it commands is based merely on heightened enthusiasm, it is likely to vanish with the collapse of such enthusiasm. Thus, to succeed, especially in the
face of adversity, a movement must command a more persistent and fixed
loyalty. This is yielded by the development of morale.

The Development of Morale

As we have seen, *esprit de corps* is a collective feeling which gives
life, enthusiasm, and vigor to a movement. Morale can be thought of as

giving persistency and determination to a movement; its test is whether solidarity can be maintained in the face of adversity. In this sense, morale can be thought of as a group will or an enduring collective purpose.

Morale seems to be based on, and yielded by, a set of convictions. In the case of a social movement these seem to be of three kinds. First is a conviction of the rectitude of the purpose of the movement. This is accompanied by the belief that the attainment of the objectives of the movement will usher in something approaching a millennial state. What is evil, unjust, improper, and wrong will be eradicated with the success of the movement. In this sense, the goal is always overvalued. Yet these beliefs yield to the members of a movement a marked confidence in themselves. A second conviction closely identified with these beliefs is a faith in the ultimate attainment, by the movement, of its goal. There is believed to be a certain inevitability about this. Since the movement is felt to be a necessary agent for the regeneration of the world, it is regarded as being in line with the higher moral values of the universe, and in this sense as divinely favored. Hence, there arises the belief that success is inevitable, even though it be only after a hard struggle. Finally, as part of this complex of convictions, there is the belief that the movement is charged with a sacred mission. Together, these convictions serve to give an enduring and unchangeable character to the goal of a movement and a tenacity to its effort. Obstructions, checks, and reversals are occasions for renewed effort instead of for disheartenment and despair, since they do not seriously impair the faith in the rectitude of the movement nor in the inevitability of its success.

It is clear from this explanation that the development of morale in a movement is essentially a matter of developing a sectarian attitude and a religious faith. This provides a cue to the more prominent means by which morale is built up in a movement. One of these is found in the emergence of a saint cult which is to be discerned in every enduring and persisting social movement. There is usually a major saint and a series of minor saints, chosen from the popular leaders of the movement. Hitler, Lenin, Marx, Mary Baker Eddy, and Sun Yat-sen will serve as convenient examples of major saints. Such leaders become essentially deified and endowed with miraculous power. They are regarded as grossly superior, intelligent, and infallible. People develop toward them attitudes of reverence and awe, and resent efforts to depict them as ordinary human beings. The pictures or other mementos of such individuals come to have the character of religious idols. Allied with the saints of a movement are its heroes and its martyrs. They also come to be regarded as sacred figures. The development of this whole saint cult is an important means of imparting essentially a religious faith to the movement and of helping to build up the kinds of convictions spoken of above.

Similar in function is the emergence in the movement of a creed and of a sacred literature. These, again, are to be found in all persisting social movements. Thus, as has been said frequently, *Das Kapital* and *Mein Kampf* have been the bibles respectively of the communist movement and of the National Socialist movement. The role of a creed and literature of this sort in imparting religious conviction to a movement should be clear.

Finally, great importance must be attached to myths in the development of morale in a social movement. Such myths may be varied. They may be myths of being a select group or a chosen people; myths of the inhumanity of one's opponents; myths about the destiny of the movement; myths depicting a glorious and millennial society to be realized by the movement. Such myths usually grow out of, and in response to, the desires and hopes of the people in the movement and acquire by virtue of their collective character a solidity, a permanency, and an unquestioned acceptance. It is primarily through them that the members of the movement achieve the dogmatic fixity of their convictions, and seek to justify their actions to the rest of the world.

The Development of Group Ideology

Without an ideology a social movement would grope along in an uncertain fashion and could scarcely maintain itself in the face of pointed opposition from outside groups. Hence, the ideology plays a significant role in the life of a movement; it is a mechanism essential to the persistency and development of a movement. The ideology of a movement consists of a body of doctrine, beliefs, and myths. More specifically, it seems to consist of the following: *first*, a statement of the objective, purpose, and premises of the movement; *second*, a body of criticism and condemnation of the existing structure which the movement is attacking and seeking to change; *third*, a body of defense doctrine which serves as a justification of the movement and of its objectives; *fourth*, a body of belief dealing with policies, tactics, and practical operation of the movement; and, *fifth*, the myths of the movement.

This ideology is almost certain to be of a twofold character. In the first place, much of it is erudite and scholarly. This is the form in which it is developed by the intellectuals of the movement. It is likely to consist of elaborate treatises of an abstract and highly logical character. It grows up usually in response to the criticism of outside intellectuals, and seeks to gain for its tenets a respectable and defensible position in this world of higher learning and higher intellectual values. The ideology has another character, however—a popular character. In this guise, it seeks to appeal to the uneducated and to the masses. In its popular character, the ideology takes the form of emotional symbols, shibboleths, stereotypes, smooth and graphic phrases, and folk arguments. It deals, also, with the tenets of the movement, but presents them in a form that makes for their ready comprehension and consumption.

The ideology of a movement may be thought of as providing a movement with its philosophy and its psychology. It gives a set of values, a set of convictions, a set of criticisms, a set of arguments, and a set of defenses. As such, it furnishes to a movement (a) direction, (b) justification, (c) weapons of attack, (d) weapons of defense, and (e) inspiration and hope. To be effective in these respects, the ideology must carry respectability and prestige—a character that is provided primarily by the intelligentsia of the movement. More important than this, however, is the need of the ideology to answer to the distress, wishes, and hopes of the people. Unless it has this popular appeal, it will be of no value to the movement.

The Role of Tactics

We have referred to tactics as the fifth major mechanism essential to the development of a social movement. Obviously the tactics are evolved along three lines: gaining adherents, holding adherents, and reaching objectives. Little more can be said than this, unless one deals with specific kinds of movements in specific kinds of situations. For tactics are always dependent on the nature of the situation in which a movement is operating and always with reference to the cultural background of the movement. This functional dependency of tactics on the peculiarity of the situation helps to explain the ludicrous failures that frequently attend the application of certain tactics to one situation even though they may have been successful in other situations. To attempt revolutionary tactics these days in terms of the tactics of two centuries ago would be palpably foolish. Similarly, to seek to develop a movement in this country in terms of tactics employed in a similar movement in some different cultural setting would probably bring very discouraging results. In general, it may be said that tactics are almost by definition flexible and variable, taking their form from the nature of the situation, the exigencies of the circumstances, and the ingenuity of the people.

THE ANATOMY OF ORGANIZATION
Herbert A. Simon*

In the preceding selections we have viewed organizations with emphasis upon special aspects: as bureaucratic, mechanistic entities; as adaptive social systems; and as social movements. The present selection emphasizes still another approach—namely, the decision processes at work in organizations. The selection itself is the last chapter of Herbert Simon's classic book *Administrative Behavior*. The theme of this book is that organization behavior is a complex network of decisional processes. The material presented here summarizes Simon's analysis. Underlying it is the assumption that people do not necessarily make rational decisions.

In the present chapter, as in previous ones, no attempt will be made to offer advice as to how organizations *should* be constructed and operated.

* Reprinted with the permission of The Macmillan Company from *Administrative Behavior* by Herbert Simon (New York: The Macmillan Co., 1948), Chap. XI, pp. 220-247. Copyright 1945, 1947 by Herbert Simon.

The reader has been warned before that this volume deals with the anatomy and physiology of organization and does not attempt to prescribe for the ills of organization. Its field is organizational biology, rather than medicine; and its only claim of contribution to the practical problems of administration is that sound medical practice can only be founded on thorough knowledge of the biology of the organism. Any prescriptions for administrative practice will be only incidental to the main purpose of description and analysis.

The central theme around which the analysis has been developed is that organization behavior is a complex network of decisional processes, all pointed toward their influence upon the behaviors of the operatives—those who do the actual "physical" work of the organization. The anatomy of the organization is to be found in the distribution and allocation of decision-making functions. The physiology of the organization is to be found in the processes whereby the organization influences the decisions of each of its members—supplying these decisions with their premises.

THE PROCESS OF COMPOSITE DECISION

It should be perfectly apparent that almost no decision made in an organization is the task of a single individual. Even though the final responsibility for taking a particular action rests with some definite person, we shall always find, in studying the manner in which this decision was reached, that its various components can be traced through the formal and informal channels of communication to many individuals who have participated in forming its premises. When all of these components have been identified, it may appear that the contribution of the individual who made the formal decision was a minor one, indeed.[1]

We may see the treasurer of a corporation affix his signature to a contract whereby the corporation borrows a sum of money to finance a particular project. The treasurer evidently has authority to make this decision for the organization and to commit the organization to it; but what steps preceded his decision? Perhaps the chief engineer (acting, no doubt, on information and analyses communicated to him by his subordinates) decides that for the adequate operation of a technological system there should be a particular structure that his department has designed at an anticipated cost of five hundred thousand dollars. The general manager to whom he reports does not object to the proposal from the technological standpoint, but doubts that its value is sufficient to justify so large an expenditure; but before making a decision he consults the president or some members of the board as to their willingness to approve the risk of additional investment, as to the feasibility of financing, and as to the time of financing. This results in a decision to ask for a revision and curtailment of the proposal, and plans are redrafted in the engineering department to reduce the cost to four hundred thousand dollars. The proposal is then

[1] I am indebted to Mr. Barnard, through correspondence, both for the term "composite decision" and for the particular example of composite decision that is given here. The reader can undoubtedly supply many comparable examples from his own organizational experience.

formally drawn up, approved by the chief engineer and the officers, and presented to the board. The questions then are: should the project be approved, and how should it be financed? It is approved; but it is suggested that in view of the danger of error of estimate, financing to the amount of four hundred fifty thousand dollars should be sought because otherwise the financial position of the company would be embarrassed if the cost should exceed four hundred thousand. Then, after much discussion, it is decided to finance by means of a mortgage loan at an interest rate not exceeding a certain amount, preferably placed with Company X, and the officers are authorized by the board of directors to proceed. Company X, however, when consulted is not interested in the proposal at the interest rate suggested and on examination of the plans thinks the engineering aspects call for revision. The matter goes through the same process again, and so on.

In the end, the officer making the final negotiation or signing the contract, though appearing to decide at least the major questions, is reduced almost to performing a ministerial function. The major decisions were made neither by the board nor by any officer, nor formally by any group; they evolved through the interaction of many decisions both of individuals and by committees and boards. No one man is likely to be aware of all the decisions entering into the process or of who made them, or of the interaction through a period of time that modified decisions at one point and another. That decision is almost always a composite process of this sort will be illustrated further in a later section of this chapter that deals with the planning process.

From the standpoint of process, it is useful to view composite decision from the standpoint of the individual who makes a decision, in order to see (a) how much discretion is actually left him, and (b) what methods the organization uses to influence the decisional premises he selects.

The Degrees of Influence

Influence is exercised in its most complete form when a decision promulgated by one person governs every aspect of the behavior of another. On the parade ground, the marching soldier is permitted no discretion whatsoever. His every step, his bearing, the length of his pace are all governed by authority. Frederick the Great is reported to have found the parade-ground deportment of his Guards perfect—with one flaw. "They breathe," he complained. Few other examples could be cited, however, of the exercise of influence in unlimited form.

Most often, influence places only partial limits upon the exercise of discretion. A subordinate may be told *what* to do, but given considerable leeway as to *how* he will carry out the task. The "what" is, of course, a matter of degree, and may be specified within narrower or broader limits. A charter which states in general terms the function of a city fire department places much less severe limits upon the discretion of the fire chief than the commands of a captain at the scene of a conflagration place on the discretion of the firemen.

A realistic analysis of influence in general and authority in particular must recognize that influence can be exercised with all degrees of specificity. To determine the scope of influence or authority which is exercised in any concrete case, it is necessary to dissect the decisions of the subordinate into their component parts, and then determine which of these parts are determined by the superior and which are left to the subordinate's discretion.

In Chapter III it was shown that a rational decision can be viewed as a conclusion reached from premises of two different kinds: value premises and factual premises. Given a complete set of value and factual premises, there is only one decision which is consistent with rationality. That is, with a given system of values, and a specified set of alternatives, there is one alternative that is preferable to the others.

The behavior of a rational person can be controlled, therefore, if the value and factual premises upon which he bases his decisions are specified for him. This control can be complete or partial—all the premises can be specified, or some can be left to his discretion. Influence, then, is exercised through control over the premises of decision. It is required that the decisions of the subordinate shall be consistent with premises selected for him by his superior. The scope of authority and, conversely, the scope of discretion are determined by the number and importance of the premises which are specified, and the number and importance of those which are left unspecified.

As pointed out previously, discretion over value premises has a different logical status from discretion over factual premises. The latter can always be evaluated as "right" or "wrong" in an objective, empirical sense. To the former, the terms "right" and "wrong" do not apply. Hence, if only factual premises are left to the subordinate's discretion, there is, under the given circumstances, only one decision which he can "correctly" reach. On the other hand, if value premises are left to the subordinate's discretion, the "correctness" of a decision will depend upon the value premises he has selected, and there is no criterion of right or wrong which can be applied to his selection.

When it is admitted that authority need extend to only a few of the premises of decision, it follows that more than one order can govern a given decision, provided that no two orders extend to the same premise. An analysis of almost any decision of a member of a formal organization would reveal that the decision is responsive to a very complex structure of influence.

Military organization affords an excellent illustration of this. In ancient warfare, the battlefield was not unlike the parade ground. An entire army was often commanded by a single man, and his authority extended in a very complete form to the lowest man in the ranks. This was possible because the entire battlefield was within range of a man's voice and vision, and because tactics were for the most part executed by the entire army in unison.

The modern battlefield presents a very different picture. Authority is exercised through a complex hierarchy of command. Each level of the hierarchy leaves an extensive area of discretion to the level below, and even the private soldier, under combat conditions, exercises a considerable measure of discretion.

Under these circumstances, how does the authority of the commander extend to the soldiers in the ranks? How does he limit and guide their behavior? He does this by specifying the general mission and objective of each unit on the next level below, and by determining such elements of time and place as will assure a proper coordination among units. The colonel assigns to each battalion in his regiment its task; the major, to each company in his battalion; the captain, to each platoon in his company. Beyond this, the officer does not ordinarily go. The internal arrangements of Army Field Service Regulations specify that "an order should not trespass upon the province of a subordinate. It should contain everything beyond the independent authority of the subordinate, but nothing more."[2]

So far as field orders go, then, the discretion of an officer is limited only by the specification of the objective of his unit, and its general schedule. He proceeds to narrow further the discretion of his subordinates so far as is necessary to specify what part each sub-unit is to play in accomplishing the task of the unit.

Does this mean that the discretion of the officer is limited only by his objective or mission? Not at all. To be sure, the field order does not go beyond this point. It specifies the *what* of his action. But the officer is also governed by the tactical doctrine and general orders of the army which specify in some detail the *how*. When the captain receives field orders to deploy his company for an attack, he is expected to carry out the deployment in accordance with the accepted tactical principles in the army. In leading his unit, he will be held accountable for the *how* as well as the *what*.

When we turn our attention, finally, to the man who carries out the army's task—the private soldier—we see that a great mass of influences bear upon the decisions which he makes. The decision that he will participate in an attack may have been made by a divisional, or even a corps, commander. His precise geographical location and place in the attack will be determined with ever increasing degrees of specificity by general, colonel, major, captain, lieutenant, sergeant in turn. But that is not all. The plan of attack which the captain determines upon will be a result not only of the field orders he receives, but also of the tactical training he has received, and his intelligence of the disposition of the enemy. So also the private, as he moves forward to the attack in the skirmish line, must thenceforth rely more and more upon the influences of his training and indoctrination.

To understand the process of decision in an organization, it is necessary to go far beyond the on-the-spot orders that are given by superior to subordinate. It is necessary to discover how the subordinate is influenced by standing orders, by training, and by review of his actions. It is necessary to study the channels of communication in the organization in order to determine what information reaches him which may be relevant to his decisions. The broader the sphere of discretion left to the subordinate, the more important become those types of influence which do not depend upon the exercise of formal authority.

[2] *U.S. Army Field Service Regulations*, 1923, p. 7.

The Modes of Influence

The ways in which the organization brings its influence to bear on the decisions of the individual have been enumerated in Chapter I. The "external" influences include authority, advice and information, and training. The "internal" influences include the criterion of efficiency and organizational identifications. Each of these has been discussed at length in preceding chapters, and that discussion does not need repetition here.

It is a fundamental problem of organization to determine the extent to which, and the manner in which, each of these forms of influence is to be employed. To a very great extent, these various forms of influence are interchangeable, a fact that is far more often appreciated in small than in large organizations.

The simplest example of this is the gradual increase in discretion that can be permitted to an employee as he becomes familiar with his job. A secretary learns to draft routine correspondence; a statistical clerk learns to lay out his own calculations. In each case training has taken the place of authority in guiding the employee's decisions.

"Functional supervision" often takes the form of advice rather than authority. This substitution of advice for authority may prove necessary in many situations in order to prevent conflicts of authority between line officers, organized on a geographical basis, and experts organized on a functional basis.

To the extent to which these forms of influence supplement, or are substituted for, authority, the problem of influence becomes one of internal education and public relations. Following is an example of this kind of influence:

> To the administration of a big department, the staff of the department themselves constitute a kind of inner "public," the right orientation of whose attitudes to each other in their mutual office contacts, in the inevitable absence of the direct personal touch which secures it in a small organization, would seem *prima facie* to call for just the same kind of attention, the same "practical psychology" or "salesmanship," as their attitude to members of the outside public. . . .
>
> Consider, for example, the machinery for preparing official instructions to the staff. . . . Do not official instructions tend to be drafted too rationalistically? Is not the draftsman's attention often concentrated too exclusively on framing a logical statement setting accurately and comprehensively what *ought* to be done? . . . But after all, the primary object of an instruction is not to be admired by critical specialists in the same office; an instruction is intended to be acted on, and that by people who are as a rule neither critical, nor specialists, nor in the same office—in other words, to produce such an impression on the *ultimate* recipient that on receiving it, he *will* forthwith proceed to do what is required of him.[3]

Administrators have increasingly recognized in recent years that

[3] H. Townshend, " 'Practical Psychology' in Departmental Organization," *Journal of Public Administration*, 12:66.

authority, unless buttressed by other forms of influence, is relatively impotent to control decision in any but a negative way. The elements entering into all but the most routine decisions are so numerous and so complex that it is impossible to control positively more than a few. Unless the subordinate is himself able to supply most of the premises of decision, and to synthesize them adequately, the task of supervision becomes hopelessly burdensome.

When viewed from this standpoint, the problem of organization becomes inextricably interwoven with the problem of recruitment. For the system of influence which can effectively be used in the organization will depend directly upon the training and competence of the employees at the various levels of the hierarchy. If a welfare agency can secure trained social workers as interviewers and case workers, broad discretion can be permitted them in determining eligibility, subject only to a sampling review, and a review of particularly difficult cases.

If trained workers can be obtained only for supervisory positions, then the supervisors will need to exercise a much more complete supervision over their subordinates, perhaps reviewing each decision, and issuing frequent instructions. The supervisory problem will be correspondingly more burdensome than in the first example, and the effective span of control of supervisors correspondingly narrower.

Likewise, when an organization unit is large enough to retain within its own boundaries the specialized expertise that is required for some of its decisions, the need for functional supervision from other portions of the organization becomes correspondingly less. When a department can secure its own legal, medical, or other expert assistance, the problems of functional organization become correspondingly simpler, and the lines of direct authority over the department need less supplementation by advisory and informational services.

Hence, problems of organization cannot be considered apart from the specifications of the employees who are to fill the positions established by the organization. The whole subject of job classification needs to be brought into much closer coordination with the theory of organization. The optimum organizational structure is a variable, depending for its form upon the staffing of the agency. Conversely, the classification of a position is a variable, depending upon the degree of centralization or decentralization which is desired or anticipated in the operation of the organizational form.

PLANNING AND REVIEW IN THE PROCESS OF COMPOSITE DECISION

There are two administrative techniques that are of key importance in the process of composite decision and in bringing to bear on a single decision a multiplicity of influences. Reference has already been made to them from time to time, but they deserve more systematic discussion as a part of the over-all decisional structure of the organization. The first of these is planning—a technique whereby the skills of a variety of specialists can be brought to bear on a problem before the formal stage of decision-making is reached. The second is review—a technique whereby the individual can be held accountable for the "internal" as well as the "external" premises that determine his decision.

The Planning Process

Plans and schedules are perhaps not strictly distinguishable from commands, since they usually derive their authority from an order. None the less, they are of special interest as devices for influencing decisions because of the immense amount of detail which it is possible to include in them, and because of the broad participation that can be secured, when desirable, in their formulation. Let us consider the last point first. An example is given by Sir Oswyn Murray:

> There is very little that is haphazard or disconnected about the array of Admiralty Departments. The noteworthy thing about them is not their number or variety, so much as their close inter-connection and the manner in which they combine to serve those administrative ends which I mentioned at the beginning of my paper. Perhaps I can best illustrate this by describing briefly the procedure followed in the design and production of a new battleship, which always seems to me to be the very romance of cooperation.
>
> We start with the First Sea Lord and his Assistant Chief of Naval Staff laying down in general terms the features that they desire to see embodied in the new design—the speed, the radius of action, the offensive qualities, the armour protection. Thereupon the Director of Naval Construction, acting under and in consultation with the Controller, formulates provisional schemes outlining the kind of ship desired, together with forecasts of the size and cost involved by the different arrangements. To do this he and his officers must have a good general knowledge—in itself only obtainable by close relations with those in charge of these matters—of the latest developments and ideas in regard to a great range of subjects —gunnery, torpedo, engineering, armour, fire-control, navigation, signalling, accommodation, and so on—in order to be reasonably sure that the provision included in his schemes is such as is likely to satisfy the experts in all these subjects, when the time for active cooperation arrives.
>
> With these alternative schemes before them, the Sea Lords agree on the general lines of the new ship, which done, the actual preparation of the actual designs begins. The dimensions and shape of the ship are drawn out approximately by the naval constructors. Then the Engineer-in-Chief and his Department are called in to agree upon the arrangement of the propelling machinery, the positions of shafts, propellers, bunkers, funnels, etc., and at the same time the cooperation of the Director of Naval Ordnance is required to settle the positions of the guns with their barbettes, and magazines and shell rooms and the means of supplying ammunition to the guns in action.
>
> An understanding between these three main departments enables further progress to be made. The cooperation of the Director of Torpedoes and the Director of Electrical Engineering is now called for to settle the arrangements for torpedo armament, electric generating ma-

chinery, electric lighting, etc. So the design progresses and is elaborated from the lower portions upwards, and presently the Director of Naval Construction is able to consult the Director of Naval Equipment as to the proposed arrangements in regard to the sizes and stowage of the motor boats, steamboats, rowing and sailing boats to be carried, as well as of the anchors and cables; the Director of the Signal Department as to the wireless telegraphy arrangements; the Director of Navigation as to the arrangements for navigating the ship; and so on. In this way the scheme goes on growing in a tentative manner, its progress always being dependent on the efficiency of different parts, until ultimately a more or less complete whole is arrived at in the shape of drawings and specifications provisionally embodying all the agreements. This really is the most difficult and interesting stage, for generally it becomes apparent at this point that requirements overlap, and that the best possible cannot be achieved in regard to numbers of points within the limit set to the contractors. These difficulties are cleared up by discussion at round-table conferences, where the compromises which will least impair the value of the ship are agreed upon, and the completed design is then finally submitted for the Board's approval. Some fourteen departments are concerned in the settlement of the final detailed arrangements.[4]

The point which is so clearly illustrated here is that the planning procedure permits expertise of every kind to be drawn into the decision without any difficulties being imposed by the lines of authority in the organization. The final design undoubtedly received authoritative approval; but, during the entire process of formulation, suggestions and recommendations flowed freely from all parts of the organization without raising the problem of "unity of command." It follows from this that to the extent to which planning procedures are used in reaching decisions, the formal organization has relevance only in the final stages of the whole process. So long as the appropriate experts are consulted, their exact location in the hierarchy of authority need not much affect the decision.

This statement must be qualified by one important reservation. Organizational factors are apt to take on considerable importance if the decision requires a compromise among a number of competing values which are somewhat incompatible with one another. In such a case, the focus of attention and the identification of the person who actually makes the decision are apt to affect the degree to which advice offered him by persons elsewhere in the organization actually influences him. This factor is present in the example of the warship just cited.

This same illustration throws in relief the other aspect of the planning procedure which was mentioned above—that the plan may control, down to minute details, a whole complex pattern of behavior. The completed plan of the battleship will specify the design of the ship down to the last rivet. The task of the construction crew is minutely specified by this design.

[4] Sir Oswyn A. R. Murray, "The Administration of a Fighting Service," *Journal of Public Administration*, 1:216–217 (July, 1923).

The Process of Review

Review enables those who are in a position of authority in the administrative hierarchy to determine what actually is being done by their subordinates.

Methods of review. Review may extend to the *results* of the subordinates' activities, measured in terms of their objectives; the tangible *products*, if there are such, of their activities; or the method of their *performance*.

When authority is exercised through the specification of the objective of the organizational unit, then a primary method of review is to ascertain the degree to which the organizational objective is attained—its results. A city manager, for instance, may use measurements of results as a principal means of reviewing city departments. He may evaluate the fire department in terms of fire losses, the police department in terms of crime and accident rates, the public works department in terms of the condition of streets and the frequency of refuse collection.

A second very important method of review is one which examines the piece of completed work to see whether it meets the requirements of quantity and quality. This method assumes that the reviewing officer is able to judge the quality and quantity of the completed work with a certain degree of competence. Thus, a superior may review all outgoing letters written by his subordinates, or the work of typists may be checked by a chief clerk, or the work of a street repair crew may be examined by a superintendent.

It has not often enough been recognized that in many cases the review of work can just as well be confined to a randomly selected sample of the work as extended to all that is produced. A highly developed example of such a sampling procedure is found in the personnel administration of the Farm Credit Administration. This organization carries out its personnel functions on an almost completely decentralized basis, except for a small central staff which lays down standards and procedures. As a means of assuring that local practices follow these standards, field supervisors inspect the work of the local agencies, and in the case of certain personnel procedures, such as classification, the setting of compensation scales, and the development of testing materials, assure themselves of the quality of the work by an actual inspection of a sample. The same type of procedure is usually followed by state boards of equalization which review local assessments. Finally, welfare agencies in California, New York, and perhaps other states have developed an auditing procedure on a sampling basis, in order to review the work of local welfare agencies.

The third, and perhaps simplest, method of review is to watch the employee at work, either to see that he puts in the required number of hours, or to see that he is engaging in certain movements which if continued will result in the completion of the work. In this case, the review extends to procedures and techniques, rather than product or results. It is the prevalent form of review at the foremanship level.

Functions of review. To determine what method of review should be employed in any concrete administrative situation, it is necessary to be quite clear as to what this particular review process is to accomplish. There are at least four different functions that a review process may perform: diagnosis of the quality of decisions being made by subordinates, modification through influence on subsequent decisions, the correction of incorrect decisions that have already been made, and enforcement of sanctions against subordinates so that they will accept authority in making their decisions.[5]

In the first place, review is the means whereby the administrative hierarchy learns whether decisions are being made correctly or incorrectly, whether work is being done well or badly at the lower levels of the hierarchy. It is a fundamental source of information, then, upon which the higher levels of the hierarchy must rely heavily for their decisions. With the help of this information, improvements can be introduced into the decision-making process.

This leads to the second function of review—to influence subsequent decisions. This is achieved in a variety of ways. Orders may be issued covering particular points on which incorrect decisions have been made, or laying down new policies to govern decisions. Employees may be given training or retraining with regard to those aspects of their work which review has proved faulty. Information may be supplied to them, the lack of which has led to incorrect decisions. In brief, change may be brought about in any of the several ways in which decisions can be influenced.

Third, review may perform an appellate function. If the individual decision has grave consequences, it may be reviewed by a higher authority, to make certain that it is correct. This review may be a matter of course, or it may occur only on appeal by a party at interest. The justifications of such a process of review are that (1) it permits the decision to be weighed twice, and (2) the appellate review requires less time per decision than the original decision, and hence conserves the time of better-trained personnel for the more difficult decisions. The appellate review may, to use the language of administrative law, consist in a consideration *de novo*, or may merely review the original decision for substantial conformity to important rules of policy.

Fourth, review is often essential to the effective exercise of authority. As we have seen in Chapter VII, authority depends, to a certain extent, upon the availability of sanctions to give it force. Sanctions can be applied only if there is some means of ascertaining when authority has been respected, and when it has been disobeyed. Review supplies the person in authority with this information.

When we recall the "rule of anticipated reactions," we see that the anticipation of review and the invocation of sanctions secure conformity to authority of the decision made prior to review. It is for this reason that review can influence a prior decision.

CENTRALIZATION AND DECENTRALIZATION

Our examination of the process of composite decision, and particularly of the methods and functions of review in an organization, casts con-

[5] A somewhat similar, but not identical, analysis of the function of review can be found in Sir H. N. Bunbury's paper, "Efficiency as an Alternative to Control," *Journal of Public Administration*, 6:97–98 (Apr., 1928).

siderable light on the way in which decisional processes can best be distributed through the organization, and on the relative advantages and disadvantages in centralizing the processes of decision.

What has already been said with respect to this issue? In Chapter VII it was pointed out that the specialization and centralization of decision-making serves three purposes: it secures coordination, expertise, and responsibility. In Chapter III some pragmatic tests were suggested for arriving at a division of function between legislator and administrator. In Chapter VIII, the relation between centralization of decisions and the problems of communication was explored. In Chapter X, it was seen that a need for centralization sometimes arises from the faulty institutional identifications of the members of an organization. In the present chapter, it was urged that the capabilities of the members of an organization would be one determinant of the possible degree of decentralization. Are there additional considerations, beyond those already mentioned, that should carry weight in the allocation of decisions?

At the outset, one important distinction must be clearly understood. There are two very different aspects to centralization. On the one hand, decision-making powers may be centralized by using general rules to limit the discretion of the subordinate. On the other hand, decision-making powers may be centralized by taking out of the hands of the subordinate the actual decision-making function. Both processes may be designated as "centralization" because their result is to take out of the hands of the subordinate the actual weighing of competing considerations and to require that he accept the conclusions reached by other members of the organization.

The very close relationship between the manner in which the function of review is exercised, and the degree of centralization or decentralization should also be pointed out. Review influences decisions by evaluating them, and thereby subjecting the subordinate to discipline and control. Review is sometimes conceived as a means of detecting wrong decisions and correcting them. This concept may be very useful as applied to those very important decisions where an appellate procedure is necessary to conserve individual rights or democratic responsibility. Under ordinary circumstances, however, the function of correcting the *decisional processes* of the subordinate which lead to wrong decisions is more important than the function of correcting *wrong decisions*. As the resources of the subordinate for making correct decisions are strengthened, decentralization becomes increasingly possible. Hence, review can have three consequences: (1) if it is used to correct individual decisions, it leads to centralization, and an actual transfer of the decision-making function; (2) if it is used to discover where the subordinate needs additional guidance, it leads to centralization through the promulgation of more and more complete rules and regulations limiting the subordinate's discretion; (3) if it is used to discover where the subordinate's own resources need to be strengthened, it leads to decentralization. All three elements can be, and usually are, combined, in varying proportions.

But why should administration aim at decentralization? All of our analysis to this point has emphasized the important functions which the centralization of decision-making performs. Nevertheless, we are warned against a naïve acceptance of the advantages of centralization by the distrust which careful students of administration express for it. Sir Charles Harris, for example, has this to say:

> If I appear before you as a throughgoing advocate of decentralization, it is as a convert to the faith in middle age.... At the beginning of my service I was greatly impressed by the lack of general knowledge and grasp of central principle displayed in the local decisions and actions that came under my notice. For years the conviction grew upon me that a larger measure of active control from the centre would conduce to both efficiency and economy of administration; and today, if I were to confine my view to particular details and to immediate results, I should still feel on that point no possible doubt whatever. It is when one falls back to Capability Brown's view-point, and tries to see the wood as well as the trees, that the certainty disappears.
>
> ...Simple centralization drives up the functions of decision and authorization to the top centre; it leaves action, when decided upon, to be carried out by the subordinate authority.
>
> Don't cut down the discretion of the man below, or his class, by requiring submission to higher authority in the future, because he has made a mistake. Teach him and try him again; but if he is unteachable, shunt him.[6]

Almost any person, unless he recognizes the long-term consequences, feels "safer" if he makes decisions himself instead of delegating them to a subordinate. The superior rationalizes this centralization on a variety of grounds: he is more highly skilled or trained than the subordinate; if he makes the decision, he can be certain that it is decided as he would want it. What he does not always realize is that by concentrating the entire function of decision in himself, he is multiplying his work, and making the subordinate superfluous.

There are two principal reasons for decentralizing decisions even in cases where the superior is more highly trained than the subordinate. The first harks back to the distinction in Chapter IX between efficiency and adequacy. It is not enough to take into consideration the accuracy of the decision; its cost must be weighed as well. The superior is presumably a higher-paid individual than the subordinate. His time must be conserved for the more important aspects of the work of the organization. If it is necessary, in order that he may make a particular decision, that he sacrifice time which should be devoted to more important decisions, the greater accuracy secured for the former may be bought at too high a price.

The second reason why decentralization is often preferable to centralization is that the referral of a decision upward in the hierarchy introduces new money and time costs into the decision-making process. Against any advantages of accuracy when the decision is made at the center must be balanced the cost of duplicating the decisional process, together with the cost of communicating the decisions.

[6] Sir Charles Harris, "Decentralization," *Journal of Public Administration*, 3:117–133 (Apr., 1925).

To emphasize the costs of uneconomic standards of review, we cannot do better than quote an example cited by Ian Hamilton from his personal experience:

> In 1896 I was Deputy Quartermaster-General at Simla; then, perhaps still, one of the hardest-worked billets in Asia. After a long office day I used to get back home to dinner pursued by a pile of files three to four feet high. The Quartermaster-General, my boss, was a clever, delightful work-glutton. So we sweated and ran together for a while a neck-and-neck race with our piles of files, but I was the younger and he was the first to be ordered off by the doctors to Europe. Then I, at the age of forty-three, stepped into the shoes and became officiating Quartermaster-General in India. Unluckily, the Government at that moment was in a very stingy mood. They refused to provide pay to fill the post I was vacating and Sir George White, the Commander-in-Chief, asked me to duplicate myself and do the double work. My heart sank, but there was nothing for it but to have a try. The day came; the Quartermaster-General went home and with him went the whole of his share of the work. As for my own share, the hard twelve hours' task melted by some magic into the Socialist's dream of a six hours' day. How was that? Because, when a question came up from one of the Departments I had formerly been forced to compose a long minute upon it, explaining the case, putting my own views, and endeavoring to persuade the Quartermaster-General to accept them. He was a highly conscientious man and if he differed from me he liked to put on record his reasons—several pages of reasons. Or, if he agreed with me, still he liked to agree in his own words and to "put them on record." Now, when I became Quartermaster-General and Deputy Quartermaster-General rolled into one, I studied the case as formerly, but there my work ended: I had not to persuade my own subordinates: I had no superior except the Commander-in-Chief, who was delighted to be left alone: I just gave an order—quite a simple matter unless a man's afraid: "Yes," I said, or "No!"[7]

There is an additional objection to centralization that goes beyond those already considered. It has been assumed thus far that, given ample time, the superior could make more accurate decisions than the subordinate. This will be true, however, only if the information upon which the decision is to be based is equally accessible to both. When decisions must be made against a deadline, or when the organization is characterized by geographical dispersion, this may be far from the case. The "facts of the case" may be directly present to the subordinate, but highly difficult to communicate to the superior. The insulation of the higher levels of the administrative hierarchy from the world of fact known at first hand by the lower levels is a familiar administrative phenomenon.

Centralization is sometimes urged as a necessary concomitant of the specialization of work. If work is specialized, then procedures must be introduced to secure coordination among the members of the group; and

[7] Sir Ian Hamilton, *The Soul and Body of an Army* (London: E. Arnold & Co., 1921), pp. 235–236.

among the most powerful of coordinative procedures is the centralization of decisions. This is true; but in accepting this conclusion we must not blind ourselves to the very real disadvantages and costs that accompany specialization.

Interpersonal coordination involves communication of a plan. Complex and powerful as are the devices which can be used for such coordination, their effectiveness is in no way comparable to the coordinating power of the individual human nervous system. When the elements of the plan can be reduced to diagrams and maps, as in the case of a design for a ship or a bridge, interpersonal coordination can reach even minute detail. But the coordinative mechanisms of a skilled pianist, or of an engineer bringing all his skill and knowledge to bear on a problem of design, are far more intricate.

Successful use of the device of specialization to increase efficiency implies either that no coordination is required among the specialized segments of the complete task, or that this coordination can be achieved with the available techniques of interpersonal coordination. If neither of these conditions is fulfilled, then specialization must be sacrificed in order to retain the use of the individual brain as the coordinating mechanism. It is not very easy to thread a needle if one person holds the thread and another the needle. Here the task is to get thread and needle to the *same* place, and interpersonal coordination accomplishes this much less successfully than the coordination of the movements of the two hands by the human nervous system.

The quotation in which the procedure for designing a battleship was described is another case in point. A careful analysis of the procedure reveals that there were involved in it not only the experts on various aspects of battleship design, but also a group of functionaries who might be described as "expert jacks-of-all-trades in battleship design." The Director of Naval Construction, and not the functional experts, lays down the general lines of the ship. To repeat:

> Thereupon the Director of Naval Construction, acting under and in consultation with the Controller, formulates provisional schemes outlining the kind of ship desired, together with forecasts of the size and cost involved by the different arrangements. To do this he and his officers must have a good general knowledge—in itself only attainable by close relations with those in charge of these matters—of the latest developments and ideas in regard to a great range of subjects—gunnery, torpedo, engineering, armour, fire-control, navigation, signalling, accommodation, and so on—in order to be reasonably sure that the provision included in his schemes is such as is likely to satisfy the experts in all these subjects, when the time for active cooperation arrives.[8]

Only after the "jack-of-all-trades" has done his job are the experts called in for their suggestions. Next, a technique of interpersonal coordination, the conference, is used to reconcile the competing claims of experts. Finally, the plan is turned over again to the non-specialist for authorization.

[8] Sir Oswyn A. R. Murray, *loc. cit.*

We may conclude, then, that some measure of centralization is indispensable to secure the advantages of organization: coordination, expertise, and responsibility. On the other hand, the costs of centralization must not be forgotten. It may place in the hands of highly paid personnel decisions which do not deserve their attention. It may lead to a duplication of function which makes the subordinate superfluous. Facilities for communication must be available, sometimes at considerable cost. The information needed for a correct decision may be available only to the subordinate. Finally, centralization leaves idle and unused the powerful coordinative capacity of the human nervous system, and substitutes for it an interpersonal coordinative mechanism. These are the considerations which must be weighed in determining the degree to which decisions should be centralized or decentralized.

LESSONS FOR ADMINISTRATIVE THEORY

In Chapter II the position was taken that the currently accepted "principles of administration" are little more than ambiguous and mutually contradictory proverbs, and that a new approach is needed to establish a consistent and useful administrative theory. This is a fact that is beginning to be recognized in the literature of administration. If we study the chain of publications extending from Mooney and Reiley through Gulick, the President's Committee controversy, to Schuyler Wallace and Benson, we see a steady shift of emphasis from the "principles of administration" themselves to a study of the *conditions* under which competing principles are respectively applicable. We no longer say that organization should be by purpose, but rather that under such and such conditions purpose organization is desirable, but under such and such other conditions, process organization is desirable. It is the central thesis of this study that an understanding of these underlying conditions for the applicability of administrative principles is to be obtained from an analysis of the administrative process in terms of decisions.

If this approach be taken, the rationality of decisions—that is, their appropriateness for the accomplishment of specified goals—becomes the central concern of administrative theory. As was pointed out, however, in Chapter II, if there were no limits to human rationality, administrative theory would be barren. It would consist of the single precept: Always select that alternative, among those available, which will lead to the most complete achievement of your goals. The need for an administrative theory resides in the fact that there *are* practical limits to human rationality, and that these limits are not static, but depend upon the organizational environment in which the individual's decision takes place. The task of administration is so to design this environment that the individual will approach as close as practicable to rationality (judged in terms of the organization's goals) in his decisions.

The Area of Rationality

As has also been explained in Chapter II, when the limits to rationality are viewed from the individual's standpoint, they fall into three categories: he is limited by his unconscious skills, habits, and reflexes; he is limited by his values and conceptions of purpose, which may diverge from the organization goals; he is limited by the extent of his knowledge and information. The individual can be rational in terms of the organization's goals only to the extent that he is *able* to pursue a particular course of action, he has a correct conception of the *goal* of the action, and he is correctly *informed* about the conditions surrounding his action. Within the boundaries laid down by these factors, his choices are rational—goal-oriented.

Rationality, then, does not determine behavior. Within the area of rationality, behavior is perfectly flexible and adaptable to abilities, goals, and knowledge. Instead, behavior is determined by the irrational and non-rational elements that bound the area of rationality. The area of rationality is the area of adaptability to these nonrational elements. Two persons, given the same possible alternatives, the same values, the same knowledge, can rationally reach only the same decision. Hence, administrative theory must be concerned with the limits of rationality, and the manner in which organization affects these limits for the person making a decision. The theory must determine—as suggested in Chapter X—how institutionalized decisions can be made to conform to values developed within a broader organizational structure. The theory must be a critique of the effect (judged from the point of view of the whole organization) of the organizational structure upon the decisions of its component parts and its individual members.

Perhaps an example of the way in which the organization can alter each of the three types of limits enumerated above will make the problem more concrete:

Limited alternatives. Suppose a bricklayer is unable to work at an acceptable speed. There may be no lack of rationality in his behavior. The fact may be that his skills are not sufficiently developed to enable him to lay bricks rapidly. However, if attention were to be given to the skills themselves, if he were given instruction and training in proper methods, the impossible might readily become possible. Skills are examples of behavior patterns that in the short run limit the sphere of adaptability or rationality, but in the long run may, by training, open up entirely new behavior possibilities.

Reorientation of values. Sometimes rationality is limited by the individual's failure to identify himself correctly with the goals of the whole organization. In certain situations, at least, it is possible to reorient an individual from identification with a subgoal of the organization to identification with a broader and more inclusive goal. The writer has had occasion in another context to point to this method for reorienting the behavior of a "rational person" by altering his framework of values. The problem dealt with in that situation was to control and modify the motivation of a group of social workers who were participating in an administrative experiment:

> To the worker, the experiment might seem inconsistent with the objectives he was trying to attain in his daily job. The cooperation of such a worker could be obtained only by interpreting the study in terms of his more fundamental values and by showing him that these broader

values would be benefited by a temporary sacrifice of some of his immediate objectives and attitudes. In this way his attention might be detached from the narrower frame of reference—the conditioned reflexes, so to speak—forced on him by his regular daily schedule of work.[9]

Limits of knowledge. Where a particular item of knowledge is needed repeatedly in decision, the organization can anticipate this need and, by providing the individual with this knowledge prior to decision, can extend his area of rationality. This is particularly important when there are time limits on decision. Thus, a policeman is trained in methods of making arrests, handling unruly prisoners, and the like, so that he will not have to figure these things out on the spot when occasion requires.

Individual and Group Rationality

A decision is rational from the standpoint of the individual (subjectively rational) if it is consistent with the values, the alternatives, and the information which he weighed in reaching it. A decision is rational from the standpoint of the group (objectively rational) if it is consistent with the values governing the group, and the information that the group possesses relevant to the decision. Hence, the organization must be so constructed that a decision which is (subjectively) rational from the standpoint of the deciding individual will remain rational when reassessed from the standpoint of the group.

Suppose than an officer orders a soldier under his command to capture a particular hill. Rationality (subjective) demands of him that he combine this objective, or value, with the skills he possesses for approaching hostile positions, and with the information his senses provide him regarding his situation.

On the other hand, rationality requires of the officer that the objective he assigns the soldier shall contribute to the broader objective of his unit (which usually implies that the soldier's objective must have a reasonable possibility of successful attainment), and that he provide the soldier with all available information that may assist him in his task. To say that the officer is rational means that the soldier's behavior continues to appear rational when evaluated from the broader viewpoint which the officer's position affords him.

This is the basic task of administration—to provide each "operative" employee with an environment of decision of such a kind that behavior which is rational from the standpoint of this environment is also rational from the standpoint of the group values and the group situation. Moreover, it must be taken into consideration that the establishment of an environment of decision for the individual involves problems of communication for the organization. These, then, are the basic elements from which a theory of organization can be constructed: (1) a decision made above the operative level must be communicated; (2) wherever a decision is made, its quality will depend on the environment that bounds the area of rationality of the person making the decision. With respect to the first element, the technology of communication (in the very broadest sense) is the limiting factor; with respect to the second, the limiting factors are the very factors that limit the area of individual rationality.

[9] Simon and Divine, *op. cit.,* p. 487.

Importance of Organizational Location

Since the administrative theory is concerned with control of the non-rational, it follows that the larger the area of rationality, the less important is the administrative organization. For example, the function of plan preparation, or design, if it results in a written plan that can be communicated interpersonally without difficulty, can be located almost anywhere in the organization without affecting results. All that is needed is a procedure whereby the plan can be given authoritative status; and that can be provided in a number of ways. A discussion, then, of the proper location for a planning or designing unit is apt to be highly inconclusive, and may hinge on the personalities in the organization and their relative enthusiasm, or lack of it, toward the planning function.[10]

On the other hand, when factors of communication or identification are crucial to the making of a decision, the location of the decision in the organization is of great importance. The method of allocating decisions in the army, for instance, automatically (and "theoretically," I hasten to add) provides, at least in the period prior to the actual battle, that each decision will be made where the knowledge is available for coordinating it with other decisions. Similarly, we may note that final decisions regarding budget allowances are always entrusted to administrators who are not identified with the particular items to be allowed, but must weigh these items against alternative items.

THE ROLE OF THE ADMINISTRATOR

It may be appropriate to conclude this volume with a brief statement about the role and training of administrators. It has been suggested earlier that the decisions which might be uniquely designated as "administrative" decisions are those which are concerned with the decision-making process itself. That is, such decisions do not determine the content of the organization's work, but rather how the decision-making function is to be allocated and influenced in that particular organization.

But to say that in any organization certain "administrative" decisions have to be made is not to say that the person who happens to be designated an "administrator" in that organization makes, or should make, only administrative decisions. Whether or not it is desirable that there *should* be functionaries whose tasks are confined within these limits, it is certainly not an accurate description of administrative organizations as they exist today to define the administrator's task in those terms.

In almost all organizations he has a responsibility not only to establish and maintain the organizational structure, but also to make some of the broader and more important decisions regarding the content of the organization's work. To mention only one of these decisions, the higher

---

[10] See, for instance, Robert A. Walker, *The Planning Function in Urban Government* (Chicago: University of Chicago Press, 1941), pp. 166–175. Walker makes out a case for attaching the planning agency to the chief executive. But he rests his entire case on the rather slender reed that "as long as the planning agency is outside the governmental structure, however, planning will tend to encounter resistance from public officials as an invasion of their responsibility and jurisdiction." The verb "will" seems entirely too strong for the facts of the case.

administrator ordinarily has a considerable responsibility for budget decisions—that is, decisions as to the directions in which the organization's efforts should be applied. Further, to him falls the responsibility, within the limits of his discretion, of formulating organizational objectives—that is, the values that will guide decisions at all lower levels of the organization.

The statement, then, that as we proceed upward in the hierarchy "administrative" duties come to occupy more and more of the administrator's time, and "technical" duties less, must be interpreted with considerable caution. It is not true if the term "administrative duties" is taken to refer only to the organization-determining functions. It is true if the broader decisional functions which fall to the administrator are considered as "administrative duties."

What is the difference between these latter functions and the "technical" functions at the lower levels of the hierarchy? Simply that the content decisions of the higher administrator deal with more ultimate purposes and more general processes than the decisions of the lower administrator. We might say that the lower administrator's purposes are the upper administrator's processes.

The stenographer's rationality is exercised in translating a piece of copy, whatever its content, into a typewritten manuscript. Her employer's rationality is exercised in determining the content of the copy, taking for granted the very element with which the stenographer is concerned—its translation into typewritten form.

If the Chief Engineer's decisions are less concerned with engineering technology than those of his designing engineers, with what are they concerned? If the Health Officer's decisions do not involve the minutiae of medical knowledge, what do they involve? They involve the application of the criterion of efficiency to the broader purposes of the organization. Since the broader purposes of governmental organizations (and, to a lesser extent, commercial organizations) are predominantly social, and the larger problems of means are principally economic and fiscal, this means that the decisions of the higher administrators involve social science principles and economic calculations.

One further point should be noted that applies even to those decisions which deal with the organization structure itself. If, as has been suggested, administrative theory cannot be entirely freed from concern with the content of the organization's work, it follows that sound organizational decisions require also a knowledge of that content.

We see, then, that the work of the administrator, as organizations are now constituted, involves (1) decisions about the organization structure, and (2) the broader decisions as to the content of the organization's work. Decisions of neither type can rest entirely, or even primarily, upon a knowledge of or facility with administrative theory. The former must be firmly grounded in the organization's technology. The latter must be grounded in the organization's technology and requires in addition (a) a thorough appreciation of the theory of efficiency, and (b) a knowledge of those aspects of the social sciences which are relevant to the broader purposes of the organization.

If this analysis is correct, it has direct implications for the training of an "administrative class," that is, for the training of persons who are skilled in higher administration. In the first place, it casts grave doubts on the possibility of developing administrative ability apart from subject-matter competence except at the very highest levels of the hierarchy. In the second place, it indicates that the proper training of "administrators" lies not in the narrow field of administrative theory, but in the broader field of the social sciences generally.

CONCLUSION

Our study has not led us to any definitive administrative principles. It has, however, provided us with a framework for the analysis and description of administrative situations, and with a set of factors that must be weighed in arriving at any valid proposal for administrative organization. It has shown us, further, that currently accepted "principles" of administration suffer from internal ambiguity and mutual contradiction.

What are the next steps that research must take? First, it must develop adequate case studies of existing administrative situations. It will do well to initiate these on a small scale—dealing in minute detail with organizational units of moderate size. Only in this way can superficiality be avoided.

Second, techniques must be developed and improved for measuring the success of particular administrative arrangements. Specifically, the assumption so often made in administrative studies, that an arrangement is effective because it exists, is a circular argument of the worst sort. Students of administration are possessed of no occult vision which permits them, by simply observing an administrative organization, to determine whether it is "working" or not. The only procedure of evaluation that can possibly be valid is the comparison of alternative administrative schemes in terms of their objective results.

Finally, the valuable investigations already initiated of the "conditions" under which different administrative principles are validly applicable might well be extended with the use of the "decisional" framework described in this study.

THE NATURE OF LEADERSHIP
Chester I. Barnard*

In this selection Chester I. Barnard systematically analyzes leadership. In so doing, he eliminates much of the confusion surrounding the subject, and develops a rudimentary theory of managerial behavior.

* Reprinted by permission of the publishers from Chester I. Barnard, *Organization and Management* (Cambridge, Mass.: Harvard University Press, 1948), Chap. IV, pp. 80–110. Copyright 1940, 1948, by The President and Fellows of Harvard College.

INTRODUCTION

Leadership has been the subject of an extraordinary amount of dogmatically stated nonsense. Some, it is true, has been enunciated by observers who have had no experience themselves in coordinating and directing the activities of others; but much of it has come from men of ample experience, often of established reputations as leaders. As to the latter, we may assume that they know how to do well what they do not know how to describe or explain. At any rate, I have found it difficult not to magnify superficial aspects and catch-phrases of the subject to the status of fundamental propositions, generalized beyond all possibility of useful application, and fostering misunderstanding.

Seeking to avoid such errors, I shall not tell you what leadership is or even how to determine when it is present; for I do not know how to do so. Indeed, I shall venture to assert that probably no one else knows. These statements may seem strange and extreme, but I hope to convince you that they are not expressions of false modesty or of ill-considered judgment. At any rate, what I intend to discuss is *the problem of understanding the nature of leadership*.

The need for wide consideration of this subject was most forcibly impressed upon me by two observations, made on a single occasion, which revealed the extent of public misunderstanding of it. Some time ago I attended a large joint conference of laymen and members of the faculty of an important university to consider the subject of educational preparation for leadership. At this meeting my first observation was that *leadership* was confused with *preeminence* or *extraordinary usefulness* both by speakers and by audience. In their view a leading writer, artist, pianist, mathematician, or scientist exemplifies leadership substantially as does an executive or leader of an organization. No one appeared to be aware of the double meaning of "leadership" and its implications for the discussion of the subject of preparing "leaders." Among the meanings of the verb "to lead" we may say that one is "to excel, to be in advance, to be preeminent"; and another is "to guide others, to govern their activities, to be head of an organization or some part of it, to hold command." I think the distinction between these meanings is rather easy to see. Most individuals matured in a well-organized effort recognize it as a matter of course, so that it may be difficult for many who from long experience thoroughly understand the distinction to believe such a confusion common. I fear that it is common, however, and is making cooperation and adequate organization increasingly difficult.

My second observation at this meeting, further evidence of the same fact, was this: During the period of open discussion, a well-known engineer protested the subjection of engineers to supervision or management by those not engineers. The superiority of engineers in nearly all respects, especially in intellect, training, and science, was implied. Though the audience was not one of engineers, it expressed derision generally at the absurd state of affairs portrayed. Could there have been a more striking proof of the misconception of the subject these several hundred earnest, intelligent, educated people were discussing—how better to prepare people to be leaders?

These observations show the importance of public discussion of the problem. Mere knowledge of how to solve it would not be sufficient. Often, in similar matters, when a solution is available it will not be accepted unless the problem itself is either acknowledged as such by reliance upon a responsible authority or is recognized and accepted by agreement and understanding. Otherwise a correct solution is merely "one man's idea, a little queer"; and a "solution" is something that cannot be made effective because it *will* not be used. This seems often not to be adequately taken into account in the discussion of social and organization "remedies."

Now it seems to me evident that the problem of leadership, like some others which now obsess us, is not yet suitably formulated. For this reason, if for no other, it is not generally understood. This needs emphasis because within our own organizations we usually do not experience much difficulty on this account; for we already have an approximately common understanding or sense, coming from long interconnected experience, which is workably adequate. Such an understanding is a substitute, and a superior one, for abstract knowledge of the matter—at least for any I imagine being available for a long time. But outside these circles of intimate experiential knowledge, understanding fails, even among leaders.

Not only misunderstanding but positive need for leaders warrants our attention to this subject. The large-scale integrations of our present societies—the great nations, the immense organizations of war and peace, of culture and religion—make the needs of leadership relatively greater and its functions more complex than heretofore, so that the necessary proportion of leaders to the population has greatly increased. In other words, the "overhead" of any organization or society clearly tends to expand more rapidly than its size. Moreover, technology and specialization make the arts of leadership even more complex than consideration of size alone would indicate. These facts suggest that scarcity of leaders of requisite quality may already limit the possibility of stable cooperation in our societies.

I think we may agree, then, that public misunderstanding and misinformation, and the need for provision of more adequate leadership, both urge our effort to understand the nature of leadership. My present attempt to contribute to this end ought chiefly, I think, to make evident the present obscurity of the subject and the complexity of the functions and conditions involved in it. This method of approach will surely try our patience and may be discouraging to some; but we shall be wise in this matter not to give answers before we have found out what are the questions. The attitude that I think we may best have has been admirably stated by T. S. Eliot:

> The fact that a problem will certainly take a long time to solve, and that it will demand the attention of many minds for several generations, is no justification for postponing the study. And, in times of emergency, it may prove in the long run that the problems we have postponed or ignored, rather than those we have failed to attack successfully, will return to plague us. Our difficulties of the moment must always be dealt

with somehow; but our permanent difficulties are difficulties of every moment.[1]

In the light of these preliminary remarks it may be well for me to state the meaning of the word "leadership." As I use it herein it refers to the quality of the behavior of individuals whereby they guide people or their activities in organized effort. This is its primary significance. Organized effort takes place, however, in systems of cooperation which often include property or plants. When this is so, the activities coordinated relate to, or are connected with, the property or plant, and the two are not separate. Hence, the management or administration of such properties, as distinguished from the command or supervision of personnel, is also included as a secondary aspect of leadership.

Whatever leadership is, I shall now make the much oversimplified statement that it depends upon three things—(1) the individual, (2) the followers, and (3) the conditions. We shall agree at once, no doubt; but unless we are careful, I suspect that within an hour we shall be talking of the qualities, capacities, talents, and personalities of leaders as if the individual were the exclusive component of leadership. Therefore, let me emphasize the interdependence by restating it in quasi-mathematical language, thus: Leadership appears to be a function of at least three complex variables—the individual, the group of followers, the conditions.

Now the points to note here are two. First, these are variables obviously within wide limits, so that leadership may in practice mean an almost infinite number of possible combinations. Second, if we are to have a good understanding of leadership we shall need a good understanding of individuals, of organizations, and of conditions, and of their interrelationships so far as relevant to our topic. Do we have that now? I am sure we do not. Yet I fear this may be thought an extreme theoretical view unless I give some demonstration of its correctness, and at the same time give some idea of how we might at least approach some better practical understanding.

In undertaking this, I shall depart from the scheme of the three variables and proceed along more everyday lines. To present my suggestions of possibilities as to the nature of leadership, I shall give the following: (i) a general description of what leaders have to do in four sectors of leadership behavior; (ii) thoughts concerning certain differences of conditions of leadership; (iii) some remarks about the active personal qualities of leaders; (iv) a few notes on the problem of the development of leaders; and (v) observations about the selection of leaders.

FOUR SECTORS OF LEADERSHIP BEHAVIOR

Leaders lead. This implies activity, and suggests the obvious question "What is it that they have to do?" Now, I must confess that heretofore on the few occasions when I have been asked: "What do you *do?*" I have been unable to reply intelligibly. Yet I shall attempt here to say generally what leaders do, dividing their work under four topics, which

[1] T. S. Eliot, *The Idea of a Christian Society*, Harcourt, Brace & Co., New York, 1940.

for present purposes will be sufficient. The topics I shall use are: The Determination of Objectives; The Manipulation of Means; The Control of the Instrumentality of Action; and The Stimulation of Coordinated Action.

Unfortunately it is necessary to discuss these topics separately. This is misleading unless it is remembered that, except in special cases or when specially organized, these kinds of action are not separate but closely interrelated, interdependent, and often overlapping or simultaneous. Therein lies one reason why it is so difficult for a leader to say what he does or to avoid misrepresenting himself. He does not know how to untangle his acts in a way suitable for verbal expression. His business is leading, not explaining his own behavior, at which, though sometimes voluble, he is usually rather inept, as we doubtless all are. Indeed, as I shall show later, it is *impossible* for him to be aware of this behavior in the sense necessary to explain it except very generally on the basis of his observations of others as well as of himself.

First Sector—Determination of Objectives

Let us consider the first sector of behavior.

An obvious function of a leader is to know and say what to do, what not to do, where to go, and when to stop, with reference to the general purpose or objective of the undertaking in which he is engaged. Such a statement appears to exhaust the ideas of many individuals as to a leader's *raison d'être*. But if they are able to observe the operations closely, it often disconcerts them to note that many things a leader tells others to do were suggested to him by the very people he leads. Unless he is very dynamic—too dynamic, full of his own ideas—or pompous or Napoleonic, this sometimes gives the impression that he is a rather stupid fellow, an arbitrary functionary, a mere channel of communication, and a filcher of ideas. In a measure this is correct. He has to be stupid enough to listen a great deal, he certainly must arbitrate to maintain order, and he has to be at times a mere center of communication. If he used only his own ideas he would be somewhat like a one-man orchestra, rather than a good conductor, who is a very high type of leader.

However, one thing should make us cautious about drawing false conclusions from this description. It is that experience has shown it to be difficult to secure leaders who are able to be properly stupid, to function arbitrarily, to be effective channels of communication, and to steal the right ideas, in such ways that they still retain followers. I do not pretend to be able to explain this very well. It seems to be connected with knowing whom to believe, with accepting the right suggestions, with selecting appropriate occasions and times. It also seems to be so related to conditions that a good leader in one field is not necessarily good in others, and not equally good under all circumstances. But at any rate, to say what to do, and when, requires an understanding of a great many things "on the whole," "taking everything into account," in their relations to some purpose or intention or result—an understanding that leads to distinguishing effectively between the important and the unimportant *in the particular concrete situation*, between what can and what cannot be done, between what will probably succeed and what will probably not, between what will weaken cooperation and what will increase it.

Second Sector—Manipulation of Means

There is undoubtedly an important difference between the kind of effort we have just considered and the direction of detailed activities that are parts of technical procedures and technological[2] operations as the subsidiary means and instruments of accomplishing specific objectives already determined. Sometimes an exceptional leader can effectively guide technical operations in which he has no special competence, whereas those of high competence are often not successful leaders. I shall not attempt a general explanation of these facts; but on the whole we may regard leadership without technical competence as increasingly exceptional, unless for the most general work. Usually leaders, even though not extraordinarily expert, appear to have an understanding of the technological or technical work which they guide, particularly in its relation to the activities and situations with which they deal. In fact, we usually assume that a leader will have considerable knowledge and experience in the specifically technical aspects of the work he directs. I need not say much about this, for it seems to me that at present we overestimate the importance of technical skill and competence and undervalue, or even exclude, the less tangible and less obvious factors in leadership.

Nevertheless, the technical and technological factors in leadership not only constitute a variable of great importance, but they introduce serious difficulties, which should be mentioned, especially in respect to (1) the development of types of leaders, and to (2) the limitations these technical factors place upon the "mobility" of the leaders in an organization or society, and also (3) because of the restrictive effect of technical study and experience on the *general* or "social" development of individuals.

(1) It is almost a matter of course that leadership "material" will be inducted into organization through some particular technical channel. Such channels are now highly specialized. When the course has been run, the man has been trained for leadership only with respect to a narrow range of activities. Otherwise he is untrained, and hence (2) the mobility of leadership resources may be seriously reduced because it is difficult to use a good leader of one narrow field in another field or in more general work—a fact which I suppose is now well recognized at least in all large organizations of industry and government and education. This difficulty, which is real, has become exaggerated in our minds, so that in my opinion we all—leaders and followers—tend to overlook superior leaders who at the moment may be lacking particular technical qualifications.

(3) Concerning the third difficulty—the effect of specialization upon the individual—it is only necessary to note that while men are concentrat-

---

[2] Throughout I use "technological" exclusively to refer to conditions of physical technology—plants, machines, chemical processes; and "technical" to refer either to systems of procedure in accounting, management, etc., or in a more general sense to cover both ideas.

ing upon techniques, machines, processes, and abstract knowledge, *they are necessarily diverted to a considerable extent from experience with men, organizations, and the social situations, the distinctive fields of application of leadership ability*. Thus at the most impressionable period they become so well grounded in "mechanical" attitudes toward non-human resources and processes that they transfer these attitudes, then and later, toward men also.

The technical sector of leadership behavior is not a new thing in the world, but its importance has greatly increased. By technology and specialization we have accomplished much; but the resulting complexity of leadership functions and the restriction of the development and supply of general leaders seems to me one of the important problems of our times.

Third Sector—Instrumentality of Action

Leadership obviously relates to the coordination of certain efforts of people. There is little coordination or cooperation without leadership, and leadership implies cooperation. Coordinated efforts constitute organization. *An organization is the instrumentality of action so far as leaders are concerned, and it is the indispensable instrumentality*. Many promising men never comprehend this because of early emphasis upon plants, structures, techniques, and abstract institutions, especially legal institutions such as the law of corporations.

The primary efforts of leaders need to be directed to the maintenance and guidance of organizations as whole systems of activities. I believe this to be the most distinctive and characteristic sector of leadership behavior, but it is the least obvious and least understood. Since most of the acts which constitute organization have a specific function which superficially is independent of the maintenance of organization—for example, the accomplishment of specific tasks of the organization—it may not be observed that such acts at the same time also constitute organization and that this, not the technical and instrumental, is the primary aspect of such acts from the viewpoint of leadership. Probably most leaders are not ordinarily conscious of this, though intuitively they are governed by it. For any act done in such a way as to disrupt cooperation destroys the capacity of organization. Thus the leader has to guide all in such a way as to preserve organization as the instrumentality of action.[3]

Up to the present time, leaders have understood organization chiefly in an intuitive and experiential way. The properties, limitations, and processes of organization as systems of coordinated action have been little known in abstraction from concrete activities and situations; but the persistence and effectiveness of many organizations are evidence that leaders know how to behave with respect to them. On the other hand, we know that many very able, intelligent, and learned persons have neither understanding nor correct intuitions about concrete organizations.

---

[3] The conception of the nature of organization—as a system of coordinated *activities*—involved in this paragraph is carefully developed and defended in *The Functions*, chapter vii, "The Theory of Formal Organization," and is made more explicit in the article "Comments on the Job of an Executive." See the preliminary note of the title page.

Fourth Section—Stimulation of Coordinated Action

To repeat a commonplace, it is one thing to say what should be done, and quite another to get it done. A potential act lies outside organization, and it is one task of leaders to change potentiality into the stuff of action. In other words, one important kind of thing that leaders do is to induce people to convert abilities into coordinated effort, thereby maintaining an organization while simultaneously getting its work done. I need hardly say that this kind of activity of leaders is sometimes the most striking aspect of what they do. In a broad sense this is the business of persuasion. Nor need I say that the sorts of acts or behavior by which executives "persuade" to coordinated action are innumerable. They vary from providing the example in "going over the top," or calm poise inspiring confidence, or quiet commands in tense moments, to fervid oratory, or flattery, or promises to reward in money, prestige, position, glory, or to threats and coercion. Why do they vary? Some obvious differences of combination in leaders, in followers, in organizations, in technology, in objectives, in conditions, will occur to you. But the effective combinations are often so subtle and so involved in the personalities of both leaders and followers that to be self-conscious about them, or for others to examine them when in process, would disrupt them.

My chief purpose in this brief account of four sectors of leadership behavior has been to indicate how interconnected and interdependent they are and to suggest how great is the variation in what "leadership" means specifically, depending upon the relative importance of the kinds of behavior required.

THE CONDITIONS OF LEADERSHIP

Already it has been necessary to allude at least by implication to differences in conditions of leadership, such for example as are involved in the degrees and kinds of technological operations. I shall now confine the discussion to differences of conditions of another sort, relating to the degree of tension of the action of leaders, followers, or both. It will be sufficient to consider only the two extremes.

The first is that which we may call stable conditions. These may be complex and of very large scale; but they are comparatively free from violent changes or extreme uncertainties of *unusual* character or implying important hazards. The behavior of leaders under such conditions may be calm, deliberate, reflective, and anticipatory of future contingencies. Leadership then is lacking in the dramatic characteristics often observed at the other extreme, and this is one of its difficulties; for its function of persuasion must be carried on without the aid of emotional drives and of obvious necessities and against the indifference often accompanying lack of danger, excitement, and sentiment. Stable conditions call for self-restraint, deliberation, and refinement of technique, qualities that some men who are good leaders under tense conditions are unable to develop.

The other extreme is that of great instability, uncertainty, speed, intense action, great risks, important stakes, life and death issues. Here leaders must have physical or moral courage, decisiveness, inventiveness, initiative, even audacity; but I believe we tend to overstate the qualities required for this extreme, due to its dramatic aspects and because the outcome of action is more easily judged.

This is enough to suggest that differences of conditions of this type, that is, differences in tension, are important factors in leadership behavior. It should be apparent that we could expect only rarely to find men equally adapted to both extremes, and that quite different types of leaders are to be expected for this reason. Yet it is obvious that emergencies may be encountered in any kind of cooperative effort, and that leaders have to be adapted to function under wide ranges of conditions. Indeed, intermittent periods of severe stress are the rule in navigation, in military organizations, in some kinds of public utility work, in political activity, to cite a few examples in which particular types of *flexibility* are necessary to continuous leadership. It may be apparent here, as perhaps it was in considering the sectors of leadership behavior, that the practical problem in selecting specific leaders would be to ascertain the *balance of qualities* most probably adapted to the conditions or to the variations of conditions.

THE ACTIVE QUALITIES OF LEADERS

I have already stated why I do not think it useful to discuss leadership exclusively in personal terms. Leaders, I think, are made quite as much by conditions and by organizations and followers as by any qualities and propensities which they themselves have. Indeed, in this connection, I should put much more emphasis upon the character of organizations than upon individuals. But this is not the common opinion; and I certainly should not fail to discuss that quite variable component, the individual.

I shall list and discuss briefly five fundamental qualities or characteristics of those who are leaders, in their order of importance as regarded for very *general* purposes. Probably I shall not include qualities that some think essential. I would not quarrel about what may be only a difference in names or emphasis. Perhaps, also, there will be disagreement about the order I have chosen. This I shall mildly defend, my chief purpose being to correct for a current exaggerated and false emphasis. The list follows: (i) Vitality and Endurance; (ii) Decisiveness; (iii) Persuasiveness; (iv) Responsibility; and (v) Intellectual Capacity.

Vitality and Endurance

We should not confuse these qualities with good health. There are many people of good health who have little or moderate vitality—energy, alertness, spring, vigilance, dynamic qualities—or endurance. Conversely, there are some who have poor health and even suffer much who at least have great endurance. Generally, it seems to me, vitality and endurance are fundamental qualities of leadership, though they may wane before leadership capacity does.

Notwithstanding the exceptions, these qualities are important for several reasons. The first is that they both promote and permit the unremitting acquirement of exceptional experience and knowledge, which in general underlies extraordinary personal capacity for leadership.

The second is that vitality is usually an element in personal attractiveness or force which is a great aid to persuasiveness. It is sometimes even a compelling characteristic. Thus, few can be unaffected by the violent energy with which Mussolini throws his arm in the Fascist salute, or by the vehemence of Hitler's speech, or by the strenuous life of Theodore Roosevelt. Similarly, we are impressed by the endurance of Franklin D. Roosevelt in campaign.

The third reason for the importance of vitality and endurance is that leadership often involves prolonged periods of work and extreme tension without relief, when failure to endure may mean permanent inability to lead. To maintain confidence depends partly on uninterrupted leadership.

Decisiveness

I shall be unable to discuss here precisely what decision is or involves as a process, but I regard it as the element of critical importance in all leadership, and I believe that all formal organization depends upon it. Ability to make decisions is the characteristic of leaders I think most to be noted. It depends upon a propensity or willingness to decide and a capacity to do so. I neglect almost entirely the appearance or mannerism of being decisive, which seems often to be a harmful characteristic, at least frequently misleading, usually implying an improper understanding and use of authority, and undermining confidence. Leadership requires making actual appropriate decisions and only such as are warranted.

For present purposes decisiveness needs to be considered in both its positive and negative aspects. Positively, decision is necessary to get the right things done at the right time and to prevent erroneous action. Negatively, failure to decide undoubtedly creates an exceedingly destructive condition in organized effort. For delay either to direct or to approve or disapprove, that is, mere suspense, checks the decisiveness of others, introduces indecisiveness or lethargy throughout the whole process of co-operation, and thus restricts experience, experiment, and adaptation to changing conditions.

Persuasiveness

The fundamental importance of persuasiveness I have already mentioned. Here I refer to the ability in the individual to persuade, and the propensity to do so. Just what these qualities are defies description; but without them all other qualities may become ineffective. These other qualities seem to be involved, yet not to be equivalent. In addition, persuasiveness appears often to involve or utilize talents, such as that of effective public speaking or of exposition or special physical skills or even extraordinary physique, and many others. The relation of specific talents to leadership we cannot usefully consider further here. But at least we may say that persuasiveness involves a *sense* or understanding of the point of view, the interests, and the conditions of those to be persuaded.

Responsibility

I shall define responsibility as an emotional condition that gives an individual a sense of acute dissatisfaction because of failure to do what he feels he is morally bound to do or because of doing what he thinks he is morally bound not to do, in particular concrete situations. Such dissatisfaction he will avoid; and therefore his behavior, if he is "responsible" and if his beliefs and his sense of what is right are known, can be approximately relied upon. That this stability of behavior is important to leadership from several points of view will be recognized without difficulty; but it is especially so from that of those who follow. Capricious and irresponsible leadership is rarely successful.

Intellectual Capacity

I have intentionally relegated "brains" to the fifth place. I thereby still make it important, but nevertheless subsidiary to physical capacity, decisiveness, persuasiveness, and responsibility. Many find this hard to believe, for leaders especially seem to me frequently to be inordinately proud of their intellectual abilities, whatever they may be, rather than of their more important or effective qualities.

A Digression on the Importance of the Non-intellectual Abilities

This attitude may be partly due to a confusion between preeminence and leadership—an instance of which I gave in my introduction—and partly to the high social status now given to intellect, to which I shall refer later. Disagreement as to the subordinate place to which I here assign intellect may also be partly due to a matter of definition; for I think we usually confuse *acquirement* by intellectual processes with responsive, habitual, intuitive *expression* or *application* of what has been acquired, which I take to involve processes largely non-intellectual.

However, I believe sensitiveness about our intellects is often due especially to the fact that the part of behavior *of which we are most conscious* is at least largely intellectual, whereas much of our most effective behavior, such as reflects vitality, decisiveness, and responsibility, is largely matter-of-course, unconscious, responsive, and on the whole has to be so to be effective. Self-consciousness in these respects would at least often check their force, speed, or accuracy. Moreover, leaders, like others, are for the most part unaware of their most effective faculties in actual behavior, for they cannot see themselves as others do.

This last point is so important both in theory and in practical administration that I think it worth further consideration here. The point is easy to prove, but its implications are difficult to explain. For the proof we may take, as an example, speaking and its accompanying gestures. It is well known that no one hears his own voice as it sounds to others, chiefly because many of the vibrations of the speaker's voice are conducted within the structure and passages of the head. I believe that an individual without previous experience rarely recognizes his own voice from a good reproduction. Some are greatly surprised and often displeased at hearing such a reproduction for the first time. Obviously, too, an individual cannot see his own demeanor or many of his movements. Yet in all our relations to others the use of voice and gestures is of first importance, and both are effectively controlled to a considerable extent so as to accomplish specific reactions in listeners. If we cannot hear and see ourselves as others do, how can we accomplish such control of our behavior?

I think the explanation may be as follows: We learn to correlate our own speech and action, as we hear and feel them, with certain effects upon others. We are only approximately successful, and some are much more so than others. Listeners and observers, on the other hand, learn to correlate the entirely different thing, our observable behavior, with our meanings and intentions. This is also only approximate, and is done more successfully by some than by others. Since leadership primarily involves the guidance of the conduct of others, in general leaders need to be more effective than others both in conveying meanings and intentions and in receiving them.

These fundamental processes are certainly not to any great extent intellectual. We all know that the capacity to understand the logical significance of sentences, even when written or printed, is limited, and that repeatedly we understand by the manner of speaking. We can with some success teach by logical processes what to do in the operation of a machine or process, though even here we know that often to state a direction correctly in language is to mislead, whereas an incorrect statement, especially with appropriate gesture or facial expression, may well convey the precise meaning. But to teach by logical exposition how to behave with other people is a slow process of limited effectiveness at best. This is why I think it will be widely observed that good leaders seldom undertake to tell followers *how* to behave, though they tell what should be done, and will properly criticize the manner of its doing *afterward*. Whereas inferior leaders often fail by trying, as it were, to tell others how to live their lives.

Whatever may be the explanation of our strong predilection for our intellectual attainments, it is difficult to evade the emphasis I have placed on other qualities in leadership. We all know persons, in and out of practical affairs, of superior intellects and intellectual accomplishments who do not work well as leaders. In matters of *leadership*, for example, they prove to be irresponsible (absent-minded, non-punctual), non-decisive (ultra-judicial, see so many sides they can never make up their minds), non-persuasive (a little "queer," not interested in people). Moreover, we can observe that intellectual capacity rarely rises above physiological disabilities in active life, that the utmost perspicacity is useless for leadership if it does not decide issues, that persuasive processes must take full account of the irrational by which all are largely governed, that responsibility is a moral or emotional condition.

Intellectual abilities of high order may achieve preeminent usefulness. They are sometimes an important element in leadership but not sufficient to maintain it. However, as a differential factor—that is, other qualities being granted and adequate—intellectual capacity is of unquestioned importance, and especially so in the age in which complex techniques and elaborate technologies are among the conditions of leadership. Leaders of the future, in my opinion, will generally need to be intellectually competent. However, the main point, which I wish greatly to emphasize, is that intellectual competency is *not* a substitute, at least in an important degree, for the other essential qualities of leadership.

Though it may be unpleasant to some, I have laid stress upon my opinion in this matter for two principal reasons. The first is that under present trends an excessive emphasis is placed upon intellectual (and pseudo-intellectual) qualifications by responsible "selecting" authorities, which artificially limits the supply of leaders. The same excessive emphasis upon the intellectual is made by followers who are intellectuals. Thus it is often difficult for them (experts and professionals of many kinds, who have no administrative capacity or interest) to follow even extraordinary leaders. This is a form of conceit frequently accompanied by exhibitions of temperament and disruptiveness, and by false, ruthless, and irresponsible professions of individualism and freedom, especially professional and academic freedom. All of this tends to a limitation of the supply of competent leaders, because it discourages men from undertaking the work of leadership, and it restricts their effectiveness.

My second reason is that a general condition amounting to intellectual snobbishness, it seems to me, has a great deal to do with industrial unrest. I see this in the propensity of educated people, whatever their economic status or social position, to underestimate the intelligence and other important personal qualities of workmen; in the tendency of some supervisors, quite honestly and sincerely, to blame failure to lack of brains in subordinates instead of to the stupidity of instructions; in the assumption of some men that "pure bunk" dressed up in "highbrow" jargon is effective in dealing with people; in the excessive popularity of white-collar occupations; in the desire of so many intellectuals to tell others how to eat, save money, dress, marry, raise families, take care of their own interests. These are symptoms of attitudes, and it is the latter, not the symptoms, which are important. They cause division of interest artificially and lack of sympathetic understanding, that are destructive of cooperation and cannot be corrected by mere "measures of good will."

I am well aware that there are differences in the intellectual capacities of men and know that such differences are important, especially as respects the ability to acquire knowledge and understanding by study in those matters which can only be learned in this way. Nevertheless, after a fairly long experience in dealing with many classes of men and women individually and collectively, the destructive attitudes I am attacking seem to me to be unwarranted by anything I know about intellect, education, or leadership. Intellectual superiority is an obtrusive thing, which even intellectuals dislike in others except as they *voluntarily* give it their respect.

Our Ignorance of the Qualities of Leadership

After this long digression it may have been forgotten, though observed, that in this discussion of personal qualifications I have failed, with one exception, to define my terms. Though in a general way I am confident that my meaning is understood, greater precision of meaning seems quite impossible, at least without extended space, and is not needed here. Indeed, a significant fact to emphasize is that neither in science nor in practical affairs has there yet been attained a degree of understanding of these qualities now vaguely described which permits much clear definition even for special purposes.

It is worthwhile to illustrate this with reference to "decisiveness." The making of decisions is one of the most common of the events of which we are conscious both in ourselves and others. We believe that many decisions are momentous either to ourselves, to our enterprises, or to our society. We may agree that those incapable of making *any* decisions are at least morons if not insane. We are aware that to make decisions is a leading function of executives. We also know that decisions are made collectively, as in committees, boards, legislatures, juries, and that such work is one of the most characteristic features of our social life. Yet decisive behavior, as contrasted with responsive behavior, seems to have received little attention in the psychologies,[4] in the literature of logical operations, in sociology, and seldom in economics. Moreover, in business I rarely hear appraisals of men in terms of their capacity for decision, except when they fail apparently for lack of ability to decide. It seems clear that we know so little of this quality or process that we do not discuss it as such, though "decision," "decisive," and "decisiveness" are words frequently on our lips.

Interdependence of Leadership Qualities

I am aware, as I said earlier, that I have omitted several qualifications of leadership which are commonly stated. In my intention, they are all comprehended in the five I have named or in some combination or derivation of them. Three omitted qualifications are great favorites: "honesty" ("character"), "courage," and "initiative." They may be added; but for myself I find them words which depend for their meaning in the specific case upon the *situation*, not merely the individual, either as interpreted by the actor or leader or others, and that his interpretation will often differ from the interpretations made by different observers.

In any case, the important point is that the qualifications of leadership, however discriminated and however named, are interacting and interdependent. We do not assemble them as we would the ingredients of a compound, yet we may suppose that different combinations of qualities produce quite different kinds of leaders, and that the qualities and their combinations change with experience and with conditions.

[4] While writing this sentence I have taken off the shelf at random more than a dozen books on psychology and social psychology. In only two is "decision" indexed (Lewin: *Principles of Topological Psychology* and Guthrie: *The Psychology of Human Conflict*) and in both cases the citations are few and quite secondary. Of course, perhaps all of the elements of the decisive processes may be covered in all these books, though from my recollection of them I doubt it. The fact is that one of the most conspicuous factors in common current observable behavior simply has not been recognized as such, notwithstanding that decision is the culmination of whatever we mean by "free will," "will," "voluntary," "determined" (in some meanings). The situation recalls what one psychologist has said of others, though in another connection: "All such explanations fail to explain why we think that A is A. For, even when the psychologists told us that A really was B, we stubbornly persisted in calling it A and not B . . . For in the long run it has proved to be more profitable to accept an A as an A and explain it as such..." (K. Koffka, *Gestalt Psychology*, Harcourt, Brace and Co., Inc., 1935, p. 179.)

THE DEVELOPMENT OF LEADERS

I think I have now shown that my profession of ignorance of this subject and my doubts with respect to the knowledge of others concerning it were both justified. Yet I recognize that however lacking in knowledge we may be, we nevertheless endeavor in our educational systems and at least in the larger organizations to increase the number of available leaders and their competence. It might be suggested that I should say something on this aspect of the subject in the light of my earlier remarks. I shall confine myself briefly to development methods and, in the next section, to the processes of selection.

Concerning the development of leaders, I shall in this section discuss the following topics: (i) Training; (ii) Balance and Perspective; and (iii) Experience.

Training

As I understand it, the only qualification for leadership that is subject to specific preparatory training by formal processes is the intellectual, including therein the inculcation of general and special knowledge. My opinion as to the relative importance and status of intellectual qualities has already been stated to the effect that such qualities are increasingly necessary to effective leadership in technical and technological fields and also in large-scale organizations where complexity and the remoteness of concrete activities call for capacity in the handling of abstract material. The latter are the conditions in which leadership also usually involves management of extensive cooperative systems as well as of organizations.

Nevertheless, I believe it should be recognized that intellectual preparation by itself tends to check propensities indispensable to leadership. For example, study and reflection on abstract facts do not promote decisiveness and often seem to have the opposite effect. Analysis, which broadly is characteristic of intellectual processes especially in the early stages of education and experience, is the reverse of the process of combining elements, of the treatment of them as whole systems involved in concrete decisive action—for instance, in persuasion. As a result of intellectual training many prefer to recognize only what has been stated or is susceptible of statement and to disregard what has not been stated or is not susceptible of statement. The emphasis upon abstract facts, characteristic now of the "more intelligent" and dominant classes of our population, has its results, in innumerable instances, in the "fallacy of misplaced concreteness," the confusion of the fact with the thing and of *an aspect* with an indescribable whole, in the disregard of the interdependence of the known and the unknown.

An example of this or of its general effects may be found in the excessive emphasis upon knowledge as against skill in nearly all fields except sports and individual artistic performance. Yet but a moment's reflection is needed to acknowledge that many of the noteworthy efforts of scientist, teacher, lawyer, physician, architect, engineer, clergyman—to take professions in which intellectual discipline and experience are indispensable—are expressions not of intellect but of skills, the effective behavior by which the appropriate adjustment to the infinite complexity of the concrete is accomplished. Indeed, we repeatedly confess the point in our practical emphasis upon experience, if not upon intuition, in every profession.

Nowhere is the emphasis upon fact to the exclusion of the thing to which it relates more harmful, it seems to me, than in the human side of industrial relations. We may think of employees as mechanics, clerks, laborers, or as members of an organization, but to lead requires to *feel* them as embodying a thousand emotions and relationships with others and with the physical environment, of which for the most part we can have no knowledge.

The dilemma which this state of affairs presents is, I think, concealed by the increasing extent to which prestige and status based on education are the basis of general social and industrial discrimination. I mean by this that a certain intellectual and educational status has become important, to the relative disregard of other qualifications, in getting a job, or at least a job generally regarded as desirable or distinctive. We can hardly help believing that an attitude is useful to society as a whole if we find that same attitude socially imposed upon us as individuals.[5]

Balance and Perspective

It may be thought that changes in curricula might be sufficient to correct for the tendency toward distortion of judgment which I have described. This may be possible in the future but not yet. So far as I know there is not developed the basic material for such changes, and it is unlikely that there will be unless my view of this problem, assuming it to be correct, should be accepted widely. But at best I should expect such studies only to offset the prejudices inculcated, possibly excepting the humanities, by higher education.

Hence, for the present, it seems to me that balance, perspective, and proportion in the senses relevant to leadership are to be acquired almost exclusively from responsible experience in leading.

Experience

In speaking of experience, it will be well to avoid the common error of regarding it as primarily a matter of repetition through a period of time. When experience is merely repetition of action, it is better called practice to acquire patterns of behavior. It is often convenient as a rough approximation to speak of hours, days, months, or years of experience, but we know that some men learn slowly, others quickly. Moreover, the possibility of learning depends upon activity. If nothing happens, little can be learned. Significant experience is secured largely by adapting one's self to varieties of conditions and by acquiring the sense of the appropriate in variations of action.

The acquirement of experience under modern conditions presents us with another dilemma; for the refined specialization and the technical complexity through which men are now introduced into the world of affairs

[5] An analogous problem is presented in "oversaving" theories of depressions, in which it is asserted that it is possible for a society as a whole to oversave, whereas the desire to save is commendable as to individuals.

give limited opportunity for general experience in leadership. The most "natural" opportunities at present formally available seem to me to be the small *general* business, political party work in communities, and, perhaps to a less extent, labor union leadership. These are insufficient sources for the supply of general leaders. Hence, we need to develop the artificial methods of giving wide experience which are now attempted to some extent in large organizations.

The effect of technical work is so strongly opposed to the acquirement of experience in the arts of leadership that I cannot forbear to add a suggestion that encouragement should be given in gaining experience informally in "extracurricular" activities. In fact, though we can as yet apparently do little in a formal way to develop leaders, we can encourage potential leaders to develop themselves, to seek for themselves the occasions and opportunities when leadership is needed, to learn the ways of making themselves sought as leaders, to acquire experience in leading by doing it. I have myself been so encouraged and inspired in my youth and since then, as no doubt we all have, so that to give such encouragement seems to me an important private and social duty; but I believe whatever we do in this respect will be harmful if not done in full realization that *there is no substitute for the experience of recognizing and seizing opportunities, or for making one's own place unaided and against interference and obstacles;* for these kinds of ability are precisely those that followers expect in leaders.

SELECTION OF LEADERS

Thus we have to recognize that leaders, almost blindly created by physiology, physical environments, social conditions, and experience, are now secured chiefly by selection, not by formal preparation. Our success is relative in the sense that we select as best we may of the quality that is presented but are little able to affect favorably that quality as a whole except as to the intellectual element. If this is a fact, it is admittedly difficult to observe, because to do so requires comparison of what we have with what we think we might have. Yet if we believe it to be a fact, it implies a precarious position; for the most perfect selection would not suffice to give adequate leadership if the supply of the "raw material" were of inferior quality, any more, for example, than the best selection among untutored electricians would be likely to afford an adequate supply of superior electrical engineers.

The test of the adequacy of leadership is the extent of cooperation, or lack of it, in relation to our ideals; and this is largely a matter of the disposition of followers. Even in this brief discussion it should be stated that in all formal organizations selection is made simultaneously by two authorities, the formal and the informal. That which is made by formal authority we may call appointment (or dismissal); that by the informal authority we may call acceptance[6] (or rejection). Of *the two, the in-*

---

[6] Under some, usually small or local, situations leaders are acclaimed spontaneously and are induced or forced to lead by pressure of social opinion. There is often some element of this even in large and institutionalized organizations, chiefly

formal authority is fundamental and controlling. It lies in or consists of the willingness and ability of followers to follow.

To many who have struggled and worried regarding appointment or dismissal of leaders, and to whom the maintenance of formal authority is the very keystone of cooperation, order, and efficiency, what I say may seem absurd or even subversive. But we have all many times proved it correct. For has not our first question always been in effect "Can he lead and will they follow?" If our answer were "No!" would we not appoint at the peril of our own leadership? And when there has been failure of followers to follow, writhe as we would, were not our only recourses to change the leader or possibly to change the followers?

If it is thought that this doctrine is subversive, this may be because it is thought to be what uninformed preachers of the vague thing called "industrial democracy" want, and we suppose they know less of leadership and organization than even we do. But what they advocate and what we fear is the transfer of *formal* authority from leaders to voters, forgetting that the informal authority must finally determine, whatever be the nature of the formal authority. Indeed, this latter fact is the chief reason for our fear; for we recall the men who have been enthusiastically elected but never followed. As to most (but not all) leadership, *appointment* by responsible leaders has proved, and I believe will continue to prove, more effective and more satisfactory to followers than any other formal process. And the followers make the leader, though the latter also may affect and must guide the followers.

I turn now to the process of selection, by formal authority of appointment or dismissal. In the selective process we eliminate for positive disqualifications—bad health, lack of ability to decide, irresponsibility, lack of adequate intellectual or technical ability. Frequently this is all disregarded most conveniently by saying "lack of experience" when what we mean is "lack of successful experience." For although a few eliminations are made for positive disqualifications, the really important basis of selection is that of prior achievement. Since we know so little about the qualifications for leadership, this often proves a fallacious method, sometimes resulting in tragic errors and often in a great deal of foolish rationalization. Nevertheless, we must confess that the past record is the best basis of selection we have. Thirty years ago Mr. Theodore N. Vail, a great leader and organizer in his day, and then president of the American Telephone and Telegraph Company, said to me: "You never can tell what a man will do by what he has done; but it is the best guide you have." I believe this still to be true; but I do not think it is an adequate basis for selection of leaders for our society of the future.

If leadership depends, as I have said, upon the individual, the followers, and the conditions, there must be many failures that are not the result of original errors of selection. For men, followers, and conditions all change. We are prone to forget this and to condemn, perhaps because it imposes upon us one of the most serious problems in the selective process.

---

expressed on the negative side, i.e., it is socially or organizationally not countenanced to quit leading or to refuse promotion, and loss of "caste" would be involved.

Failure of leadership if not corrected by replacement means the checking of the experience and development of potential leaders. Hence the elimination of super-annuated, obsolete, and incompetent leaders is recognized as extremely important in most organizations, perhaps most systematically in the Army and Navy. But this process is extremely delicate; for though followers cannot follow those who cannot lead, those who have been superior leaders embody or personify the spirit of an organization and represent the aspirations of their followers. Crude dismissal at any level of organization destroys morale and ambition and thus does violence to organization itself. In all types of organizations I believe this often means retaining a leader in the interest of everyone concerned after he has passed the peak of his capacities and sometimes even when the latter have become inadequate. When this is a matter of favoritism there can be no good defense of it; but when it is a part of the process of *organizing leadership*, involving the supplementing of incapacities by auxiliary leaders, it must be defended.

Here we are confronted with another problem of balance—another of the dilemmas of our subject. Who will say that we now know enough about it or are sufficiently successful with respect to it?

CONCLUSION

In this short study of one aspect of life, I have tried to emphasize the extent of our limitations and the importance of overcoming them, both from the standpoint of the effect of public blindness to the nature of the problem—which results so often in obstruction and in destructive criticism—and also from the standpoint of preparation to meet the future needs for leaders. These are ever increasing as the integrations of our societies grow larger, and as specialization and technological progress continue. Whether such an account is depressing, perhaps appalling, or is challenging and inspiring, will depend, I suppose, upon one's philosophy, outlook, or temperament.

It is in the nature of a leader's work that he should be a realist and should recognize the need for action, even when the outcome cannot be foreseen, but also that he should be an idealist and in the broadest sense pursue goals some of which can only be attained in a succeeding generation of leaders. Many leaders when they reach the apex of their powers have not long to go, and they press onward by paths the ends of which they will not themselves reach. In business, in education, in government, in religion, again and again I see men who, I am sure, are dominated by this motive, though unexpressed, and by some queer twist of our present attitudes often disavowed.

Yet, "Old men plant trees." To neglect today for tomorrow surely reflects a treacherous sentimentalism; but to shape the present for the future by the surplus of thought and purpose which we now can muster seems the very expression of the idealism which underlies such social coherence as we presently achieve, and without this idealism we see no worthy meaning in our lives, our institutions, or our culture.

COMMUNICATION
William B. Wolf*

Without communication there can be no organization or management. This selection provides an overview of the communication process. It does so by (1) considering the elementary model developed in the mathematical theory of communication; (2) describing the symbolic nature of languages (the theory of verbal and nonverbal communication); and (3) analyzing the communication process as it occurs in formal organizations.

Much of the discussion in the previous chapters can be thought of as part of the subject of *communication*. For, directly and indirectly, we have been concerned with the manner in which an organization coordinates its parts. Underlying coordination and inseparable from it is the pervasive process of communication. Without communication, there can be no organization.[1] Thus, this chapter—focusing directly on certain aspects of communication in organizations—explores the communication process and suggests what management can do to maintain efficient communication. Our procedure is first to consider the general communication process. Once we have developed background materials, we will consider the problems of communication within organizations and, finally, an approach for dealing with these problems.

THE COMMUNICATION PROCESS

The word *communication* appears frequently in the management literature. It is used in a variety of ways. In its broadest interpretation, it is defined as "all of the procedures by which one mind may affect another."[2] Probably a more useful definition is provided by Keith Davis, who defines communication as "the process of passing information and understanding from one person to another."[3] The difference between "passing information" and "passing understanding" should be emphasized. Anything and everything a person does may be considered the passing of information. Passing understanding is more difficult: it involves passing selected information with a definite goal in mind. In other words, com-

---

* From *The Management of Personnel* (Belmont, Calif.: Wadsworth Publishing Co., Inc., 1961), pp. 167–178. © 1961 by Wadsworth Publishing Company, Inc.
[1] Chester I. Barnard, *The Functions of the Executive* (Cambridge, Mass.: Harvard University Press, 1938), p. 82.
[2] Claude E. Shannon and Warren Weaver, *The Mathematical Theory of Communication* (Urbana: University of Illinois Press, 1949), p. 95.
[3] *Human Relations in Business* (New York: McGraw-Hill Book Co., Inc., 1957), p. 228.

munication includes both the passing of information in general and the flow of information directed toward a specific goal (i.e., understanding).

Mathematical Theory of Communication

One of the best theoretical presentations of the process of communicating is found in the work of Warren Weaver and Claude Shannon on the mathematical theory of communication.[4] They view communication as occurring in a system: an *information source* (such as a person or machine) selects a desired message from a set of possible messages; the selected *message* is then changed into a form to be transmitted over the *communication channel* to the *receiver;* the receiver changes the transmitted signal back into a message. For example, you ask a friend to open the door: your brain is the information source, your friend's brain is the destination, your vocal system is the transmitter, the sound waves serve as the principal channel of communication, and your friend's ear is the receiver.

In actuality, transmission of information is seldom precise. The signal transmitted by the information source may not give the intended results. It may be distorted by unwanted additions such as errors in sending the message, distortion of the message while in the process of being sent, and problems of reception. In the language of communication theory, all such changes in the transmitted signal are called *noise.*

Language Systems

As mentioned, problems may arise at any or all points in the communication process—that is, at the point of origination, or transmission, or reception of a message. However, the principal problems in communication are best understood by considering the process as a whole. These problems arise mainly because all communication involves symbols. Generally, communication is carried on through a variety of systems of codified symbols. Such systems are languages—that is, they consist of a plurality of signs that have a known interpretation to a number of people, and they are capable of being reproduced. Four types of language systems are used in the process of communication.

Verbal language. Verbal language consists of written or spoken words. It depends upon logic made up of a set of rules that have been agreed upon. Examples of verbal language abound: the written memo, the boss's speech, the employees' handbook, the union contract—all of these contain primarily verbal language. Verbal language is used so extensively that the terms *language* and *verbal language* are often considered synony-

---

[4] See note 2 above. One of the major scientific breakthroughs in recent years is the mathematical theory of communication. In it a new conceptualization, which will significantly affect the social and physical sciences, has crystallized. Already its influence is apparent in the development of automatic controls, operations research techniques, quantum physics, psychology, and sociology. For some of the implications of communication theory, see Richard L. Meier, "Communications and Social Change," *Behavioral Science,* 1, No. 1 (Jan. 1956), 43–58. See also James G. Miller, "Discussion and Reviews; Three Symposia: Problems in Human Communication and Control; Information Theory in Psychology; Toward a Unified Theory of Human Behavior," *Behavioral Science,* 1, No. 4 (Oct. 1956), 303–326.

mous. However, *actions, objects,* and *signs* (since they, too, may have a known interpretation to a number of people, and can be reproduced) often constitute languages.[5] Jurgen Ruesch and Weldon Kees describe these languages as follows:

Sign language. "Sign language includes all forms of codification in which words, numbers, and punctuation signs have been supplanted by gestures; these vary from the 'monosyllabic' gesture of the hitchhiker to such complete systems as the language of the deaf."

Action language. Action language "embraces all movements that are not used exclusively as signals. Such acts as walking and drinking, for example, have a dual function: on the one hand they serve personal needs, and on the other they constitute statements to those who may perceive them."

Object language. Object language "comprises all intentional and non-intentional display of material things, such as implements, machines, art objects, architectural structures, and—last but not least—the human body and whatever clothes cover it."

Functions of Verbal Language

During most of their waking hours, people are responding to words. Even when alone, they tend to use words in thinking. Moreover, they use words not only to communicate ideas but also to let off steam, to impress others, or to ease social tensions. Roethlisberger has pointed out that verbal language has three primary functions: (1) to refer to external events outside the body; (2) to express personal attitudes, emotions, and ideas; and (3) to satisfy desires and needs as in daydreaming and the emotional release that comes from counseling.[6] Thus, what is said may be related to the speaker's needs or feelings rather than to the concrete event about which he appears to be talking.

Examples of these usages of verbal language are found every day—for instance, in normal social intercourse when two people first meet: generally they will talk about external events, neutral or trivial subjects, merely to establish rapport; often, in such situations, it is not *what* is said that is important, but the fact that *something* is said. Similarly, in talking to people who are upset, one may find that the mere act of verbalizing has therapeutic value for them. In fact, one approach to psychotherapy emphasizes the emotional catharsis that occurs through verbalization.[7]

Another function of verbal language is to develop group cohesiveness. This function is noticeable as one moves from one field of study to another. For example, before one talks to a sociologist or an economist or some other social scientist, he should have a knowledge of the specialized

[5] This classification (action, object, and sign languages) has been developed by Jurgen Ruesch and Weldon Kees in their interesting book *Nonverbal Communication* (Berkeley: University of California Press, 1956), p. 189.

[6] F. J. Roethlisberger, *Management and Morale* (Cambridge, Mass.: Harvard University Press, 1941), pp. 89–91.

[7] Carl R. Rogers, *Client-Centered Therapy* (Boston: Houghton Mifflin Co., 1951).

vocabulary of the respective disciplines. These specialized vocabularies add to precision in communication; they also serve to exclude outsiders. The result is that cross-discipline communications are apt to be difficult to understand. Almost every relatively permanent group develops its own jargon. Waitresses, for instance, have unique terms for practically everything on the menu; and probably only a logger knows what is meant by "choker boys," "bull bucks," or "donkey drivers."

Verbal language not only helps to develop group esprit de corps; it also tends to reflect the group's spirit or aroma (i.e., the character of the group). For example, the writer once took a colleague out on an assignment in a very successful luggage-manufacturing firm. It was a hard-selling operation, and the men in the organization had their own pattern of verbalization. Shortly after we entered the manufacturing area, the loudspeaker went on. It was the president calling the vice-president. He started, "Bill, you stupid _____," and kept right on in the same vein. We were shocked—but the rest of the people in the organization were obviously unaffected. In fact, after several weeks in the organization it became apparent that "plain talk" in this company would probably be interpreted as "vile abuse" in some other firms.

Ambiguities in Verbal Language

One problem to be emphasized is that words may have the same *denotation* but different *connotations*. Hence, what a person hears or understands is a function of his background and perception. Aldous Huxley stated this problem clearly when he said, "There ought to be some way of dry cleaning and disinfecting words." The difficulties of translating words into meaning become dramatic as one moves from the subculture of an organization to the culture of nations as a whole. For example, Kluckhohn asked a Japanese with a fair knowledge of English to translate from the Japanese the phrase in the new Japanese constitution that represents our "life, liberty, and pursuit of happiness." The translation was "license to commit lustful pleasure."[8]

A less startling example of the problem of disinfecting words occurred in a midwestern manufacturing plant. The management issued orders that the workers were to wear "smocks." To the workers, smocks were women's garments, and these men refused to obey the order. They called a "wildcat" strike. When management changed its order and insisted that the workers wear "coveralls," the dispute was ended.

The confusion arising from the ambiguity of words has been studied by semanticists. Closely related to this area is that of the study of *meaning*, known as general semantics.[9] In order to recognize the difficulty of com-

---

[8] Clyde Kluckhohn, *Mirror for Man* (New York: Fawcett World Library, 1957), p. 120.

[9] The growth of general semantics is traceable to the work of Alfred Korzybski, a Polish-American mathematician who published *Science and Sanity* in 1933 (4th ed.; New York: Institute of General Semantics, 1948). See also Stuart Chase, *The Tyranny of Words* (New York: Harcourt, Brace and Co., Inc., 1938); S. I. Hayakawa, *Language in Action* (New York: Harcourt, Brace and Co., Inc., 1941) and *Language, Meaning and Maturity* (New York: Harper & Brothers, 1954); and the periodical *ETC*, The Bulletin of the General Semantics Society.

munications, it is helpful to consider the manner in which *meaning* is influenced. Transmission of meaning, fundamental to successful communications, is complicated and difficult to deal with. Meaning appears to be a function of a number of interrelated factors. In part, it is a personal matter. One's perceptions are influenced by his past experience as well as his present needs. For example, a woman quit her job as a factory worker in a midwestern company. She was so provoked by her supervisor that she wrote a letter to the president of the company. The letter mentioned the lack of consideration and the insults her foreman had heaped upon her. The president dispatched a staff assistant to investigate what was wrong. The assistant's report indicated that the woman's foreman had repeatedly told her "to get on the team," and had talked of "the team pulling together." This woman was from a farm community. She had never been exposed to team sports. The only team she thought of was a team of horses. She "knew when she was being insulted!"

In this example, cultural background appears to have been an important factor in creating misunderstanding. However, it could be that the needs of the worker caused her to *want* to misunderstand. In other words, she may have had a desire to leave the job.[10] The error in semantics was her excuse.

A person's background and feelings not only cause misinterpretation of words, but also may lead to emotional reactions. This is seen in the "smock versus coverall" example. It is also encountered in the field of union-management relations. For numerous union men, words such as "scab," "rate buster," and "speed up" trigger off strong emotional responses. This emotional reaction to the words is then frequently transferred to the broader situation. For example, the writer had a guest speak to his class about merit rating. The class consisted primarily of junior executives. As soon as they discovered the guest speaker was a union organizer, they became hypercritical of everything he said—despite the fact that in a previous discussion they had reacted very favorably to similar ideas. In this and similar cases, a stereotyped attitude shapes the interpretation placed upon what is said. Moreover, one's attitudes are in part shaped by the group to which he belongs (i.e., his *reference group*). Because these students identified with management, they had assumed a set of concepts about unions and union leaders.

In summary, it is apparent that transmitting meaning is a difficult task, mainly because individuals differ in their interpretations of words; they tend to get the message they want to receive; they have emotional responses to certain words and situations; and frequently they do not know how others are perceiving a given situation or message.

COMMUNICATION WITHIN ORGANIZATIONS

Within an organization, all four of the previously described language systems (verbal, sign, object, action) tend to be used in transmitting mes-

[10] Misunderstanding may be related to poor morale. For example, it has been noted that in an environment of authoritarian leadership, workers may purposely misunderstand instructions. Cf. J. A. C. Brown, *The Social Psychology of Industry* (Baltimore: Penguin Books, Inc., 1956), pp. 230–231.

sages. Thus, objects of status (type of clothing, location of work station, type of desk, number of telephones) provide a language for telling people where a man stands in the social hierarchy of the organization. Actions that complement words also provide a language for communicating. Frequently the meaning given to a specific message is a function of the interaction of all four languages.

Factors Limiting Effective Communication

The ambiguities in verbal language cause special communication problems within organizations. The general hypothesis underlying the discussion to follow is that a number of forces operating within organizations tend to interfere with effective communication.

Protection of specialized interests. One of the most noticeable factors limiting effective communication is found in the structure of organizations. Almost every large organization is based upon the concepts of division of labor and specialization. Thus, there are specialized groups—personnel, sales, engineering, and so forth. These groups tend to have their own biases and unique connotations of words. Moreover, they sometimes have a need to misunderstand in order to protect their specialized interests. This is seen in the committee meetings of problem-solving groups in which representatives of sales, accounting, and other specialized departments are present. An impartial observer will notice that there tends to be considerable rambling, digression, and apparent misunderstanding. What really is happening is that each man has his own special interests to represent. He has his own personalized, hidden agenda, which reflects the pressures of the organization on the individual.[11]

Superior-subordinate relationship. The effectiveness of communication is also limited by the hierarchy of authority found in organizations. The superior-subordinate relationship is a dependency relationship; that is, since the subordinate is dependent upon his superior for such things as advancement, job security, work assignments, and pay raises, he is under pressure to impress the boss; and any intelligent subordinate will tend to play a role that presents him in a favorable light.[12]

It appears that a principle of organization life is, "A subordinate shouldn't tell the boss anything that will cause him (i.e., the subordinate) to appear to be doing poorly unless the boss will find it out anyway. If this is the case, the subordinate had better tell the boss the facts rather than let someone else do it." Many people fail to recognize, however, that frequently the boss also withholds information. He too has his boss, and he may not feel too secure in his role as an intermediary. Thus, in order to maintain among his subordinates the image of a competent boss, the supervisor in middle management is apt to filter the information that he passes up to his boss and to screen the information passed down to subordinates.

---

[11] For a discussion of hidden agendas, see Chapter 12.

[12] Erving Goffman, *The Presentation of Self in Everyday Life* (Garden City, N.Y.: Doubleday & Co., Inc., Anchor Book, 1959).

Restrictive lines of communication. Another limitation arising from the nature of organizations is the tendency to rely on bureaucratic methods. The formal procedures for communicating usually involve going up and down the hierarchy, whereas accuracy in communication is usually facilitated by direct interaction of parties concerned about specific issues. This means that in many instances lines of communication should be horizontal rather than vertical. The establishment of lateral communication channels is generally handled through the informal organization. Yet, management may fail to recognize the need for informal channels. In fact, in many organizations it is dangerous for a subordinate to cut across the hierarchy. But if communication is not to be warped and perverted, there is a need for direct contacts of this nature.

The usefulness of informal channels of communication becomes apparent in studying the functioning of large organizations. For example, this writer had an opportunity to study one of the large airplane-manufacturing companies. In spite of an amazing amount of red tape involved in its activities, the organization moved rapidly and effectively in times of crisis—largely because of ties established through such informal groups as the supervisors' club and the 20-year club. In these social situations the key men established personal friendships upon which they could trade. Thus, they communicated across lines of authority, and cut through bureaucratic rules to accomplish the major tasks before them.

Emphasis on written communication. Another problem of communication within organizations is the tendency to "put it in writing." Writing is, of course, an excellent way to prove what was said; but it is often a poor way to communicate understanding. Certainly, if one writes an order he has tangible proof that it was given, but it doesn't necessarily follow that this is the best way to develop understanding; for writing is a discrete means of communicating:[13] it relies only on verbal language and does not permit rapid feedback; whereas oral, face-to-face communication allows almost instant feedback and brings into play other languages as well as the verbal.

Inconsistent communication. Still another problem of communication within organizations arises from the fact that executives "wear many hats." Because they are under a variety of pressures, their statements may not be consistent with their actions. Thus, in one instance an executive may reassure his staff that he trusts them and is pleased with what they are doing; yet at the same time he may set up formalized systems of controls that automatically check on the performance of the staff.

Misinterpretations and rumors. Another major obstacle to communication in numerous large organizations occurs because the organization necessarily tends to be impersonal and bureaucratic. In such a setting, the organization comes first; the individual is subordinate to the organization. As a result, many of the individuals, especially those of middle manage-

---

[13] Cf. Jurgen Ruesch and Gregory Bateson, *Communication: The Social Matrix of Psychiatry* (New York: W. W. Norton & Co., Inc., 1951), pp. 170–172.

ment, can be and are frustrated.[14] With their frustrations come rumor, apathy, and low morale. They lose faith and perspective. In a sense, they want to misinterpret data. One aspect of this is seen in the growth and spread of rumors within organizations. An event occurs and news of it spreads by informal channels throughout the organization. As it spreads, the message becomes garbled. "Joe is quitting because he has a better position." As this story circulates, it is distorted: each person gets only part of the story and tends to inject into it his own interpretation. Thus, by the time the story has circulated to a number of people, it is significantly changed. It may be reported as, "Joe was fired for hitting his boss."

Rumor tends to develop in an organization in proportion to the importance and ambiguity of its subject matter in the lives of the individual members of the group. "Although some rumors are simply idle conversation to facilitate social intercourse," most rumors circulate primarily because they provide an explanation and at the same time relieve emotional tensions felt by individuals.[15]

The process of spreading a rumor follows a general pattern. As the rumor travels, it tends to grow shorter and more concise: events are described in the immediate present, and relatively large or dominant objects are emphasized. Each reporter adds his explanation so that the incomplete facts are tied together. In this process the individuals involved inject into the rumor obliterations, falsifications, and distortions based on their respective sentiments, interests, and habits of feeling, thinking, perceiving, and acting.

Lack of mutual trust. On many subjects it is impossible to communicate without mutual trust. For example, if a salesman in a used-car lot tells a prospective buyer that he has a 1952 Ford driven only 20,000 miles, in perfect condition, whose only previous owner was a 70-year-old lady, etc., the listener probably *receives* and *understands* the message; but he probably does not *believe* it. Similarly, within organizations, management may profess interest in its employees and may declare certain policies such as promotion from within or maintaining wages above the prevailing rates. But such policies may not be believed. Effective communication, then—in the sense of sending messages with specific meaning—depends not only on the message and the channel of communication, but on the attitude of the receiver. No matter how correct the message and how efficient the channel of communication, the message will not be transmitted if the receiver is not receptive. Thus, failure of a communication system may be due to a lack of mutual trust rather than to inaccuracy in coding or transmitting the message.

Communication Systems in Organizations

It was pointed out at the beginning of this chapter that communication is a pervasive process essential to the existence of the organization.

---

[14] This is a point developed by Chris Argyris, "Understanding Human Behavior in Organizations: One Viewpoint," in *Modern Organization Theory*, ed. Mason Haire (New York: John Wiley & Sons, Inc., 1959).

[15] Gordon W. Allport and Leo F. Postman, "The Basic Psychology of Rumor," in *Readings in Social Psychology*, ed. Theodore M. Newcomb and Eugene L. Hartley (New York: Henry Holt & Co., Inc., 1947), pp. 547–548.

For our purpose, the organization may be considered as *a number of interrelated systems of communication.* The more obvious of these systems are the controls (embodied in budgets, accounting records, and statements of policy) formally established within the organization, and transmitted to employees or supervisors through *one-way* or *two-way communication.* One-way communication consists of messages being sent *down* the management hierarchy without an upward flow. Two-way communication involves a two-directional flow of information—in both directions, up and down—so that feedback is possible, and both management and workers give and receive information.

Methods of one-way communication involve:

1. Written memos.
2. Bulletin boards.
3. Public-address systems.
4. Published reports such as financial reports and employee handbooks.
5. Company publications such as a newspaper or a monthly magazine.
6. General meetings involving presentation of data, as contrasted with the discussion of a problem.

These all involve the downward flow of information. In communicating within a business, they are important but incomplete. An upward flow of data is also necessary. The principal means of attaining an upward flow are:

1. Group discussions.
2. Grievances.
3. Suggestion systems.
4. The grapevine.
5. Face-to-face contacts between people at different levels in the organization.
6. Attitude surveys.
7. Accounting data and other statistical reports designed to indicate what has happened or is happening in the organization.

The difficulties of one-way communication arise from the lack of feedback: the sender has no assurance that the desired message has been received or understood. The difficulties of two-way communication center around implementation. The methods or techniques are fallible. They need to be administered with a great deal of wisdom if they are to be effective. For example, group discussion does not guarantee the upward flow of information. Only if a proper *climate* is established will group discussion result in a relatively free exchange of ideas.[16] Similarly, grievances are usually received by management in a garbled and confused form, and the stated grievance may be significantly different from what *really* bothers the worker. Suggestions, as presented through a formal suggestion system, may actually have an adverse effect on the flow of ideas;[17] and since the grapevine consists of rumors, its reliability and accuracy are questionable.

In other words, communication involves more than techniques, more than the passing of information by mass media or the manipulation of

[16] See Chapter 9, on leadership styles.
[17] See Chapter 17, on suggestion systems.

techniques such as nondirective interviewing and merit rating. For communication to be highly efficient, there must be a desire to communicate and an esprit de corps in the organization.

CONCLUSION

This brings us to the concept of communication that permeates this book: communication and the organization are inseparable, and the management of personnel can be thought of as a problem in communication. The development of an organization involves structuring the flow of information. But for the transmission of understanding there needs to be an esprit de corps. As Harriet Ronken points out:

> [A person] cannot communicate effectively in an organization until he understands the workers' ways of thinking, the attitudes which underlie their expressions, their jargon and their codes of acceptable conduct. That is, one needs to understand the social factors coloring the words and messages people use.
>
> The primary problems of communication in industry arise because each of us tends to talk and to listen in terms of his own private world, with inadequate reference to the others.[18]

What can management do about maintaining effective communications?

First, it can be aware of the social factors in the organization, and it can attempt to select workers who tend to fit into the social climate of the job. It can develop induction and training programs that help to create common experiences and facilitate becoming a "member" of the organization. It can publish papers, bulletins, and the like, to increase the common context of organization life. It can promote styles of supervision that facilitate two-way communication, and it can render all sorts of services to create common bonds between people so that there is less of a discrepancy between what is said or heard or read, and what is understood.

In short, management can engage in a number of activities that will help workers understand their place in the organization society. Most important in this framework for developing effective communication is the structuring of day-to-day interactions in a frame of reference encompassing *empathy*, so that the meaning of what a person says or does is correctly interpreted.[19]

Finally, in transmitting communications, management can keep in mind the following essentials of effective communication:

1. The message must be as clear and precise as possible.
2. There should be provision for feedback.
3. The recipient must want to understand or be motivated to understand and accept the message.

[18] Harriet O. Ronken, "Communication in the Work Group," *Harvard Business Review*, 29, No. 4 (July 1951), 108–114.
[19] Fred Massarik and I. R. Weschler, "Empathy Revisited," *California Management Review*, 1, No. 2 (Winter 1959), 36–46.

BUREAUPATHOLOGY
Victor A. Thompson*

In this selection Victor Thompson describes behavior patterns which are functional for less than the organization as a whole. He brings into focus a number of commonly encountered problem areas, and provides an analysis of why they tend to develop.

BUREAUPATHIC BEHAVIOR

Dependence upon specialization imparts to modern organizations certain qualities which we discussed in chapter two. Among these are routinization, strong attachment to subgoals, impersonality, categorization, resistance to change, etc. The individual must adjust to these qualities because they cannot be eliminated from bureaucratic organization. In our society there are many people who have been unable to make this adjustment and who therefore find modern organization a constant source of frustration. They suffer from the social disease of "bureausis." In the last part of this chapter we shall try to diagnose this disease.

Personal behavior patterns are frequently encountered which exaggerate the characteristic qualities of bureaucratic organization. Within bureaucracy we often find excessive aloofness, ritualistic attachment to routines and procedures, and resistance to change; and associated with these behavior patterns is a petty insistence upon rights of authority and status. From the standpoint of organizational goal accomplishment, these personal behavior patterns are pathological because they do not advance organizational goals. They reflect the personal needs of individuals. To the extent that criticism of modern bureaucracy is not "bureautic," it is directed at these self-serving personal behavior patterns. Responsible criticism of bureaucratic pathology does not constitute a nostalgic longing to go back to a simpler era, but is an attempt to find the causes of pathological behavior with the hope of eliminating it. When people use the term "bureaucratic" in a critical sense, they are frequently referring to these personally oriented behavior patterns. Because the term is also used in a descriptive, noncritical sense, as Weber used it and as it has been used throughout this book, we shall avoid this critical use of the term and use in its stead a word which clearly denotes the pathological. We shall call these behaviors "bureaupathic."

The appropriation of major aspects of bureaucratic organization as means for the satisfaction of personal needs is pathological. It is a form of behavior which is functional for less than the system as a whole, including in this connection the clientele as part of the system. It involves a shifting

* Reprinted from *Modern Organization* by Victor A. Thompson (New York: Alfred A. Knopf, Inc., 1961), Chap. 8, pp. 152–169. By permission of Alfred A. Knopf, Inc. Copyright © 1961 by Victor A. Thompson.

in the costs[1] of the system by those with more authority to those with less, be they subordinates or clientele. It is a kind of behavior possible to those in the organization who have the best opportunity to use the organization to satisfy personal needs, namely, those in authority positions. It can only be exercised "downward." It cannot be exercised by clientele over authoritative officials, and it cannot be exercised by subordinates over superiors. It is, in short, a phenomenon of the system of authority, both hierarchical and nonhierarchical.[2]

INSECURITY AND THE NEED TO CONTROL

This pathological behavior starts with a need on the part of the person in an authority position to control those subordinate to himself. To "control" means to have subordinate behavior correspond as closely as possible with one set of preconceived standards. While the need to control arises in large part from personal insecurity in the superior, it has conceptual sources as well, which we shall briefly state.

In the United States, we have still the ghost of the absolute king in the guise of the theory of sovereignty. Sovereignty theory supports the monistic conception of bureaucratic organization, with its associated institution of hierarchy. The superior has the right, by delegation ultimately from the absolute sovereign, to obtain a unique outcome; and he has the duty, or the responsibility to his superior, to obtain it. In profit organizations, it is held that there is only one outcome which will satisfy profit maximization under the specific conditions of the market. It is also held that the duty to seek this outcome is an overriding one because only in this way can the welfare of all be best promoted, even though in individual instances it may not seem so. In the monocratic society of Russia, only one outcome can be tolerated because only one is consistent with the laws of history; only one is possible. (Why it is necessary to seek bureaucratic control in the face of this historical determinism has never been satisfactorily explained so far as we know.)

Although these conceptual sources for the need to control exist, they

[1] The obligation to accept another's decision may have a number of negative aspects, or *costs*. First is the dislike of subordination itself. Furthermore, the decision may not accord with one's moral beliefs, or it may conflict with one's self-interest. It may not appeal to one's reason and is likely in any case to require some change in habits. Therefore, the possible costs involved in being a subordinate or a regulated client are subordination costs, moral costs, self-interest costs, rationality costs, and inertial costs. See Herbert A. Simon, Donald W. Smithburg, and Victor A. Thompson: *Public Administration* (New York: Alfred A. Knopf; 1959), ch. xxi.

[2] Writers on bureaucracy like Merton, Selznick, Gouldner and others use essentially the same concept of "bureaucratic," although, except by Gouldner, the distinction between the descriptive and critical sense of the term is never made clear. In general, they start with a need of some authority figure for control, followed by behavior which creates conditions exaggerating the need for control, etc., in a vicious circle. On this point see James G. March and Herbert A. Simon: *Organizations* (New York: John Wiley & Sons, Inc.; 1958), pp. 36–46; and Chris Argyris: "The Individual and Organization: Some Problems of Mutual Adjustment," *Admin. Sci. Q.*, Vol. II (1957), pp. 1–22, and "Understanding Human Behavior in Organizations: One Viewpoint," in Mason Haire, ed.: *Modern Organization Theory* (New York: John Wiley & Sons, Inc.; 1959).

are hardly compelling. Much more important in explaining the authoritative need to control is personal insecurity.[3] Here we may well recap these sources of personal insecurity and anxiety in modern bureaucratic organization.

Hierarchical structure with its monopoly of "success" is a potent source of anxiety. The person in a superordinate position has a near final control over the satisfaction of subordinates' needs, their personal goals.[4] While at the bottom of the hierarchy the standards which must be met are frequently made explicit and objectively measurable, managerial personnel have generally resisted a like invasion of their own superordinate rights.[5] As we have said before, the objectivity of performance standards decreases as one mounts the hierarchy until at some point they become largely subjective. At the same time, we would expect an increasing concentration of success-hungry people in the upper reaches of the hierarchy. Strong status needs and strong doubts as to what will please the person who can satisfy those needs can only result in anxiety and, for many, in "automaton conformity"[6] to the wishes of the boss. Hierarchical anxiety is much like Calvinism in that it generates painful doubt as to who is chosen. Like Calvinism, these doubts can be reduced, not only by automaton conformity but by excessive activity and the appearance of extreme busyness.[7]

Anxiety is also associated with insecurity of function. To occupy a position not fully accepted by significant others in the organization tends to make one isolated, a minority in a hostile world. This kind of insecurity may result from a new specialty not yet fully accredited and accepted; or it may result from the authoritative assignment of jurisdiction (the delegation of nonhierarchical authority) in defiance of the needs of specialization.

Finally, the source of insecurity which is becoming the most significant in modern organizations is the growing gap between the rights of

[3] Although the conceptual basis for the need to control is more thoroughly worked out in Russia, it has been observed that the attempt by Russian top management to concentrate power and control in its own hands results from insecurity generated by pressure from above. See Reinhard Bendix: *Work and Authority in Industry* (New York: John Wiley & Sons, Inc.; 1956), ch. vi.

[4] For a theory of individual accommodation to the organization based on hierarchically generated anxiety, see Robert V. Presthus: "Toward a Theory of Organizational Behavior," *Admin. Sci. Q.*, Vol. III, No. 1 (June 1958), pp. 48 ff. See also Peter Blau: *The Dynamics of Bureaucracy* (Chicago: University of Chicago Press; 1955), p. 173.

[5] This resistance was apparently the basis of the managerial opposition to Taylorism and Scientific Management generally. See Bendix: *op. cit.*, pp. 274–81.

[6] See Erich Fromm: *Escape from Freedom* (New York: Holt, Rinehart and Winston, Inc.; 1941), p. 185. See also Clara Thompson: *Psychoanalysis: Evolution and Development* (New York: Thomas Nelson & Sons; 1950), p. 208. See also Fromm: *Man for Himself: An Inquiry into the Psychology of Ethics* (New York: Holt, Rinehart and Winston, Inc.; 1947), p. 72. Of 75 middle-management people questioned by Harold Leavitt, most thought that conformance to the wishes of the boss was the principal criterion for evaluating subordinates. Harold J. Leavitt: *Managerial Psychology* (Chicago: University of Chicago Press; 1958), p. 288.

[7] See Rollo May: *The Meaning of Anxiety* (New York: The Ronald Press Company; 1950), p. 172.

authority (to review, to veto, to affirm) and the specialized ability or skill required to solve most organizational problems. The intellectual, problem-solving, content of executive positions is being increasingly diverted to specialists, leaving hierarchical rights (and duties) as the principal components of executive posts.[8] Persons in hierarchical positions are therefore increasingly dependent upon subordinate and nonsubordinate specialists for the achievement of organizational (or unit) goals. The superior tends to be caught between the two horns of a dilemma. He must satisfy the non-explicit and nonoperational demands of a superior through the agency of specialized subordinates and nonsubordinates whose skills he only dimly understands.[9] And yet, to be counted a success he must accept this dilemma and live with its increasing viciousness throughout his life. He must live with increasing insecurity and anxiety.[10] Although a particular person may have great maturity and general psychological security, an insecure superior at any point in the hierarchy above him can, and probably will, generate pressures which must inevitably be passed down the line, creating insecurity and tensions all the way to the bottom.[11] Given a person's hierarchical relationship with his superior, he is always subject to blame for outcomes which he could control only remotely, if at all.

THE BUREAUPATHIC REACTION

Insecurity gives rise to personal (nonorganizational) needs which may be generalized in the need for control. This need often results in behavior which appears irrational from the standpoint of the organization's goals because it does not advance them; it advances only personal goals and satisfies only personal needs. In so doing, it creates conditions which do not eliminate the need for control but rather enhance it.[12]

[8] For a discussion of this process in industrial management, see Bendix: *op. cit.*, pp. 226 ff. His discussion is based on a work by Ernest Dale: *Planning and Developing the Company Organization Structure* (New York: American Management Association, Inc.; 1952), Research Report No. 20. Advancing specialization in the problem-solving aspect of organizations is further reflected in these figures from Bendix: *op. cit.*, pp. 211 ff. Between 1899 and 1947 the proportion of administrative to production workers in American industry increased from 7.7 percent to 21.6 percent. From 1910 to 1940 the work force in America increased by 49 percent. Entrepreneurs increased by 17 percent; manual workers, by 49 percent; and salaried employees, by 127 percent. Bendix sees bureaucratization in industry as the continuing subdivision of the functions of the early owner-manager.

[9] Of course, the extent of the dilemma varies with position in the hierarchy and with the extent to which complex specialities are required by the particular organization. The ongoing process of specialization will move the dilemma down the hierarchy and to more and more organizations.

[10] Middle-management executives interviewed by William H. Whyte referred to their lives as "treadmills" or "rat races," thereby expressing the tensions generated by this dilemma. *The Organization Man* (Garden City, New York: Doubleday & Company, Inc.; 1953), p. 176.

[11] William Caudill has shown that tensions starting at the very top of a mental hospital were easily communicated all the way down to the patients, creating symptoms in them that were generated entirely within the hospital. *The Psychiatric Hospital as a Small Society* (Cambridge: Harvard University Press; 1958).

[12] March and Simon (*op. cit.*) criticize some of the sociological treatments of bureaupathic behavior because they feel that these theories do not explain why func-

Alvin W. Gouldner studied the succession to the position of plant manager by a man from outside the plant.[13] This man was obligated to upper management and felt duty-bound to realize its efficiency and production values. He started out, therefore, with heavy pressure from above. Coming from outside, he did not understand the informal system prevailing in the plant and was unable to use it. As his insecurity and anxiety mounted, he turned more and more to the formal system of rules, defined competencies, impersonality, and close supervision. He met resistance and felt his position between the horns of the dilemma, between those above and those below, increasingly insecure. He reacted with increased aloofness and formality. He exaggerated the characteristics of bureaucratic organization. He became bureaupathic.

The example illustrates the circularity in the bureaupathic reaction. Since the manager's behavior was so strongly influenced by his personal needs to reduce his own anxiety, the employees' responses deviated more and more from organizational needs, thereby increasing the manager's anxiety and completing the circle. The mechanisms underlying this process are not difficult to understand. Control standards encourage minimal participation.[14] They encourage employees to meet the standards and no more. Furthermore, meeting the control devices tends to become the aim of the subordinates because that is how they manage their own insecurities and avoid sanctions. For example, if agents are rated on the number of violations they uncover, cases of compliance are not likely to give them great joy.[15] Strict control from above encourages employees to "go by the book," to avoid innovations and chances of errors which put black marks on the record. It encourages the accumulation of records to prove compliance, resulting in *paperasserie*, as the French call it.[16] It encourages decision by precedent, and unwillingness to exercise initiative or take a chance. It encourages employees to wait for orders and do only what they are told. It is not hard to understand, therefore, why the superior may

---

tional learning on the part of authority figures does not take place. It will be recalled that these theories posit a need for control, followed by behaviors which create conditions which exaggerate the need for control. If this behavior is conceived as organization problem solving, there is indeed a problem of functional learning involved. However, bureaupathic behavior is functional in personal rather than organizational terms. It must be admitted that most of these sociological treatments do not clearly distinguish between personal and organizational goals—between bureaupathic and bureaucratic behavior. The "dysfunctional learning" involved is failure to learn that employees cannot very effectively be treated according to the machine model. However, this learning can be considered dysfunctional only by applying the machine model to management. If management operated like a rational machine, it would learn that employees are not machines. The basic methodological flaw of the "management" approach is that it assumes that persons described by the term "management" behave according to sociopsychological laws different from those governing the behavior of others—that the manager is an independent variable in the organization.

    [13] The following discussion of succession is taken from his *Patterns of Industrial Bureaucracy* (Glencoe, Illinois: The Free Press; 1954), Part Two.
    [14] *Ibid.*, pp. 174-6.
    [15] See Blau: *op. cit.*, p. 192.
    [16] Walter Rice Sharp: *The French Civil Service: Bureaucracy in Transition* (New York: The Macmillan Co.; 1931), pp. 446-50.

come to feel that he must apply more control. If he is also subject to strict bureaupathic control from above, this situation is likely to contribute to ulcers, if not, indeed, to complete breakdown.

THE DRIFT TO QUANTITATIVE COMPLIANCE

An exaggerated dependence upon regulations and quantitative standards is likely to stem from a supervisor's personal insecurity in the parent-like role of the boss. It has been observed that women supervisors are more likely to insist upon strict compliance with all organizational rules and regulations than are men. The bureaupathic tendency of women has been attributed to their greater insecurity in the superordinate role because the general role of women in our society is somewhat subordinate.[17] A battery of regulations makes it unnecessary for the superior to give the detailed face-to-face order very often. Everybody, including the supervisor, is simply carrying out instructions imposed from above. If they are unpleasant instructions, it is not the supervisor's fault. For much the same reason, an insecure superior will probably appreciate a large number of quantitative control standards because his ratings of his subordinates then appear to be inevitable results of the performances of the subordinates, not merely the personal judgments of the superior. The anger and aggressions of the subordinates can then be displaced to the impersonal "system," and the superior can continue to get their indispensable co-operation upon which his own "success" depends.[18] Furthermore, disparities of power are hidden by the rules, and if punishment is meted out, it comes from the rules, not from the superior. In all of these ways, the rules and regulations make the parentlike role less uncomfortable for insecure people.[19]

Only the observable and measurable aspects of behavior can be controlled. These aspects are often the most trivial and unimportant from the standpoint of the long-range success of the organization. Where the need to control exists, therefore, it often manifests itself in procedures, reports, and clearances governing trivia, while at the same time very important matters are left to discretion because controlling them is not feasible. The need to control is sufficiently widespread to have given sometimes a petty and ludicrous quality to modern organization. We venture to predict that if one looks hard enough in any modern organization, he will find instructions just as ridiculous as those of the military on how to wash a dog, pick a flower, or use a fork.[20] Since the controls can successfully be applied

[17] See Arnold W. Green and Eleanor Melnick: "What Has Happened to the Feminist Movement," Alvin W. Gouldner, ed.: *Studies in Leadership: Leadership and Democratic Action* (New York: Harper & Brothers; 1950), pp. 277–302.

[18] See Blau: *op. cit.*, pp. 175–6.

[19] Gouldner: *Patterns of Industrial Bureaucracy*, ch. ix. On the relationship between ritualistic compliance with regulations and personal insecurity, see Rose Laub Coser: "Authority and Decision Making in a Hospital: A Comparative Analysis," *Am. Sociol. Rev.* (February 1958). See also Reinhard Bendix: *Higher Civil Servants in American Society* (Boulder, Colorado Press; 1949), pp. 14–19, 112–22.

[20] There is another source of extreme, detailed controls in modern organizations, one which can be dealt with rationally. Units are frequently established whose goals are defined *entirely* in terms of writing instructions. Since they have nothing assigned to them except to write instructions, in time they can be expected to "cover"

only to the observable and measurable aspects of a job, and since the employee must concentrate on satisfying the control standards in order to reduce his own personal insecurities, his emphasis shifts from the more important, qualitative aspects of the job to the less important, quantitative aspects. In an employment office, for example, the goal shifted from good placement, in the beginning, to the highest possible number of people put to work. Interviewers felt constrained to use whatever sanctions they had to induce a client to take a job, whether he wanted it and was suited to it or not.[21]

EXAGGERATED ALOOFNESS

Organizational relationships are by nature less warm and personal than the relations of friendship. It is only when this impersonality is exaggerated to cold aloofness and apparent disinterest that we can with any fairness call it pathological. As with other kinds of bureaupathic behavior, exaggerated aloofness can usually be attributed to personal insecurity.

A cold aloofness protects an insecure superior from commitments to his subordinates which he fears will be inconsistent with demands upon him from above. It makes it easier for him to mete out punishment or to perform other aspects of his hierarchical role, such as rating his subordinates. It protects him from the aggressions of his subordinates by maintaining a psychic distance between him and them. In extreme cases it can come close to a complete breakdown of communication between the superior and his subordinates.

The same considerations apply to relations between officials and clients. A certain impersonality is necessary both to protect the goals of the organization and to secure objective and therefore effective service to the client. This impersonality may be exaggerated into a cold disinterest by an insecure official. When officials are caught between demands or "rights" of clients and tight administrative controls from above, dissociation from the clients and disinterest in their problems may seem to be the only way out of the dilemma. Client hostility, generated by what appears to be official emphasis on the wrong goals, creates tension. Inconsiderate treatment of the clients may become a device for reducing tensions and maintaining the cohesion of the officials. Blau has shown how such a situation leads to backstage demeaning of clients, which, by putting psychic distance between the officials and the clients, protects the officials. Officials then tend to seek satisfactions from the abstract values of the enterprise rather than from the concrete values of personal service to a client.[22]

Within the organization, technically unnecessary interdependence creates insecurity of function. As we have seen in previous chapters, authority is sometimes delegated for political rather than technical reasons, to meet personal rather than organizational needs. Because the resulting

---

everything—even as a monkey, if given enough time on the typewriter, would eventually type out the complete works of Shakespeare. Involved in this situation is goal factoring, not bureaupathic behavior.

[21] Blau: *op. cit.*, p. 96.

[22] *Ibid.*, pp. 91–5. See also Erving Goffman: *The Presentation of Self in Everyday Life* (Garden City, New York: Doubleday & Company, Inc.; 1959), p. 177.

relationship is not accepted and is constantly under attack, the person with the delegated authority lives in insecurity. Here, also, patterns of cold and imperious aloofness are often observed, and abstract values rather than personal service become goals. Officials exercising such disputed, delegated authority frequently demean their clients as narrow-minded, if not stupid. Procedures to govern the relationship are elaborated and, because they stabilize the relationship, such procedures acquire an exaggerated value for these officials.

RESISTANCE TO CHANGE

Bureaucratic organizations have to administer change carefully, as we pointed out in chapter two. Perhaps most people resist change just for the sake of change. The burden of proof is on the side of those advocating change. However, resistance to change may also be exaggerated by insecure officials; it may become bureaupathic. In an organizational context dominated by the need to control, innovation is dangerous because, by definition, it is not controlled behavior. It creates risks of errors and therefore of sanctions. To encourage innovation, an insecure superior would have to extend the initiative to subordinates and thereby lose control. Furthermore, in an insecure, competitive group situation, innovation threatens the security of all members of the group and for this reason tends to be suppressed by informal group action, as well as by the insecure superior. Innovation is facilitated by a secure, noncompetitive group administrative effort dominated by a professional outlook. Since this kind of situation is thought to be rare in modern bureaucracy, some people might regard excessive resistance to change as an inherent feature of bureaucratic organization, rather than as a form of bureaupathology. We feel, however, that excessive bureaucratic inertia is much less widespread than is supposed.[23] In an era of ever more rapid change, it seems unlikely that man has evolved a kind of organization which is particularly resistive to innovation. The traditionalistic organization was the kind most resistive, and in many places it had to be blasted off the scene by revolutionary action. The bureaucratic form replaced it, partly because it was able to accommodate to a changing world.

There is another source of resistance to change which is not bureaupathic and which is therefore subject to rational corrective procedures. The communication pattern determines who gets feedback information. A particular official may never get intimate knowledge of the results of his own actions. Consequently, he may feel no need for a change which others who do have this knowledge think should be made. Bringing the

---

[23] In a state employment office and a federal enforcement agency, Blau found little evidence of resistance to change. The cases he did find were based upon the fear of a superior and fear of the loss of security in relations with subordinates or clients. (*Op. cit.*, pp. 184–9.) He found that new employees and less competent employees were more resistive to change than others. (*Ibid.*, p. 197.) He found also that ritualistic compliance with rules and regulations stemmed from personal insecurity in important relationships at work. (*Ibid.*, p. 188.) Secure officials welcomed change because it made their work interesting by providing new challenges.

"offending" official into direct communication with respondents might cure in a hurry this particular case of resistance to change.

INSISTENCE ON THE RIGHTS OF OFFICE

The bureaupathic official usually exaggerates the official, nontechnical aspects of relationships and suppresses the technical and the informal. He stresses rights, not abilities. Since his behavior stems from insecurity, he may be expected to insist on petty rights and prerogatives, on protocol, on procedure—in short, on those things least likely to affect directly the goal accomplishment of the organization. For example, a rather functionless reviewing officer will often insist most violently on his right of review and scream like an injured animal if he is by-passed. He will often insist on petty changes, such as minor changes in the wording of a document. If he has a counterpart at a higher organizational level, he will probably insist on exclusive contact with that higher clearance point. By controlling this particular communication channel he protects his authority and influence, even perhaps enhancing them somewhat by being the sole interpreter of the higher clearance point's requirements.[24] In like fashion and for the same reasons, an insecure superior can be expected to exert his right to the monopoly of outgoing and incoming communication. Everything must go through "formal channels." In this way he can hide his weakness and suppress information which might reveal his insecurity. He also hopes to maintain his influence and authority by suppressing the influence of external specialists, the "staff." One of the great difficulties of modern organization arises from the inescapable fact that specialist communication must break through such blockades.

Insistence upon the full rights of the superordinate role is what is meant by "close supervision." It seems to be related to doubts about the loyalty or ability of subordinates, combined with pressure from above.[25] Close supervision can be regarded as bureaupathic under conditions where the right to act and the ability to do so have become separated because of the advance of specialization. However, where the position has a great deal of technical content so that subordinates are technically dependent upon their supervisor, as in a railroad maintenance section, close supervision may be tolerated and even demanded by subordinates. It may be a necessary means to the organization's goal. The right to supervise closely gets further legitimation from the technical ability to do so.[26]

[24] See Victor A. Thompson: *The Regulatory Process in OPA Rationing* (New York: King's Crown Press; 1950), pp. 298–303.

[25] In addition to other references cited throughout this chapter, see Walter L. Dorn: "The Prussian Bureaucracy in the 18th Century," *Polit. Sci. Rev.*, Vol. XLVI (September 1931). See also Alexander Barmine: *One Who Survived* (New York: G. P. Putnam's Sons; 1945); and "The Stewardship of Sewell Avery," *Fortune*, Vol. XXXIII (May 1946).

[26] See D. Katy, N. Maccoby, G. Gurin, and L. G. Floor: *Productivity, Supervision and Morale among Railroad Workers* (Ann Arbor: Survey Research Center, University of Michigan; 1951). See also A. W. Halpin: "The Leadership Behavior and Combat Performance of Airplane Commanders," *J. Abnorm. and Soc. Psychol.*, Vol. XLIX (1954), pp. 19–22.

BUREAUPATHOLOGY AND ORGANIZATION STRUCTURE

Institutions are staffed by persons, and so personality is always an element in institutional behavior. It will account for differences of degree and minor variations in form. For the major outlines of institutional behavior, however, we must seek the causes in the institutions themselves. Bureaupathic behavior is caused by the structures and conditions within our bureaucratic organizations. To say this is not to deny the reinforcing impact of personality. Some people are undoubtedly more inclined than others to be aloof, to get enmeshed in details, to be officious, to be excessively cautious, to be insensitive to others, to be insecure. What we do deny is that there is a bureaupathic personality type, or that observed cases of bureaupathic behavior will always, or even usually, be associated with one type of person.[27] Any person, regardless of personality type, may behave in some or all of the ways we have just described under the appropriate conditions, and these conditions occur very frequently in the modern bureaucratic organization.

It has been argued that a kind of rigidity grows out of prolonged role enactment, and that bureaucrats, over a period of time, become insensitive to the needs of clients.[28] We have shown that a certain impersonal treatment is inherent in bureaucratic structure. The charge of insensitivity may therefore be a bureautic reaction. One must not forget that clients are notoriously insensitive to the needs of bureaucrats. The question is, when does bureaucratic insensitivity become pathological? In many bureaucratic organizations, relations with clients are warm and cordial, as, for example, between the postman and the householder.

Although prolonged role enactment undoubtedly has a profound effect on a person,[29] what is the "bureaucratic role"? People move around

[27] For example, attempts have been made to show that "compulsive neurotics" predominate in bureaucracy. See Otto Sperling: "Psychoanalytic Aspects of Bureaucracy," *Psychoan. Q.*, Vol. XIX (1950), pp. 88–100.

[28] Theodore R. Sarbin: "Role Theory," in Gardner Lindzey, ed.: *Handbook of Social Psychology* (Reading, Massachusetts: Addison-Wesley Publishing Company, Inc.; 1954), Vol. I, pp. 223–58. Sarbin points out that this proposition is only an hypothesis, and one would have to find these qualities of rigidity and impersonality in nonoccupational behavior as well in order to demonstrate it. We might point out that one would also have to show that these qualities were not present at the beginning of the period of "prolonged role enactment." Sarbin relies somewhat on Robert K. Merton's well-known essay, "Bureaucratic Structure and Personality," in *Social Theory and Social Structure*, rev. ed. (Glencoe, Illinois: The Free Press; 1957). However, Merton does not seem to be talking about the interaction of self and role. Generally, he is explaining "bureaucratic" behavior by reference to bureaucratic structure (graded careers, seniority, *esprit de corps*, the appropriateness of secondary, i.e., impersonal, relations, etc.). He also suggests that the ideal patterns of bureaucratic behavior become exaggerated by being affectively backed, as we have argued. However, he does not explain the origin of this affect ("sentiments") to our satisfaction. We have argued that it comes from personal insecurity in an authority position. Merton does not distinguish between the descriptive and critical uses of the term "bureaucratic."

[29] See Willard Waller: *The Sociology of Teaching* (New York: John Wiley & Sons, Inc.; 1932).

quite freely in bureaucracies. They perform various roles. We do not think it makes sense to speak of the "bureaucratic role." We have emphasized specialist roles and hierarchical roles. In the hierarchy, people go from position to position as they advance. Specialists often move from organization to organization. The truly prolonged role is the entrepreneurial professional role, such as the physician. It seems doubtful that physicians, as a group, are "insensitive to the needs of clients."

Although there is no "bureaucratic role," there is bureaucratic structure. It is obvious that some people are able to achieve personal goals within this structure more easily and comfortably than others. These people have been called bureaucratic types; but they are not necessarily bureaupathic. In fact, it may be that the person who moves most easily within the bureaucratic structure is the one who can hide his insecurity, his "inner rumblings," as Whyte puts it. His insecurity may express itself internally as ulcers but not externally as bureaupathic behavior.

Bureaupathic behavior is one result of the growing insecurity of authority in modern organizations. This insecurity exists because non-hierarchical authority is so frequently delegated without regard to the ability to exercise it; such is the practice of politics.[30] More important, however, is the fact that the culturally defined institution of hierarchy, with its rather extreme claim of rights, is increasingly uncomfortable with advancing specialization. Hierarchical rights change slowly; specialization, the result of technology, changes with increasing speed. The situation is unstable. The legitimacy of organizational authority is in danger. Bureaupathic behavior is one result of this situation.

BUREAUPATHOLOGY AND ROUTINIZATION

The bureaupathic response to insecurity is facilitated by the routinization of organizational problem solving. When the development of appropriate routines is the dominant imperative, when technical problems must be solved, the emphasis must be on abilities rather than rights.[31] Charismatic patterns predominate. These facts are illustrated by wartime experience.

When World War II broke out, a large regulatory structure had to be quickly created. People with many types of skill, from many walks of life, and with many different statuses were quickly assembled in Washing-

[30] In organizational terms, politics means those activities concerned with the delegation of authority on bases other than a generally recognized ability to exercise it. It involves some kind of exchange between the person desiring the authority and the authority figure who has it to give. It is made possible by the fact that authority may be delegated. Since the specialist content of executive positions is increasingly attenuated as one mounts the hierarchy, so that ability criteria become less and less relevant, placement in these positions becomes more and more a political phenomenon, a matter of "office politics"; the incumbents are "political types." See Harold Lasswell: *Politics: Who Gets What, When, How* (New York: McGraw-Hill Book Co.; 1936).

[31] Studies of decision-making groups in business and government show that the groups prefer strict and formal performances by the conference leader when the subject matter is trivial but not when the subject is important. L. Berkowitz: "Sharing Leadership in Small, Decision-Making Groups," *J. Abnorm. and Soc. Psychol.*, Vol. XLVIII (1953), pp. 231–8.

ton. A whole host of brand-new problems was given to them. In those early days, emphasis was on technical problem solving. Anyone who could come up with an idea on how to proceed "got ahead." Bureaupathic patterns were almost nonexistent. The emphasis was on what one could do, not on rights and prerogatives. People became quite scrambled up, with permanently low-status people temporarily elevated to high-status positions. Very young people found themselves in high positions.

Gradually technical problems were mastered and reduced to procedures and programs. Bureaupathic patterns became more pronounced. There were constant reorganizations, a growing volume of reports, increasing insistence upon clearance protocol, authority impressed for its own sake, not as a problem-solving device. Hierarchical dominance was pressed through a great variety of rituals—"control" boards, frequent staff meetings, calls to the "front office," progress reports, increasing insistence upon formal channels, etc.[32] These manifestations of authority were ritualistic because they were not related to winning the war, but to the "need for control." The organization product was not affected by them, because it was secured through an elaborate routine, of which no one comprehended more than a small part. Bureaupathic behavior occupied much more of the time of officials. They became kings' messengers after the kings were gone.[33] . . .

[32] See Victor A. Thompson: *op. cit.*, Part Two.
[33] The technical problem military organizations must solve is winning a war. In peacetime, with no technical problem to solve, bureaupathic patterns are more pronounced. Arthur K. Davis says they live and survive in peacetime on ritual. "Bureaucratic Patterns in the Navy Officers Corps," *Social Forces*, Vol. XXVII (1948), pp. 143–53. He hypothesizes that "the effectiveness of military leaders tends to vary inversely with their exposure to a conventionally routinized military career." This study is reproduced in Merton, *et al.*, eds.: *Reader in Bureaucracy* (Glencoe, Illinois: The Free Press, 1952), pp. 380 ff.

3

THE DYNAMICS OF ORGANIZATIONS

To understand what an organization is and how it functions, one needs more than Weber's general description of bureaucracy, more than an understanding of social movements. These approaches contribute to general understanding, but they are incomplete. They leave out much of the human aspect—how people behave in organizations. Accordingly, this chapter provides reports on the behavior of workers in various organizations.

"BANANA TIME": JOB SATISFACTION AND INFORMAL INTERACTION

Donald F. Roy*

This article is a participant-observer's report of the way in which a small group of machine operators performing monotonous work developed their own informal organization. It builds on the point made by Selznick that people bring themselves as whole individuals to the work environment, and thus do not restrict their behavior to the performance of formalized tasks or organizationally defined roles.

This paper undertakes description and exploratory analysis of the social interaction which took place within a small work group of factory machine operatives during a two-month period of participant observation. The factual and ideational materials which it presents lie at an intersection of two lines of research interest and should, in their dual bearing, contribute to both. Since the operatives were engaged in work which involved the repetition of very simple operations over an extra-long workday, six days a week, they were faced with the problem of dealing with a formidable "beast of monotony." Revelation of how the group utilized its resources to combat that "beast" should merit the attention of those who are seeking solution to the practical problem of job satisfaction, or employee morale. It should also provide insights for those who are trying to penetrate the mysteries of the small group.

Convergence of these two lines of interest is, of course, no new thing. Among the host of writers and researchers who have suggested connections between "group" and "joy in work" are Walker and Guest, observers of social interaction on the automobile assembly line.[1] They quote assembly-line workers as saying, "We have a lot of fun and talk all the time,"[2] and, "If it weren't for the talking and fooling, you'd go nuts."[3]

My account of how one group of machine operators kept from "going nuts" in a situation of monotonous work activity attempts to lay bare the tissues of interaction which made up the content of their adjustment. The talking, fun, and fooling which provided solution to the elemental problem of "psychological survival" will be described according to their embodiment in intra-group relations. In addition, an unusual opportunity for close observation of behavior involved in the maintenance of group equilibrium was afforded by the fortuitous introduction of a "natural experiment." My unwitting injection of explosive materials into the stream of interaction resulted in sudden, but temporary, loss of group interaction.

* From *Human Organization*, 18, No. 4 (Winter 1959–60), 158–168. Reprinted with permission.
[1] Charles R. Walker and Robert H. Guest, *The Man on the Assembly Line*, Harvard University Press, Cambridge, 1952.
[2] *Ibid.*, p. 77.
[3] *Ibid.*, p. 68.

My fellow operatives and I spent our long days of simple, repetitive work in relative isolation from other employees of the factory. Our line of machines was sealed off from other work areas of the plant by the four walls of the clicking room. The one door of this room was usually closed. Even when it was kept open, during periods of hot weather, the consequences were not social; it opened on an uninhabited storage room of the shipping department. Not even the sounds of work activity going on elsewhere in the factory carried to this isolated work place. There were occasional contacts with "outside" employees, usually on matters connected with the work; but, with the exception of the daily calls of one fellow who came to pick up finished materials for the next step in processing, such visits were sporadic and infrequent.

Moreover, face-to-face contact with members of the managerial hierarchy were few and far between. No one bearing the title of foreman ever came around. The only company official who showed himself more than once during the two-month observation period was the plant superintendent. Evidently overloaded with supervisory duties and production problems which kept him busy elsewhere, he managed to pay his respects every week or two. His visits were in the nature of short, businesslike, but friendly exchanges. Otherwise he confined his observable communications with the group to occasional utilization of a public address system. During the two-month period, the company president and the chief chemist paid one friendly call apiece. One man, who may or may not have been of managerial status, was seen on various occasions lurking about in a manner which excited suspicion. Although no observable consequences accrued from the peculiar visitations of this silent fellow, it was assumed that he was some sort of efficiency expert, and he was referred to as "The Snooper."

As far as our work group was concerned, this was truly a situation of laissez-faire management. There was no interference from staff experts, no hounding by time-study engineers or personnel men hot on the scent of efficiency or good human relations. Nor were there any signs of industrial democracy in the form of safety, recreational, or production committees. There was an international union, and there was a highly publicized union-management cooperation program; but actual interactional processes of cooperation were carried on somewhere beyond my range of observation and without participation of members of my work group. Furthermore, these union-management get-togethers had no determinable connection with the problem of "toughing out" a twelve-hour day at monotonous work.

Our work group was thus not only abandoned to its own resources for creating job satisfaction, but left without that basic reservoir of ill-will toward management which can sometimes be counted on to stimulate the development of interesting activities to occupy hand and brain. Lacking was the challenge of intergroup conflict, that perennial source of creative experience to fill the otherwise empty hours of meaningless work routine.[4]

The clicking machines were housed in a room approximately thirty

[4] Donald F. Roy, "Work Satisfaction and Social Reward in Quota Achievement: An Analysis of Piecework Incentive," *American Sociological Review*, XVIII (October 1953), 507–514.

by twenty-four feet. They were four in number, set in a row, and so arranged along one wall that the busy operator could, merely by raising his head from his work, freshen his reveries with a glance through one of three large barred windows. To the rear of one of the end machines sat a long cutting table; here the operators cut up rolls of plastic materials into small sheets manageable for further processing at the clickers. Behind the machine at the opposite end of the line sat another table which was intermittently the work station of a female employee who performed sundry scissors operations of a more intricate nature on raincoat parts. Boxed in on all sides by shelves and stocks of materials, this latter locus of work appeared a cell within a cell.

The clickers were of the genus punching machines; of mechanical construction similar to that of the better-known punch presses, their leading features were hammer and block. The hammer, or punching head, was approximately eight inches by twelve inches at its flat striking surface. The descent upon the block was initially forced by the operator, who exerted pressure on a handle attached to the side of the hammer head. A few inches of travel downward established electrical connection for a sharp, power-driven blow. The hammer also traveled, by manual guidance, in a horizontal plane to and from, and in an arc around, the central column of the machine. Thus the operator, up to the point of establishing electrical connections for the sudden and irrevocable downward thrust, had flexibility in maneuvering his instrument over the larger surface of the block. The latter, approximately twenty-four inches wide, eighteen inches deep, and ten inches thick, was made, like a butcher's block, of inlaid hardwood; was set in the machine at a convenient waist height. On it the operator placed his materials, one sheet at a time if leather, stacks of sheets if plastic, to be cut with steel dies of assorted sizes and shapes. The particular die in use would be moved, by hand, from spot to spot over the materials each time a cut was made; less frequently, materials would be shifted on the block as the operator saw need for such adjustment.

Introduction to the new job, with its relatively simple machine skills and work routines, was accomplished with what proved to be, in my experience, an all-time minimum of job training. The clicking machine assigned to me was situated at one end of the row. Here the superintendent and one of the operators gave a few brief demonstrations, accompanied by bits of advice which included a warning to keep hands clear of the descending hammer. After a short practice period, at the end of which the superintendent expressed satisfaction with progress and potentialities, I was left to develop my learning curve with no other supervision than that afforded by members of the work group. Further advice and assistance did come, from time to time, from my fellow operatives, sometimes upon request, sometimes unsolicited.

THE WORK GROUP

Absorbed at first in three related goals of improving my clicking skill, increasing my rate of output, and keeping my left hand unclicked, I paid little attention to my fellow operatives save to observe that they were friendly, middle-aged, foreign-born, full of advice, and very talkative. Their names, according to the way they addressed each other, were George, Ike, and Sammy.[5] George, a stocky fellow in his late fifties, operated the machine at the opposite end of the line; he, I later discovered, had emigrated in early youth from a country in southeastern Europe. Ike, stationed at George's left, was tall, slender, in his early fifties, and Jewish; he had come from eastern Europe in his youth. Sammy, number-three man in the line, and my neighbor, was heavy set, in his late fifties, and Jewish; he had escaped from a country in eastern Europe just before Hitler's legions had moved in. All three men had been downwardly mobile as to occupation in recent years. George and Sammy had been proprietors of small businesses; the former had been "wiped out" when his uninsured establishment burned down; the latter had been entrepreneuring on a small scale before he left all behind him to flee the Germans. According to his account, Ike had left a highly skilled trade which he had practiced for years in Chicago.

I discovered also that the clicker line represented a ranking system in descending order from George to myself. George not only had top seniority for the group, but functioned as a sort of leadman. His superior status was marked in the fact that he received five cents more per hour than the other clickermen, put in the longest workday, made daily contact, outside the workroom, with the superintendent on work matters which concerned the entire line, and communicated to the rest of us the directives which he received. The narrow margin of superordination was seen in the fact that directives were always relayed in the superindendent's name; they were on the order of "You'd better let that go now, and get on the green. Joe says they're running low on the fifth floor," or "Joe says he wants two boxes of the 3-die today." The narrow margin was also seen in the fact that the superintendent would communicate directly with his operatives over the public address system; and, on occasion, Ike or Sammy would leave the workroom to confer with him for decisions or advice in regard to work orders.

Ike was next to George in seniority, then Sammy. I was, of course, low man on the totem pole. Other indices to status differentiation lay in informal interaction, to be described later.

With one exception, job status tended to be matched by length of workday. George worked a thirteen-hour day, from 7 A.M. to 8:30 P.M. Ike worked eleven hours, from 7 A.M. to 6:30 P.M.; occasionally he worked until 7 or 7:30 for an eleven and a half- or a twelve-hour day. Sammy put in a nine-hour day, from 8 A.M. to 5:30 P.M. My twelve hours spanned from 8 A.M. to 8:30 P.M. We had a half hour for lunch, from 12 to 12:30.

The female who worked at the secluded table behind George's machine put in a regular plant-wide eight-hour shift, from 8 to 4:30. Two women held this job during the period of my employment; Mable was succeeded by Baby. Both were Negroes, and in their late twenties.

A fifth clicker operator, an Arabian *emigré* called Boo, worked a

---

[5] All names used are fictitious.

night shift by himself. He usually arrived about 7 P.M. to take over Ike's machine.

THE WORK

It was evident to me, before my first workday drew to a weary close, that my clicking career was going to be a grim process of fighting the clock, the particular timepiece in this situation being an old-fashioned alarm clock which ticked away on a shelf near George's machine. I had struggled through many dreary rounds with the minutes and hours during the various phases of my industrial experience, but never had I been confronted with such a dismal combination of working conditions as the extra-long workday, the infinitesimal cerebral excitation, and the extreme limitation of physical movement. The contrast with a recent stint in the California oil fields was striking. This was no eight-hour day of racing hither and yon over desert and foothills with a rollicking crew of "roustabouts" on a variety of repair missions at oil wells, pipe lines, and storage tanks. Here there were no afternoon dallyings to search the sands for horned toads, tarantulas, and rattlesnakes, or to climb old wooden derricks for raven's nests, with an eye out, of course, for the tell-tale streak of dust in the distance which gave ample warning of the approach of the boss. This was standing all day in one spot beside three old codgers in a dingy room looking out through barred windows at the bare walls of a brick warehouse, leg movements largely restricted to the shifting of body weight from one foot to the other, hand and arm movements confined, for the most part, to a simple repetitive sequence of place the die, _____ punch the clicker, _____ place the die, _____ punch the clicker, and intellectual activity reduced to computing the hours to quitting time. It is true that from time to time a fresh stack of sheets would have to be substituted for the clicked-out old one; but the stack would have been prepared by someone else, and the exchange would be only a minute or two in the making. Now and then a box of finished work would have to be moved back out of the way, and an empty box brought up; but the moving back and the bringing up involved only a step or two. And there was the half hour for lunch, and occasional trips to the lavatory or the drinking fountain to break up the day into digestible parts. But after each momentary respite, hammer and die were moving again: click, _____ move die, _____ click, _____ move die.

Before the end of the first day, Monotony was joined by his twin brother, Fatigue. I got tired. My legs ached, and my feet hurt. Early in the afternoon I discovered a tall stool and moved it up to my machine to "take the load off my feet." But the superintendent dropped in to see how I was "doing" and promptly informed me that "we don't sit down on this job." My reverie toyed with the idea of quitting the job and looking for other work.

The next day was the same: the monotony of the work, the tired legs and sore feet and thoughts of quitting.

THE GAME OF WORK

In discussing the factory operative's struggle to "cling to the remnants of joy in work," Henri de Man makes the general observations that "it is psychologically impossible to deprive any kind of work of all its positive emotional elements," that the worker will find *some* meaning in any activity assigned to him, a "certain scope for initiative which can satisfy after a fashion the instinct for play and the creative impulse," that "even in the Taylor system there is found luxury of self-determination."[6] De Man cites the case of one worker who wrapped 13,000 incandescent bulbs a day; she found her outlet for creative impulse, her self-determination, her meaning in work by varying her wrapping movements a little from time to time.[7]

So did I search for *some* meaning in my continuous mincing of plastic sheets into small ovals, fingers, and trapezoids. The richness of possibility for creative expression previously discovered in my experience with the "Taylor system"[8] did not reveal itself here. There was no piecework, so no piecework game. There was no conflict with management, so no war game. But, like the light-bulb wrapper, I did find a "certain scope for initiative," and out of this slight freedom to vary activity, I developed a game of work.

The game developed was quite simple, so elementary, in fact, that its playing was reminiscent of rainy-day preoccupations in childhood, when attention could be centered by the hour on colored bits of things of assorted sizes and shapes. But this adult activity was not mere pottering and piddling; what it lacked in the earlier imaginative content, it made up for in clean-cut structure. Fundamentally involved were: (a) variation in color of the materials cut, (b) variation in shapes of the dies used, and (c) a process called "scraping the block." The basic procedure which ordered the particular combination of components employed could be stated in the form: "As soon as I do so many of these, I'll get to do those." If, for example, production scheduled for the day featured small, rectangular strips in three colors, the game might go: "As soon as I finish a thousand of the green ones, I'll click some brown ones." And, with success in attaining the objective of working with brown materials, a new goal of "I'll get to do the white ones" might be set. Or the new goal might involve switching dies.

Scraping the block made the game more interesting by adding to the number of possible variations in its playing; and, what was perhaps more important, provided the only substantial reward, save for going to the lavatory or getting a drink of water, on days when work with one die and one color of material was scheduled. As a physical operation, scraping the block was fairly simple; it involved application of a coarse file to the upper surface of the block to remove roughness and unevenness resulting from the wear and tear of die penetration. But, as part of the intellectual

---

[6] Henri de Man, *The Psychology of Socialism*, Henry Holt and Company, New York, 1927, pp. 80–81.

[7] *Ibid.*, p. 81.

[8] Roy, *op. cit.*

and emotional content of the game of work, it could be in itself a source of variation in activity. The upper left-hand corner of the block could be chewed up in the clicking of 1,000 white trapezoid pieces, then scraped. Next, the upper right-hand corner, and so on until the entire block had been worked over. Then, on the next round of scraping by quadrants, there was the possibility of a change of color or die to green trapezoid or white oval pieces.

Thus the game of work might be described as a continuous sequence of short-range production goals with achievement rewards in the form of activity change. The superiority of this relatively complex and self-determined system over the technically simple and outside-controlled job-satisfaction injections experienced by Milner at the beginner's table in a shop of the feather industry should be immediately apparent:

> Twice a day our work was completely changed to break the monotony. First Jennie would give us feathers of a brilliant green, then bright orange or a light blue or black. The "ohs" and "ahs" that came from the girls at each change was proof enough that this was an effective way of breaking the monotony of the tedious work.[9]

But a hasty conclusion that I was having lots of fun playing my clicking game should be avoided. These games were not as interesting in the experiencing as they might seem to be from the telling. Emotional tone of the activity was low, and intellectual currents weak. Such rewards as scraping the block or "getting to do the blue ones" were not very exciting, and the stretches of repetitive movement involved in achieving them were long enough to permit lapses into obsessive reverie. Henri de Man speaks of "clinging to the remnants of joy in work," and this situation represented just that. How tenacious the clinging was, how long I could have "stuck it out" with my remnants, was never determined. Before the first week was out this adjustment to the work situation was complicated by other developments. The game of work continued, but in a different context. Its influence became decidedly subordinated to, if not completely overshadowed by, another source of job satisfaction.

INFORMAL SOCIAL ACTIVITY OF THE WORK GROUP: TIMES AND THEMES

The change came about when I began to take serious note of the social activity going on around me; my attentiveness to this activity came with growing involvement in it. What I heard at first, before I started to listen, was a stream of disconnected bits of communication which did not make much sense. Foreign accents were strong and referents were not joined to coherent contexts of meaning. It was just "jabbering." What I saw at first, before I began to observe, was occasional flurries of horseplay so simple and unvarying in pattern and so childish in quality that they made no strong bid for attention. For example, Ike would regularly switch off the power at Sammy's machine whenever Sammy made a trip to the lava-

[9] Lucille Milner, *Education of an American Liberal*, Horizon Press, New York, 1954, p. 97.

tory or the drinking fountain. Correlatively, Sammy invariably fell victim to the plot by making an attempt to operate his clicking hammer after returning to the shop. And, as the simple pattern went, this blind stumbling into the trap was always followed by indignation and reproach from Sammy, smirking satisfaction from Ike, and mild paternal scolding from George. My interest in this procedure was at first confined to wondering when Ike would weary of his tedious joke or when Sammy would learn to check his power switch before trying the hammer.

But, as I began to pay closer attention, as I began to develop familiarity with the communication system, the disconnected became connected, the nonsense made sense, the obscure became clear, and the silly actually funny. And, as the content of the interaction took on more and more meaning, the interaction began to reveal structure. There were "times" and "themes," and roles to serve their enaction. The interaction had subtleties, and I began to savor and appreciate them. I started to record what hitherto had seemed unimportant.

Times

This emerging awareness of structure and meaning included recognition that the long day's grind was broken by interruptions of a kind other than the formally instituted or idiosyncratically developed disjunctions in work routine previously described. These additional interruptions appeared in daily repetition in an ordered series of informal interactions. They were, in part, but only in part and in very rough comparison, similar to those common fractures of the production process known as the coffee break, the coke break, and the cigarette break. Their distinction lay in frequency of occurrence and in brevity. As phases of the daily series, they occurred almost hourly, and so short were they in duration that they disrupted work activity only slightly. Their significance lay not so much in their function as rest pauses, although it cannot be denied that physical refreshment was involved. Nor did their chief importance lie in the accentuation of progress points in the passage of time, although they could perform that function far more strikingly than the hour hand on the dull face of George's alarm clock. If the daily series of interruptions be likened to a clock, then the comparison might best be made with a special kind of cuckoo clock, one with a cuckoo which can provide variation in its announcements and can create such an interest in them that the intervening minutes become filled with intellectual content. The major significance of the interactional interruptions lay in such a carryover of interest. The physical interplay which momentarily halted work activity would initiate verbal exchanges and thought processes to occupy group members until the next interruption. The group interactions thus not only marked off the time; they gave it content and hurried it along.

Most of the breaks in the daily series were designated as "times" in the parlance of the clicker operators, and they featured the consumption of food or drink of one sort or another. There was coffee time, peach time, banana time, fish time, coke time, and, of course, lunch time. Other interruptions, which formed part of the series but were not verbally recognized as times, were window time, pickup time, and the staggered quitting times

of Sammy and Ike. These latter unnamed times did not involve the par-
taking of refreshments.

My attention was first drawn to this times business during my first
week of employment when I was encouraged to join in the sharing of two
peaches. It was Sammy who provided the peaches; he drew them from his
lunch box after making the announcement, "Peach time!" On this first
occasion I refused the proffered fruit, but thereafter regularly consumed
my half peach. Sammy continued to provide the peaches and to make the
"Peach time!" announcement, although there were days when Ike would
remind him that it was peach time, urging him to hurry up with the mid-
morning snack. Ike invariably complained about the quality of the fruit,
and his complaints fed the fires of continued banter between peach donor
and critical recipient. I did find the fruit a bit on the scrubby side but
felt, before I achieved insight into the function of peach time, that Ike was
showing poor manners by looking a gift horse in the mouth. I wondered
why Sammy continued to share his peaches with such an ingrate.

Banana time followed peach time by approximately an hour. Sammy
again provided the refreshments, namely, one banana. There was, however,
no four-way sharing of Sammy's banana. Ike would gulp it down by himself after surreptitiously extracting it from Sammy's lunch box, kept on a
shelf behind Sammy's work station. Each morning, after making the
snatch, Ike would call out, "Banana time!" and proceed to down his prize
while Sammy made futile protests and denunciations. George would join
in with mild remonstrances, sometimes scolding Sammy for making so
much fuss. The banana was one which Sammy brought for his own consumption at lunch time; he never did get to eat his banana, but kept bringing one for his lunch. At first this daily theft startled and amazed me. Then
I grew to look forward to the daily seizure and the verbal interaction
which followed.

Window time came next. It followed banana time as a regular consequence of Ike's castigation by the indignant Sammy. After "taking" repeated references to himself as a person badly lacking in morality and
character, Ike would "finally" retaliate by opening the window which
faced Sammy's machine, to let the "cold air" blow in on Sammy. The
slandering which would, in its echolalic repetition, wear down Ike's patience and forbearance usually took the form of the invidious comparison:
"George is a good daddy! Ike is a bad man! A very bad man!" Opening the
window would take a little time to accomplish and would involve a great
deal of verbal interplay between Ike and Sammy, both before and after the
event. Ike would threaten, make feints toward the window, then finally
open it. Sammy would protest, argue, and make claims that the air blowing
in on him would give him a cold; he would eventually have to leave his
machine to close the window. Sometimes the weather was slightly chilly,
and the draft from the window unpleasant; but cool or hot, windy or still,
window time arrived each day. (I assume that it was originally a cold
season development.) George's part in this interplay, in spite of the "good
daddy" laudations, was to encourage Ike in his window work. He would
stress the tonic values of fresh air and chide Sammy for his unappreciative-
ness.

Following window time came lunch time, a formally designated half-hour for the midday repast and rest break. At this time, informal interaction would feature exchanges between Ike and George. The former would start eating his lunch a few minutes before noon, and the latter, in his role as straw boss, would censure him for malobservance of the rules. Ike's off-beat luncheon usually involved a previous tampering with George's alarm clock. Ike would set the clock ahead a few minutes in order to maintain his eating schedule without detection, and George would discover these small daylight-saving changes.

The first "time" interruption of the day I did not share. It occurred soon after I arrived on the job, at eight o'clock. George and Ike would share a small pot of coffee brewed on George's hot plate.

Pickup time, fish time, and coke time came in the afternoon. I name it pickup time to represent the official visit of the man who made daily calls to cart away boxes of clicked materials. The arrival of the pickup man, a Negro, was always a noisy one, like the arrival of a daily passenger train in an isolated small town. Interaction attained a quick peak of intensity to crowd into a few minutes all communications, necessary and otherwise. Exchanges invariably included loud depreciations by the pickup man of the amount of work accomplished in the clicking department during the preceding twenty-four hours. Such scoffing would be on the order of "Is that all you've got done? What do you boys do all day?" These devaluations would be countered with allusions to the "soft job" enjoyed by the pickup man. During the course of the exchanges news items would be dropped, some of serious import, such as reports of accomplished or impending layoffs in the various plants of the company, or of gains or losses in orders for company products. Most of the news items, however, involved bits of information on plant employees told in a light vein. Information relayed by the clicker operators was usually told about each other, mainly in the form of summaries of the most recent kidding sequences. Some of this material was repetitive, carried over from day to day. Sammy would be the butt of most of this newscasting, although he would make occasional counter-reports on Ike and George. An invariable part of the interactional content of pickup time was Ike's introduction of the pickup man to George. "Meet Mr. Papeatis!" Ike would say in mock solemnity and dignity. Each day the pickup man "met" Mr. Papeatis, to the obvious irritation of the latter. Another pickup time invariably would bring Baby (or Mable) into the interaction. George would always issue the loud warning to the pickup man: "Now I want you to stay away from Baby! She's Henry's girl!" Henry was a burly Negro with a booming bass voice who made infrequent trips to the clicking room with lift-truck loads of materials. He was reputedly quite a ladies' man among the colored population of the factory. George's warning to "Stay away from Baby!" was issued to every Negro who entered the shop. Baby's only part in this was to laugh at the horseplay.

About mid-afternoon came fish time. George and Ike would stop work for a few minutes to consume some sort of pickled fish which Ike provided. Neither Sammy nor I partook of this nourishment, nor were we invited. For this omission I was grateful; the fish, brought in a newspaper and with head and tail intact, produced a reverse effect on my appetite. George and Ike seemed to share a great liking for fish. Each Friday night, as a regular ritual, they would enjoy a fish dinner together at a nearby restaurant. On these nights Ike would work until 8:30 and leave the plant with George.

Coke time came late in the afternoon, and was an occasion for total participation. The four of us took turns in buying the drinks and in making the trip for them to a fourth-floor vending machine. Through George's manipulation of the situation, it eventually became my daily chore to go after the cokes; the straw boss had noted that I made a much faster trip to the fourth floor and back than Sammy or Ike.

Sammy left the plant at 5:30, and Ike ordinarily retired from the scene an hour and a half later. These quitting times were not marked by any distinctive interaction save the one regular exchange between Sammy and George over the former's "early washup." Sammy's tendency was to crowd his washing up toward five o'clock, and it was George's concern to keep it from further creeping advance. After Ike's departure came Boo's arrival. Boo's was a striking personality productive of a change in topics of conversation to fill in the last hour of the long workday.

Themes

To put flesh, so to speak, on this interactional frame of "times," my work group had developed various "themes" of verbal interplay which had become standardized in their repetition. These topics of conversation ranged in quality from an extreme of nonsensical chatter to another extreme of serious discourse. Unlike the times, these themes flowed one into the other in no particular sequence of predictability. Serious conversation could suddenly melt into horseplay, and vice versa. In the middle of a serious discussion on the high cost of living, Ike might drop a weight behind the easily startled Sammy, or hit him over the head with a dusty paper sack. Interaction would immediately drop to a low-comedy exchange of slaps, threats, guffaws, and disapprobations which would invariably include a ten-minute echolalia of "Ike is a bad man, a very bad man! George is a good daddy, a very fine man!" Or, on the other hand, a stream of such invidious comparisons as followed a surreptitious switching-off of Sammy's machine by the playful Ike might merge suddenly into a discussion of the pros and cons of saving for one's funeral.

"Kidding themes" were usually started by George or Ike, and Sammy was usually the butt of the joke. Sometimes Ike would have to "take it," seldom George. One favorite kidding theme involved Sammy's alleged receipt of $100 a month from his son. The points stressed were that Sammy did not have to work long hours, or did not have to work at all, because he had a son to support him. George would always point out that he sent money to his daughter; she did not send money to him. Sammy received occasional calls from his wife, and his claim that these calls were requests to shop for groceries on the way home were greeted with feigned disbelief. Sammy was ribbed for being closely watched, bossed, and henpecked by his wife, and the expression "Are you man or mouse?" became an echolalic utterance, used both in and out of the original context.

Ike, who shared his machine and the work scheduled for it with Boo, the night operator, came in for constant invidious comparison on the subject of output. The socially isolated Boo, who chose work rather than sleep on his lonely night shift, kept up a high level of performance, and George never tired of pointing this out to Ike. It so happened that Boo, an Arabian Moslem from Palestine, had no use for Jews in general; and Ike, who was Jewish, had no use for Boo in particular. Whenever George would extol Boo's previous night's production, Ike would try to turn the conversation into a general discussion on the need for educating the Arabs. George, never permitting the development of serious discussion on this topic, would repeat a smirking warning, "You watch out for Boo! He's got a long knife!"

The "poom poom" theme was one that caused no sting. It would come up several times a day to be enjoyed as unbarbed fun by the three older clicker operators. Ike was usually the one to raise the question "How many times you go poom poom last night?" The person questioned usually replied with claims of being "too old for poom poom." If this theme did develop a goat, it was I. When it was pointed out that I was a younger man, this provided further grist for the poom poom mill. I soon grew weary of this poom poom business, so dear to the hearts of the three old satyrs, and, knowing where the conversation would inevitably lead, winced whenever Ike brought up the subject.

I grew almost as sick of a kidding theme which developed from some personal information contributed during a serious conversation on property ownership and high taxes. I dropped a few remarks about two acres of land which I owned in one of the western states, and from then on I had to listen to questions, advice, and general nonsensical comment in regard to "Danelly's farm."[10] This "farm" soon became stocked with horses, cows, pigs, chickens, ducks, and the various and sundry domesticated beasts so tunefully listed in "Old MacDonald Had a Farm." George was a persistent offender with this theme. Where the others seemed to be mainly interested in statistics on livestock, crops, etc., George's teasing centered on a generous offering to help with the household chores while I worked in the fields. He would drone on, *ad nauseam*, "when I come to visit you, you will never have to worry about the housework, Danelly. I'll stay around the house when you go out to dig the potatoes and milk the cows, I'll stay in and peel potatoes and help your wife do the dishes." Danelly always found it difficult to change the subject on George, once the latter started to bear down on the farm theme.

Another kidding theme which developed out of serious discussion could be labeled "helping Danelly find a cheaper apartment." It became known to the group that Danelly had a pending housing problem, that he would need new quarters for his family when the permanent resident of his temporary summer dwelling returned from a vacation. This information engendered at first a great deal of sympathetic concern and, of course, advice on apartment hunting. Development into a kidding theme was immediately related to previous exchanges between Ike and George on the

---

[10] This spelling is the closest I can come to the appellation given me in George's broken English and adopted by other members of the group.

quality of their respective dwelling areas. Ike lived in "Lawndale," and George dwelt in the "Woodlawn" area. The new pattern featured the reading aloud of bogus "apartment for rent" ads in newspapers which were brought into the shop. Studying his paper at lunch time, George would call out, "Here's an apartment for you, Danelly! Five rooms, stove heat, $20 a month, Lawndale Avenue!" Later, Ike would read from his paper, "Here's one! Six rooms, stove heat, dirt floor. $18.50 a month! At 55th and Woodlawn." Bantering would then go on in regard to the quality of housing or population in the two areas. The search for an apartment for Danelly was not successful.

Serious themes included the relating of major misfortunes suffered in the past by group members. George referred again and again to the loss, by fire, of his business establishment. Ike's chief complaints centered around a chronically ill wife who had undergone various operations and periods of hospital care. Ike spoke with discouragement of the expenses attendant upon hiring a housekeeper for himself and his children; he referred with disappointment and disgust to a teen-age son, an inept lad who "couldn't even fix his own lunch. He couldn't even make himself a sandwich!" Sammy's reminiscences centered on the loss of a flourishing business when he had to flee Europe ahead of Nazi invasion.

But all serious topics were not tales of woe. One favorite serious theme which was optimistic in tone could be called either "Danelly's future" or "getting Danelly a better job." It was known that I had been attending "college," the magic door to opportunity, although my specific course of study remained somewhat obscure. Suggestions poured forth on good lines of work to get into, and these suggestions were backed with accounts of friends, and friends of friends, who had made good via the academic route. My answer to the expected question, "Why are you working here?" always stressed the "lots of overtime" feature, and this explanation seemed to suffice for short-range goals.

There was one theme of especially solemn import, the "professor theme." This theme might also be termed "George's daughter's marriage theme"; for the recent marriage of George's only child was inextricably bound up with George's connection with higher learning. The daughter had married the son of a professor who instructed in one of the local colleges. This professor theme was not in the strictest sense a conversation piece; when the subject came up, George did all the talking. The two Jewish operatives remained silent as they listened with deep respect, if not actual awe, to George's accounts of the Big Wedding which, including the wedding pictures, entailed an expense of $1,000. It was monologue, but there was listening, there was communication, the sacred communication of a temple, when George told of going for Sunday-afternoon walks on the Midway with the professor, or of joining the professor for a Sunday dinner. Whenever he spoke of the professor, his daughter, the wedding, or even of the new son-in-law, who remained for the most part in the background, a sort of incidental like the wedding cake, George was complete master of the interaction. His manner, in speaking to the rank-and-file of clicker operators, was indeed that of master deigning to notice his underlings. I came to the conclusion that it was the professor connection, not the straw-boss-ship or the extra nickel an hour, which provided the fount of George's superior status in the group.

If the professor theme may be regarded as the cream of verbal interaction, the "chatter themes" should be classed as the dregs. The chatter themes were hardly themes at all; perhaps they should be labeled "verbal states," or "oral autisms." Some were of doubtful status as communication; they were like the howl or cry of an animal responding to its own physiological state. They were exclamations, ejaculations, snatches of song or doggerel, talkings-to-oneself, mutterings. Their classification as themes would rest on their repetitive character. They were echolalic utterances, repeated over and over. An already mentioned example would be Sammy's repetition of "George is a good daddy, a very fine man! Ike is a bad man, a very bad man!" Also, Sammy's repetition of "Don't bother me! Can't you see I'm busy? I'm a very busy man!" for ten minutes after Ike had dropped a weight behind him would fit the classification. Ike would shout "Mamariba!" at intervals between repetition of bits of verse, such as:

> Mamma on the bed,
> Papa on the floor,
> Baby in the crib
> Says giver some more!

Sometimes the three operators would pick up one of these simple chatterings in a sort of chorus. "Are you man or mouse? I ask you, are you man or mouse?" was a favorite of this type.

So initial discouragement with the meagerness of social interaction I now recognized as due to lack of observation. The interaction was there, in constant flow. It captured attention and held interest to make the long day pass. The twelve hours of "click, _____ move die, _____ click, _____ move die" became as easy to endure as eight hours of varied activity in the oil fields or eight hours of playing the piecework game in a machine shop. The "beast of boredom" was gentled to the harmlessness of a kitten.

BLACK FRIDAY: DISINTEGRATION OF THE GROUP

But all this was before "Black Friday." Events of that dark day shattered the edifice of interaction, its framework of times and mosaic of themes, and reduced the work situation to a state of social atomization and machine-tending drudgery. The explosive element was introduced deliberately, but without prevision of its consequences.

On Black Friday, Sammy was not present; he was on vacation. There was no peach time that morning, of course, and no banana time. But George and Ike held their coffee time, as usual, and a steady flow of themes was filling the morning quite adequately. It seemed like a normal day in the making, at least one which was going to meet the somewhat reduced expectations created by Sammy's absence.

Suddenly I was possessed of an inspiration for modification of the professor theme. When the idea struck, I was working at Sammy's machine, clicking out leather parts for billfolds. It was not difficult to get the attention of close neighbor Ike to suggest *sotto voce*, "Why don't you tell him you saw the professor teaching in a barber college on Madison Street? . . . Make it near Halsted Street."

Ike thought this one over for a few minutes, and caught the vision of its possibilities. After an interval of steady application to his clicking, he informed the unsuspecting George of his near West Side discovery; he had seen the professor busy at his instructing in a barber college in the lower reaches of Hobohemia.

George reacted to this announcement with stony silence. The burden of questioning Ike for further details on his discovery fell upon me. Ike had not elaborated his story very much before we realized that the show was not going over. George kept getting redder in the face, and more tight-lipped; he slammed into his clicking with increased vigor. I made one last weak attempt to keep the play on the road by remarking that barber colleges paid pretty well. George turned to hiss at me, "You'll have to go to Kankakee with Ike!" I dropped the subject. Ike whispered to me, "George is sore!"

George was indeed sore. He didn't say another word the rest of the morning. There was no conversation at lunchtime, nor was there any after lunch. A pall of silence had fallen over the clicker room. Fish time fell a casualty. George did not touch the coke I brought for him. A very long, very dreary afternoon dragged on. Finally, after Ike left for home, George broke the silence to reveal his feelings to me:

> Ike acts like a five-year-old, not a man! He doesn't even have the respect of the niggers. But he's got to act like a man around here! He's always fooling around! I'm going to stop that! I'm going to show him his place!
>
> . . . Jews will ruin you, if you let them. I don't care if he sings, but the first time he mentions my name, I'm going to shut him up! It's always "Meet Mr. Papeatis! George is a good daddy!" And all that. He's paid to work! If he doesn't work, I'm going to tell Joe [the superintendent]!

Then came a succession of dismal workdays devoid of times and barren of themes. Ike did not sing, nor did he recite bawdy verse. The shop songbird was caught in the grip of icy winter. What meager communication there was took a sequence of patterns which proved interesting only in retrospect.

For three days, George would not speak to Ike. Ike made several weak attempts to break the wall of silence which George had put between them, but George did not respond; it was as if he did not hear. George would speak to me, on infrequent occasions, and so would Ike. They did not speak to each other.

On the third day George advised me of his new communication policy, designed for dealing with Ike, and for Sammy, too, when the latter returned to work. Interaction was now on a "strictly business" basis, with emphasis to be placed on raising the level of shop output. The effect of this new policy on production remained indeterminate. Before the fourth day had ended, George got carried away by his narrowed interests

to the point of making sarcastic remarks about the poor work performances of the absent Sammy. Although addressed to me, these caustic depreciations were obviously for the benefit of Ike. Later in the day Ike
spoke to me, for George's benefit, of Sammy's outstanding ability to turn
out billfold parts. For the next four days, the prevailing silence of the
shop was occasionally broken by either harsh criticism or fulsome praise
of Sammy's outstanding workmanship. I did not risk replying to either im-
peachment or panegyric for fear of involvement in further situational de-
teriorations.

Twelve-hour days were creeping again at snail's pace. The strictly
business communications were of no help, and the sporadic bursts of dis-
taste or enthusiasm for Sammy's clicking ability helped very little. With
the return of boredom came a return of fatigue. My legs tired as the after-
noons dragged on, and I became engaged in conscious efforts to rest one
by shifting my weight to the other. I would pause in my work to stare
through the barred windows at the grimy brick wall across the alley; and,
turning my head, I would notice that Ike was staring at the wall too.
George would do very little work after Ike left the shop at night. He
would sit in a chair and complain of weariness and sore feet.

In desperation, I fell back on my game of work, my blues and greens
and whites, my ovals and trapezoids, and my scraping the block. I came
to surpass Boo, the energetic night worker, in volume of output. George
referred to me as a "day Boo" (day-shift Boo) and suggested that I
"keep" Sammy's machine. I managed to avoid this promotion, and consequent estrangement with Sammy, by pleading attachment to my own
machine.

When Sammy returned to work, discovery of the cleavage between
George and Ike left him stunned. "They were the best of friends!" he said
to me in bewilderment.

George now offered Sammy direct, savage criticisms of his work.
For several days the good-natured Sammy endured these verbal aggressions without losing his temper; but when George shouted at him "You
work like a preacher!" Sammy became very angry, indeed. I had a few
anxious moments when I thought that the two old friends were going to
come to blows.

Then, thirteen days after Black Friday, came an abrupt change in
the pattern of interaction. George and Ike spoke to each other again, in
friendly conversation. I noticed Ike talking to George after lunch. The
two had newspapers of fish at George's cabinet. Ike was excited; he said,
"I'll pull up a chair!" The two ate for ten minutes. It seems that they went
up to the 22nd Street Exchange together during lunch period to cash pay
checks.

That afternoon Ike and Sammy started to play again, and Ike burst
once more into song. Old themes reappeared as suddenly as the desert
flowers in spring. At first, George managed to maintain some show of the
dignity of superordination. When Ike started to sing snatches of "You Are
My Sunshine," George suggested that he get "more production." Then
Ike backed up George in pressuring Sammy for more production. Sammy
turned this exhortation into low comedy by calling Ike a "slave driver"

and by shouting over and over again, "Don't bother me! I'm a busy man!" On one occasion, as if almost overcome with joy and excitement, Sammy cried out, "Don't bother me! I'll tell Rothman [the company president]! I'll tell the union! Don't mention my name! I hate you!"

I knew that George was definitely back into the spirit of the thing when he called to Sammy, "Are you man or mouse?" He kept up the "man or mouse" chatter for some time.

George was for a time reluctant to accept fruit when it was offered to him, and he did not make a final capitulation to coke time until five days after renewal of the fun and fooling. Strictly speaking, there never was a return to banana time, peach time, or window time. However, the sharing and snitching of fruit did go on once more, and the window in front of Sammy's machine played a more prominent part than ever in the renaissance of horseplay in the clicker room. In fact, the "rush to the window" became an integral part of increasingly complex themes and repeated sequences of interaction. This window rushing became especially bound up with new developments which featured what may be termed the "anal gesture."[11] Introduced by Ike, and given backing by an enthusiastic, very playful George, the anal gesture became a key component of fun and fooling during the remaining weeks of my stay in the shop. Ike broke wind, and put his head in his hand on the block as Sammy grabbed a rod and made a mock rush to open the window. He beat Ike on the head, and George threw some water on him, playfully. In came the Negro head of the Leather Department; he remarked jokingly that we should take out the machines and make a playroom out of the shop.

Of course, George's demand for greater production was metamorphized into horseplay. His shout of "Production please!" became a chatter theme to accompany the varied antics of Ike and Sammy.

The professor theme was dropped completely. George never again mentioned his Sunday walks on the Midway with the professor.

CONCLUSIONS

Speculative assessment of the possible significance of my observations on information interaction in the clicking room may be set forth in a series of general statements.

Practical Application

First, in regard to possible practical application to problems of industrial management, these observations seem to support the generally accepted notion that one key source of job satisfaction lies in the informal interaction shared by members of a work group. In the clicking-room situation the spontaneous development of a patterned combination of

---

[11] I have been puzzled to note widespread appreciation of this gesture in the "consumatory" communication of the working men of this nation. For the present I leave it to clinical psychologists to account for the nature and pervasiveness of this social bond and confine myself to joining offended readers in the hope that some day our industrial workers will achieve such a level of refinement in thought and action that their behavior will be no more distressing to us than that of the college students who fill out our questionnaires or form groups for laboratory experimentation.

horseplay, serious conversation, and frequent sharing of food and drink reduced the monotony of simple, repetitive operations to the point where a regular schedule of long workdays became livable. This kind of group interplay may be termed "consumatory" in the sense indicated by Dewey, when he makes a basic distinction between "instrumental" and "consumatory" communication.[12] The enjoyment of communication "for its own sake" as "mere sociabilities," as "free, aimless social intercourse," brings job satisfaction, at least job endurance, to work situations largely bereft of creative experience.

In regard to another managerial concern, employee productivity, any appraisal of the influence of group interaction upon clicking-room output could be no more than roughly impressionistic. I obtained no evidence to warrant a claim that banana time, or any of its accompaniments in consumatory interaction, boosted production. To the contrary, my diary recordings express an occasional perplexity in the form of "How does this company manage to stay in business?" However, I did not obtain sufficient evidence to indicate that, under the prevailing conditions of laissez-faire management, the output of our group would have been more impressive if the playful cavorting of three middle-aged gentlemen about the barred windows had never been. As far as achievement of managerial goals is concerned, the most that could be suggested is that leavening the deadly boredom of individualized work routines with a concurrent flow of group festivities had a negative effect on turnover. I left the group, with sad reluctance, under the pressure of strong urgings to accept a research fellowship which would involve no factory toil. My fellow clickers stayed with their machines to carry on their labors in the spirit of banana time.

Theoretical Considerations

Secondly, possible contribution to ongoing sociological inquiry into the behavior of small groups in general, and factory work groups in particular, may lie in one or more of the following ideational products of my clicking-room experience:

1. In their day-long confinement together in a small room spatially and socially isolated from other work areas of the factory the Clicking Department employees found themselves ecologically situated for development of a "natural" group. Such a development did take place; from worker intercommunications did emerge the full-blown sociocultural system of consumatory interactions which I came to share, observe, and record in the process of my socialization.

2. These interactions had a content which could be abstracted from the total existential flow of observable doings and sayings for labelling and objective consideration. That is, they represented a distinctive sub-culture, with its recurring patterns of reciprocal influencings which I have described as times and themes.

3. From these interactions may also be abstracted a social structure of statuses and roles. This structure may be discerned in the carrying out of the various informal activities which provide the content of the sub-culture of the group. The times and themes were performed with a system

[12] John Dewey, *Experience and Nature*, Open Court Publishing Co., Chicago, 1925, pp. 202–206.

of roles which formed a sort of pecking hierarchy. Horseplay had its initiators and its victims, its amplifiers and its chorus; kidding had its attackers and attacked, its least attacked and its most attacked, its ready acceptors of attack and its strong resistors to attack. The fun went on with the participation of all, but within the controlling frame of status, a matter of who can say or do what to whom and get away with it.

4. In both the cultural content and the social structure of clicker-group interaction could be seen the permeation of influences which flowed from the various multiple group memberships of the participants. Past and present "other-group" experiences or anticipated "outside" social connections provided significant materials for the building of themes and for the establishment and maintenance of status and role relationships. The impact of reference-group affiliations on clicking-room interaction was notably revealed in the sacred, status-conferring expression of the professor theme. This impact was brought into very sharp focus in developments which followed my attempt to degrade the topic, and correlatively, to demote George.

5. Stability of the clicking-room social system was never threatened by immediate outside pressures. Ours was not an instrumental group, subject to disintegration in a losing struggle against environmental obstacles or oppositions. It was not striving for corporate goals; nor was it faced with the enmity of other groups. It was strictly a consummatory group, devoted to the maintenance of patterns of self-entertainment. Under existing conditions, disruption of unity could come only from within.

Potentials for breakdown were endemic in the interpersonal interactions involved in conducting the group's activities. Patterns of fun and fooling had developed within a matrix of frustration. Tensions born of long hours of relatively meaningless work were released in the mock aggressions of horseplay. In the recurrent attack, defense, and counter-attack there continually lurked the possibility that words or gestures harmless in conscious intent might cross the subtle boundary of accepted, playful aggression to be perceived as real assault. While such an occurrence might incur displeasure no more lasting than necessary for the quick clarification or creation of kidding norms, it might also spark a charge of hostility sufficient to disorganize the group.

A contributory potential for breakdown from within lay in the dissimilar "other-group" experiences of the operators. These other-group affiliations and identifications could provide differences in tastes and sensitivities, including appreciation of humor, differences which could make maintenance of consensus in regard to kidding norms a hazardous process of trial and error adjustments.

6. The risk involved in this trial and error determination of consensus on fun and fooling in a touchy situation of frustration—mock aggression—was made evident when I attempted to introduce alterations in the professor theme. The group disintegrated, *instanter*. That is, there was an abrupt cessation of the interactions which constituted our groupness. Although both George and I were solidly linked in other-group affiliations with the higher learning, there was not enough agreement in our attitudes toward university professors to prevent the interactional development which shattered our factory play group. George perceived my offered alterations as a

real attack, and he responded with strong hostility directed against Ike, the perceived assailant, and Sammy, a fellow traveler.

My innovations, if accepted, would have lowered the tone of the sacred professor theme, if not to "Stay Away from Baby" ribaldry, then at least to the verbal slapstick level of "finding Danelly an apartment." Such a downgrading of George's reference group would, in turn, have downgraded George. His status in the shop group hinged largely upon his claimed relations with the professor.

7. Integration of our group was fully restored after a series of changes in the patterning and quality of clicking-room interaction. It might be said that reintegration took place *in* these changes, that the series was a progressive one of step-by-step improvement in relations, that re-equilibration was in process during the three weeks that passed between initial communication collapse and complete return to "normal" interaction.

The cycle of loss and recovery of equilibrium may be crudely charted according to the following sequence of phases: (a) the stony silence of "not speaking"; (b) the confining of communication to formal matters connected with work routines; (c) the return of informal give-and-take in the form of harshly sarcastic kidding, mainly on the subject of work performance, addressed to a neutral go-between for the "benefit" of the object of aggression; (d) highly emotional direct attack, and counter-attack, in the form of criticism and defense of work performance; (e) a sudden rapprochement expressed in serious, dignified, but friendly conversation; (f) return to informal interaction in the form of mutually enjoyed mock aggression; (g) return to informal interaction in the form of regular patterns of sharing food and drink.

The group had disintegrated when George withdrew from participation; and, since the rest of us were at all times ready for rapprochement, reintegration was dependent upon his "return." Therefore, each change of phase in interaction on the road to recovery could be said to represent an increment of return on George's part. Or, conversely, each phase could represent an increment of reacceptance of punished deviants. Perhaps more generally applicable to description of a variety of reunion situations would be conceptualization of the phase changes as increments of re-association without an atomistic differentiation of the "movements" of individuals.

8. To point out that George played a key role in this particular case of re-equilibration is not to suggest that the homeostatic controls of a social system may be located in a type of role or in a patterning of role relationships. Such controls could be but partially described in terms of human interaction; they would be functional to the total configuration of conditions within the field of influence. The automatic controls of a mechanical system operate as such only under certain achieved and controlled conditions. The human body recovers from disease when conditions for such homeostasis are "right." The clicking-room group regained equilibrium under certain undetermined conditions. One of a number of other possible outcomes could have developed had conditions not been favorable for recovery.

For purposes of illustration, and from reflection on the case, I would consider the following as possibly necessary conditions for reintegration of our group: (a) Continued monotony of work operations. (b) Continued lack of a comparatively adequate substitute for the fun and fooling release from work tensions. (c) Inability of the operatives to escape from the work situation or from each other, within the work situation. George could not fire Ike or Sammy to remove them from his presence, and it would have been difficult for the three middle-aged men to find other jobs if they were to quit the shop. Shop space was small, and the machines close together. Like a submarine crew, they had to "live together." (d) Lack of conflicting definitions of the situation after Ike's perception of George's reaction to the "barber college" attack. George's anger and his punishment of the offenders was perceived as justified. (e) Lack of introduction of new issues or causes which might have carried justification for new attacks and counter-attacks, thus leading interaction into a spiral of conflict and crystallization of conflict norms. For instance, had George reported his offenders to the superintendent for their poor work performance; had he, in his anger, committed some offense which would have led to reporting of a grievance to local union officials; had he made his anti-Semitic remarks in the presence of Ike or Sammy, or had I relayed these remarks to them; had I tried to "take over" Sammy's machine, as George had urged—then the interactional outcome might have been permanent disintegration of the group.

9. Whether or not the particular patterning of interactional change previously noted is somehow typical of a "re-equilibration process" is not a major question here. My purpose in discriminating the seven changes is primarily to suggest that re-equilibration, when it does occur, may be described in observable phases and that the emergence of each succeeding phase should be dependent upon the configuration of conditions of the preceding one. Alternative eventual outcomes may change in their probabilities, as the phases succeed each other, just as prognosis for recovery in sickness may change as the disease situation changes.

10. Finally, discrimination of phase changes in social process may have practical as well as scientific value. Trained and skillful administrators might follow the practice in medicine of introducing aids to re-equilibration when diagnosis shows that they are needed.

CONFLICTS BETWEEN STAFF AND LINE MANAGERIAL OFFICERS

*Melville Dalton**

In almost all large organizations there exist sections or departments consisting of highly specialized personnel. Usually, this personnel is identified

* From *American Sociological Review*, 15 (June 1950), 342–351. Reprinted with permission.

as "staff" as opposed to "line" employees. The staff is supposed to advise, educate, inspect, and render service; but it has no formal authority over the "line." One aspect of understanding organizations involves appreciation of the "staff" concept (i.e., the use of specialists to advise and assist in getting the work done) and the functional role actually played by the staff.

In this article by Melville Dalton, we have a report of a study of the relationship between line and staff personnel, and an analysis of why it tends to develop as an area of conflict.

In its concentration on union-management relations, industrial sociology has tended to neglect the study of processes inside the ranks of industrial management. Obviously the doors to this research area are more closely guarded than the entry to industrial processes through the avenue of production workers, but an industrial sociology worthy of the name must sooner or later extend its inquiries to include the activities of all industrial personnel.

The present paper is the result of an attempt to study processes among industrial managers. It is specifically a report on the functioning interaction between the two major vertical groupings of industrial management: (1) the *staff* organization, the functions of which are research and advisory; and (2) the *line* organization, which has exclusive authority over production processes.

Industrial staff organizations are relatively new. Their appearance is a response to many complex interrelated forces, such as economic competition, scientific advance, industrial expansion, growth of the labor movement, and so on. During the last four or five decades these rapid changes and resulting unstable conditions have caused top industrial officials more and more to call in "specialists" to aid them toward the goal of greater production and efficiency. These specialists are of many kinds including chemists, statisticians, public and industrial relations officers, personnel officers, accountants, and a great variety of engineers, such as mechanical, draughting, electrical, chemical, fuel, lubricating, and industrial engineers. In industry these individuals are usually known as "staff people." Their functions, again, for the most part are to increase and apply their specialized knowledge in problem areas, and to advise those officers who make up the "line" organization and have authority[1] over production processes.

This theoretically satisfying industrial structure of specialized experts advising busy administrators has in a number of significant cases failed to function as expected. The assumptions that (a) the staff specialists would be reasonably content to function without a measure of formal authority[2] over production, and that (b) their suggestions regarding improvement of processes and techniques for control over personnel and production would be welcomed by line officers and be applied, require closer examination. In practice there is often much conflict between industrial

[1] *Inside* their particular staff organization, staff officers also may have authority over their subordinates, but not over production personnel.

[2] To the extent that staff officers influence line policy they do, of course, have a certain *informal* authority.

staff and line organizations, and in varying degrees the members of these organizations oppose each other.[3]

The aim of this paper is, therefore, to present and analyze data dealing with staff-line tensions.

Data were drawn from three industrial plants[4] in which the writer had been either a participating member of one or both of the groups or was intimate with reliable informants among the officers who were.

Approached sociologically, relations among members of management in the plants could be viewed as a general conflict system caused and perpetuated chiefly by (1) power struggles in the organization stemming in the main from competition among departments to maintain low operating costs; (2) drives by numerous members to increase their status in the hierarchy; (3) conflict between union and management; and (4) the staff-line friction which is the subject of this paper.[5] This milieu of tensions was not only unaccounted for by the blue-print organizations of the plants, but was often contradictory to, and even destructive of, the organizations' formal aims. All members of management, especially in the middle and lower ranks,[6] were caught up in this conflict system. Even

[3] Some social scientists have noted the possibility of staff-line friction, and industrial executives themselves have expressed strong feelings on the matter. See Burleigh B. Gardner, *Human Relations in Industry* (Chicago: Richard D. Irwin, Inc., 1945) and H. E. Dimock, *The Executive in Action* (New York: Harper & Brothers, 1945). Dimock believes that we are too "staff-minded" and that we should become more "executive-minded" (p. 241). A high line officer in a large corporation denounced staff organizations to the writer on the ground of their "costing more than they're worth," and that "They stir up too much trouble and are too theoretical." He felt that their function (excepting that of accountants, chemists, and "a few mechanical engineers") could be better carried out by replacing them with "highly-select front-line foremen [the lowest placed line officers] who are really the backbone of management, and pay them ten or twelve thousand dollars a year."

[4] These plants were in related industries and ranged in size from 4,500 to 20,000 employees, with the managerial groups numbering from 200 to nearly 1,000. Details concerning the plants and their location are confidential. Methodological details concerning an intensive study embracing staff-line relations and several other areas of behavior in one of the plants are given in the writer's unpublished doctoral thesis, "A Study of Informal Organization Among the Managers of an Industrial Plant" (Department of Sociology, University of Chicago, 1949).

[5] Because these conflict areas were interrelated and continually shifting and reorganizing, discussion of any one of them separately—as in the case of staff-line relations—will, of course, be unrealistic to some extent.

[6] From bottom to top, the line hierarchy consisted of the following strata of officers: (1) first-line foremen, who were directly in charge of production workmen; (2) general foremen; (3) departmental superintendents; (4) divisional superintendents; (5) assistant plant manager; (6) plant manager. In the preceding strata there were often "assistants," such as "assistant general foreman," "assistant superintendent," etc., in which case the total strata of the line hierarchy could be almost double that indicated here.

In the staff organizations the order from bottom to top was: (1) supervisor (equivalent to the first-line foreman); (2) general supervisor (equivalent to the general foreman); (3) staff head—sometimes "superintendent" (equivalent to departmental superintendent in the line organization). Occasionally there were strata of assistant supervisors and assistant staff heads.

The term "upper line" will refer to all strata above the departmental superintendent. "Middle line" will include the departmental superintendent and assistants. "Lower line" will refer to general and first-line foremen and their assistants.

though they might wish to escape, the obligation of at least appearing to carry out formal functions compelled individuals to take sides in order to protect themselves against the aggressions of others. And the intensity of the conflict was aggravated by the fact that it was formally unacceptable and had to be hidden.

For analytical convenience, staff-line friction may be examined apart from the reciprocal effects of the general conflict system. Regarded in this way, the data indicated that three conditions were basic to staff-line struggles: (1) the conspicuous ambition and "individualistic" behavior among staff officers; (2) the complication arising from staff efforts to justify its existence and get acceptance of its contributions; and, related to point two, (3) the fact that incumbency of the higher staff offices was dependent on line approval. The significance of these conditions will be discussed in order.

MOBILE BEHAVIOR OF STAFF PERSONNEL

As a group, staff personnel in the three plants were markedly ambitious, restless, and individualistic. There was much concern to win rapid promotion, to make the "right impressions," and to receive individual recognition. Data showed that the desire among staff members for personal distinctions often overrode their sentiments of group consciousness and caused intra-staff tensions.[7]

The relatively high turnover of staff personnel[8] quite possibly reflected the dissatisfactions and frustrations of members over inability to achieve the distinction and status they hoped for. Several factors appeared to be of importance in this restlessness of staff personnel. Among these were age and social differences between line and staff officers, structural differences in the hierarchy of the two groups, and the staff group's lack of authority over production.

With respect to age, the staff officers were significantly younger than

---

"Lower," "middle," and "upper" staff will refer respectively to the supervisor, general supervisor and staff head.

"Top management" will refer to the upper line and the few staff heads with whom upper line officers were especially intimate on matters of policy.

[7] In a typical case in one of the plants, a young staff officer developed a plan for increasing the life of certain equipment in the plant. He carried the plan directly to the superintendent of the department in which he hoped to introduce it, but was rebuffed by the superintendent who privately acknowledged the merit of the scheme but resented the staff officer's "trying to lord it over" him. The staff organization condemned the behavior of its member and felt that he should have allowed the plan to appear as a contribution of the staff group rather than as one of its members. The officer himself declared that "By G— it's my idea and I want credit. There's not a damn one of you guys [the staff group] that wouldn't make the same squawk if you were in my place!"

[8] During the period between 1944 and 1950 turnover of staff personnel in these plants was between two and four times as great as that of line personnel. This grouping included all the non-managerial members of staff and line and all the hourly-paid (non-salaried) members of management (about 60 assistant first-line foremen). Turnover was determined by dividing the average number of employees for a given year (in line or staff) into the accessions or separations, whichever was the smaller.

line officers.[9] This would account to some extent for their restlessness. Being presumably less well established in life in terms of material accumulations, occupational status, and security, while having greater expectations (see below), and more energy, as well as more life ahead in which to make new starts elsewhere if necessary, the staff groups were understandably more dynamic and driving.[10]

Age-conflict[11] was also significant in staff-line antagonisms. The incident just noted of the young staff officer seeking to get direct acceptance by the line of his contribution failed in part—judging from the strong sentiments later expressed by the line superintendent—because of an age antipathy. The older line officers disliked receiving what they regarded as instruction from men so much younger than themselves, and staff personnel clearly were conscious of this attitude among line officers.[12] In staff-line meetings staff officers frequently had their ideas slighted or even treated with amusement by line incumbents. Whether such treatment was warranted or not, the effects were disillusioning to the younger, less experienced staff officers. Often selected by the organization because of their outstanding academic records, they had entered industry with the belief that they had much to contribute, and that their efforts would win early recognition and rapid advancement. Certainly they had no thought that their contributions would be in any degree unwelcome. This naiveté[13] was

[9] Complete age data were available in one of the larger plants. Here the 36 staff heads, staff specialists, and assistants had a mean age of 42.9 years. This value would have been less than 40 years, except for the inclusion of several older former line officers, but even a mean of 42.9 years was significantly less (C.R. 2.8) than that of the 35 line superintendents in the plant who had a mean age of 48.7 years. The age difference was even more significant when the staff heads were compared with the 61 general foremen who had a mean age of 50.0 years. And between the 93 salaried first-line foremen (mean age of 48.5 years) and the 270 salaried nonsupervisory staff personnel (mean age of 31.0 years) the difference was still greater.

[10] One might also hypothesize that the drive of staff officers was reflected in the fact that the staff heads and specialists gained their positions (those held when the data were collected) in less time than did members of the line groups. E.g., the 36 staff officers discussed above had spent a median of 10 years attaining their positions, as against a median of 11 years for the first-line foremen, 17 years for the general foremen, and 19 years for the superintendents. But one must consider that some of the staff groups were relatively new (13–15 years old) and had grown rapidly, which probably accelerated their rate of promotions as compared with that of the older line organization.

[11] E. A. Ross in *Principles of Sociology* (New York: D. Appleton-Century Co., 1938), pp. 238–48, has some pertinent comments on age conflict.

[12] Explaining the relatively few cases in which his staff had succeeded in "selling ideas" to the line, an assistant staff head remarked: "We're always in hot water with these old guys on the line. You can't tell them a damn thing. They're bullheaded as hell! Most of the time we offer a suggestion it's either laughed at or not considered at all. The same idea in the mouth of some old codger on the line'd get a round of applause. They treat us like kids."

Line officers in these plants often referred to staff personnel (especially members of the auditing, production planning, industrial engineering, and industrial relations staffs) as "college punks," "slide-rules," "crackpots," "pretty boys," and "chairwarmers."

[13] John Mills, a research engineer retired from the telephone industry, has noted the worldly naiveté of research engineers in that field in his *The Engineer in Society* (New York: D. Van Nostrand Co., 1946).

apparently due to lack of earlier first-hand experience in industry (or acquaintance with those who had such experience), and to omission of realistic instruction in the social sciences from their academic training. The unsophisticated staff officer's initial contacts wth the shifting, covert, expedient arrangements between members of staff and line usually gave him a severe shock. He had entered industry prepared to engage in logical, well-formulated relations with members of the managerial hierarchy, and to carry out precise, methodical functions for which his training had equipped him. Now he learned that (1) his freedom to function was snared in a web of informal commitments; (2) his academic specialty (on which he leaned for support in his new position) was often not relevant[14] for carrying out his formal assignments; and that (3) the important thing to do was to learn who the informally powerful line officers were and what ideas they would welcome which at the same time would be acceptable to his superiors.

Usually the staff officer's reaction to these conditions is to look elsewhere for a job or make an accommodation in the direction of protecting himself and finding a niche where he can make his existence in the plant tolerable and safe. If he chooses the latter course, he is likely to be less concerned with creative effort for his employer than with attempts to develop reliable social relations that will aid his personal advancement. The staff officer's recourse to this behavior and his use of other status-increasing devices will be discussed below in another connection.

The formal structure, or hierarchy of statuses, of the two larger plants from which data were drawn offered a frustration to the ambitious staff officer. That is, in these plants the strata, or levels of authority, in the staff organizations ranged from three to five as against from five to ten in the line organization. Consequently there were fewer possible positions for exercise of authority into which staff personnel could move. This condition may have been an irritant to expansion among the staff groups. Unable to move vertically to the degree possible in the line organization, the ambitious staff officer could enlarge his area of authority in a given position only by lateral expansion—by increasing his personnel. Whether or not aspiring staff incumbents revolted against the relatively low hierarchy through which they could move, the fact remains that (1) they appeared eager to increase the number of personnel under their authority,[15] (2) the

[14] Among the staff heads and assistants referred to earlier, only 50 per cent of those with college training (32 of the 36 officers) were occupied with duties related to their specialized training. E.g., the head of the industrial relations staff had a B.S. degree in aeronautical engineering; his assistant had a similar degree in chemical engineering. Considering that staff officers are assumed to be specialists trained to aid and advise management in a particular function, the condition presented here raises a question as to what the criteria of selection were. (As will be shown in a separate paper, the answer appeared to be that personal—as well as impersonal—criteria were used.) Among the college-trained of 190 line officers in the same plant, the gap between training and function was still greater, with 61 per cent in positions not related to the specialized part of their college work.

[15] This was suggested by unnecessary references among some staff officers to "the number of men under me," and by their somewhat fanciful excuses for increase of personnel. These excuses included statements of needing more personnel to (1) carry on research, (2) control new processes, (3) keep records and reports up-to-

personnel of staff groups *did* increase disproportionately to those of the line,[16] and (3) there was a trend of personnel movement from staff to line,[17] rather than the reverse, presumably (reflecting the drive and ambition of staff members) because there were more positions of authority, as well as more authority to be exercised, more prestige, and usually more income in the line.

Behavior in the plants indicated that line and staff personnel belonged to different social status groups and that line and staff antipathies were at least in part related to these social distinctions. For example, with respect to the item of formal education, the staff group stood on a higher level than members of the line. In the plant from which the age data were taken, the 36 staff officers had a mean of 14.6 years of schooling as compared with 13.1 years for 35 line superintendents, 11.2 years for 60 general foremen, and 10.5 years for 93 first-line foremen. The difference between the mean education of the staff group and that of the highest line group (14.6–13.1) was statistically significant at better than the one per cent level. The 270 non-supervisory staff personnel had a mean of 13.1 years—the same as that of the line superintendents. Consciousness of this difference probably contributed to a feeling of superiority among staff members, while the

date. These statements often did not square with (1) the excessive concern among staff people about their "privileges" (such as arriving on the job late, leaving early, leaving the plant for long periods during working hours, having a radio in the office during the World Series, etc.); (2) the great amount of time (relative to that of line officers) spent by lower staff personnel in social activities on the job, and (3) the constantly recurring (but not always provoked) claims among staff personnel of their functional importance for production. The duties of middle and lower staff personnel allowed them sufficient time to argue a great deal over their respective functions (as well as many irrelevant topics) and to challenge the relative merit of one another's contributions or "ideas." In some of the staffs these discussions could go on intermittently for hours and develop into highly theoretical jousts and wit battles. Where staff people regarded such behavior as a privilege of their status, line officers considered it as a threat to themselves. This lax control (in terms of line discipline) was in part a tacit reward from staff heads to their subordinates. The reward was expected because staff superiors (especially in the industrial relations, industrial engineering, and planning staffs) often overlooked and/or perverted the work of subordinates (which was resented) in response to pressures from the line. This behavior will be noted later.

   16 In one of the larger plants, where exact data were available, the total staff personnel had by 1945 exceeded that of the line. At that time the staff included 400 members as against 317 line personnel composed of managerial officers and their clerical workers, but not production workers. By 1948 the staff had increased to 517 as compared with 387 for the line (during this period *total* plant personnel declined over 400). The staff had grown from 20.8 per cent larger than the line in 1945 to 33.6 per cent larger in 1948, and had itself increased by 29.3 per cent during the three years as against a growth in the line of 22.1 per cent. Assuming the conditions essential for use of probability theory, the increase in staff personnel could have resulted from chance about 1.5 times in a hundred. Possibly post-war and other factors of social change were also at work but, if so, their force was not readily assessable.

   17 This movement from staff to line can disorganize the formal managerial structure, especially when (1) the transferring staff personnel have had little or no supervisory experience in the staff but have an academic background which causes them to regard human beings as mechanisms that will respond as expected; (2) older, experienced line officers have hoped—for years in some cases—to occupy the newly vacated (or created) positions.

sentiment of line officers toward staff personnel was reflected in the name-calling noted earlier.

Staff members were also much concerned about their dress, a daily shave, and a weekly hair-cut. On the other hand line officers, especially below the level of departmental superintendent, were relatively indifferent to such matters. Usually they were in such intimate contact with production processes that dirt and grime prevented the concern with meticulous dress shown by staff members. The latter also used better English in speaking and in writing reports, and were more suave and poised in social intercourse. These factors, and the recreational preferences of staff officers for night clubs and "hot parties," assisted in raising a barrier between them and most line officers.

The social antipathies of the two groups and the status concern of staff officers were indicated by the behavior of each toward the established practice of dining together in the cafeterias reserved for management in the two larger plants. Theoretically, all managerial officers upward from the level of general foremen in the line, and general supervisors in the staff, were eligible to eat in these cafeterias. However, in practice the mere taking of one of these offices did not automatically assure the incumbent the privilege of eating in the cafeteria. One had first to be invited to "join the association." Staff officers were very eager to "get in" and did considerable fantasying on the impressions, with respect to dress and behavior, that were believed essential for an invitation. One such staff officer, a cost supervisor, dropped the following remarks:

> There seems to be a committee that passes on you. I've had my application in for three years, but no soap. Harry [his superior] had his in for over three years before he made it. You have to have something, because if a man who's in moves up to another position the man who replaces him doesn't get it because of the position—and he might not get it at all. I think I'm about due.

Many line officers who were officially members of the association avoided the cafeteria, however, and had to be *ordered* by the assistant plant manager to attend. One of these officers made the following statement, which expressed more pointedly the many similar spontaneous utterances of resentment and dislike made by other line officers:

> There's a lot of good discussion in the cafeteria. I'd like to get in on more of it but I don't like to go there—sometimes I have to go. Most of the white collar people [staff officers] that eat there are stuck-up. I've been introduced three times to Svendsen [engineer], yet when I meet him he pretends to not even know me. When he meets me on the street he always manages to be looking someplace else. G____ d____ such people as that! They don't go in the cafeteria to eat and relax while they talk over their problems. They go in there to look around and see how somebody is dressed or to talk over the hot party they had last night. Well, that kind of damn stuff don't go with me. I haven't any time to put on airs and make out I'm something that I'm not.

COMPLICATIONS OF STAFF NEED
TO PROVE ITS WORTH

To the thinking of many line officers, the staff functioned as an agent on trial rather than as a managerial division that might be of equal importance with the line organization in achieving production goals. Staff members were very conscious of this sentiment toward them and of their need to prove themselves. They strained to develop new techniques and to get them accepted by the line. But in doing this they frequently became impatient, and gave already suspicious line officers the impression of reaching for authority over production.

Since the line officer regards his authority over production as something sacred, and resents the implication that after many years in the line he needs the guidance of a newcomer who lacks such experience, an obstacle to staff-line cooperation develops the moment this sore spot is touched. On the other hand, the staff officer's ideology of his function leads him to precipitate a power struggle with the line organization. By and large he considers himself as an agent of top management. He feels bound to contribute something significant in the form of research or ideas helpful to management. By virtue of his greater education and intimacy with the latest theories of production, he regards himself as a managerial consultant and an expert, and feels that he must be, or appear to be, almost infallible once he has committed himself to top management on some point. With this orientation, he is usually disposed to approach middle and lower line with an attitude of condescension that often reveals itself in the heat of discussion. Consequently, many staff officers involve themselves in trouble and report their failures as due to "ignorance" and "bullheadedness" among these line officers.

On this point, relations between staff and line in all three of the plants were further irritated by a rift inside the line organization. First-line foremen were inclined to feel that top management had brought in the production planning, industrial relations, and industrial engineering staffs as clubs with which to control the lower line. Hence they frequently regarded the projects of staff personnel as manipulative devices, and reacted by cooperating with production workers and/or general foremen (whichever course was the more expedient) in order to defeat insistent and uncompromising members of the staff. Also, on occasion (see below), the lower line could cooperate evasively with lower staff personnel who were in trouble with staff superiors.

EFFECT OF LINE AUTHORITY
OVER STAFF PROMOTION

The fact that entry to the higher staff offices in the three plants was dependent on approval of top line officers had a profound effect on the behavior of staff personnel. Every member of the staff knew that if he aspired to higher office he must make a record for himself, a good part of which would be a reputation among upper line officers of ability to "understand" their informal problems without being told. This knowledge worked in varying degrees to pervert the theory of staff-line relations. Ideally the two organizations cooperate to improve existing methods of output, to introduce new methods, to plan the work, and to solve problems of production and the scheduling of orders that might arise. But when the line offers resistance to the findings and recommendations of the staff, the latter is reduced to evasive practices of getting some degree of acceptance of its programs, and at the same time of convincing top management that "good relations" exist with officers down the line. This necessity becomes even more acute when the staff officer aspires (for some of the reasons given above) to move over to the line organization, for then he must convince powerful line officers that he is worthy. In building a convincing record, however, he may compromise with line demands and bring charges from his staff colleagues that he is "selling out," so that after moving into the line organization he will then have to live with enemies he made in the staff. In any case, the need among staff incumbents of pleasing line officers in order to perfect their careers called for accommodation in three major areas:[18] (1) the observance of staff rules, (2) the introduction of new techniques, and (3) the use of appropriations for staff research and experiment.

With respect to point one, staff personnel, particularly in the middle and lower levels, carried on expedient relations with the line that daily evaded formal rules. Even those officers most devoted to rules found that, in order not to arouse enmity in the line on a scale sufficient to be communicated *up* the line, compromising devices were frequently helpful and sometimes almost unavoidable both for organizational and career aims. The usual practice was to tolerate minor breaking of staff rules by line personnel, or even to cooperate with the line in evading rules,[19] and in exchange lay a claim on the line for cooperation on critical issues. In some cases line aid was enlisted to conceal lower staff blunders from the upper staff and the upper line.[20]

[18] The relative importance of one or more of these areas would vary with the function of a given staff.

[19] In a processing department in one of the plants the chemical solution in a series of vats was supposed to have a specific strength and temperature, and a fixed rate of inflow and outflow. Chemists (members of the chemical staff) twice daily checked these properties of the solution and submitted reports showing that all points met the laboratory ideal. Actually, the solution was usually nearly triple the standard strength, the temperature was about 10 degrees Centigrade higher than standard, and the rate of flow was in excess of double the standard. There are, of course, varying discrepancies between laboratory theory and plant practice, but the condition described here resulted from production pressures that forced line foremen into behavior upsetting the conditions expected by chemical theory. The chemists were sympathetic with the hard-pressed foremen, who compensated by (1) notifying the chemists (rather than their superior, the chief chemist) if anything "went wrong" for which the laboratory was responsible and thus sparing them criticism; and by (2) cooperating with the chemists to reduce the number of analyses which the chemists would ordinarily have to make.

[20] Failure of middle and lower staff personnel to "cooperate" with line officers might cause the latter to "stand pat" in observance of line rules at a time when the pressures of a dynamic situation would make the former eager to welcome line cooperation in rule-breaking. For example, a staff officer was confronted with the combined effect of (1) a delay in production on the line that was due to an inde-

Concerning point two, while the staff organizations gave much time to developing new techniques, they were simultaneously thinking about how their plans would be received by the line. They knew from experience that middle and lower line officers could always give a "black eye" to staff contributions by deliberate malpractices. Repeatedly top management had approved, and incorporated, staff proposals that had been verbally accepted down the line. Often the latter officers had privately opposed the changes, but had feared that saying so would incur the resentment of powerful superiors who could informally hurt them. Later they would seek to discredit the charge by deliberate malpractice and hope to bring a return to the former arrangement. For this reason there was a tendency for staff members to withhold improved production schemes or other plans when they knew that an attempt to introduce them might fail or even bring personal disrepute.

Line officers fear staff innovations for a number of reasons. In view of their longer experience, presumably intimate knowledge of the work, and their greater remuneration, they fear[21] being "shown up" before their line superiors for not having thought of the processual refinements themselves. They fear that changes in methods may bring personnel changes which will threaten the break-up of cliques and existing informal arrangements and quite possibly reduce their area of authority. Finally, changes in techniques may expose forbidden practices and departmental inefficiency. In some cases these fears have stimulated line officers to compromise staff men to the point where the latter will agree to postpone the initiation of new practices for specific periods.

In one such case an assistant staff head agreed with a line superintendent to delay the application of a bonus plan for nearly three months so that the superintendent could live up to the expedient agreement he had made earlier with his grievance committeeman to avoid a "wildcat" strike by a group of production workmen.[22] The lower engineers who had devised the plan were suspicious of the formal reasons given to them for withholding it, so the assistant staff head prevented them (by means of "busy work") from attending staff-line meetings lest they inadvertently reveal to top management that the plan was ready.

The third area of staff-line accommodations growing out of authority relations revolved around staff use of funds granted it by top management. Middle and lower line charged that staff research and experimentation was

---

fensible staff error; (2) pressure on the line superintendent—with whom he was working—to hurry a special order; and (3) the presence in his force of new inexperienced staff personnel who were (a) irritating to line officers, and (b) by their inexperience constituted an invitation to line aggression. Without aid from the line superintendent (which could have been withheld by observance of formal rules) in covering up the staff error and in controlling line personnel, the staff officer might have put himself in permanent disfavor with all his superiors.

[21] Though there was little evidence that top management expected line officers to refine production techniques, the fear of such an expectation existed nevertheless. As noted earlier, however, some of the top executives *were* thinking that development of a "higher type" of first-line foreman might enable most of the staff groups to be eliminated.

[22] This case indicates the overlapping of conflict areas referred to earlier. A later paper will deal with the area of informal union-management relations.

little more than "money wasted on blunders," and that various departments of the line could have "accomplished much more with less money." According to staff officers, those of their plans that failed usually did so because line personnel "sabotaged" them and refused to "cooperate." Specific costs of "crack-pot experimentation" in certain staff groups were pointed to by line officers. Whatever the truth of the charges and counter-charges, evidence indicated (confidants in both groups supported this) that pressures from the line organization (below the top level) forced some of the staff groups to "kick over" parts of the funds appropriated for staff use[23] by top management. These compromises were of course hidden from top management, but the relations described were carried on to such an extent that by means of them—and line pressures for manipulation of accounts in the presumably impersonal auditing departments—certain line officers were able to show impressively low operating costs and thus win favor[24] with top management that would relieve pressures and be useful in personal advancement. In their turn the staff officers involved would receive more "cooperation" from the line and/or recommendation for transfer to the line. The data indicated that in a few such cases men from accounting and auditing staffs were given general foremanships (without previous line experience) as a reward for their understanding behavior.

SUMMARY

Research in three industrial plants showed conflict between the managerial staff and line groups that hindered the attainment of organizational goals. Privately expressed attitudes among some of the higher line executives revealed their hope that greater control of staff groups could be achieved, or that the groups might be eliminated and their functions taken over in great part by carefully selected and highly remunerated lower line officers. On their side, staff members wanted more recognition and a greater voice in control of the plants.

All of the various functioning groups of the plants were caught up in a general conflict system; but apart from the effects of involvement in this complex, the struggles between line and staff organizations were attributable mainly to (1) functional differences between the two groups; (2) differentials in the ages, formal education, potential occupational ceilings, and status group affiliations of members of the two groups (the staff officers being younger, having more education but lower occupational potential, and forming a prestige-oriented group with distinctive dress and recreational tastes); (3) need of the staff groups to justify their existence; (4) fear in the line that staff bodies, by their expansion and well-financed research activities, would undermine line authority; and (5) the fact that aspirants to higher staff offices could gain promotion only through approval of influential line executives.

[23] In two of the plants a somewhat similar relation, rising from different causes, existed *inside* the line organization with the *operating* branch of the line successfully applying pressures for a share in funds assigned to the *maintenance* division of the line.

[24] The reader must appreciate the fact that constant demands are made by top management to maintain low operating costs.

If further research should prove that staff-line behavior of the character presented here is widespread in industry, and *if* top management should realize how such behavior affects its cost and production goals—and be concerned to improve the condition—then remedial measures could be considered. For example, a corrective approach might move in the direction of (1) creating a separate body[25] whose sole function would be the coordination of staff and line efforts; (2) increasing the gradations of awards and promotions in staff organizations (without increase of staff personnel); (3) granting of more nearly equal pay to staff officers, but with increased responsibility (without authority over line processes or personnel) for the practical working of their projects; (4) requiring that staff personnel have a minimum supervisory experience and have shared repeatedly in successful collaborative staff-line projects before transferring to the line; (5) steps by top management to remove the fear of veiled personal reprisal felt by officers in most levels of both staff and line hierarchies (this fear—rising from a disbelief in the possibility of bureaucratic impersonality—is probably the greatest obstacle to communication inside the ranks of management); (6) more emphasis in colleges and universities on realistic instruction in the social sciences for students preparing for industrial careers.

[25] This body, or "Board of Coordination," would be empowered to enforce its decisions. Membership would consist of staff and line men who had had wide experience in the plant over a period of years. The Board would (a) serve as an arbiter between staff and line; (b) review, screen, and approve individual recommendations submitted; and (c) evaluate contributions after a trial period. Such a body would incidentally be another high status goal for seasoned, capable, and ambitious officers who too often are trapped by the converging walls of the pyramidal hierarchy.

POWER AND POLITICS

*John Pfiffner and Frank Sherwood**

Power and politics are important aspects of functioning organizations and need to be explored as part of the dynamic processes found in every organization. The authors have drawn heavily from Melville Dalton's book *Men Who Manage*, a pioneering study of behavior in four organizations. This selection alerts us to the politics of organizations—i.e., who gets what, when, and how.

POWER AND POLITICS IN ORGANIZATIONS

Power and politics are terms that have not traditionally been a part of management literature. Indeed they have been popularly limited to those

* From *Administrative Organization* (Englewood Cliffs, N.J.: Prentice-Hall, Inc., 1960). © 1960. Prentice-Hall, Inc., Englewood Cliffs, N.J. Reprinted by permission.

activities which surround campaigns for elected public office and those which have to do with governmental policy-making. This orientation has led to the assumption that business organizations do not possess within themselves a political structure. Even in government one of the central purposes of reform groups has been to rid the organization of "politics," this to be done by placing the administrative apparatus under civil service. Thus in both business and government there has been an implicit expectation that the internal structure of the organization may be free of politics while the organization as a whole reacts to its external environment on a political basis.

Is such a simplified view of the way in which power is acquired and exercised really tenable? Bear in mind that in an earlier chapter we pointed out that authority and power are not the same thing. Hierarchical status suggests official legitimacy, the right to make decisions and supervise others. It does not necessarily mean that individual occupants of such status positions possess the *capacity* to see that their will dominates. Nor does the concept of the formal authority pyramid really tell us anything about the interpersonal systems of influence that prevail over decision-making in the official hierarchy. Those in high-level positions have to depend on someone to provide information and advice; and in some cases there is such a regularized pattern of assistance that real power shifts to the adviser. The official structure remains the same. Finally, the concept of the authority pyramid tells us nothing about how particular individuals advance to positions of status in the hierarchy. Are we to assume that all promotions and appointments are highly routinized and according to merit? We of course know this is not the case; and hence there is discretion exercised by someone in deciding who is to receive a certain post. As a consequence there is just as much jockeying, just as much contest, for many hierarchical posts where the succession is not as clear as in a public election.

It seems fairly apparent, then, that the forces which dominate and control the internal organization cannot be explained entirely in terms of traditional managerial concepts of hierarchy and authority.

At this point we may refer briefly to definitions of the two basic terms in this chapter. *Power* was earlier defined as "the capacity to secure the dominance of one's values or goals." For our purposes influence may be roughly regarded as synonymous with power. Thus power and influence are in a sense static. They reside in someone or some office. Therefore, we need to have another term to describe the network of interactions by which power is acquired, transferred, and exercised upon others. We call this process *politics*. Many years ago Lasswell put it simply and most meaningfully when he titled a book *Politics—Who Gets What, When, How*. He went on to say that in politics the "unifying frame of reference . . . is the rich and variable meaning of 'influence and the influential,' 'power and the powerful.' "[1]

The basic proposition of this chapter is that the "who gets what" dynamic is endemic to every organization, regardless of size, function, or

[1] Harold Lasswell, *Politics—Who Gets What, When, How* (New York: Whittlesey House, 1936), p. 19.

character of ownership. Furthermore, it is to be found at every level of the hierarchy; and it intensifies as the stakes become more important and the area of decision possibilities greater. Although it is common to think of policy and politics as synonymous because we are most aware of the exercise of power on the big decisions, it is nevertheless important to recognize that they are not the same. Policy suggests broadly the setting or articulating of goals. Politics concerns what is frequently a raw contest for power without any particular reference to the directions or goals of the organization.

It might be said, for example, that authoritarian leaders gather up much of the policy setting in their own hands. They seem formally to make all the big decisions, leaving the impression that the arena of political activity has been thereby lessened. But this does not necessarily occur. Indeed, there is some evidence that the struggle for influence and influential alignments within a dictatorship becomes more frantic than ever. To summarize, politics is the *process* by which power and influence are acquired and exercised. The particular goals sought may fall in the "policy" category or may concern a relatively low-level contest for promotion.

Organizational politics is a subject that seems destined to command increasing interest in the years ahead. In this sense it is a part of the more general concern with the social processes which lie at the heart of organization behavior. Noteworthy, too, is the fact that this more intensive look at the totality of organization life, not just its formal mechanisms, has served to spotlight the realities of political life in such units. Miller and Form have reported that "... political processes run through the social structure of industry." Those who participate in such hierarchies "must learn to play the appropriate roles. Such roles require adaptability to the techniques of conflict, accommodation, and cooperation. If they are successful, they may gain power and status. If they fail, others rise to take their places."[2] Three articles appearing in the *Harvard Business Review* in the late fifties also emphasize this trend toward political realism. One, by Martin and Sims, returned to Machiavelli and his somewhat stark and naked theory of power.[3]

In the field of public administration a similar note of political realism has been injected by Albert Somit in his plea for "realpolitik" in the teaching of administration. Somit says that from the administrator's point of view, "the administrative structure is also the scene of an unending and desperate battle for personal survival, power and prestige. In large part, his career depends upon his skill at the game of bureaucratic realpolitik, i.e., his mastery of the administrative verson of 'who gets what, when, and how' "[4]

[2] Delbert C. Miller and William H. Form, *Industrial Sociology* (New York: Harper and Brothers, 1951), p. 339.

[3] See N. H. Martin and J. H. Sims, "Thinking Ahead: Power Tactics," *Harvard Business Review* 34:25–36 ff; November–December 1956; Malcolm McNair, "What Price Human Relations?" *Harvard Business Review* 35:15–39, March–April 1957; Robert N. McMurry, "The Case for Benevolent Autocracy," *Harvard Business Review* 36:82–90, January–February 1958.

[4] Albert Somit, "Bureaucratic Realpolitik and the Teaching of Administration," *Public Administration Review* 16:292–295, Autumn 1956.

THE MILO STUDY

It may now prove profitable to take a look at power and politics as they actually operated within one organization. Fortunately, the writing of this section has been made easier by the published research of sociologist Melville Dalton.[5] Dalton's thesis was much the same as that of this book. He recognized that organizations did not function strictly according to the official prescriptions; and he therefore wanted to discover the ways in which the official was modified by the unofficial.

In order to pursue this objective Dalton literally lived in an organization. He was officially a member of the staff of an industrial firm of 8,000 employees, to which he gave the fictional name of Milo Fractionating Center. The locale was the area of Mobile Acres, a heavily industrialized region of the central United States. In addition, two other manufacturing firms and one department store came under his surveillance. But it is particularly the story of Milo that provides a rich insight into the actual workings of a large private organization. Before proceeding further in a description of this research, however, we must insert one caution. This was the kind of study of human behavior that dug very deeply and probed a veritable hornet's nest of interests and involvements. It could be done only by promising anonymity. Thus there is no possibility of another researcher validating the Dalton findings. And we have had enough experience with the studies of anthropologists to know that no human is free of error and bias. Even with this reservation, the Dalton research made a real contribution because it dug so deeply. Dalton revealed himself as a perceptive and resourceful observer. In very few places in the management literature can the reader obtain such a sense of the fullness of organization life as here.

Dalton discovered that there were six problem areas which seemed continually to recur. These were: (1) pressures for economy; (2) "cooperation" of officially powerless experts with their administrative superiors, involving the relationship of the line and the staff; (3) the conflict between unions and management in interpreting at the plant level labor agreements made at the corporate level; (4) uncertainty about standards and strategies of promotion, particularly at the middle and top management levels; (5) the difficulty of identifying and rewarding employees who were making different degrees of contributions to the organization; and (6) the dilemma of the individual executive in seeking to resolve the official doctrines of the firm with the reality-oriented claims of subordinates and associates.[6]

The significance of this list lies in the fact that without exception Dalton found politics—that is, influence maneuvering—a central feature. In each case it will be noted that there was a wide latitude of behavior possibilities; and this, of course, meant that decisions were inevitably made in terms of the power resources available to any individual or group at a particular time. The pressure for economy may not at first seem to fit

---

[5] Melville Dalton, *Men Who Manage* (New York: John F. Wiley and Sons, Inc., 1959).

[6] *Ibid.*, p. 4.

into this category, but deep in this pressure lies a conflict of great potential political consequence—that between production and maintenance. As will be seen later in this section, this conflict had much to do with the nature of political activity, in respect to the plant and corporate headquarters, among the production executives and between production and maintenance officials.

Did these problem areas develop because the four firms studied by Dalton were atypical? Would other organizations reduce the arena of political activity by invoking more prescriptions and rules from the top? Dalton produced rather voluminous evidence that answers to these kinds of problems are not easily or routinely come by. The answers arise from the situation; and any attempt to prescribe in advance may very well result in strangulation of the organization through bureaucratic red tape. In the end, then, such decisions inevitably attract struggles for power and influence because they involve choice between alternatives. It is no answer to say that decisions should not be made or that choice should somehow be removed from the decision-making process. On balance, there is every reason to believe that the firms studied by Dalton were rather typical.

Power Structure at Milo

One of the most interesting aspects of Dalton's work is his attempt to put on paper the working power structure in the Milo plant. In Chart 1 there is a simplified version of the "official map" of Milo. Contrast this assignment of formal authority with what Dalton considered to be the actual distribution of power in Chart 2. The differences are quite striking. Dalton arrived at his appraisal by asking fifteen Milo participants to rank the various officers in terms of the "relative deference of associates, superiors, and subordinates to his known attitudes, wishes, and informally

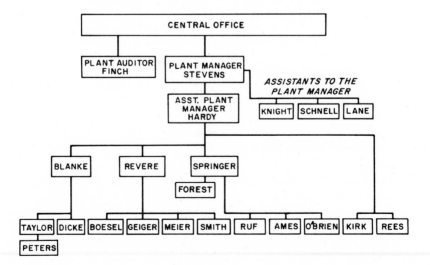

CHART 1. *Milo formal chart simplified* (SOURCE: Dalton, *Men Who Manage*, p. 21).

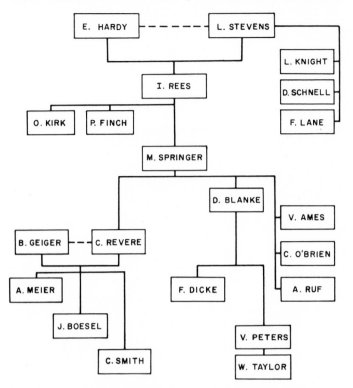

CHART 2. *Milo chart of unofficial influence* (SOURCE: Dalton, *Men Who Manage*, p. 22).

expressed opinions, and the concern to respect, prefer, or act on them."[7] The assumption that such power structures can be identified and that they do have operational significance has been accepted increasingly in recent years. Hunter's research suggests its operation at the community level; Mills in particular has written persuasively of its existence on the national plane.[8]

[7] Dalton, *Men Who Manage*, p. 20.

[8] Hunter used a roughly similar technique to that of Dalton in identifying the power structure in Atlanta, Georgia. See Floyd Hunter, *Community Power Structures* (Chapel Hill: University of North Carolina Press, 1953).

Mills' work is based on a wide examination of studies in the field, yet it is highly controversial because of its interpretations and basic propositions. He identifies five power eras. The first, from the revolution through the administration of John Adams, exemplified power in the hands of many-sided, gifted individuals who were equally at home in the social, economic, political, and military realms. The period from Jefferson to Lincoln was characterized by a loose coalition of power in the hands of economic interests, with a rather dispersed pluralism tempered strongly by Jacksonian concepts of status. The third period, beginning in the fourth quarter of the nineteenth century, saw the rise of corporate industrial interests as masters of the power structure, an era which continued, with a brief fourth interlude of the New Deal, until it merged into a contemporary fifth phase. This was characterized by a coalition between corporate ownership, corporate management, and the military.

Although Dalton's unofficial power structure showed a substantial number of discrepancies from the official authority chart, three are particularly worthy of note:

(a) The assistant plant manager, Hardy, was accorded equal status with the manager, Stevens.

(b) The third most powerful man in the organization was a staff person, Rees, who was superintendent of industrial relations. Note, too, that those particularly responsible to him were Finch, the plant auditor who was supposed to report to corporate headquarters, and Kirk, the head of production planning.

(c) The superintendents of the three manufacturing units in the plant, Divisions A, B, and C, did not enjoy the same actual power status in the organization; and in one case the relationship between the division superintendent himself and his assistant was the same as between Stevens and Hardy.

Hardy and Stevens. The placement of Hardy on the same status level as the plant superintendent was based on a number of considerations. It was observed, for example, that while Stevens usually opened staff meetings, he quickly gave way to Hardy, who dominated thereafter. Hardy's approval was deemed indispensable in the more important promotions; during breakdowns and emergency stops, it was fear of Hardy, rather than Stevens, that caused alarm among the supervisors; and in many significant cases staff officers saw Hardy as the principal man to convince concerning the value of a project.

Dalton also pointed out that Hardy's social activities, his occupation experience, and perhaps even his physical appearance were important to him in achieving his power status. Hardy was under forty, athletic, and "very handsome." He was active socially; Stevens was withdrawn.

The position of Rees. The role of Rees, the superintendent of industrial relations, is of particular importance because the staff unit he headed had not typically been a significant one at Milo. His "weak" predecessor had been promoted out of the position to an ambiguous and unimportant status as "assistant to" Stevens. Rees, who was also under forty, apparently acquired his power through his close associations with corporate headquarters. Indeed, he was presumably sent out from the "office" to strengthen the department. Because of this he had power alignments outside the plant itself, and thus he was in a different relationship to Stevens and particularly to Hardy. It is a situation quite familiar to those in government service, where not infrequently some of the key administrative officials are elective and therefore freed from the usual command restraints.

In this instance Rees was the only one who really challenged Hardy. On one issue he came into open conflict and he said, "The Office put that

---

"The seemingly permanent military threat places a premium on the military and upon their control of men, material, money and power; virtually all political and economic actions are now judged in terms of military definitions of reality; the higher warlords have ascended to a firm position within the power elite of the fifth epoch." See C. Wright Mills, *The Power Elite* (New York: Oxford University Press, 1956), p. 275; also available in the paper Galaxy Books series.

system in here and by God we're going to make it work, not just tolerate it!'"[9] Dalton's general analysis was that Hardy exceeded his official authority in every field of plant activity except those Rees interpreted as lying within his industrial relations sphere, which he defined rather broadly. Thus Rees had real power in the organization because he was regarded as the unofficial spokesman for corporate headquarters.

Power of Division Superintendent Springer. Just below Rees in the power structure was Springer, superintendent of Division C, who in the formal chart ranked equally with the superintendents of Divisions A and B. In this instance Springer's influence over his two colleagues was rather clearly evidenced in that they first conferred with him before asking important favors from Hardy. How did Springer achieve this status? Largely it was a reflection of Hardy's power. Springer, who had come from corporate headquarters, worked for four years in Division B when Hardy was its chief. The two had an extremely close relationship.

One division chief, Revere, was the lowest ranked of the three superintendents. Indeed one of his subordinates, Geiger, was considered to possess as much influence. Here Dalton noted two reciprocal factors at work. In the first place, Revere was relatively near retirement and living out his time. He was not interested in dominating plant events. On the other hand, the 42-year-old Geiger headed the major production unit in the division. Thus the nature of his official responsibility enhanced his power position, even in the relationship to his immediate superior.

Summary. Dalton suggests rather strongly that the nature of the power configuration in Milo developed from the personalities who occupied key positions. He finds that those who possessed power were the "promoters," those who saw the organization as dynamic, who viewed risk-taking as a way of life. Age seems to have been an important factor in the structuring of these attitudes. The most influential group, for example, had an average age of 42.2 years; the least influential averaged 55.5 years.[10] These basic tendencies were then reinforced by official position, relationship to corporate headquarters, and other social attributes.

With personalities as a key variable in the struggle for power at Milo, it is not surprising that various types of alliances among these individuals would be the prime means of acquiring and expanding influence. Dalton calls such alliances *cliques* and suggests that there are three general types: vertical, horizontal, and random. The vertical cliques involve people at various levels in the hierarchy and may provide a reciprocal relationship where the higher officer protects his subordinates and they in turn tell him of threats to his position. In some cases, however, the clique is formed largely to provide protection from the top. The horizontal alliance is composed of people of the same status who combine either to combat a threat or to effect a change. The random clique follows no particular axis of the hierarchy and tends more to be based on social attractiveness than other factors.

[9] Dalton, *Men Who Manage*, p. 25.
[10] *Ibid.*, p. 31.

Politics and Promotions

There were a number of ways in which Dalton found the power structure operative at Milo—in staff-line relations, in labor-management contacts, and in the system of rewards. Two particularly significant areas, however, will serve to illustrate the fundamental proposition of this chapter that power and politics are an intrinsic part of organization life. One reveals the way in which pressure for production creates political problems. The other concerns the ever present problem of promotions, the struggle upward.

The politics of promotion is certainly not a new idea to anyone who has had even the briefest glimpse of organization life. Why should this be an area of such intense maneuver? Dalton suggests the reason is that we have so few criteria by which to judge people. The business of fitting people to jobs remains highly judgmental and personal; hence it is inevitable that there should be a struggle for the dominance of one set of values over another. At Milo, Dalton made an analysis of 190 line officers. He found that age and years of experience were not important for appointment and promotion. There was no regular progression through the hierarchical levels, as would occur where age and length of service were major criteria of promotion. Similar analyses of educational backgrounds showed some correlation between position and years of schooling. Yet very frequently the specialization in school had nothing whatsoever to do with the present job; and there were enough people without extensive schooling to suggest that education was not a controlling consideration for most managerial positions.

Thus the result at Milo was a quest for competence intermingled simultaneously with the imposition of some stringent unofficial prescriptions. These included (1) membership in the Masons and not in the Roman Catholic Church, (2) Anglo-Saxon or German ethnic background, (3) membership in a local yacht club, and (4) Republican orientation in politics. Dalton found that nearly 70 per cent of all management people were Masons and only 13 per cent were Catholics. He also discovered that over 90 per cent of all management people were from the Anglo-Saxon, German, and Scandinavian ethnic groups. The Yacht Club had 114 management people as members; and the only appropriate newspaper for a management person to carry into the plant was a famous "isolationist" journal. No executives had served the government except as Republicans.[11]

Without any well-established official standards of executive performance, Dalton believes that managers tend to place their greatest confidence in people who are generally like themselves. Thus unofficial requirements develop. They serve to solidify and perpetuate existing power patterns within the organization.

The very nature of the system suggests, too, that a process subject to so many influences outside individual and official control must be a prime focus of political activity. Its very inconsistencies as to the official

[11] Dalton, *Men Who Manage*, pp. 178 ff.

route upward "naturally provoked fears, speculation, and search for un-official routes."[12]

Politics and Production Pressure

Although production would seem to be a value upon which every-one can agree, the goal of maintenance is often in conflict with it. The supervisor on the line is judged by the amount of work he gets out, the maintenance supervisor by the consistency with which the machines operate. The maintenance man has the tendency to worry, to want pro-duction stopped at the least sign of trouble. The production man wants to take a chance, or at least hopes the breakdown will occur on the next shift. In many ways, then, the maintenance-production battle is another version of the standing debate over long-term and short-term goals.

Dalton captured some of the components of this type of struggle at the Milo plant. He noted that direct costs of labor and material were easy to control but it was in the general area of equipment upkeep that "cush-ions" were sought. He wrote:

> Hence this area of upkeep was used by the department chief as one means of relieving cost pressures on himself. In using the escape he of course competed obscurely with other heads groping for similar devices. Hence at times calculating alliances were formed to share an expedient. As pressures for economy increased, many operation executives placed low short-run production costs above concern for equipment. That is, they favored continuous use of the equipment with shutdowns only for breakdowns followed by minimum repair and quick resumption of pro-duction.[13]

For a decade Milo had operated a system of shops where different types of maintenance functions were performed. When the work was done, the appropriate operating unit was billed for the cost. Dissatisfac-tion was mounting in certain parts of the plant, however, for two reasons. Some heads of operations complained because there was a backlog of 1,500 orders, which hit almost entirely at those units with the least powerful and assertive leaders. The other problem was that charges for work varied a great deal, with some departments having to pay more for the same kinds of services than others. Clearly there was a system of favoritism operating in which the less effective of the production chiefs were taking the beating.

Ultimately top plant management concerned itself with the prob-lem. First, an incentive wage scheme was established for maintenance workers in order to beat the backlog problem. Second, a new central con-trol unit was established to receive and route all maintenance orders to the shops. The new unit's major function was to lessen the possibility of favor-itism by reducing contact between operations and maintenance units and by adhering to a fixed numerical sequence in processing orders. Further-more, cost estimates were to be made on each job and this was to be compared with actual cost.

[12] *Ibid.*, p. 167.
[13] *Ibid.*, p. 33.

The new system was successful in that it did eliminate the backlog and revise charges for maintenance work. But in accomplishing these goals, it was alienating all the aggressive supervisors who had prospered under the old system. They were no longer getting the same breaks and their maintenance costs were soaring. Actually the two groups of supervisors were reversing their positions. Some members of the less aggressive group had cut their maintenance costs in half; and they were now engaging in various informal arrangements to obtain favors. This became more pronounced as the aggressive supervisors increased the vigor of their attack on the new system as one of "red tape," "slowing down production," and "no good estimates." Ultimately the new system was abolished and maintenance was almost completely decentralized to the individual departments.

In the debate that surrounded the scrapping of the system, Dalton reports that the real issues were never discussed. Although the system was created to "check 'politics' it was undone by politics because such relations were not understood and were officially rejected as improper...."[14] Furthermore, the political conflicts now continued *within* the departments. Assistant Manager Hardy sought to settle these problems by suggesting that responsibility for maintenance costs be placed on the maintenance men. What this did, however, was to free operations from any sense of responsibility for maintenance.

At about this time the focus of the conflict shifted. Corporate headquarters was now interesting itself in the problem. It was no longer a question of *who* in Milo was to control but *how*, to combat infringements on local autonomy. The struggle thus became one between the office and the plant.

The corporate approach emphasized the purchase of replacement parts. All parts costing $500 or more were to be inventoried and a permanent system for record-keeping was to be installed. Henceforth all purchases would require corporate approval. To administer the program the office proposed that two new supervisory positions be created. In filling these positions, we again see the Milo plant power structure in operation. The Hardy group selected the two men and made sure they were notable people. The purpose, of course, was to insure that the two men could be controlled at the plant level even though they were officially to have free and direct contact with corporate headquarters. The situation was further complicated by the fact that the two men were relatively independent of each other. It was hoped that each man would be free of local pressures and that the new system of control would prove "simple, direct, and manageable."

The first maneuver after the appointments of the two supervisors was a request for the parts inventory. But plant officials dragged their feet. They did not supply the information. Six weeks went by; and finally the new supervisor responsible for this part of the work defied the Hardy group and reported to the office that he was receiving no cooperation. Six officials from corporate headquarters came out, praised the new supervisor, and censured plant heads for failing to cooperate. It was clear to the plant people that the supervisor had to be won over. They gave him

14 Dalton, *Men Who Manage*, p. 4.

a bigger office, flattered him, consulted him. Finally these blandishments, along with a fear of reprisals and the assurance that he would be protected by appearances, caused the difficult supervisor to go along.

Parts inventories of a type were furnished. "Surprise" inspections ordered by corporate headquarters to insure the accuracy of reports were made. There developed a system of cooperation among the various production chiefs to use each other's storage areas when the inspections came. The reports, "roughly accurate," did flow into corporate headquarters and they apparently did serve a planning purpose. Within the plant the tensions between operations and maintenance were reduced by the common threat from corporate headquarters. As Dalton summarized the results of the conflict, ". . . the Milo chiefs preserved their conception of local rights and at the same time raised morale. Conflict between principle and action in this area had not, of course, 'ended' but it was contained and existed latently."[15]

The purpose of this rather extended description of political activities at the Milo Fractionating Center is to emphasize the universality of this aspect of human behavior. Put another way, there is still the necessity of demonstrating to many readers the extent to which power and influence form a part of the sum of organization behavior. The Dalton study reveals very clearly the way in which the "official map" of the command structure is amended by individual and group abilities to acquire and exercise power, in short, to operate politically.

[15] *Ibid.*, p. 49.

PRIMARY CONTROLS IN FORMAL WORK ORGANIZATIONS
*Edward Gross**

In this article we are alerted to some of the weaknesses of institutional or formal controls such as division of labor, formal authority systems, and the procedure for recruiting and selecting workers. Moreover, the author points out that *informal* (primary) controls tend to reinforce and compensate for the inadequacies of formal controls. Thus, Gross exposes us to additional dimensions of the management of organizations, and suggests concepts which are useful guides to managers (e.g., the work-leisure cycle, informal cliques, implications of cliques to selection).

The present paper concerns the proposition that primary controls may be functional within instituted social organizations. For this purpose,

* From "Some Functional Consequences of Primary Controls in Formal Work Organizations," *American Sociological Review*, 18 (August 1953), 368–373. Reprinted with permission.

evidence will be submitted which suggests that such primary controls may make their appearance precisely when formal or institutional controls prove inadequate. As such, these primary controls enable the organization to accomplish its formal purpose.

The study uses two sources of data—one, a manufacturing concern in Chicago, with approximately 1500 workers, which produces plastic raincoats, belts, jewelry, and other items; and second, a radar air site in the Air Defense Command, United States Air Force.[1] The two cases are utilized, first, in order partially to avoid the dangers of the unique case and, second, in order to provide a comparison between a small, independent civilian factory on the one hand, and a huge interlocking military organization on the other. The data in both cases were gathered by means of interview and participant observation techniques.[2] It is necessary to emphasize that the writer is still very much in the midst of the Air Force study, so that findings with reference to it are highly tentative.

Work organizations are characterized by purposiveness. Each has one or more specified goals or objectives which it seeks to achieve. In the case of the factory, these are, mainly, the manufacture, sale, and distribution of certain physical goods, while in the case of the air site, there is the one objective or "mission" of maintaining radar surveillance against hostile aircraft. The fact of purpose creates the need for institutional or segmented controls on behavior so that this purpose or mission may be realized. To this end, it is necessary only that a segment of the personality be controlled; namely, the role as worker, but it is essential that *that* one role be controlled. This control is provided in the following manner in the two organizations under examination.

Formal control is instituted through a division of labor which serves to relate specialisms and specialists to one another, through an authority system which serves to coordinate specialists and to evaluate their contributions to the objective, and finally, through a selection system which serves to recruit personnel who, it is felt, can assume the work roles required.

We proceed next to discuss each of these instituted controls and the manner in which they may break down or prove inadequate, and how, in each case, primary controls then make their appearance. The paramount

---

[1] The research reported here was supported in part by the United States Air Force under Contract Number AF 33(038)26823, monitored by the Human Resources Research Institute, Air University, Maxwell Air Force Base, Alabama.

[2] For a full description of method in the factory study, see Edward Gross, "Informal Relations and the Social Organization of Work in an Industrial Office," unpublished Ph.D. Dissertation, University of Chicago, 1949, Chapter 1. The research the writer did there was concentrated in the office among the white-collar workers, though he also did some work with the factory personnel. There were approximately 100 workers in the office at the time of the study, and a total of 319 interviews (nondirective) were gathered. It is difficult to specify the nature of the Air Force population because of security regulations. However, it may be said that the writer has been with the project on a full-time basis for one and a half years, of which approximately one half has been spent at air sites. The writer is concentrating the major part of his efforts at one air site.

problem which any division of labor system must solve, as stated above, is that of relating the specialisms and specialists it creates to one another. Observation revealed that the following instituted means were used to attempt to solve this problem: (1) minute specialization, and (2) provision for formal horizontal communication. In general, specialization became more minute as operations increased in complexity. Each predictable act was planned for in advance and assigned to one or more persons. These acts were related to one another in flow charts, with the underlying conception that, if each person did what was expected of him, then specialisms would mesh and the goal be reached. It was felt that the more minute the division of labor, the easier it is to train persons and replace them. Further, the more carefully specialisms were defined, it was felt, the less likely would it be that specialists would overlap and conflict with one another. Formal horizontal communication between specialists, in turn, was expected to take place through a common supervisor, so that appropriate permission was secured and relevant persons informed of the action.[3]

But in actual practice, at both the factory and the air site, these instituted procedures gave rise to problems. The provision for formal communication through a common supervisor was found to be cumbersome and time-consuming. The required person was often busy, or, at the air site, which is on 24-hour shift duty, he was off-shift, and thus action came to a standstill. Yet some persons were loath to take action by simply going directly to the specialist concerned, while others did so, but in interviews, expressed anxiety about possible reprimand.

The minuteness of the division of labor had two effects in both organizations.

1. While *specialties* were related to one another, the very minuteness of the division of labor and the restriction of persons to their specialties operated effectively to isolate *specialists* from one another. Thus, when pressure was imposed for each person to do his job, persons sometimes refused to help others in difficulties. Most interesting was the expression in interviews of what might be called a "sphere of concern." One office worker in the Credit Department at the factory stated:

> I check ledger cards to see what a man's past credit record with the Company is. All I want from the Accounting Department is clear, up-to-date postings on the cards. I don't know where they get their information and I don't care. I'm paid to do a job here, and how they do theirs is none of my affair.

On a later occasion, when mailing lists for the company catalogue were being drawn up, extensive checking of accounting records was necessary to determine who were to receive catalogues. The company experienced difficulty in getting persons from other departments in the office to assist in this emergency work, which required meeting a publication deadline. Persons stated that they were unfamiliar with accounting records, and,

---

[3] See B. B. Gardner, *Human Relations in Industry,* Chicago: Richard D. Irwin, Inc., 1945, Chap. 2, for a discussion of this point.

more important, could see no point in leaving their own work to assist the accounting personnel. The formal division of labor provided no way for rewarding such effort, unless a supervisor saw fit to recommend a raise or promotion, because such extra effort came to his personal attention. It is noteworthy that such a reward is only possible in an organization small enough for higher supervisors to be in close touch with lower employees.

At the radar site, a similar problem occurred in connection with specialty classification. Men are originally classified at induction depots by AFSC[4] and given commensurate training. In order to justify the time and money spent on a man, it is required that he spend at least one year in his AFSC before he is eligible for a change. Further, promotions in rank for airmen depend to a considerable extent on time spent in the AFSC. The job of radar operator was reported in interviews to be a highly tedious one for which it is apparently difficult to recruit volunteers in large numbers; therefore, some men are given that AFSC even though their primary wishes lie elsewhere. Now, some commanding officers have adopted the procedure of shifting men temporarily to other specialties wherein there are personnel shortages, and where those specialties are more in accord with the men's interests and wishes. This informal practice might actually assist the air site in accomplishing its mission more effectively. However, the restriction on promotion interferes, and men discover they are not accumulating time in their official AFSC's. Thus, they find themselves caught in the midst of a dilemma for which the formal system provides no solution. One consequence is considerable anxiety, "griping," and requests for return to the official AFSC. Thus, as in the industrial office, specialization made it difficult for men to cross specialty lines when such action was necessary to the mission of the organization, and the promotions system is tied up inextricably with the specialization system.

2. The restriction of persons to their specialisms had the further effect of tending to strip work of meaning. Indeed, it seemed that the greater the restriction, the more meaningless the work. This was found to be the case in the small civilian organization but it seemed to be much more the case in the Air Force organization. Radar surveillance is but a minuscule segment of Air Force activities, and, in spite of movies and the Information and Education program, men in interviews expressed difficulty in being able to see where their particular activity fitted into the whole. This led, in some cases, to a loss of faith in the mission, with consequent depression and feelings of uselessness. The phenomena of payday sprees and debauches may be, in part, a function of this problem.

However, further examination revealed that a second set of controls was operative, which lessened the severity of these problems and even prevented their occurrence in some cases. These controls were primary in nature, and took the form of the clique or informal group, wherein workers met one another as more than segmented personalities. In the case of the office, it was discovered that the 11 cliques that were found in the office tended to cut across work sections, and thus brought together, on an informal basis, persons from various segments of the structure. Within

----

[4] An abbreviation for Air Force Specialty Code, a system of classifying specialties.

these groups, horizontal communication was easy, persons volunteered assistance to one another, and, by being able to compare their specialisms with one another, gained some conception of the relation of their work to the whole. At the same time, isolates proved to be peculiarly vulnerable to the inadequacies of the institutional controls.[5]

In the case of the air force organization, a special situation prevailed by virtue of the fact of 24-hour-a-day shift operations. It is the practice to change men continually from one shift to another, so that, in a short period of time, in certain sections, a man has worked every shift. The writer, with two graduate student associates, L. W. Wager and H. J. Loether, became aware of what we have since called "work leisure cycles." The concept of work leisure refers to the amount of opportunity afforded by a specialty for informal recreational contacts while on the job. Some shifts coincide, but others run at different rates around the clock. Preliminary findings suggest that cliques tend to develop between work sections when their work leisure opportunities coincide. This, in turn, makes possible inter-specialty informal communication.

By contrast, one work section operates a special piece of equipment, while another work section does this section's maintenance work for it. Their shifts coincide, but here we have a case where work leisure periods do not coincide. When the operators of the equipment are working, maintenance personnel merely stand by. When the equipment requires repairs, or is given periodic maintenance checks, operators have leisure, but it is just then that maintenance personnel are busiest. Observation has revealed an almost complete absence of cliquing between these two work sections. Instead, there is considerable conflict between them, refusals to make allowance for each other's problems, and actual lack of knowledge, in some cases, of how interdependent they in fact are and must be. Solution of these conflicts requires intervention by the commanding officer. These data, while only suggestive, imply that cliques which cross specialty lines act to reduce conflicts between work sections, by virtue of the intimacy provided by clique interaction. But if cliques are prevented from forming by a lack of coincidence of leisure periods, then conflict may, and does, occur. The writer has not had the opportunity to observe this work leisure phenomenon in civilian industries, but it is noteworthy that cliques in the civilian office tended to be composed of persons who had coffee "breaks" at the same time of day, and who ate lunch at the same hour. The times for the latter were different for different departments.

We turn next to the formal authority system. A work organization requires some means for coordinating and evaluating the work done in order that it shall be consistent with the purposes of the organization. In organizations of any size, this is usually accomplished by establishing a set of supervisors of graded rank who are held responsible for segments of the organization.[6] Institutional requirements in both organizations under ex-

[5] For a fuller discussion, see Edward Gross, "Characteristics of Cliques in Office Organizations," *Research Studies of the State College of Washington,* Vol. XIX (June, 1951), pp. 131–136.

[6] W. L. Warner, M. Meeker, and E. Eells, *Social Class in America,* Chicago: Science Research Associates, Chap. 1, for a discussion of the functions of supervision.

amination provide that supervisors shall perform their work by reporting on their sections to the next higher supervisor, and so on. In the case of the factory, by virtue of its small size, much of this reporting was done personally, but in the case of the air force organization, a large amount of paper work is created by this requirement and the specter of SOP[7] is everywhere in evidence. Two consequences tend to occur: first, a fairly elaborate "covering-up" process, whereby higher supervisors were sometimes almost isolated from their work sections and were thus only partially aware of their degree of success in reaching organizational goals; and, second, a tendency for persons to get buried in paper-work to such an extent that they were able to spend only a little time actually coordinating their departments.

At the air site, the informal organization related itself to these institutional concomitants as follows. Preliminary findings suggest that in addition to cliquing between specialties, there is also a considerable tendency for cliques to be confined to a given specialty. We are working now on the hypothesis that this phenomenon is related to the work section's ability to accomplish its mission without formal direction or in spite of ineffective direction. There is some evidence that the work section may be operated informally. The paper-work problem is in part solved by informal sessions —one commanding officer sees to it that officers report to the club daily for coffee—where experiences are traded and higher-ranking officers gain knowledge of what is taking place in their work sections. This serves also to protect them should paper reveal inadequacies; they have at least been forewarned. It seems to serve the further function of providing opportunities for supervisors to evaluate one another's capabilities and thus develop confidence in one another.

This leads us to the third institutional control; namely, the selection system. At the factory, this is handled in the usual manner by a personnel office. Here, the individual's qualifications are examined and a decision reached concerning whether he can perform the work role for which there is a vacancy. In the Air Force, as in military organizations generally, entrance is facilitated, but the individual is then given a set of tests to determine aptitude and interests. Persons are then sent to a school (if necessary) in large numbers to equip them for jobs to which they are later assigned. Theoretically, if persons have been well trained and have appropriate interests and aptitudes, the organization should succeed in filling its vacancies in this manner.

What is noteworthy about the approach in both instances is that it focuses attention completely on the individual and his abilities, and ignores completely the cooperative nature of the organization in which he must play a role. The individual may have the requisite skills, but before he can play the role successfully, other workers must be willing to accept him in that role. At the factory, it was discovered that employees engaged in a continuous process of mutual evaluation in terms of the following criteria: personal characteristics, marital ties, religion, education, race, ethnicity and

---

[7] Abbreviation for Standard Operating Procedure.

language, experience, and union membership.[8] There were sentiments expressed that these characteristics made a difference in terms of the amount of respect or confidence one should have in fellow workers, and that the formal organization did not sufficiently reward possessors of what were considered desirable characteristics. Said the secretary to the office manager:

> You know, there are quite a few refugees from Nazi Germany here. They don't seem to get along so well in the office. They seem to be set in their ways. I don't know what it is, but they just form a group apart. Fred [her husband] says it's because of their background. Most of them have never worked before in their life. They don't fit into our industrial system at all. They just don't seem to have the knack. Many times, Mr. Hanson [her supervisor] and I are going over a form and I see immediately what the trouble is, but he has to go slowly and ploddingly around, taking small steps, until he eventually comes to the same conclusion that I do. But he has to do it in the roundabout, slow, methodical way.

Another worker, commenting on the problem of trying to work with Mr. Hanson said, "Talking to Hanson is like talking to yourself."

Cliques, by their very nature, tend to be made up of persons who feel at ease in one another's presence and feel confidence in one another. Indeed, it is through clique experience that such confidence may be highly developed. As the secretary to a vice-president explained:

> A private secretary is the top of the heap. You need something else besides the ability to type and take shorthand. You've got to feel you're working for the company and not just for yourself. Now Mildred and Emma (other private secretaries)—we see eye to eye on that. Louise—she's a good little stenographer, but she'll never be a secretary. She doesn't fit into our crowd. When we go out for coffee, she tags along. Then she'll usually complain about her boss. She can't accept the idea that you don't work for a boss, you work for the company.

In the air force organization, the following situation prevailed. The air site, like all military organizations, is required to make best use of the men assigned to it, whether they have what are regarded as desirable qualities or not. Since a large proportion of the personnel are either draftees or involuntary recalls,[9] one of the most important criteria for success in a work role is likely to be an identification with the Air Force and the mission of the squadron. The implicit question arises: Where do you feel you belong? Are you one of us, or do you still regard yourself as a civilian? The problem is complicated in surveillance work for two reasons. First, there exists a split between personnel with and without wings. Ability to fly is not related to the mission of the site; yet those with wings exhibit a tendency to identify with the flying air force outside the site.

---

[8] For a full discussion, see Chapter 3 of the reference cited in footnote 2 above.

[9] A considerable proportion qualify as "volunteers," but on questionnaires gave overwhelmingly as their reason for volunteering: "To avoid getting drafted into the Army."

Second, not all radar personnel desire to remain in that work after their one-year AFSC requirement has been met.

There is some evidence that the informal organization is used to discover primary identifications and also to change those identifications. Thus, the commanding officer at one site organized a duty night, which, after two hours of work, turned into a stag party till 3:00 A.M. There were later objections from the wives of officers present, about which the commanding officer said in an interview:

> I called that a duty night because that's exactly what it was. There's too much of this dashing for the gate right after a man's shift is over to get home, or to get in flying time. I wanted to take this means of informing my men that radar comes first, family and flying second. If I, as their CO, want them to stay till 3 in the morning to work, they'll do it. If I want them to play poker till 3, they'll do it, because I said so. Let the wives gripe. It's time they found out their husbands are in the Air Force.

It was significant that the commanding officer employed an informal means of driving the point home, for the formal regulations are quite clear on this point. The point here is that the selection system does not insure a supply, either in the office or the Air Force, of persons who have what are regarded as "desirable" characteristics by persons within the organization. In the case of both the office and the air site, primary-control devices are employed both to discover these characteristics and to try to develop them if they are absent.

Evidence has been submitted which suggests that primary controls on behavior are far from being inconsistent with institutional controls. There is an unfortunate tendency in the literature on the sociology of work to regard cliques as innocuous play groups, or else as being antithetical to the purposes of the organization, as exemplified in restriction of output.[10] While this is unquestionably the case in some situations, it is suggested here that cliques may have quite another purpose—they may actually be essential to the very functioning of instituted organizations.

The data presented here, based as they are on only two work organizations, are inconclusive. But they do suggest that the relation between primary and institutional controls is by no means a simple one, and that further research on this relation may prove fruitful in the examination of behavior in formal work organizations.[11]

---

[10] Cf. F. J. Roethlisberger and W. J. Dickson, *Management and the Worker*, Cambridge: Harvard University Press, 1947, Chapters XXII and XXIII, and W. E. Moore, *Industrial Relations and the Social Order*, New York: The Macmillan Co., 1947, Chapter XV. An exception to this emphasis is provided in D. C. Miller and W. H. Form, *Industrial Sociology*, New York: Harper and Bros., 1951, Chapter IX.

[11] See also W. F. Whyte, *Street Corner Society*, Chicago: University of Chicago Press, 1943, for a discussion of the significance of informal organization in the slum, which deals with roughly the same theme as that discussed here, though in a different social situation.

OBSERVATION OF A BUSINESS DECISION
Richard M. Cyert, Herbert A. Simon, and Donald B. Trow*

This selection presents a case study of decision-making in a large organization. It illustrates the procedures followed in making a basic, long-range decision dealing with a problem of a non-repetitive nature, and suggests the requirements of a theory dealing with making choices in the decision processes.

Decision-making—choosing one course of action rather than another, finding an appropriate solution to a new problem posed by a changing world—is commonly asserted to be the heart of executive activity in business. If this is so, a realistic description and theory of the decision-making process are of central importance to business administration and organization theory. Moreover, it is extremely doubtful whether the only considerable body of decision-making theory that has been available in the past—that provided by economics—does in fact provide a realistic account of decision-making in large organizations operating in a complex world.

In economics and statistics the rational choice process is described somewhat as follows:

1. An individual is confronted with a number of different, specified alternative courses of action.

2. To each of these alternatives is attached a set of consequences that will ensue if that alternative is chosen.

3. The individual has a system of preferences or "utilities" that permit him to rank all sets of consequences according to preference and to choose that alternative that has the preferred consequences. In the case of business decisions the criterion for ranking is generally assumed to be profit.

If we try to use this framework to describe how real human beings go about making choices in a real world, we soon recognize that we need to incorporate in our description of the choice process several elements that are missing from the economic model:

1. The alternatives are not usually "given" but must be sought, and hence it is necessary to include the search for alternatives as an important part of the process.

2. The information as to what consequences are attached to which alternatives is seldom a "given," but, instead, the search for consequences is another important segment of the decision-making task.

* Reprinted from *The Journal of Business*, XXIX, No. 4 (1956), 237–248, by permission of The University of Chicago Press. Copyright 1956 by The University of Chicago.

3. The comparisons among alternatives are not usually made in terms of a simple, single criterion like profit. One reason is that there are often important consequences that are so intangible as to make an evaluation in terms of profit difficult or impossible. In place of searching for the "best" alternative, the decision-maker is usually concerned with finding a *satisfactory* alternative—one that will attain a specified goal and at the same time satisfy a number of auxiliary conditions.

4. Often, in the real world, the problem itself is not a "given," but, instead, searching for significant problems to which organizational attention should be turned becomes an important organizational task.

Decisions in organizations vary widely with respect to the extent to which the decision-making process is *programmed*. At one extreme we have repetitive, well-defined problems (e.g., quality control or production lot-size problems) involving tangible considerations, to which the economic models that call for finding the best among a set of pre-established alternatives can be applied rather literally. In contrast to these highly programmed and usually rather detailed decisions are problems of a non-repetitive sort, often involving basic long-range questions about the whole strategy of the firm or some part of it, arising initially in a highly unstructured form and requiring a great deal of the kinds of search processes listed above. In this whole continuum, from great specificity and repetition to extreme vagueness and uniqueness, we will call decisions that lie toward the former extreme *programmed*, and those lying toward the latter end *non-programmed*. This simple dichotomy is just a shorthand for the range of possibilities we have indicated.

It is our aim in the present paper to illustrate the distinctions we have introduced between the traditional theory of decision, which appears applicable only to highly programmed decision problems, and a revised theory, which will have to take account of the search processes and other information processes that are so prominent in and characteristic of non-programmed decision-making. We shall do this by recounting the stages through which an actual problem proceeded in an actual company and then commenting upon the significance of various items in this narrative for future decision-making theory.

The decision was captured and recorded by securing the company's permission to have a member of the research team present as an observer in the company's offices on substantially a full-time basis during the most active phases of the decision process. The observer spent most of his time with the executive who had been assigned the principal responsibility for handling this particular problem. In addition, he had full access to the files for information about events that preceded his period of observation and also interviewed all the participants who were involved to a major degree in the decision.

THE ELECTRONIC DATA-PROCESSING DECISION

The decision process to be described here concerns the feasibility of using electronic data-processing equipment in a medium size corporation that engages both in manufacturing and in selling through its own widely scattered outlets. In July, 1952, the company's controller assigned to Ronald Middleton, an assistant who was handling several special studies in the accounting department, the task of keeping abreast of electronic developments. The controller, and other accounting executives, thought that some of the current developments in electronic equipment might have application to the company's accounting processes. He gave Middleton the task of investigation, because the latter had a good background for understanding the technical aspects of computers.

Middleton used three procedures to obtain information: letters to persons in established computer firms, discussions with computer salesmen, and discussions with persons in other companies that were experimenting with the use of electronic equipment in accounting. He also read the current journal literature about computer developments. He informed the controller about these matters principally through memorandums that described the current status of equipment and some of the procedures that would be necessary for an applications study in the company. Memorandums were written in November, 1952, October, 1953, and January, 1954. In them, in addition to summarizing developments, he recommended that two computer companies be asked to propose possible installations in the company and that the company begin to adapt its accounting procedures to future electronic processing.

In the spring of 1954 a computer company representative took the initiative to propose and make a brief equipment application study. In August he submitted a report to the company recommending an installation, but this was not acted upon—doubt as to the adequacy of the computer company's experience and knowledge in application being a major factor in the decision. A similar approach was made by another computer company in September, 1954, but terminated at an early stage without positive action. These experiences convinced Middleton and other executives, including the controller, that outside help was needed to develop and evaluate possible applications of electronic equipment.

Middleton drew up a list of potential consultants and, by checking outside sources and using his own information, selected Alpha as the most suitable. After preliminary meetings in October and November, 1954, between representatives of Alpha and the company accounting executives, Alpha was asked to develop a plan for a study of the application of electronic data-processing to sales accounting. Additional meetings between Alpha and company personnel were held in February, 1955, and the proposal for the study was submitted to the controller in March.

Although the proposal seemed competent and the price reasonable, it was felt that proposals should be obtained from another consulting firm as a double check. The controller agreed to this and himself selected Beta from Middleton's list. Subsequently representatives of Beta met with Middleton and other department executives. Middleton, in a memorandum to the controller, listed criteria for choosing between the two consultants. On the assumption that the written report from Beta was similar to the oral proposal made, the comparison indicated several advantages for Beta over Alpha.

After the written report was received, on May 2, the company's management committee authorized a consulting agreement with Beta, and work began in July, 1955. The controller established a committee, headed by Middleton, to work on the project. Middleton was to devote full time to the assignment; the other two committee members, one from sales accounting and one from auditing, were to devote one-third time.

The consulting firm assigned two staff members, Drs. Able and Baker, to the study. Their initial meetings with Middleton served the purpose of outlining a general approach to the problem and planning the first few steps. Twenty-three information-gathering studies were defined, which Middleton agreed to carry out, and it was also decided that the consultants would spend some time in field observation of the actual activities that the computer might replace.

During July, Middleton devoted most of his time to the twenty-three studies on volume of transactions and information flow, obtaining data from the sales department and from the field staffs of the other two committee members. Simultaneously, steps were taken to secure the cooperation of the field personnel who would be visited by the consultants early in August.

On July 22 Middleton submitted a progress report to the controller, describing the data-gathering studies, estimating completion dates, and summarizing the program's objectives. On July 25 the consultants met with Middleton and discussed a method of approach to the design of the data-processing system. The field trip took place early in August. The consultants obtained from field personnel information as to how accounting tasks were actually handled and as to the use actually made of information generated by the existing system.

On August 8 Middleton submitted another progress report, giving the status of the data-gathering studies and recording some ideas originating in the field trip for possible changes in the existing information-processing system. On August 10 he arranged with the assistant controller to obtain clerical assistance on the data-gathering studies, so that the consultants would not be held up by lack of this information, and on August 17 the work was completed.

On the following day the consultants met with the company committee to review the results of the twenty-three studies. They then listed the outputs, files, and inputs required by any sales accounting system the company might adopt and drew a diagram showing the flow of the accounting information. The group also met with the assistant controller and with the controller. The latter took the opportunity to emphasize his basic decentralization philosophy.

Upon returning from his vacation early in September, Middleton discussed the flow diagram in greater detail with Able and Baker, and revisions were made on the basis of information Middleton supplied about the present accounting system. Baker pointed out that all the alternative systems available to the company could be defined by the location of seven principal functions and records. Further analysis reduced this number to three: stock records, pricing of orders, and accounts receivable. The possible combinations of locations of these gave eighteen basic alternative systems, of which eight that were obviously undesirable were eliminated.

Middleton was to make a cost analysis of the existing system and the most decentralized of the proposed systems, while the consultants were to begin costing the most centralized system.

Middleton reviewed these tentative decisions with the other members of the company committee, and the group divided up the work of costing. Middleton also reported to the controller on the conference, and the latter expressed his attitudes about the location of the various functions and the resulting implications for the development of executive responsibility.

During the next week, in addition to working on his current assignments, Middleton gave an equipment salesman a preliminary overview of the probable requirements of a new system. Next, there was a two-day meeting of the consultants and the company's committee to discuss the form and implications of a centralized electronic system. The consultants presented a method of organizing the records for electronic processing and together with the committee calculated the requirements which this organization and company's volume of transactions would impose on a computer. The group then discussed several problems raised by the system, including the auditing problems, and then met with the assistant controller to review the areas they had discussed.

On the following day, Middleton summarized progress to date for the controller, emphasizing particularly the work that had been done on the centralized system. The controller expressed satisfaction with several new procedures that would be made possible by an electronic computer. During the next several days the committee members continued to gather the information necessary to determine the cost of the present system. Middleton also checked with the assistant controller on the proposed solutions for certain problems that the consultants had indicated could not be handled readily by a computer and relayed his reactions to the consultants.

A week later the consultants returned for another series of meetings. They discussed changes that might be necessary in current practices to make centralized electronic processing possible and the way in which they would compare the centralized and decentralized proposals. The comparison presented some difficulties, since the data provided by the two systems would not be identical. A general form for a preliminary report was cleared with the assistant controller, and a date was set for its submission. The processing, outputs, and costs for the two alternatives would be described, so that additional information required for a final report could be determined.

During the next week Middleton continued collecting cost data. He phoned to the consultants to provide them with important new figures and to inform them of the controller's favorable reaction to certain proposed changes in the system that had implications for the company's policies.

On October 17 Baker met with Middleton to review the content of the accounting reports that would be produced by the centralized system, to discuss plans for the preliminary report, and to discuss the relative advantages and disadvantages of the centralized and decentralized systems. On the next day, Middleton checked on their decisions relative to the report with the controller and assistant controller and raised the possibility of an outside expert being retained by the company to review the final report submitted by Beta. During the last days of this week, Middleton attended the national meeting of a management society, where he obtained information about the availability of computers and computer personnel and the existence of other installations comparable to that contemplated for the company.

Work continued on the planning and costing of the two systems—Middleton worked primarily on the decentralized plan, and the consultants on the centralized. On October 27 the two consultants met with Middleton and they informed each other of the status of their work. Baker discussed methods for evaluating system reliability. Plans for the preliminary report were discussed with the company committee and the assistant controller. Since the controller strongly favored decentralization of authority, the question was raised of the compatibility of this with electronic processing in general and with the centralized system in particular. The groups concluded, however, that centralization of purely clerical data-processing operations was compatible with decentralization of responsibility and authority.

After several meetings between the committee and the consultants to iron out details, the preliminary report was presented to the company committee, the controller, and the assistant controller on November 3. The report was devoted primarily to the centralized system. The following points were made in the oral presentation: (1) that both the centralized and decentralized proposals would yield substantial and roughly equivalent savings but that the centralized system would provide more and better accounting data; (2) that the alternatives had been costed conservatively; (3) that the centralized system involved centralization of paper work, not of management; (4) that not all problems raised by the centralized system had been worked out in detail but that these did not appear insurmountable; (5) that the centralized system would facilitate improved inventory control; and (6) that its installation would require nine to twelve months at a specified cost. At this meeting the group decided that in the final report only the two systems already considered would be costed, that the final report would be submitted on December 1, and that investigation of other accounting applications of the system would be postponed.

In informal conversations after the meeting the controller told Middleton he had the impression that the consultants strongly favored the centralized system and that he believed the cost considerations were relatively minor compared with the impact the system would have on executives' operating philosophies. The assistant controller told Middleton he thought the preliminary report did not adequately support the conclusions. The committee then reviewed with the assistant controller the reasons for analyzing in detail only the two extreme systems: the others either produced less information or were more costly.

The next day the committee met with the controller and assistant controller to determine what additional information should be requested for the final report. The controller outlined certain questions of practicability that the final report should answer and expressed the view that the report should contain a section summarizing the specific changes that the system would bring about at various levels of the organization. He thought the comparison between systems in the preliminary report had emphasized equivalence of savings, without detailing other less tangible benefits of the centralized system.

Middleton reported these discussions to the consultants and with them developed flow charts and organization charts for inclusion in the final report, settled on some intermediate deadlines, and worked up an outline of the report. Within the company he discussed with the controller and assistant controller the personnel and organizational requirements for installation of an electronic system and for operation after installation. Discussion focused on the general character and organizational location of the eventual electronic-data-processing group, its relation to the sales accounting division, and long-term relations with manufacturing accounting and with a possible operations research group.

On November 14 the controller, on recommendation of Middleton, attended a conference on automation for company senior executives. There he expressed the view that three to five years would be required for full installation of a centralized electronic system but that the fear of obsolescence of equipment should not deter the company in making the investment. He also concluded that a computer installation would not reverse his long-range program for decentralizing information and responsibility.

Middleton, his suggestion being accepted, made tentative arrangements with an independent expert and with two large computer companies for the review of the consultants' report. Middleton presented to the controller and assistant controller a memorandum he had prepared at the latter's request, establishing a new comparison of the centralized and a modified decentralized system. The modification made the two systems more nearly comparable in data-processing capacity, hence clarified the cost comparison, which was now in favor of the centralized system. Consideration of the possibility of starting with a partially electronic decentralized system as a step toward a completely electronic system led to the decision that this procedure had no special advantages. The controller reported that conversations with the sales manager and the president had secured agreement with the concept of removal of stock record-keeping from field locations—an aspect of the plan to which it had been assumed there would be sales department opposition. The group discussed several other specific topics and reaffirmed that the final report should discuss more fully the relative advantages and disadvantages of centralized and decentralized systems.

Toward the end of November there was further consultation on the report, and final arrangements for its review were made with the two equipment companies and the independent expert. Each equipment company was expected to determine the method for setting up the proposed system on its computer and to check the consultants' estimates of computer capacity. During this week the controller informed the company's management committee that the report from the consultants would be submitted shortly and would recommend a rather radical change to electronic data-processing.

The final report, which recommended installation of the centralized system, was submitted on December 1. The report consisted of a summary of recommendations, general description of the centralized system, a discussion of the installation program, and six appendixes: (1) statistics on volume of transactions (the twenty-three studies); (2) costs of the present system; (3) the requirements of a fully centralized system; (4) changes in allocation of functions required by the system; (5) an outline of the alternative decentralized system; and (6) a description of the existing system in verbal and flow-chart form. When the report was received and reviewed initially, the company's committee members and the consultants made some further computations on installation costs.

At a meeting the following Monday the assistant controller proposed an action program: send copies of the report to equipment companies, send copies to the sales department, and await the report of the independent expert. The controller decided that the second and third steps should be taken before giving the report to the machine companies, and the assistant controller indicated to Middleton some points requiring further clarification and elaboration.

By January 7 Middleton had prepared an outline for a presentation of the report to the sales department. This was revised on the basis of a meeting with the other interested accounting executives. A final outline was agreed upon after two more revisions and three more meetings. The report was presented on January 28 to the president and to six of the top executives of the sales department. The presentation discussed large-scale computers briefly, described with flow charts the proposed system, emphasized the completeness and accuracy of the information produced, discussed costs and savings, and mentioned the current trend in other companies toward electronic data-processing.

At Middleton's recommendation the same presentation was made subsequently to top members of the accounting department and still later to a group from the manufacturing department. At the same time the preliminary report of the independent expert was received, agreeing that the electronic installation seemed justifiable and stating that there might not be any cost savings but that it would make possible numerous other profitable applications of the computer. The consultants' report was then distributed to the computer companies, and Middleton began more detailed planning of the installation.

Middleton, the assistant controller, and the controller now met with the independent expert, who reported his conclusions: the feasibility study was excellent, the estimates of processing time were probably optimistic, the installation program should provide for an early test run, and the two principal available computers were highly competitive. Independent confirmation had been obtained on the last two points from another outside source. Middleton now proposed that the company proceed with its planning while awaiting the final written report from the independent expert and the proposals of the equipment companies. The assistant controller preferred to wait until these reports were actually in hand.

During the next week the equipment companies proceeded with their analysis, meeting several times with Middleton. Baker sent a memorandum on his estimates of processing time to meet the criticism of the independent expert. Middleton prepared two charts, one proposing a schedule and the staffing requirements for the installation phase, the other proposing organizational arrangements for the computer center. Middleton and the assistant controller presented these to the controller at the beginning of February, discussion centering responsibility for accuracy of input information.

Middleton and the assistant controller also had a meeting with sales executives who reported that on the basis of their own internal departmental discussions of the consultants' report they were in general agreement with the program. Middleton and one of the other committee members then spent two days inspecting computer installations in two other companies.

In the middle of February the two equipment companies presented their reports, each bringing a team of three or four men to present their recommendations orally. The two recommendations were substantially alike (except for the brand of the machine recommended!), but one report emphasized the availability of its personnel to give help during the installation planning stage.

Discussions were held in the accounting department and with consultant Baker about these reports and the next steps to be taken. The question was debated whether a commitment should be made to one equipment company or whether a small group should continue planning the system in detail, postponing the equipment decision until fall. Most of the group preferred the former alternative.

On February 15 the controller, in conference with the assistant controller and Middleton, dictated a letter to the company's president summarizing the conclusions and recommendations of the study and requesting that the accounting department be authorized to proceed with the electronics program.

On the following day the controller read the letter to the management committee. The letter reviewed briefly the history of the project and summarized the conclusions contained in the consultants' report: that there was ample justification for an electronic-data-processing installation; that the installation would warrant use of the largest computers; and that it would produce savings, many intangible benefits, and excess computer capacity for other applications. The letter quoted the consultants' estimate of the cost of the installation and their recommendation that the company proceed at once to make such a conversion and to acquire the necessary equipment. It then cited the various cross-checks that had been made of the consultants' report and concluded with a repetition of the conclusions of the report—but estimating more conservatively the operating and installation costs—and a request for favorable management committee action. Supplementary information presented included a comparison of consultant and equipment company cost estimates and a list of present and proposed computer installations in other companies. After a few questions and brief discussion, the management committee voted favorably on the recommendation, and the controller informed Middleton of the decision when the meeting ended.

THE ANATOMY OF DECISION

From this narrative, or more specifically from the actual data on which the narrative is based, one can list chronologically the various activities of which the decision process is composed. If we wish to describe a program for making a decision of this kind, each of these activities might be taken as one of the steps of the program. If the rules that determined when action would switch from one program step to another were specified, and if the program steps were described in enough detail, it would be possible to replicate the decision process.

The program steps taken together define in retrospect, then, a program for an originally unprogrammed decision. The program would be an inefficient one because it would contain all the false starts and blind alleys of the original process, and some of these could presumably be avoided if the process were repeated. However, describing the process that took place in terms of such a program is a useful way of organizing the data for purposes of analysis.

In order to make very specific what is meant here by a "program," Chart 1 has been prepared to show the broad outlines of the actual program for the first stages of the decision process (through the first seven paragraphs of the narrative).

CHART 1
Program Steps from Inception of the Problem to Selection of a Consultant

KEEPING-UP PROGRAM (paragraphs 1 and 2 of narrative):
    Search for and correspond with experts;
    Discuss with salesmen and with equipment users;
    Search for and read journals;
PROCUREMENT PROGRAM (paragraph 3):
    Discuss applications study with salesmen who propose it;
    Choice: accept or reject proposed study;
    (If accepted) transfer control to salesmen;
    Choice: accept or reject applications proposal;
    (If rejected) switch to consultant program;
CONSULTANT PROGRAM (paragraphs 4 through 7):
    Search for consultants;
    Choice: best consultant of several;
    Transfer control to chosen consultant;
    Choice: accept or reject proposal;
    (If accepted): begin double-check routine;
    Request expenditure of funds;
    (If authorized) transfer control to consultants;
    And so on.

Subprograms. The various program steps of the decision process fall into several subprograms, some of which have been indicated in Chart 1. These subprograms are ways of organizing the activities *post factum*, and in Chart 1 the organizing principle is the method of approach taken by the company to the total problem. It remains a question as to whether this organizing principle will be useful in all cases. As in the present example, these subprograms may sometimes be false starts, but these must be regarded as parts of the total program, for they may contribute information for later use, and their outcomes determine the switching of activity to new subprograms.

In this particular case the reasons for switching from one subprogram to another were either the proved inadequacy of the first one or a redefinition of the problem. Other reasons for switching can be imagined, and a complete theory of the decision process will have to specify the conditions under which the switch from one line of attack to another will occur.

Common processes. In the whole decision-making program there are certain steps or "routines" that recur within several of the subprograms; they represent the basic activities of which the whole decision process is composed. For purposes of discussion we have classified these common processes in two categories: the first comprises processes relating to the communication requirements of the organization; the second comprises processes relating directly to the solution of the decisional problem.

Communication processes. Organizational decision-making requires a variety of communication activities that are absent when a decision is made in a single human head. If we had written out the program steps in greater detail, many more instances of contacts among different members of the organization would be recorded than are now explicit in the narrative. The contacts may be oral or written. Oral contacts are used for such purposes as giving orders, transmitting information, obtaining approval or criticism of proposed action; written communications generally take the form of memorandums having the purpose of transmitting information or proposing action.

The information-transmitting function is crucial to organizational decision-making, for it almost always involves acts of selection or "filtering" by the informational source. In the present instance, which is rather typical in this respect, the consultants and subordinate executives are principal information sources; and the controller and other top executives must depend upon them for most of their technical information. Hence, the subordinate acts as an information filter and in this way secures a large influence over the decisions the superior can and does reach.

The influence of the information source over communications is partly controlled by checking processes—for example, retaining an independent expert to check consultants—which give the recipient an independent information source. This reduces, but by no means eliminates, filtering. The great differences in the amounts and kinds of information available to the various participants in the decision process described here emphasize the significance of filtering. It will be important to determine the relationship of the characteristics of the information to the resultant information change and to explore the effects of personal relations between people on the filtering process and hence upon the transmission of information.

Problem-solving processes. Alongside the organizational communication processes, we find in the narrative a number of important processes directed toward the decision problem itself. One of the most prominent of these is the search for alternative courses of action. The first activities recounted in the narrative—writing letters, reading journals, and so on—were attempts to discover possible action alternatives. At subsequent points in the process searches were conducted to obtain lists of qualified consultants and experts. In addition to these, there were numerous searches—most of them only implicit in the condensed narrative—to find action alternatives that would overcome specific difficulties that emerged as detail was added to the broader alternatives.

The data support strongly the assertion made in the introduction that searches for alternative courses of action constitute a significant part of non-programmed decision-making—a part that is neglected by the classical theory of rational choice. In the present case the only alternatives that became available to the company without the expenditure of time and effort were the systems proposals made early in the process by representatives of two equipment companies, and these were both rejected. An important reason for the prominent role of search in the decision process is that the "problem" to be solved was in fact a whole series of "nested" problems, each alternative solution to a problem at one level leading to a new set of problems at the next level. In addition, the process of solving the substantive problems created many procedural problems for the organization: allocating time and work, planning agendas and report presentations, and so on.

Examination of the narrative shows that there is a rich variety of search processes. Many questions remain to be answered as to what determines the particular character of the search at a particular stage in the decision process: the possible differences between searches for procedural alternatives, on the one hand, and for substantive alternatives, on the other; the factors that determine how many alternatives will be sought before a choice is made; the conditions under which an alternative that has tentatively been chosen will be subjected to further check; the general types of search strategies.

The neglect of the search for alternatives in the classical theory of decision would be inconsequential if the search were so extensive that most of the alternatives available "in principle" were generally discovered and considered. In that case the search process would have no influence upon the alternative finally selected for action. The narrative suggests that this is very far from the truth—that, in fact, the search for alternatives terminates when a satisfactory solution has been discovered even though the field of possibilities has not been exhausted. Hence, we have reason to suppose that changes in the search process or its outcome will actually have major effects on the final decision.

A second class of common processes encompasses information-gathering and similar activity aimed at determining the consequences of each of several alternatives. In many decisions, certainly in the one we observed, these activities account for the largest share of man-hours, and it is through them that subproblems are discovered. The narrative suggests that there is an adverse relation between the cost or difficulty of this investigational task and the number of alternative courses of action that are examined carefully. Further work will be needed to determine if this relation holds up in a broader range of situations. The record also raises numerous questions about the *kinds* of consequences that are examined most closely or at all and about the conditions under which selection of criteria for choice is prior to, or subsequent to, the examination of consequences.

Another set of common processes are those concerned with the choices among alternatives. Such processes appear at many points in the narrative: the selection of a particular consulting firm from a list, the choice between centralized and decentralized electronic-data-processing systems, as well as numerous more detailed choices. These are the processes most closely allied to the classical theory of choice, but even here it is notable that traditional kinds of "maximizing" procedures appear only rarely.

In some situations the choice is between competing alternatives, but in many others it is one of acceptance or rejection of a single course of action—really a choice between doing *something* at this time and doing nothing. The first such occasion was the decision by the controller to assign Middleton to the task of watching developments in electronics, a decision that initiated the whole sequence of later choices. In decisions of this type the consequences of the single alternative are judged against some kind of explicit or implicit "level of aspiration"—perhaps expressed in terms of an amount of improvement over the existing situation—while in the multiple-alternative situations, the consequences of the several alternatives are compared with each other. This observation raises a host of new questions relating to the circumstances under which the decision will be formulated in terms of the one or the other of these frameworks and the personal and organizational factors that determine the aspirational levels that will be applied in the one-alternative case.

Another observation derivable from our data—though it is not obvious from the condensed narrative given here—is that comparability and noncomparability of the criteria of choice affects the decision processes in significant ways. For one thing, the criteria are not the same from one choice to another: one choice may be made on the basis of relative costs and savings, while the next may be based entirely on non-monetary criteria. Further, few, if any, of the choices were based on a single criterion. Middleton and the others recognized and struggled with this problem of comparing consequences that were sometimes measured in different, and incomparable, units, and even more often involved completely intangible considerations. The narrative raises, but does not answer, the question of how choices are made in the face of these incommensurabilities and the degree to which tangible considerations are overemphasized or underemphasized as compared with intangibles as a result.

CONCLUSION

We do not wish to try to transform one swallow into a summer by generalizing too far from a single example of a decision process. We have tried to illustrate, however, using a large relatively non-programmed decision in a business firm, some of the processes that are involved in business decision-making and to indicate the sort of theory of the choice mechanism that is needed to accommodate these processes. Our illustration suggests that search processes and information-gathering processes constitute significant parts of decision-making and must be incorporated in a theory of decision if it is to be adequate. While the framework employed here—and particularly the analysis of a decision in terms of a hierarchical structure of *programs*—is far from a complete or finished theory, it appears to provide a useful technique of analysis for researchers interested in the theory of decision as well as for business executives who may wish to review the decision-making procedures of their own companies.

PART 2

DIFFERENTIAL ASPECTS OF
ORGANIZATION AND MANAGEMENT

4

STUDIES OF SPECIFIC ORGANIZATIONS

The goals of this chapter are to build awareness of the differences that are encountered as one moves from organization to organization, and the causes of these differences. The various readings describe research findings in specific organizational settings.

HOSPITAL ADMINISTRATION—ONE OF A SPECIES
*Edith M. Lentz**

In this article Edith Lentz delineates aspects of hospital administration which justify treating it as a separate species of management. She suggests that an analysis of (1) the social role of the organization, (2) its economic aspects, and (3) its internal structure will provide a basis for identifying the various species.

Any branch of learning that deals with complex subject matter will sooner or later develop a classification system wherein each variety of case may find its appropriate place. This article suggests the possibility of such a classification system in the science of administration. It will use hospital administration as its content, but one may hope that the same system of concepts might be applied to other types of administration as well, until all are brought into logical relationship with each other. This paper will discuss three areas of classification: (a) the social role of the institution, (b) its economic aspects, and (c) its internal structure.

THE SOCIAL ROLE OF THE INSTITUTION

First consideration, in placing any institution within a system, must be given to the way it is seen to fit into its cultural environment, the evaluation which it is given, and the configuration of other social organizations of which it is a part.

The modern hospital cannot be understood without an understanding of its traditions. Hospitals have changed. They began in our society as an expression of Christian concern and were the gift of the fortunate to the unfortunate. It was in this guise that they became rooted into the social fabric of our society. Those who donated money to them demonstrated thereby not only their virtue but their social position and their allegiance to upper-class traditions of *noblesse oblige*. People who went to the hospitals as patients, on the other hand, were seen to be the recipients of charity. The two groups fell at the opposite ends of the social scale; hence the way hospitals were perceived depended upon the social position of the perceiver.

As biological and medical sciences advanced, the hospital began to offer the hope of cure. The rich began to patronize certain hospitals, and special accommodations were set aside for them, including private rooms, a distinctive dining service, and private nurses. To go to the hospital was no longer seen as a disgrace. It was not until recently, however, that economic and social conditions made it possible for the middle classes to utilize

* From *Administrative Science Quarterly*, 1, No. 4 (March 1957), 444–463. Reprinted by permission.

hospital services. Today everybody accepts them; most of us take them for granted. The hospital may be seen as a special kind of public utility designed to serve the total community. Yet the traditions of the past, the old altruistic flavor, continue.

In many nations it is accepted as only natural that such a public utility should be operated by the government. In this country our hospitals designed for long-term illnesses such as tuberculosis and mental diseases, along with those set aside for the military, are government owned and operated. Otherwise the tradition of voluntarism which keeps American museums, symphony orchestras, and many universities in private hands has also kept the majority of our general, short-term hospitals in the control of religious, fraternal, or other civic-minded groups which operate them as nonprofit institutions.

In view of the history of hospitals, it is perhaps not surprising that one finds persons of the highest social prestige associated with hospitals and sitting on their policy-making boards. They represent the "best families in town," that is, those with traditions of civic responsibility and service as well as comfortable incomes and a propensity to share them with the less fortunate. Some hospitals have been seeking to achieve a wider representation of community groups on their boards, but this is not yet typical of the nation as a whole.

If one stops to consider the values upon which our society places highest esteem, it becomes easy to see why hospital service continues to be so prestigeful.[1] Certainly humanitarian service is one. Learning is another. Youthfulness, health, and physical vigor, so important in a pioneer society, remain highly prized out of proportion to the evaluation placed upon them in other cultures, we are told. We prize efficiency for efficiency's sake and look upon large-scale business enterprise as somehow symbolizing this virtue. And finally, we tend to attribute merit to almost any kind of scientific endeavor. Hospitals embody these virtues in varying degrees, and generally speaking their prestige varies correspondingly. The highest standing is normally attributed to the medical center associated with a university, which combines them all.

The medical center has multiple functions. Almost all hospitals do, but the medical center may be seen as an extreme example. A generalization might be made that the more varied the functions of an institution the more complex the administrative task, since shifts in emphasis through time will necessitate a series of decisions concerning the priorities among these functions.

The original function of the hospital, to go back a bit, was custodial care of the dying poor. Curative care, as contrasted to custodial care, became a second function. Custodial care was relatively easy to provide, but curative care requires highly trained personnel. The education of such personnel became the third function of the hospital. Once doctors were the only recognized therapeutic agents. Today nurses, dietitians, social workers, and a wide variety of technicians are so recognized, and the hospital has become their school and laboratory. Scientific research into the cause

[1] Robin M. Williams, "Value Orientations in American Society," in *American Society: A Sociological Interpretation* (New York, 1951), pp. 372–442.

as well as the cure of disease is a still more recent addition to hospital functions. And finally the beginnings of preventive medicine have placed upon hospital management the necessity of allocating money, time, and personnel to health education. A hospital under religious control may have additional functions. The administrator and board of trustees must constantly juggle these purposes and needs in order to maintain a suitable balance among them and to see that those deemed most important within a given institution are met first.

All of these things have greatest significance in the administrative functioning of hospitals. The administrator is responsible to a board which represents not only economic power over him but ethical and humanitarian values as well. The board expresses the voice of dominant groups in the community and its most respected minds. Their judgment, even on minor matters, is of consequence in the daily routines of the hospital. A hospital board is typically more prone to "interfere" in administrative details than is a similar board in industry, for example; it is more concerned with particular cases. Similarly the medical staff of a hospital, which represents its scientific aspects, has unusual power and prestige within the hospital's internal structure. The administrator is seen as representing the need for efficiency and smooth coordination. Hospital government is a series of accommodations and compromises among these power groups, as we shall see.

The social role of the hospital may come into better focus if it is compared to organizations of somewhat similar nature. The primary health agencies of our communities continue to be the private family and the doctor's office. We go to hospitals only when our homes and the doctor's office fail to encompass our health needs. The doctor's office shares with the hospital the overtones of humanitarian service but has the additional status of independence. Physicians normally operate as private practitioners, answerable only to themselves and their medical association. This freedom from control gives the doctor prestige, for our culture prizes individualism as it does voluntarism. The public health office, on the other hand, deals with the social and biological environment of both the sick and the well, yet has less status than the hospital because it is subject to government control. Hospitals usually are characterized by a larger scale of operation than are nursing homes or diagnostic clinics. This gives them the higher place, unless the clinic has an unusually glorified reputation, such as that afforded the Mayo clinic because of its perceived scientific excellence. Purely scientific laboratories, however, such as those operated by the great drug companies, have less status than the hospital presumably because they are considered to be dominated by the profit motive.

In many respects the hospital is closer to the university in its public character than to any of the other organizations mentioned here. Both have a public-utility aspect, yet command the voluntary services of notable people. Private universities, generally speaking, have higher prestige among us than do publicly supported ones. The university, on the other hand, serves only some of the people and thus has a narrower basis for the tradition of altruistic service which dignifies the concept of the hospital in modern society.

To summarize, the modern, general, short-term hospital is a special kind of public utility which remains for the most part in private hands, yet provides service to all the people. It is seen to be an expression of humanitarian concern, and service in its cause elevates the social position of the individual. The larger hospitals serve many functions and combine the prestige of big business and scientific endeavor with that of the humanitarian arts. This combination of factors brings about social expectations which are so extreme as to be somewhat difficult for the individual institution to realize.

THE ECONOMIC ASPECTS OF HOSPITALS

There are two ways to view the economic question: from the standpoint of the hospital industry as a whole and from that of the individual institution within the industry.

Figures relating to the industry as a whole are impressive indeed. In 1955 there were 6,970 hospitals in the United States and more than twenty million patient admissions, an increase of five million admissions in the past nine years. These hospitals employed more than 1,200,000 full-time persons and spent approximately five billion dollars, making the hospital industry the sixth largest in the nation.[2] One gets the impression of a colossus, but this is a mistaken image.

In the first place, the industry is in the service field and therefore has little effect on the economy as a whole except insofar as it bolsters it by helping provide it with healthy personnel. On the other hand, it is highly influenced by the economic pressures exerted by the other, more dominant institutions. At least, past experience has been that in times of general economic depression, occupancy rates in private hospitals drop like a plummet. Prospective patients postpone elective surgery and try to care for their medical needs at home as long as possible. At such times the hospital cannot close down its facilities to the same extent as do commercial enterprises. Staff, equipment, and beds must be held in readiness for disaster, epidemic, or other acute human need. During times of renewed prosperity occupancy rates zoom upward and overcrowdedness occurs. It still requires an average of three years to train a nurse, however, and considerably longer than that to train a doctor; hence the educational functions of a hospital continue unabated through good times or bad. Similarly, research may be curtailed, but the careful keeping of records upon which future research must be based must continue. In other words, the hospital is an agency which continues to function even when it must limp along without income from patients for prolonged periods. Whether hospitalization insurance schemes will greatly ease these crisis situations remains to be proved.

In the second place, despite its total size, the industry is relatively weak in terms of organized economic strength. Traditionally, nongovernmental hospitals operated as independent units. They did their purchasing locally, employed local people, and dedicated themselves to the service

[2] George Bugbee, in Foreword to Temple Burling, Edith M. Lentz, and Robert N. Wilson, *The Give and Take in Hospitals* (New York, 1956), pp. v–vii.

of their immediate geographical area. Record keeping was minimized, and there were few standards against which an individual institution could be measured.

Today the situation is changing. The American Hospital Association has five thousand institutional members. It acts in similar capacity to that of other trade associations, having advisory power over its members, speaking for them on public issues, and encouraging the pooling of their knowledge. It has encouraged the formation of local and regional hospital councils, which in some instances have brought about concerted action on economic problems. It is also one of five member agencies composing the Joint Commission on Accreditation of Hospitals, another voluntary agency, which acts to raise the level of medical and hospital care throughout the nation. Its powers are largely those of persuasion but are not by that account to be considered negligible.

Because hospitals used to be built at the initiative of wealthy donors, their geographical placement tended to be capricious. Areas where many wealthy people lived had many hospitals, while other parts of the nation were seriously underprivileged with respect to health care. Today, just as there is an ecumenical movement among our churches to consolidate their efforts, so among our hospitals there are forces at work to consolidate institutions and services in order to improve the level of service offered the public and to lighten the financial burden of hospital care. Federal funds are being distributed with regional-planning schemes in mind which are designed to spread hospital services rationally within the separate states.

It is important to remember, however, that despite these influences of national and regional origin, the typical community hospital continues to pride itself on its independence and has a deeply rooted habit of plotting its own course. Institutions, like people, have a sometimes fierce pride in their history and individual identity. For these reasons it is not appropriate to speak of the "hospital industry" in the United States. One must continue to see it as it is perceived by "insiders," as 6,970 institutions which are only now beginning to see themselves as possible parts of a whole.

Roughly four thousand of these seven thousand institutions have less than one hundred beds.[3] The average of all short-term hospitals, including those operated by government agencies, has only 106 beds. Hospitals can thus be classified in a category with social clubs, restaurants, and merchandizing, as characteristically taking the form of fairly small, retail-service establishments.

Any institution of comparable size can be expected to have consumer relations which might be termed intimate in nature. In the case of the general, short-term hospital this intimacy is exaggerated by the fact that the consumer remains on the premises twenty-four hours a day for an average stay of eight days per hospital admission, and the basis of his care is about as personal as one can imagine.

Hospital services, unlike those of other retail agencies, are often unplanned for, unwanted, and frequently bitterly resented as evidence of waning physical vigor. Hospitals deal with people who are involved in

[3] The statistics in this paper are drawn chiefly from *Hospitals, Administrator's Guide Issue* (Aug. 1955), pt. II.

crisis situations. The patient and the hospital employee are caught in a relationship which cannot be routinized. Emotional stress arising from acute human need, gratitude, worry, and, occasionally, personal outrage may influence behavior and understanding. The economic aspect of patient care is thus piled on top of a sometimes turbulent mass of feelings. It is perhaps obvious why public relations will continue to be an important field of specialized training within hospital administration, even after economic factors become satisfactorily adjusted.

That possibility seems to be still in the far future. As we have seen, once hospitals were accepted by the community as charitable institutions supported by the wealthy for the benefit of the poor, but changes in the structure of our society have made this institutional form outmoded. The numbers of dependent poor have diminished, and today's self-respecting working class carries hospitalization insurance to a steadily increasing degree. What is more, there is less giving of funds for charity on the grand scale. Donations to hospital fund drives today come from a fairly wide range of the social scale, and many small donations have appeared in place of the few enormous ones. Proportionally, however, donations have come to account for a steadily declining percentage of total hospital income.

The typical nonprofit hospital today is trying to maintain itself at or near the financial break-even point. It has become common practice to charge the patient the "full cost of his care," which means his share of total operating expenses depending upon the type of accommodations he selects. On the other hand, most nonprofit hospitals do not expect patients' fees to cover capital expenditures. Money for the purchase of new buildings or grounds, basic equipment, and many social services continues to be provided through private donation, public subscription, or voluntary services. Since World War II federal funds have helped subsidize new construction. In this way the modern hospital is making its adjustment to a period of social change and to the cross-pressures of a capitalistic society, which expects financial solvency of its institutions, and the humanistic tradition, which expects hospital services to be made available to all on the basis of need.

This type of accommodation is widespread and is fairly well accepted among hospital officialdom. It is not so well accepted, or even recognized in some instances, by the public at large. Where people have become accustomed to subsidized hospital care it is hard for them to accept anything else. Consequently it is not unusual to find a hospital still caught in the interim stage of development: struggling along beneath staggering deficits until faced with decay and then outraging the community by inaugurating a more realistic policy of charges based upon actual costs.

Government bureaus, like the public at large, sometimes find it hard to accept the new definition of charity as extending to facilities and not to services. Hospitals book patient fees at or near cost, then expect reimbursement either by the patients themselves or some "third-party payer," which is the term used to include insurance agencies, social-work agencies, or government welfare departments responsible for the relief of medical indigency. Great are the arguments over the definition of indigency, and many are the hospitals that are obliged to make up the difference between the monies paid them by civil authorities and the actual cost of patient care. The tradition of deficit financing, however, is definitely waning. The third-party payer, with the Blue Cross as the most popular form of prepaid insurance, is steadily moving into ascendancy as the financial mainstay of the hospital.

Prices for hospital services are now in considerable flux. The condition of minimizing record keeping is giving way sufficiently to permit the kind of accounting system which amortizes debts, minor capital expenditures, and depreciation costs. Therefore these things are beginning to be listed on the books as routine operating expenses to be charged against patients' fees. A serious effort is being made to establish cost figures on specific items in order to adjust prices rationally. As long as hospital patients were paupers, the public considered it all right for the hospital to sell services at or below cost. When a hospital provides care below cost to people well able to pay commercial rates, however, it competes with drugstores, pharmaceutical houses, and even other hospitals in supplying drugs and services. In this interim period prevailing rates continue to be the most commonly used index for many price categories.

While hospital cost and price factors remain in flux, the consumers of hospital service will doubtlessly continue to complain. They have nothing stable upon which to base their expectations; hence any price will seem too high. The situation is only aggravated by the fact that as consumers they have so little basis for judging quality of service. The local hospital, like the local doctor, may provide the best care in the world, but in the absence of a satisfactory standard of measurement, how are they to be sure of that?

So much for the economics of consumer relations.[4] The hospital's market of supplies is also somewhat unique. For a long time salesmen from hospital supply houses and drug companies acted as a major connecting link among the thousands of small institutions. They were the educators of the hospital field; it was through them that the administrators of tiny hospitals learned what was going on elsewhere, which methods were being favored, what systems of control inaugurated. Today the American Hospital Association acts as the formal coordinating body and information center, but these salesmen are still a prominent part of the communication system. They operate for profit in most instances, but yet they are not wholly unmindful of the service motif and may be found contributing to fund drives as well as working overtime on plans for hospital construction or for new services. This tradition helps to mitigate against a widespread adoption of impersonal, competitive bidding for hospital contracts or the use of national rather than local sources of supply.

Some hospital supplies come from government sources (such as biologicals and some serums). Others come from charitable organizations such as the National Foundation for Infantile Paralysis and the American

---

[4] For further observations on consumer relations, see American Council on Education, *University Education for Administration in Hospitals* (Washington, D.C., 1954), particularly Chapter II, "Characteristics of Hospital Administration," pp. 20–31.

Cancer Society. The number of medical foundations is increasing rapidly, and their donations are often accompanied by demands. The usual exchange is goods and services on the one hand and space, personnel, and occasionally voluminous record keeping on the other. While such donations are customarily welcomed by the administrator, they add to the complications of his work, too. They cannot be included in advance plans nor can they be counted on absolutely, since they are outside the control of any given hospital.

Similarly the hospital's labor market is now outside the control of any single institution. The average, short-term, nonprofit hospital today employs approximately two persons for every occupied patient bed in order to keep the hospital staffed around the clock. Payroll costs account for between 60 and 70 per cent of total operating expenses despite the fact that characteristically hospital employees receive lower wages than those prevailing in the community for comparable work. State licensure laws and the fact that practitioners in medical and auxiliary fields are organized through their professional associations help to make the hospital labor market inflexible. The increasing degree of specialization has accentuated this inflexibility by increasing the degree of blocked mobility among these groups. For example, it is no longer possible for a nurse to move into a position of laboratory supervisor in most hospitals. She would require additional formal training first. A graduate nurse doing general duty work may not even be able to move into a nursing administrative post without going back to the university for her bachelor's degree. It is thought by some that these strictures on vertical mobility within a given institution have helped cause the increased horizontal mobility or transiency among hospitals. Since a nurse (or technician or dietitian) cannot advance herself by sheer seniority, she lacks the incentive to stay in one place. It therefore has become increasingly difficult to get and keep a stable work force. Personnel problems within the hospital will be discussed at greater length in the next section of this paper.

Volunteers help to complicate the labor situation. The "gray ladies" and women's auxiliaries supplement ordinary hospital employees, but, like supplies donated by the foundations, their services cannot be planned for in advance or counted on absolutely. Approximately one thousand of the general, short-term hospitals are controlled by or closely affiliated with religious organizations, and many of these draw a considerable portion of their labor force from sisterhoods which donate their full-time services. These are people who devote their lives to the hospital and are on call around the clock. They may also remain part of the hospital family years after their physical strength has waned and their greatest contribution has become increasingly spiritual rather than material. How can one estimate the value of their services in a bookkeeping entry?

Finally, a continuing factor in the economic aspect of hospital care is the tempo of technological change in the medical and allied arts and sciences. During the depression of the 1930s there was a slowing down of the tempo of change. Buildings and equipment grew steadily more obsolete. With the beginning of World War II there was a sudden acceleration throughout the entire medical field. Military necessities demanded advances in theory and practice. The introduction of antibiotics brought a wealth of innovations in itself. In addition, wartime prosperity flooded the hospitals with patients, and this overcrowding in obsolete buildings helped necessitate a virtual revolution in hospital architecture, organization, and practices. With the end of the war came the boom in hospital construction.

There was need to hire new occupational groups to make the latest therapies available to patients. Thanks to insurance, patients began coming to the hospital earlier in their illnesses, and thanks to the new advance in medicine, they left the hospital more quickly. This turnover of patients increased the volume of work for hospital personnel. The older professions were metamorphosed: they developed extensive divisions of labor in order to permit medical specialists, whether doctors, nurses, or technicians, to concentrate upon their highest skills while auxiliaries did the more routine tasks. There was need to train and retrain personnel all along the line in order to keep them abreast of developments. Along with the problems of revamping obsolete buildings and equipment went that of working with obsolete people, and not everybody was capable of making the adjustments which were demanded of him. Educational costs continued to mount.

To summarize: although the hospital industry is sixth largest in the nation, the general, short-term hospital is characterized by small, independent units under private control. The trend is toward charging the patient the full cost of his care and limiting "charity" to the provision of buildings and other capital goods. Centralizing forces are at work to bring about standardized patterns of operating, purchasing, accounting, and therapeutic practices. The financial picture is complicated by unpredictable fluctuations in the consumer market and by consumer expectations which are now outmoded. The suppliers' market is complicated by donations and the labor market by volunteers. The labor market is, in addition, highly controlled and highly transient. Perhaps the most serious source of instability in the hospital today is the recent and continuing tempo of change in the technology of medicine and allied fields.

INTERNAL STRUCTURES OF HOSPITALS

Transition and the confusion it denotes set the tone of institutional relationships within the hospital today.

When hospitals were regarded as charitable institutions, it was considered only appropriate that employees work for subsistence wages. In some places hospital employment was seen to be one of the forms of charity. People who could not get work elsewhere came to work where housing, meals, and medical oversight were provided in lieu of more generous wages. Nurses, laundry workers, kitchen help—all lived on the hospital grounds, ate three meals a day there, and associated primarily with each other, since they all worked hours which precluded their participation in normal community activities. Hospital employment was more than just a job: it was a way of life. The employer-employee relationship was one of paternalism, benevolent for the most part, but as with paternalism elsewhere the benevolence was sometimes lost sight of.

Within the hospital the board members held highest place in the authority system. Usually these were self-perpetuating affairs, and members served as volunteers for part of their leisure-time activity. Some of them never set foot inside their institution at all but ruled it from a distance. Others seemed to regard the hospital as if it were their feudal estate and visited it daily, giving personal direction to the work of employees at all levels.

Next in standing to the board came the doctors. They donated their services to indigent patients and helped to teach the nurses and interns. Actually the medical staff dominated most hospital routines because their orders initiated activities for the nurses. The administrator, or superintendent as he was then called, hired personnel, maintained property, and saw to it that doctors' orders were faithfully carried out. He was clearly third man down in the hierarchy.

Most of the work of the hospital was done by student nurses, including much of the office detail, the cleaning, and the cooking. These young women usually were drawn from the local area, served the hospital in exchange for their training, and left it upon graduation to take up private duty nursing in people's homes. In many hospitals there was but one graduate nurse on duty on each of the two daily shifts; these were "nursing superintendents" who supervised the work and education of the students.

Within the nursing group there was strict authoritarian control. Each student was taught to obey without question all of her superiors, and these included all members of the medical staff, the administrator, the nursing superintendents, and nursing students in the more advanced classes. Medical students and interns were subject to similar controls, and emphasis was placed upon their discipline, self-sacrifice, and obedience. Relations between doctors and nurses at all levels resembled those within each professional hierarchy, being highly ritualized and formalistic. Apparently nobody dreamed of equality. It was assumed that the "good of the patients" demanded the kind of rigid control over individuals that only an authoritarian system could provide. Nonprofessional employees were subject to the same kind of discipline, except that less was expected of them, hence even less respect was accorded their individual opinions.

All of that changed, but in many cases the changes did not occur until World War II, when military demands, the technological revolution, and booming occupancy rates combined to render obsolete the ancient system of relationships. To get and keep employees in the face of extreme competition, hospitals had to raise wages, adopt modern personnel policies, and engage in extensive experimentation in order to find a division of labor which would maximize the skills of what personnel they had left. The technological revolution brought about an educational reform within the nursing profession, and students began to spend considerably more time in the classroom and less on the wards. A hospital school of nursing used to be an economic advantage to a hospital. Today it is more apt to be an economic handicap. Graduate nurses and nursing auxiliaries had to be hired in increasing numbers. Today the typical hospital is devoting half of its payroll funds to nursing personnel.

Today most hospitals have personnel policies which, on paper, look very similar to those in enlightened industry. They also have left over from the old days, be it remembered, personnel *at every level* whose mental attitudes and behavior patterns were set under the older system of relationships. The result is a welter of compromises, the traditional system impinging on the modern one at a thousand unexpected junctures. Among the most frustrating and fascinating problems of hospital administration is that of keeping the old and the new working side by side with a maximum of harmony.

This task would be considerably easier if the administrator had clear responsibility for the management and integration of his institution. As it happens, the changing times also brought about a partial shift in the power structure, but the administrator's role still is not clearly defined.

In the traditional hospital the place of the doctor was not very different from that of the professional employee in industry in the old days of the owner-manager. The owner-manager of a fairly large shop very often hired a works superintendent to look after the daily management problems, but if a chemist or engineer wanted something he thought nothing of approaching the owner-manager directly with his problem. Having settled the matter with him, the professional would then pass the decision on down to the works superintendent with the expectation that he would act upon it in suitable fashion.

When industry changed to its present form of corporate control, a very similar change must have occurred to that which is happening in hospitals. Today engineers and chemists do not carry their problems directly to the board of directors. They go through channels, and the executive director or administrator of the corporation is the one who makes final decisions on management problems.

In hospitals, as more professional personnel were hired and organizational forms grew in complexity, the role of the man whose responsibility it was to coordinate the efforts of these people grew in importance, hence in prestige. It was at this time that professional hospital-administration training at the university level became available, and high-powered and well-trained administrators became more common. Today the hospital administrator resembles his counterpart in industry; he is the head of an extensive hierarchy with control over the communication system. Members of hospital boards have learned and are learning that it pays to let their full-time representative handle the management of their institution, and doctors are being asked to go through channels when they have requests for equipment or suggestions for improved services.

That kind of submission to bureaucratic forms may or may not have come readily to chemists and engineers. It does not sit well with the medical profession. These are independent practitioners who are not on hospital salary and over whom the hospital administrator has very little authority. They are officially "guests of the institution" and continue to donate their services to the indigent patients, to the nursing school, and to intern training. They are appointed by the board and are governed by their own medical staff organization. Moreover, the bulk of the doctor's work is done outside the hospital, where his prestige as a private practitioner remains relatively undiminished. It is not easy for him to yield to bureaucratic control in one segment of his work life, particularly if he is an older man who trained at a time when hospital superintendents were considered subordinates and knew their place.

The power structure within the hospital today remains three-pronged. Board members continue to make their convictions known, and some of them feel strongly that their job is to protect the public from "case-hardened professionals." The medical staff continue to share legal responsibility for the care of their patients; hence they must have the right to initiate activity for nursing personnel who serve those patients. The administrator is responsible for coordinating the work of all hospital personnel, whether they are on the payroll or not, and for keeping the institution on as even a keel as is possible. Any given hospital employee, therefore, may find himself responsible to three sources of authority.

The split in the power structure of hospitals is not wholly unique. Universities have their cleavage between teaching staff and administrative staff. Hotels have problems in uniting the "front of the house" personnel who receive tips and the "back of the house" personnel who do not. Department stores are caught in the difference of viewpoint between the buyers on the staff and the clerks who sell. In all of these instances employees face difficulties of communication, and administration requires all the arts of persuasion to keep the staff working in harmony. In all of them, presumably, accommodation is made, and life goes on despite handicaps. In the hospital it is possible to argue that the split in authority works to the benefit of the patients since it sets up a series of checks and balances. So far as the administrator is concerned, however, there is no denying that it complicates his task sometimes to the point that the job becomes almost untenable.

It is especially difficult for the man who comes to hospital administration with a business background. In business, prestige and power normally go to the administrative group, the paper workers who make the plans and initiate the activities of others. Production workers have lower status. In the hospital the honor and glory go to production workers, namely, the doctors and nurses. Their craft is an ancient one, and the sentiments surrounding the medicine-man-priest are sometimes amazingly present among us. It is this differential in power and status which makes it so difficult for the administrator to govern the institution for which he holds responsibility.

The doctors are not the only scientifically trained professionals who present difficulties to hospital administration. Nurses, dietitians, pharmacists, anesthesiologists, and medical technicians have their own national professional associations with their codes of ethics, standards of professional conduct and freedom, rules for admission of novices, and control over their training and employment. These associations hold meetings and institutes which members are expected to attend. How much membership in such an association influences the behavior of a given hospital employee differs among individuals and hospital situations. In some instances the membership is merely symbolic of a psychological identification on the part of that employee. In others a body of employees may be found utilizing their professional association to bring standards of performance and employment relationships to as ideal a level as their combined powers of persuasion can bring to pass.

Several of these national organizations have power of accreditation over hospitals. Usually this is voluntary, that is, the organization can enter a hospital only upon official request of its board of trustees, and the board does not have to accept the conditions set by the agency for achieving its seal of approval. The difficulty, of course, is that the penalty for not having this seal of approval may be that of not appearing on an approved list, hence losing prospective applicants for training courses, discouraging potential professional employees, and losing face within the field of hospital administration. Accreditation provides official recognition that an institution is in the top group of hospitals, a recognition which is cherished by those hospital boards that wish to be known as progressive.

It may be seen that the administrator of such an institution has many pressures exerted upon him. He must keep all groups content and satisfied that their work is being maintained at a high level, that education is available to them to keep them acquainted with developments in their field, and that their working conditions are appropriate and equal to those in other good hospitals across the nation. Managing proud people can be gratifying but difficult. Working with many proud occupational groups can be likewise. The hospital administrator today cannot use authoritarian methods to coordinate his organization. Perhaps this is also true of other modern organizations, but it seems unlikely that many other institutions contain an equal number of lively, well-informed, tightly organized, and sternly principled professional groups as this one does.

Since it is so difficult, why would anybody take on the task of hospital administration? The meaning of hospital employment cannot be understood without reference to the patients, nor, I think, without reference to the ethical standards of our culture. The truth of the matter is that we are so educated that life seems worth while when we are working hard at difficult problems and when we can feel that our efforts result in easing life's burdens for others. Hospitals pay living wages now. Nobody is getting very rich on a hospital salary, but many are leading rich lives in terms of satisfaction. The reward-and-punishment system of the hospital, then, is not quite the same as in some other parts of our society. That is precisely why it has appeal for people who do not find sufficient satisfaction in highly materialistic employment. That is why, too, private citizens continue to devote their services and money to hospital causes. The satisfactions found by volunteers, by medical and auxiliary workers, and indeed by hospital personnel at all levels are shared by the administrator as well. He knows his work is significant; therefore he can accept its frustrations.

CONCLUSION

In order to understand the administrative task in any institution and to compare it to that of other types of administration, it is helpful to consider the way the institution itself is structured and how it is perceived by the community. One would want to know what functions it has and the degree to which it is experiencing change. The economic aspects of the institution help to shape the administrative task; hence it is necessary to ascertain its degree of stability, the extent of competition it must meet, the relative rate of technological change within it, its sources of supply and of labor, and its relation to its consumers. The internal structure of the institution should be noted: one would want to know how many people work within it, the degree of organizational complexity in which they find themselves, the nature of the authority system, the extent of occupational hierarchy, and any cleavages in the structure, as well as the habitual pattern of labor-management relations. Finally one would want to inquire how the people within the institution regard themselves and their work; one would want to know what are the psychological rewards and punishments of their institutional relationships. Having these things in mind, the work of the administrator may begin to come into focus.

Once such a frame of reference is established, the differences and similarities among types of administration could be compared and our total sum of knowledge made more secure.

RECRUITMENT, DEPENDENCY, AND MORALE IN THE BANKING INDUSTRY
Robert N. McMurry*

In this selection, Robert N. McMurry, an eminent industrial psychologist, analyzes the personnel problems of banks in a framework that is in many ways similar to the one suggested by Edith Lentz. He sees the bank as a unique type of organization, which derives its character from (1) its role in the broader community of which it is a part; (2) its internal environment, which is highly routinized; and (3) its tendency to attract and hold those employees who are deferential to authority and who are well suited to the autocratic, regimented, and structured bank environment.

In a recent study of human relations in a bank, a hiring officer described what he regards as the "right type" of employee.[1] In judging job applicants, he said:

* From *Administrative Science Quarterly*, 3, No. 1 (June 1958), 87–106. Reprinted by permission.
[1] Chris Argyris, "Human Relations in a Bank," *Harvard Business Review*, 32 (Sept.–Oct. 1954), 66. See also his "Some Problems of Conceptualizing Organizational Climate: A Case Study of a Bank, "*Administrative Science Quarterly*, 2 (1958), 501–520.

We always ask who recommends them and usually we know a little about the other person. We also consider the individual—is he sloppy, is he neat, are his fingernails clean, and what sort of poise does he have. His approach, you know, that's an important thing for me. For example, I had a young kid come in the other day to apply for a job. Without saying anything he pulled out a package of cigarettes and started smoking. Now imagine that—a junior in high school saunters in here and starts smoking without even asking if he could—so I knew that wasn't the type for us and I let him go. I usually like a certain kind of youngster—a quiet youngster, slightly on the nervous side. Oh, I don't mean that he or she should be completely upset, but I think that's the kind of person we are looking for. They should have a certain amount of poise and should not do too much talking.

This quotation suggests that the roots of some of the personnel and management problems confronting large banks today are to be found in the standards used in employee selection and in the personalities of the officers charged with these and allied responsibilities. That banks are having difficulties in this area is evidenced by their present concern with personnel problems, some of which are quite acute. Discussions with bankers reveal that they are particularly concerned with three conditions:

1. The lack of qualified candidates for chief executive officer (with the result that a number of banks have had to go outside to fill this position).

2. The fact that many bank employees are not up to par; they lack some important quality; they are inferior.[2]

3. The fact that there is never any assurance that even the most trusted employee will not defalcate.

Disparate as these problems may seem, they have a common source: the nature of banking as a business; the bank's special place in its community; and, as a result, the type of person who is attracted to banking as a career. In contrast to most commercial enterprises which function in a competitive enviroment, a bank is an institution characterized by dignity and conservatism. There is relatively little pressure in a bank, which partakes of some of the qualities of a juridical or governing body.

Four conditions contribute particularly to the personnel problems of banks:

1. Senior bank officers usually enjoy a position of special prestige and distinction in their communities. Not only are they regarded as authority figures, comparable to the physician and the clergyman, but in their day-to-day business dealings they tend to be in a superior status position (as contrasted, for example, to that of a salesman who is essentially a suppliant) as a result of their economic power over the borrower. Such circumstances can create in a bank officer an exalted conception of his importance and omniscience and can foster the growth of any inherent authoritarian tendencies. The very elegance of many banking houses and of the officers' quarters in them and the awe which they create in the average citizen may contribute further to the banker's idealized conception of himself.

[2] Argyris, "Human Relations in a Bank," p. 64.

2. The routine nature of the majority of the operations in a bank, with their major emphasis on checks and balances, makes the almost total structuring of each activity inevitable. Even in extending credit, bankers have well-established standards to guide them, for example, the current ratios, capital ratios, inventory ratios, sales ratios, and net profit ratios. Except at the very top levels of management no decision making or risk taking of consequence is required of anyone. In the intermediate levels a committee usually decides. At the bottom the clerk or teller simply follows instructions. Every contingency has been provided for. In the rare instance that an unusual situation arises, a superior is available to consult— and to approve the action to be taken. This makes regimentation and autocratic management almost inevitable; there is little room, at least in the lower echelons, for much freedom of action.

3. Over the years a stereotype has developed which defines the "right type" of bank employee. He is neat, clean, well groomed, comes from a good family, speaks quietly, uses good grammar, and is properly deferential to authority figures. If, as in the instance already cited, he is also a little nervous (impressed with the bank officer's position), so much the better. He is the submissive type who has always done what he was told. He has never given either his parents or his teachers a moment's concern. Obviously, not all bank employees are of this type; nevertheless, a number approximate it closely. What is more, this is a type which fits in well in the hushed, unhurried, cathedral-like milieu of many of the older banks.

4. Men and women who conform to this stereotype have been sought for and hired by banks for many years. Most of them have stayed (those who are less submissive and conformist are the ones who have left, voluntarily or by request). Through seniority many of these "right types" have become officers. In turn, they have been charged with the hiring of new employees. They have thus tended to perpetuate their type, to hire in their own images.

It is this "right type" of employee who is now being recognized as lacking in the capacity to become the bank's chief executive officer. While he is well adapted to the role of deferential subordinate in an autocratic, regimented, and structured bank environment, he is less well suited to the rough and tumble of today's competition; as business pressures become more acute, the inadequacies of this type of employee become more apparent.

Insofar as work environment and selection criteria are concerned, we have found that banks have a strong attraction to persons with a passive-dependent-submissive type of personality configuration. This personality type is defined by a relatively consistent pattern of reaction in interpersonal relationships that tends to reduce anxiety by deference to authority. While others may find withdrawal or aggression a more satisfactory mode of accommodation, the passive type has learned that submission is the most satisfactory posture for him. Dependency, then, refers "to behavior which seems to have as its goal the obtaining of nurturance from other people, or which clearly indicates that reliance upon the help of others is the individual's dominant method of striving for his goals."[3] It is such patterns of behavior that define "personality."[4] Such conclusions suggest that employment in a bank satisfies needs which are deeply embedded in the dependent individual's personality. Chief among these are:

1. A high degree of job security. (Few banks fail any longer.)
2. High social status and prestige in the community (as contrasted with work in a factory or in "trade").
3. Regularity of employment; a predictable future; a career which can be plotted well in advance. (The "right type" can hope to progress "through the chairs" from teller to senior officer if he is patient and sufficiently "other directed.")[5]
4. Pleasant working conditions (short hours, comfortable quarters, numerous holidays, little or no manual labor, little pressure).
5. Such a high degree of job structuring or routinization that there is seldom any need to make decisions, exercise judgment, or take risks (all but the senior positions require mainly diligence, conscientiousness, and a proper respect for constituted authority).

These positive features of employment in a bank have such a powerful appeal that many persons are willing to accept such less attractive features as:

1. The pay may be low (compensation in any vocation tends to be in inverse proportion to the degree to which a job is structured and is, therefore, free from risk-taking and decision-making responsibility).
2. Promotions tend to come slowly (being determined principally by seniority).
3. The routinized system under which many employees work discourages initiative, imagination, and creativeness (tradition and precedents rule).

The status needs of many bank employees are so strong that they will not join a union in spite of the fact that membership would probably better their lot. The failure of unions to organize bank employees seems due less to any special competence on the part of bank personnel officers than to the fact that employees regard unions as instruments of the working class, with which they do not care to be identified.

Security, structuring, and regimentation thus seem necessary to persons with passive, dependent, and submissive personality structures. One may even rank vocations in terms of the degree to which they offer satisfaction to particular needs and hence appeal to particular types. At the one extreme of total structuring and regimentation is the penitentiary, the inmates of which include recidivists whose need for submission and dependence has led them to make a career of life behind bars. Next come various religious orders, followed closely by the armed services in peace-

---

[3] Irvin L. Child, "Socialization," in Gardner Lindzey, ed., *Handbook of Social Psychology* (Cambridge, Mass., 1954) II, 672.

[4] Among others, see David Krech and R. Crutchfield, *Theory and Problems of Social Psychology* (New York, 1948), pp. 65, 183–186.

[5] David Riesman, *The Lonely Crowd* (New Haven, 1950).

time. After them come positions in civil service, the railroads, the utilities, insurance companies, and banks. All of these vocations (except the first two) show rather similar patterns of security, structuring, regimentation, slow advancement, little pleasure (except in a few special positions), and low pay. Once the center of the continuum is passed, however, the characteristics of the vocations begin to change and with this the type of person attracted to them. Salesmen who work on straight commission, professional men, small businessmen, entrepreneurs, and, finally, speculators enjoy progressively less security; there is little structuring and regimentation, since the individual makes his own job. On the other hand, there is usually relatively rapid advancement, a considerable amount of pressure, and at the same time opportunity for high compensation.

These propositions lead to the question why so many people, well over half the working population, seek positions which offer a high degree of security and structuring, with a consequent sacrifice of earnings and upward mobility. Why are some individuals content to remain clerks and tellers while others (not necessarily because they are well qualified) aspire to more demanding and, at the same time, more rewarding positions?

In part, the answer seems to lie in the nature of the individual's personality make-up as it is developed in childhood.[6] Either the child is never completely weaned emotionally (his parents have been overprotective or have continued to dominate him), or he has been brought up in such a loveless and threatening environment that he has never dared to become self-reliant. In either event, when he is expected to begin to stand on his own feet, to make his own decisions and to accept responsibility, he becomes terrified. On reaching late adolescence or adulthood he suddenly finds himself isolated from those who formerly provided love and reassurance. The prospect of facing a strange, formidable, and threatening world alone overwhelms him with anxiety.[7]

Some young people react to the shock by becoming mentally ill; they become schizophrenic or make use of some other flight mechanism, for example, narcotic addiction. Most, however, respond by seeking to regain the lost security of childhood. They look for parental surrogates among persons who have power, strength, and authority and attempt to establish the same type of relationship—attachment, dependence, and submission—which they enjoyed with their parents. In most cases they earned the support and approbation of the latter by being "good" boys and girls, industrious, conscientious, and docile. As employees they repeat their childhood behavior pattern; they become the "good soldiers," the loyal, conscientious workers.

In a relatively protected and structured work environment where supervision tends to be authoritarian, such persons make excellent employees. They personify bourgeois, copybook virtues. But their major

---

[6] Among others, see H. S. Sullivan, *The Interpersonal Theory of Psychiatry* (New York, 1953), pp. 49–187; E. H. Erikson, *Childhood and Society* (New York, 1950); J. Dollard *et al.*, *Frustration and Aggression* (New Haven, 1939).

[7] For an analysis of this problem, see Erich Fromm, *Escape from Freedom* (New York, 1941), pp. 29–32; Karen Horney, *The Neurotic Personality of Our Time* (New York, 1937).

weakness lies in the fact that they are typically passive, incapable of accepting responsibility, of making important decisions, of taking risks, or of exercising leadership. It is this type of person who finds security and a structured position which relieve him of the need to make decisions so necessary that to obtain them he is willing to forego adequate compensation and rapid upward mobility.

This does not mean that everyone who applies for work in a bank is of this type. Unfortunately, however, the more self-reliant applicants may not impress the hiring officers as being of the "right type." The young man who lit a cigarette without asking the hiring officer's permission was summarily rejected. He was neither anxious nor properly deferential. Perhaps this youth would not have made a good bank employee on other grounds; it is hard to say, because he was eliminated before much was learned about his qualifications. The danger is that perhaps other, potentially well-qualified applicants were eliminated because they were not properly submissive. The question may even be raised: Are the hiring standards of the banking industry such that applicants qualified to assume positions of real leadership are systematically excluded?

Inevitably, however, if only by chance, some aggressive young people will be taken into the bank. What happens to them? Probably a minority will stay because fortuitously they find a position which provides the challenge and opportunity they need. But what about the majority? If a normal labor market is assumed, for how long will they be willing to accept the low pay, the regimentation, the slow upward progress, and the stifling of initiative with which the beginner must contend? Ordinarily, not for very long. Just as their nonconformist attitudes will make their co-workers and superiors uncomfortable, so will the latter's docility and submissiveness tend to lower them in the aggressive beginners' estimation. Since these are persons with some degree of initiative and self-reliance, they are willing to take a calculated risk and seek a position elsewhere.

Thus a second negative selection device becomes operative. Not only are many potential leaders screened out initially, but of those who are hired, a substantial proportion are likely to leave after a short period of service. The result is a supersaturation of the "right type" in bank personnel—of those who are intelligent, technically competent, and socially gracious but who have high dependency needs. Not only are most of these passive, submissive employees not qualified to be top executives, but also the majority are often not even loyal to their superiors and employers. Superficially, docile and submissive employees of this kind might be thought to be automatons dedicated wholly and naïvely to meeting their superiors' expectations in as thorough, albeit sometimes mindless, a fashion as they can. This behavior seems characteristic of a few, but unfortunately far from all, owing to two peculiar psychological phenomena. (1) Dependence rarely brings with it a true sense of security. On the contrary, it tends to enhance insecurity and create fresh anxieties. This fear may be verbalized as: "What does my superior on whom I am dependent think of me? Is it possible that he no longer loves me, that he will reject and abandon me?" (2) Excessive dependence makes the individual ashamed of himself. It conflicts with his conception of himself as a man, the American stereotype in which every male is virile, aggressive, and self-reliant. Since he obviously cannot blame himself for his dependence, he must find a scapegoat. This he frequently discovers to be his superior or the bank as an institution. He convinces himself that it was not *he* who came of his own free will to depend upon his superior or his employer as a parental surrogate; it is their fault; they have, so to speak, seduced him by their provision of support and help. He feels justified, therefore, in feeling resentful toward those upon whom he is dependent.

Docility and submissiveness are thus no guarantee of loyalty. In fact, the opposite condition seems much more likely; under their veneer of obsequiousness a large number, perhaps a majority, of lower-echelon bank employees hate their superiors. Because such employees are afraid to express their hostilities openly, many do it covertly. The result is that they are often careless and uninterested in their work. They are prone to take out their dissatisfactions on the bank's customers and particularly to sabotage higher management's programs by passive resistance, by giving them lip service but never bringing them to fruition.

Most critical, this undercurrent of latent hostility makes it easy for the employee to rationalize and condone his dishonesty. Not only does he feel little guilt in theft, but also he has the tacit support of many of his associates in his activities. It is not difficult for him to rationalize that he has been mistreated and underpaid, and hence he is justified in retaliating by taking "what is justly due him," that is, by "borrowing from the bank" (it is interesting that few employees think of their defalcations as theft—all intend to repay the "loans" they make to themselves). This psychological mechanism permits otherwise conscientious and meticulously honest individuals to justify embezzlement to themselves, to steal with a clear conscience. Indeed, one of the chief problems in detecting potential embezzlers is the fact that they are frequently among the most faithful of employees. This counterattack provides them with a technique for hurting the bank in its most sensitive spot—its exchequer.

Not only do these passive, dependent individuals have limitations as rank-and-file employees; they are even less well qualified to lead in middle and top management positions. Having spent all their working lives in well-structured positions, they have had little opportunity to make decisions, to take risks, and, particularly, to work through people. When they are made supervisors they are often nonplussed. Usually no one has told them what their duties and authority are or what is expected of them. Few banks have detailed descriptions of first- and second-line supervisory positions, nor are employees instructed in even the rudiments of how to supervise. As a consequence, such employees sometimes find themselves in an almost totally strange and unstructured situation. The attributes and tactics (technical competence, industry, conformity, conservatism, and deference to superiors) which have served them so well in nonsupervisory positions are of no help.

The new supervisor's reaction may take either of two extremes. Frequently he may simply abdicate his supervisory responsibilities and permit his subordinates to do much as they wish. This appeared to be the predominant response in the bank studied by Argyris.[8] The officers here summarized the weakness in their own group as follows:

> The officers ought to command and direct more. They ought to learn how to get people to work harder. They ought to show more enthusiasm and "push" in dealing with their people.

> The officers ought to be less backward. They should not fear to reprimand, whenever that is necessary.

From the subordinates' point of view this weak supervision has some very pleasant aspects. As Argyris points out, "Since the leadership is weak, the employees have plenty of opportunity to just 'get by.' This leads them to think of the bank as 'an easy place to work,' 'no one breathes down your neck,' 'you don't have to kill yourself,' 'little pressure' and so on."[9] On the other hand, such weak superiors provide no security for their subordinates. They tend to be indecisive and incapable of providing their people the support they often need. Hence organizations with this type of leaders tend to have poor employee morale.

Other supervisors react to their anxieties by exhibiting an opposite, overcompensatory behavior. They develop into authoritarian personalities, typical pompous petty bureaucrats with many of the power-oriented values described by Adorno et al.[10] Their outstanding trait is a Januslike submissiveness to their superiors (upon whom they are still extremely dependent) combined with a thrust for unrestricted power over their subordinates.[11] Often they use their power for personal aggrandizement or, since they are somewhat sadistic, to embarrass, humiliate, or cause suffering among those subject to their authority. They are also extremely status conscious. They prefer subordinates who are bootlickers. Both the exercise of power and the possession of status with all of its symbols serve to conceal from themselves and others the extent of their own weakness and dependency.

They are also incapable of delegating authority, partly because they fear that they might be held responsible for their subordinates' mistakes and partly because delegation tends to build and strengthen those below. Since such supervisors fear strong subordinates as threats to their security, they usually see to it that those below them are weaker than they. Hence they complain about the weakness of those reporting to them and the resultant unreasonable demands upon them; thus they can rationalize their tendencies to take flight into detail. By keeping themselves overburdened with trivia they both impress their superiors with their dedication to their work and also find an excuse to avoid making decisions or initiating action.

---

[8] Argyris, "Human Relations in a Bank," p. 65.

[9] Ibid.

[10] For a detailed analysis, see T. W. Adorno et al., The Authoritarian Personality (New York, 1950). An excellent critique of this work will be found in R. Christie and M. Jahoda, Studies in the Scope and Method of "The Authoritarian Personality" (Glencoe, Ill., 1954), pp. 50–122.

[11] For a fuller description of this type, see Robert N. McMurry, "Manhunt for Top Executives," Harvard Business Review, 32 (Jan.–Feb. 1954), 54.

Such supervisors invariably tend to be "work" rather than "people" centered in dealing with their subordinates.

Under this type of weak but autocratic supervision, morale is almost invariably poor. The tendency for submissive people to be ambivalent toward authority is accentuated by real grievances and frustrations which have been repressed because the employees fear to voice them. Such dissatisfactions tend to accumulate, and the enterprise comes to be permeated with an air of quiet desperation marked by retaliatory efforts to sabotage management's objectives. In addition, "inner" and "outer" cliques tend to form about the autocratic superior. Their members constantly play politics and vie among themselves for his favor. Often, also, unusually submissive "scapegoats" are found, upon whom the superior and the members of his entourage can with impunity project their own resentments.

Because banks attract many dependent and insecure persons, it is almost inevitable that they have a disproportionate number of authoritarian supervisors. Since it is the policy of most financial organizations to promote from within, it is not unlikely that persons of this type come to be seeded throughout management and even sometimes to emerge as president. Although the presence of this type of supervisor in middle management hurts employee morale, its effect upon the day-to-day functioning of the bank is usually negligible because of the degree to which everyone's work is structured. From the vice-president down, everyone "goes by the book." The bank tends to be hidebound in its policies and practices, but unless faced with unusual stresses, it will survive. One of the advantages of such highly structured enterprises is that, once established and given momentum, they can carry on for long periods with second-rate management.

The most serious problem confronting many banks is the choice of a chief executive or operating officer (assuming that this role is not taken by one of the directors). This role is that of entrepreneur-manager. Often he alone establishes the bank's policies, makes the decisions, and takes the risks. Although even this position is structured to some extent by banking laws, practices, and so forth, it is the least structured position in the organization. The chief officer's position is qualitatively different from that of his subordinates. It demands an ability to plan, to take risks, to initiate, and, above all, to rise above mindless conformity. But the very fact that an individual's needs for security and structuring were so intense that he was willing to endure the frustrations of advancement by seniority and that he has spent from ten to thirty years in a structured environment makes his suitability for the top position questionable. Probably because many boards of directors have sensed this, a large number of bank presidents have been brought in from outside the institutions which they are to administer.

Under the most favorable circumstances the role of the chief operating officer is an exacting one. If he is lacking in the necessary courage and toughness of fiber, even though this is well concealed by a compensatory absolutism, he is headed for trouble. In the face of the problems he must meet and the risks he must take, he will be likely to develop an executive neurosis.[12] Under the pressures of his job he may become openly indecisive, be subject to chronic anxiety and worry, experience difficulty in controlling his temper, and develop an incapacity to face issues. His judgments may be increasingly influenced by his emotional needs for security, status, and power. Since judgments of this sort are prone to error, he may often find himself subsequently beset by new difficulties which, in turn, create fresh anxieties. The end result is a slowly mounting state of internal tension which may ultimately precipitate a "flight" of one sort or another. Most common are flights from decision making, in which the executive makes every excuse, including some very transparent ones, to avoid making a decision. This indecisiveness can also take the form of a literal flight from the job, that is, the executive simply ceases to devote an adequate amount of time to his work. Most common, however, is the "flight into illness." The victim begins to suffer from some type of psychogenic disorder, for example, insomnia, ulcers, colitis, hypertension, allergies, or alcoholism.

Thus the problems of developing a qualified chief executive, of weak middle management, of substandard personnel, and of employees who embezzle seem to have a common source—the type of person who is attracted to a bank as a place to work and who stays there.

SOME REMEDIAL PROPOSALS

While there is no simple, sovereign remedy for these problems any solution rests upon the personality, vision, and over-all competence of the chief executive officer of the bank. Certainly such problems cannot usually be delegated to the personnel department, which is too low in the executive hierarchy to have either the perspective or the authority to cope with them. For several reasons they must be the responsibility of the chief executive officer, who can see the operation in broad perspective, who has the necessary authority to take needed action, and upon whom depends, in the final analysis, the character of the entire institution, its practices, its policies, its management philosophy, and its goals. No scientific selection systems, no employee morale studies, and no executive development programs can have appreciable effect without his continuing and active support. If he is not convinced of the acuteness of these problems and is not motivated to correct them, little can be accomplished.

If it is assumed that the chief executive wants to attack these problems, he must first recognize that little can be accomplished overnight. A corrective program must be geared to the assumption that a minimum of five years will be required before significant results may be expected. This is because no radical replacement program can be undertaken among existing executive and supervisory personnel or, for that matter, among rank-and-file employees. To force turnover is costly and usually ill-advised. The bank therefore will have to do principally with the people it has. Moreover, it is difficult, if not impossible, to effect notable changes in individual personality, defined as a relatively consistent way of organizing experience.

[12] For a discussion of this condition see Robert N. McMurry, "The Executive Neurosis," *Harvard Business Review*, 30 (Nov.–Dec. 1952), 33–47.

Even with young people few appreciable changes can be effected because this demands therapy, and even a skilled psychiatrist can rarely bring about more than marginal alterations in a person's make-up. It seems wholly untenable that an individual who has been passive, dependent, and submissive for his entire life will respond to any influences brought about by the bank alone to make him self-reliant. For these reasons the following program is oriented toward the work milieu rather than toward individual therapy.

Such a program might well begin with a careful analysis of the nature, content, and demands of the major positions in the bank. Such a statement must encompass much more than the traditional statement of job duties and responsibilities. It must include a measure of the degree to which each position is structured. The extent to which decision making and risk taking are elements of each position is of crucial importance. Management's philosophy must also be taken into account, that is, is it autocratic, manipulative, participative, or laissez-faire? Finally, allowance must be made for the competence and personality requirements of first- and second-line and top supervision as a critical feature of the position itself. This expanded kind of job analysis serves three functions: (1) it permits the establishment of standards for use in the selection of new employees; (2) it serves as a basis for an evaluation of the qualifications of present job incumbents; and (3) it makes possible the preparation of an integrated organization chart.

Next, one might appraise the qualifications of the occupants of each of the positions for which descriptions have been prepared (see Appendix). Here a special type of merit rating known as the patterned merit review has proved useful.[13] Such a rating (1) provides an inventory of the bank's human resources, (2) yields data which can serve as a basis for a program to help those who are either under- or overqualified for their job, and (3) identifies those who clearly have potential for promotion. As previously indicated, while the attempt to change the individual to adapt him better to his work does not appear practical, this does not preclude the use of the opposite approach—the alteration of his job content and environment to adapt it better to his needs and qualifications. (In psychiatry, this is called "milieu therapy.") With both job specifications and an appraisal of each employee available, this adaptation of the job to the man through the reconstitution of the former is possible. Although not always easy, it offers greater promise than an attempt to change the man to fit the job, which is nearly always impossible of success.

After attempting to use existing personnel to the fullest, the organization can be reviewed to determine which positions cannot be filled from within. The job specifications which have been developed serve to define the characteristics of the persons needed and sometimes even to suggest where they may be found. These same standards later provide the criteria against which candidates' qualifications are measured. If management recognizes that such attributes as self-reliance, initiative, and leadership ability are more important than conformity to the "right-type" model,

---

[13] For a description of the patterned merit review procedure, see Robert E. Shaeffer, "Merit Rating as a Management Tool," *Harvard Business Review*, 27 (Nov. 1949), 693–705.

the first step in the recruitment of a more promising type of employee will have been made. This does not mean that each person employed must be a potential chief executive officer. Every bank must have career clerks and tellers. Nevertheless, candidates for supervisory and other middle-management positions will be less likely to be selected primarily because they are passive and dependent.

Where it is necessary to fill the top or other senior positions, all the more responsible bank officers must, of course, be given consideration. In such instances the appraisal procedure must be supplemented by clinical evaluation techniques, consisting of measures of intelligence, projective tests (for example, the Thematic Apperception Test), and a comprehensive patterned interview. For those applying from the outside, personnel or telephone checks must be made with universities and previous employers to verify the statements which the candidates make.[14] Through the use of these combined psychometric and clinical procedures, it is possible to assess both the applicant's technical competence and his personality make-up. Tendencies to be passive, dependent, submissive, and conformist can usually be recognized at the outset. In some instances, despite manifest limitations, the applicants who present themselves may be the best candidates available and must be hired. Nevertheless, when such candidates are employed, the nature and extent of their limitations can be recognized. In the main, however, these techniques are designed to identify a more aggressive, self-reliant type of employee. By bringing in such replacements, the management of the bank may gradually upgrade the level of potential among the employees.

In this connection, however, it must be said that the majority of the openings in a bank are thoroughly structured, are routine in nature, and will continue to offer low pay and little opportunity for advancement. There will thus always be a place for numerous passive, dependent individuals. But they must be recognized for what they are and not considered for promotion into middle management. Actually only a limited number of potential leaders and executives are required by most banks. The bulk of the clerical and lower-level supervisory positions do not demand either a high level of competence or strong leadership. In the long run the greatest hope for banks probably lies in a maximum degree of automation, which will reduce the need for the human automatons who do much of the routine work today.

THE PROBLEM OF MORALE

Although most bank jobs are already fully structured and routinized in their technical aspects, this does not mean that the employee has been given a clear statement of his supervisors' expectations. All too often he has no clear indication of the objectives of his work or of just what constitutes acceptable performance. Similar ignorance exists in the areas of interpersonal relations and policy interpretation. These expecta-

[14] For a discussion of this procedure, see Robert N. McMurry, *The Step-by-Step Selection Program* (Chicago, 1955).

tions and relationships ordinarily are not clearly spelled out. Because the employee does not know quite what to do, he tends to play it safe and do nothing. Nevertheless, ambiguity makes him anxious; it is a threat to his security and bad for his morale. One answer, therefore, at least in the lower echelons, is the provision of more detailed statements of supervisory expectations and relationships for each activity. In practice this means that almost every phase of every job must be discussed in descriptive manuals supplemented by periodic statements of supervisory expectations and close supervision so that any questions not covered in the manuals can be answered quickly.

Effective outlets for employee dissatisfaction are also difficult to establish. In theory the disgruntled employee brings his troubles to his supervisor; in practice he rarely does so. There are several reasons for this: (1) the supervisor may be the object of the grievance, in which case the employee may be understandably reluctant to discuss the problem with him; (2) the employee may lack confidence in the supervisor's integrity or in his desire to help him; (3) the supervisor may be inaccessible or unwilling to listen; and (4) the employee may be extremely introverted and reluctant or unable to discuss his problems with anyone. In addition to these barriers, many supervisors are afraid to permit their subordinates to express such dissatisfactions for fear that their superiors, that is, top management, will learn of them to their personal disadvantage. Hence they discourage any expressions of dissatisfaction, regardless of their merit. Where employees find inadequate outlets for their dissatisfactions, these, as noted, tend to emerge as a generalized anti-management sentiment.

The chief cause of poor employee morale in most banks, however, seems to be an almost total absence of clear channels of internal communication. As Argyris points out, the "right type" dislikes either to express aggression or hostility or to have these feelings expressed toward him. "Good" employees do not behave in an aggressive or hostile manner.[15] Hence most of their feelings remain bottled up. It is true that keeping these feelings "inside" and at the same time working effectively are not easy to accomplish. As one employee put it: "This takes a lot out of you. Sometimes I'm dead tired when I go home at night." As a result there is a minimum of employee interaction. Their relations are impersonal; they are polite, but few discuss personal feelings. In the bank Argyris studied, 90 per cent of the employees defined "nice people" as those who are "polite and leave you alone." Ninety-three per cent stated that they had no close friends in the organization.

Superimposed upon this inhibitive tendency of the employees is the fact that, as already noted, upward communication through supervision tends to be inadequate. Downward communication is strictly one way—from management out, without any feedback to ascertain how well the bank's message has been assimilated. Furthermore, much of what is communicated is admonitory in character and is often empty and pretentious. In consequence, even though it may wishfully be convinced to the con-

15 Argyris, "Human Relations in a Bank," p. 68.

trary, top bank management rarely knows the attitudes of its rank-and-file employees.

Nor do many of these top executives really care very much. They give "human relations" lip service but little more. In the larger banks they do not know many of their subordinates well. Having been raised in an autocratic management climate, they think of employees much as they think of the bank's cash and other assets—as a part of the complex mechanism which gets things done. They are not cruel, just impersonal. Most of them are "figure minded." They are most comfortable when dealing with the precision and tangibility of figures; people, with their unpredictability, disturb them. They have little capacity for empathy, the ability to sense and "feel themselves into" the emotional reactions of others.

On the other hand, lower-ranking employees are removed from top management by great and varied "distances." While they are similar in that they are often of the "right type," time and promotions have separated them widely. Differences in their status, authority, compensation, and resulting off-the-job social and cultural environments are often tremendous. These distances in a bank are similar to those between the general and the private in the army. Because of them the clerk knows as little about the president of the bank and the other senior officers as they do about him; in short, top management and the workers in banks are almost total strangers. As strangers they tend naturally to distrust each other; it is not surprising that bank officers refer to the bulk of employees as "not up to par" and that the employees tend to believe that they are systematically disadvantaged by the officers.

The answer to improved employee morale probably lies in a large measure in improved internal communication, together with a willingness of the chief executive officer to take action on legitimate employee complaints, for example, that of low wages. If he is unwilling to do this, the entire communication and morale program may as well be abandoned; it will simply be viewed as further proof that top management is indifferent to its employees' welfare. If the president is genuinely desirous of helping his people, an initial step might be to conduct an employee opinion poll to ascertain who is dissatisfied and why. The findings of the poll, together with proposed remedies, may then be reported by the bank to the employees whose comments have been solicited. In this way true two-way communication can be eased.

But the improvement of upward internal communication in a bank is not easy, because any proposed change will arouse fresh anxieties in every level of supervision. Each will be fearful that his control of what is reported to *his* superiors will be lost, that is, that his inability to stifle and block certain information will enable his superiors to learn of conditions which will reflect adversely upon *him*. Middle management may thus complain that a poll will only "create dissatisfactions" (presumably where none existed before) and that it "will not reveal anything that we don't already know." These rationalizations mainly represent defenses against the possibility that the poll findings will be embarrassing to the supervisors personally and that, most important, the poll will reveal to top management much that it did *not* already know.

CONCLUSION

Many banks have managed to survive during the past twenty years, partly because the economic climate has been favorable, partly because the weakest went under during the depression, partly because new fiscal controls and safeguards have been introduced, partly because they have not encountered very aggressive competition; at the same time, they have all been remiss in their personnel practices. A number have personnel departments, but few of these have either the insight or the power to be more than record-keeping employment offices, with occasional employee service facilities such as counseling, feeding, and recreation.

Yet if banks are to meet increasing competition both among themselves and with outside agencies, for example, small-loan chains, mutual funds for savings, and so on, they must recognize that employees of the "right type" are not going to keep them competitive. Banking must become more dynamic and aggressive. It can no longer survive on its dignity as an "institution." This change requires strong chief executive officers, supported by a staff which is more creative and dynamic than those revealed in our research. It must introduce as much automation as possible at the lower levels to free its clerks from drudgery and to attract and to hold employees who want challenge and opportunity rather than solely security and status. Most important, it must recognize that personnel policy is a *line* rather than a staff function, that is, it is a major responsibility of the bank's chief executive officer, not something that is limited to hiring and training methods, the management of the cafeteria and the bowling league, and the provision of counsel to aspiring but frustrated junior clerks.

THE SOCIAL STRUCTURE OF THE RESTAURANT
*William F. Whyte**

In this selection, William F. Whyte presents the results of his studies of the restaurant industry. His analysis indicates that unique factors operate in this industry, and that there are justifications for recognizing it as a "species" of administration. In addition, he points to the relationship of the characteristics of the restaurant to factors such as interaction patterns, physical lay-out of work, communication systems, status symbols.

While research has provided a large and rapidly growing fund of knowledge concerning the social organization of a factory, studies of other

* Reprinted from *The American Journal of Sociology*, LIV (January 1949), 302–310, by permission of The University of Chicago Press. Copyright 1949 by The University of Chicago.

industrial and business structures are only beginning. Sociologists who are concerned with working out the comparative structures of economic organizations must therefore look beyond as well as into the factory. This paper represents one effort in that direction. It grows out of a fourteen-month study of restaurants.[1] We do not claim to have studied a representative sample of restaurants. In an industry having so many types of operations and sizes of units, such a task would have taken years. We did aim to find out, at least in a general way, what sort of structure a restaurant is and what human problems are found within it.

Here I shall present a schematic picture of the findings as they bear upon problems of social structure. I am also using the discussion of research findings to illustrate certain points of theory and methodology in studies of social structures. Discussions of theory and methodology, divorced from the research data upon which the theory and methods are to be used, are generally fruitless. In a brief paper, discussion of our research findings must necessarily be sketchy, but that will provide a basis for at least tentative conclusions.

CHARACTERISTICS OF THE RESTAURANT

The restaurant is a combination production and service unit. It differs from the factory, which is solely a production unit, and also from the retail store, which is solely a service unit.

The restaurant operator produces a perishable product for immediate sale. Success requires a delicate adjustment of supply to demand and skilful co-ordination of production with service. The production and service tie-up not only makes for difficult human problems of co-ordinating action but adds a new dimension to the structure of the organization: the customer-employee relationship.

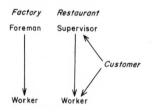

The contrast between factory and restaurant can be illustrated by this simple diagram, representing the direction of orders in the two structures:[2]

The problems of co-ordination and customer relations are relatively simple in the small restaurant, but they become much more difficult as

[1] The research was financed by the National Restaurant Association. The field work was done by Margaret Chandler, Edith Lentz, John Schaefer, and William Whyte. We made interview or participant-observation studies of twelve restaurants in Chicago and did some brief interviewing outside Chicago. From one to four months was spent upon each Chicago restaurant. In *Human Relations in the Restaurant Industry* (New York: McGraw-Hill Book Co., 1948), I report the study in detail. Since the book is primarily addressed to restaurant operators and supervisors, the sociological frame of reference given here does not duplicate the more detailed publication.

[2] This is, of course, an oversimplified picture, for many factory workers interact also with inspectors, engineers, time-study men, etc., but the frequency of such interaction does not compare with that which we observe between customers and waiters or waitresses in a restaurant.

the organization grows. This may be illustrated structurally in terms of five stages of growth.[3]

In the first stage, we have a small restaurant where the owner and several other employees dispense short orders over the counter. There is little division of labor. The owner and employees serve together as cooks, countermen, and dishwashers.

In the second stage, the business is still characterized by the informality and flexibility of its relationships. The boss knows most customers and all his employees on a personal basis. There is no need for formal controls and elaborate paper work. Still, the organization has grown in complexity as it has grown in size. The volume of business is such that it becomes necessary to divide the work, and we have dishwashers and kitchen employees, as well as those who wait on the customers. Now the problems of co-ordination begin to grow also, but the organization is still small enough so that the owner-manager can observe directly a large part of its activities and step in to straighten out friction or inefficiency.

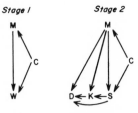

Stage 1   Stage 2

M—Manager   S—Service employees
C—Customers   K—Kitchen employees
W—Workers   D—Dishwashers

As the business continues to expand, it requires a still more complex organization as well as larger quarters. No longer able to supervise all activities directly, the owner-manager hires a service supervisor, a food production supervisor, and places one of his employees in charge of the dishroom as a working supervisor. He also employs a checker to total checks for his waitresses and see that the food is served in correct portions and style.

In time, the owner-manager finds that he can accommodate a larger number of customers if he takes one more step in the division of labor. Up to now the cooks have been serving the food to the waitresses. When these functions are divided, both cooking and serving can proceed more efficiently. Therefore, he sets up a service pantry apart from the kitchen. The cooks now concentrate on cooking, the runners carry food from kitchen to pantry and carry orders from pantry to kitchen, and the pantry girls serve the waitresses over the counter. This adds two more groups (pantry girls and runners) to be supervised, and, to cope with this and the larger scale of operation, the owner adds another level of supervision, so that there are two supervisors between himself and the workers. Somewhere along the

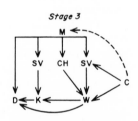

Stage 3

M—Manager   W—Waitress
SV—Supervisor   K—Kitchen worker
CH—Checker
C—Customer   D—Dishwasher

[3] I am indebted to Donald Wray for the particular structural approach presented here.

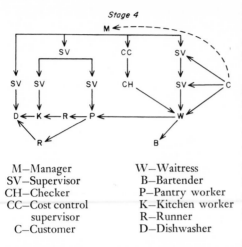

Stage 4

M—Manager
SV—Supervisor
CH—Checker
CC—Cost control
　　supervisor
C—Customer

W—Waitress
B—Bartender
P—Pantry worker
K—Kitchen worker
R—Runner
D—Dishwasher

line of development, perhaps he begins serving drinks and adds bartenders to his organization.

Stage 5 need not be diagrammed here, for it does not necessarily involve any structural changes in the individual unit. Here several units are tied together into a chain, and one or more levels of authority are set up in a main office above the individual unit structures.[4]

This expansion process magnifies old problems and gives rise to new ones. They may be considered under three headings: administration, the customer relationship, and the flow of work. Whenever we lengthen the hierarchy, adding new levels of authority to separate top executive from workers, the problem of administration becomes more complex. However, this is true for any organization, and therefore these problems of hierarchy need not be given special attention in an article on restaurants.

The particular problem of the large restaurant is to tie together its line of authority with the relations that arise along the flow of work. In the first instance, this involves the customer relationship, for here is where the flow of work begins. The handling of the customer relationship is crucial for adjustment of the restaurant personnel, and a large part of that problem can be stated in strictly quantitative interaction terms: Who originates action for whom and how often? In a large and busy restaurant a waitress may take orders from fifty to one hundred customers a day (and perhaps several times for each meal) in addition to the orders (much less frequent) she receives from her supervisor. When we add to this the problem of adjusting to service-pantry workers, bartenders, and perhaps checkers, we can readily see the possibilities of emotional tension—and, in our study, we did see a number of girls break down and cry under the strain.

Our findings suggested that emotional tension could be related directly to this quantitative interaction picture. The skilful waitress, who maintained her emotional equilibrium, did not simply respond to the initiative of customers. In various obvious and subtle ways she took the play away from customers, got them responding to her, and fitted them into the pattern of her work. She was also more aggressive than the emotionally insecure in originating action for other waitresses, service-pantry people, and supervisor.

---

[4] The structural changes arising with union organization are beyond the scope of this article. They are discussed in the book, *op. cit.*, in the chapter "The Role of Union Organization."

While in the rush hour the waitress works under a good deal of tension at best, the supervisor can either add to or relieve it. Here again we can speak in quantitative terms. In one restaurant we observed a change in dining-room management when a supervisor who was skilful in originating action for customers (thus taking pressure off waitresses) and who responded frequently to the initiation of waitresses was replaced by a supervisor who had less skill in controlling customers and who originated for the girls much more frequently and seldom responded to them. (Of the new supervisor, the waitresses would say, "She's always finding something to criticize"; "She's never around when we need her"; "She's always telling you; she doesn't care what you have to say"; etc.) This change was followed by evidences of increased nervous tension, especially among the less experienced waitresses, and finally by a series of waitress resignations.

Here we see that the customer-waitress, waitress-supervisor, waitress–service-pantry-worker relationships are interdependent parts of a social system. Changes in one part of the system will necessarily lead to changes in other parts. Furthermore, if the people involved in the system are to maintain their emotional balance, there must be some sort of compensatory activity to meet large interactional changes. For example, when waitresses are subject to a large increase in the originations of customers (at the peak of rush hours), the supervisor allows them to originate action for her with increasing frequency and diminishes the frequency with which she gives them orders. This is, in fact, the sort of behavior we have observed among supervisors who enjoy the closest co-operation with waitresses, as reported by the waitresses.

The customer relationship is, of course, only one point along the flow of work which brings orders from dining-room to kitchen and food from kitchen to dining-room. In a large restaurant operating on several floors, this is a long chain which may break down at any point, thus leading to emotional explosions in all quarters. The orders may go from waitress to pantry girl and then, as the pantry girl runs low in supplies, from pantry girl to pantry supplyman, from pantry supplyman to kitchen supplyman, and from kitchen supplyman to cook. And the food comes back along the same route in the opposite direction. Where drinks are served, the bar must be tied in with this flow of work, but there the chain is short and the problem less complex.

We have here a social system whose parts are interdependent in a highly sensitive manner. Thus the emotional tension experienced by waitresses is readily transmitted, link by link, all the way to the kitchen.

I have already noted how a skilful dining-room supervisor may help to relieve the tension on the entire system at its point of origin. Here we may consider other factors which affect the relations among employees along the flow of work: status, sex relations, and layout and equipment.

I would propose the hypothesis that relations among individuals along the flow of work will run more smoothly when those of higher status are in a position to originate for those of lower status in the organization and, conversely, that frictions will be observed more often when lower-status individuals seek to originate for those of higher status. (This is, of course, by no means a complete explanation of the friction or adjustment we observe.)

While more data are needed on this point, we made certain observations which tend to bear out the hypothesis. For example, in one kitchen we observed supplymen seeking to originate action (in getting food supplies) for cooks who were older, of greater seniority, more highly skilled, and much higher paid. This relationship was one of the sore points of the organization. Still, we discovered that there had been one supplyman who got along well with the cooks. When we got his story, we found that he had related himself to the cooks quite differently from the other supplymen. He sought to avoid calling orders to the cooks and instead just asked them to call him when a certain item was ready. In this way, he allowed them to increase the frequency of their origination for him, and, according to all accounts, he got better co-operation and service from the cooks than any other supplyman.

Much the same point is involved in the relations between the sexes. In our society most men grow up to be comfortable in a relationship in which they originate for women and to be uneasy, if not more seriously disturbed, when the originations go in the other direction. It is therefore a matter of some consequence how the sexes are distributed along the flow of work. On this question we gave particular attention to the dining-room–service pantry and dining-room–bar relationships.

In the dining-room–pantry situation there are four possible types of relationship by sex: waiter-counterman, waiter–pantry girl, waitress–pantry girl, and waitress-counterman. We were not able to give much attention to the first two types, but we did make intensive studies of two restaurants illustrating the third and fourth types. Ideally, for scientific purposes, we would want to hold everything else constant except for these sex differences. We had no such laboratory, but the two restaurants were nevertheless closely comparable. They were both large, busy establishments, operating on several floors, and serving the same price range of food in the same section of the city.

Perhaps the chief differences were found in the dining-room–pantry relationship itself. In restaurant A, waitresses gave their orders orally to the pantry girls. On the main serving floor of restaurant B, waitresses wrote out slips which they placed on spindles on top of a warming compartment separating them from the countermen. The men picked off the order slips, filled them, and put the plates in the compartment where the waitresses picked them up. In most cases there was no direct face-to-face interaction between waitresses and countermen, and, indeed, the warming compartment was so high that only the taller waitresses could see over its top.

These differences were not unrelated to the problems of sex in the flow of work. One of the countermen in restaurant B told us that, in all his years' experience, he had never before worked in such a wonderful place. Most workers who express such sentiments talk about their relations with their superiors or with fellow-employees on the same job or perhaps about wages, but this man had nothing to say about any of those subjects. He would discuss only the barrier that protected him from the waitresses. He described earlier experiences in other restaurants where there had been no such barrier and let us know that to be left out in the open where all the girls could call their orders in was an ordeal to which no man should be subjected. In such places, he said, there was constant wrangling.

This seems to check with experience in the industry. While we observed frictions arising between waitresses and pantry girls, such a relationship can at least be maintained with relative stability. On the other hand, it is difficult to prevent blowups between countermen and waitresses when the girls call their orders in. Most restaurants consciously or unconsciously interpose certain barriers to cut down waitress origination of action for countermen. It may be a warming compartment as in this case, or, as we observed in another restaurant, there was a man pantry supervisor who collected the order slips from the waitresses as they came in and passed them out to the countermen. There are a variety of ways of meeting the problem, but they all seem to involve this principle of social insulation.

The rule that all orders must be written also serves to cut down on interaction between waitresses and countermen, but this in itself is not always enough to eliminate friction. Where there is no physical barrier, there can be trouble unless the men who are on the receiving end of the orders work out their own system of getting out from under. Such systems we observed at one bar and at one of the serving counters in restaurant B. The counter in this case was only waist high. While the girls wrote out their orders, they were also able to try to spur the men on orally, and there was much pulling and hauling on this point both at the bar and at the pantry counter.

The men who did not get along in this relationship played a waiting game. That is, when the girls seemed to be putting on special pressure for speed, they would very obviously slow down or else even turn away from the bar or counter and not go back to work until the offending waitresses just left their order slips and stepped away themselves. Thus they originated action for the waitresses. While this defensive maneuver provided the men with some emotional satisfaction, it slowed down the service, increased the frustrations of the waitresses, and thus built up tensions, to be released in larger explosions later.

One bartender and one counterman not only enjoyed their work but were considered by waitresses to be highly efficient and pleasant to deal with. Both of them had independently worked out the same system of handling the job when the rush hour got under way. Instead of handling each order slip in turn as it was handed to them (thus responding to each individual waitress), they would collect several slips that came in at about the same time, lay them out on the counter before them, and fill the orders in whatever order seemed most efficient. For example, the bartender would go through the slips to see how many "Martinis," "Old Fashions," and so on were required. Then he would make up all the "Martinis" at once before he went on to the next drink.

When the work was done this way, the girl first in was not necessarily first out with her tray, but the system was so efficient that it speeded up the work on the average, and the girls were content to profit this way in the long run. The men described the system to us simply in terms of efficiency; but note that, in organizing their jobs, they had changed quantitatively the relations they had with the waitresses. Instead of responding to each waitress, they were originating action for the girls (filling their orders as the men saw fit and sending them out when the men were ready).

Along with our consideration of layout and equipment in the flow of work, we should give attention to the communication system. Where the restaurant operates on one floor, the relations at each step in the flow can be worked out on a face-to-face basis. There may be friction, but there is also the possibility of working out many problems on a friendly, informal basis.

When a restaurant operates on two or more floors, as many large ones do, face-to-face interaction must be supplemented by mechanical means of communication. We saw three such mechanical means substituted for direct interaction, and each one had its difficulties.

People can try to co-ordinate their activities through the house telephone. Without facial expressions and gestures, there is a real loss of understanding, for we do not generally respond solely to people's voices. Still, this might serve reasonably well, if the connection between kitchen and pantry could be kept constantly open. At least in the one restaurant where we gave this subject special attention, that solution was out of the question, as one call from kitchen to pantry tied up the whole house phone system and nobody could call the manager, the cashier, or anybody else on this system as long as another call was being made. Consequently, the telephone could be used only to supplement other mechanical aids (in this case, the teleautograph).

The public address system has the advantage over the telephone that it can be used all the time, but it has the great disadvantage of being a very noisy instrument. Busy kitchens and service pantries are noisy places at best, so that the addition of a public address system might be most unwelcome. We do not yet know enough of the effect of noise upon the human nervous system to evaluate the instrument from this point of view, but we should recognize the obvious fact that surrounding noise affects the ability of people to communicate with each other and becomes therefore a problem in human relations.

The teleautograph makes no noise and can be used at all times, yet it has its own disadvantages. Here we have an instrument in the service pantry and one in the kitchen. As the pantry supplyman writes his order, it appears simultaneously on the kitchen teleautograph. The kitchen's replies are transmitted upstairs in the same way. The machine records faithfully, but it does not solve the problem of meaning in interaction. We may pass over the problem of illegibility of handwriting, although we have seen that cause serious difficulties. The more interesting problem is this: How urgent is an order?

When the rush hour comes along, with customers pushing waitresses, waitresses pushing pantry girls, and pantry girls pushing supplymen, the supplyman is on the end of the line so far as face-to-face interaction is concerned, and he is likely to get nervous and excited. He may then put in a larger order than he will actually use or write "Rush" above many of his orders. If he overorders, the leftovers come back to the kitchen at the end of the meal, and the kitchen supplymen and cooks learn thus that the pantry supplyman did not really know how much he needed. They take this into account in interpreting his future orders. And, when everything is marked "Rush," the kitchen supplymen cannot tell the difference between the urgent and not so urgent ones. Thus the word becomes meaningless, and communication deteriorates. Stuck in this impasse, the pantry supplyman may abandon his machine and dash down to the kitchen to try to snatch the order himself. The kitchen people will block this move whenever they can, so, more often, the pantry supplyman appeals to his supervisor. In the heat of the rush hour, we have seen pantry supervisors running up and down stairs, trying to get orders, trying to find out what is holding up things in the kitchen. Since they have supervisor status, the kitchen workers do not resist them openly, but the invasion of an upstairs supervisor tends to disrupt relations in the kitchen. It adds to the pressures there, for it comes as an emergency that lets everybody know that the organization is not functioning smoothly.

It is not the function of this article to work out possible solutions to this problem of communication. I am concerned here with pointing out a significant new area for sociological investigation: the effects on human relations of various mechanical systems of communication. It is difficult enough to co-ordinate an organization in which the key people in the supervisory hierarchy are in direct face-to-face relations. It is a much more difficult problem (and one as yet little understood) when the coordination must be achieved in large measure through mechanical communication systems.

IMPLICATIONS FOR THEORY AND METHODOLOGY

In presenting our observations on the restaurant industry, I have discussed formal structure, quantitative measures of interaction, symbols in relation to interaction, attitudes and interaction, and layout and equipment (including mechanical systems of communication). Data of these categories must be fitted together. The uses of each type of data may be summarized here.

1. *Formal Structure*

We have ample data to show that the formal structure (the official allocation of positions) does not *determine* the pattern of human relations in an organization. Nevertheless, it does set certain limits upon the shape of that pattern. Thus, to analyze the human problems of a restaurant, it is necessary to outline its structure in terms of length of hierarchy, divisions into departments, and flow of work (as done in the five stages above).

2. *Quantitative Measures of Interaction*

Within the limits set by the formal structure, the relations among members of the organization may fall into a variety of patterns, each of which is subject to change.

The pattern we observe we call the *social system*. A social system is made up of *interdependent* parts. The parts are the *relations* of individuals in their various positions to each other. This is simply a first description of a social system, but there are important theoretical and practical conclusions which flow from it.

The relations of individuals to one another are subject to *measurement*, sufficient to allow them to be compared and classified. We can, for example, count the number of times that a waitress originates action for her customers compared with the number of times they originate it for her in a given period and observe how often she originates action for her supervisor and how often the supervisor does so for her, and so on, through the other relations in the system. So far, mathematically precise measurements of interaction have only been made in laboratory situations involving interviewer and interviewee.[5] Nevertheless, in the present state of our knowledge, we can get, through interviewing and observation, quantitative data which, though only approximate, are sufficiently accurate to allow us to predict the course of developments or explain how certain problems have arisen and point the way to their possible solution.

As the terms are used here, *interaction, origination,* and *response* are abstractions without content. That is, they are indices which have no reference to either the symbols used or the subjective reactions felt by the interacting individuals. Such measures do not, of course, tell us all it is useful to know of human relations. Indeed, many students will think it absurd to believe that any useful data can come from abstractions which leave out the "content" of human relations. To them I can only say that science is, in part, a process of abstraction, which always seems to take us away from the "real world." The value of such abstractions can be determined only by testing them in research to see whether they enable us better to control and predict social events.

Since the social system is made up of *interdependent relations*, it follows that a change in one part of the system necessarily has repercussions in other parts of the system. For example, a change in origin-response ratio between waitresses and supervisor necessarily affects the waitress-customer and waitress–service-pantry-girl relations, and changes in those parts lead to other changes in the system. Therefore, in order to study the social system or to deal with it effectively, it is necessary to discover the *pattern* of relations existing at a given time and to observe changes within that pattern. The nature of the interdependence of the parts of the system can be discovered only through observing how a change in Part A is followed by change in Part B, is followed by change in Part C, etc. Therefore, social systems must be studied *through time*. A static picture of the social structure of an organization is of little value. Science requires that we develop methods of study and tools of analysis to deal with constantly changing relations.

[5] Eliot D. Chapple, with the collaboration of Conrad M. Arensberg, *Measuring Human Relations: An Introduction to the Study of the Interaction of Individuals* ("Genetic Psychology Monographs," No. 22 [Provincetown, Mass.: Journal Press, 1940]); Eliot D. Chapple and Carleton S. Coon, *Principles of Anthropology* (New York: Henry Holt & Co., 1941), esp. first four chapters; Eliot D. Chapple and Erich Lindemann, "Clinical Implications of Measurement of Interaction Rates in Psychiatric Interviews," *Applied Anthropology*, I, No. 2 (January–March, 1942), 1–12.

3. Symbols in Relation to Interaction

We cannot be content simply with quantitative descriptions of interaction. We need to know why A responds to B in one situation and not in another or why A responds to B and not to C. In part, this is a matter of habituation, for we respond to the people we are accustomed to responding to and in the sorts of situations to which we are accustomed. But we must go beyond that to explain the development of new patterns and changes in old patterns of interaction.

We observe that individuals respond to certain symbols in interaction. I have discussed here status and sex as symbols affecting interaction (the problems of the originating from below of action for high-status individual or by woman for man).

I have noted some problems in language symbols in the discussion of mechanical means of communication. That leaves the whole field of symbols in face-to-face interaction untouched, so that it represents only the barest beginning of an attempted formulation of the relations between symbols of communication and interaction.

Especially in economic institutions, it is important to examine the bearing of *economic symbols*[6] on interaction, but this is a large subject and can only be mentioned here.

As we analyze social systems, symbols should always be seen in terms of their effects upon interaction. They are *incentives* or *inhibitors* to interaction with specific people in certain social situations. Thus, to put it in practical terms, the manager of an organization will find it useful to know both the pattern of interaction which will bring about harmonious relations and also how to use symbols so as to achieve that pattern.

4. Attitudes and Interaction

Changes in relations of individuals to one another are accompanied by changes in their *attitudes* toward one another and toward their organizations. In recent years we have developed excellent methods for attitude measurement, but the measurement in itself never tells us how the attitudes came about. The whole experience of our research program leads us to believe that the dynamics of attitude formation and change can best be worked out as we correlate attitudes with human relations in the organizations we study.

5. Layout and Equipment

Here the sociologist is not directly concerned with the problems of the mechanical or industrial engineer. He does not undertake to say which machine or which arrangement of work space and machines will be most productively efficient. However, he cannot help but observe that, for example, the height of the barrier between waitresses and countermen or the nature of the mechanical communication system has important effects upon human relations. Only as these effects are observed do the physical

[6] See Whyte's "Economics and Human Relations in Industry" to be published in *Industrial and Labor Relations Review*.

conditions come in for sociological analysis. (Of course, human relations have a bearing upon efficiency, but the sociologist, if he tackles the problem of efficiency, uses types of data and schemes of analysis quite different from those used by the engineer.)

A few years ago there was a great debate raging: statistics versus the case study. That debate is no longer waged publicly, but it still troubles many of us. On the one hand, we see that an individual case study, skilfully analyzed, yields interesting insights—but not scientific knowledge. On the other hand, we find that nearly all statistical work in sociology has dealt with the characteristics of aggregates: How much of a given phenomenon is to be found in a given population? Such an approach does not tell us anything about the relations among the individuals making up that population. And yet, if we are to believe the textbooks, the relations among individuals, the *group* life they lead, are the very heart of sociology.

So let us have more individual case studies, but let us also place the individual in the social systems in which he participates and note how his attitudes and goals change with changes in the relations he experiences. And let us have more quantitative work, but let us at last bring it to bear upon the heart of sociology, measuring the relations among individuals in their organizations.

BASIC OBJECTIVES WHICH SHAPE THE CHARACTER OF A COMPANY
William H. Newman*

Each company, according to Newman, develops its own traditions, habits, and reputation; and managers will be more effective if they are in tune with the character of their firms. Company character, though elusive, can be revealed through the basic objectives of the organization. Newman discusses various such objectives and thus provides a useful checklist in diagnosing a specific organization.

A business firm may have "no body to be kicked," but it does have character. In addition to a separate legal existence, every company develops its own traditions, habits, and reputation which give it individuality. This body of habits and attitudes endows a company with character or personality quite beyond the people who work for it at any given time.

There is nothing strange in the idea of a social institution which has an individuality separate from its members. When we speak of the Ki-

* Reprinted from *The Journal of Business*, XXVI, No. 4 (October 1953), 211–223, by permission of The University of Chicago Press. Copyright 1953 by The University of Chicago.

wanis Club, the Episcopal church, or the city government, the words have fairly definite meanings. The people who happen to be officers, or the buildings these institutions occupy, are only parts of the picture; these could be changed and yet the organizations would continue much as they had been before. More enduring are the purposes, the activities sponsored, the services rendered, and the relationships engendered.

Similarly, business firms become social institutions. For example, Macy's in New York, Marshall Field's in Chicago, and Bullock's in Los Angeles each have clear-cut identity in the minds of their respective employees and customers. Consulting firms, banks, manufacturers, and other enterprises each have their own objectives and customs which make them separate entities.

An understanding of business character has practical value. Operating executives and operators will be more effective in their daily activities when they appreciate, and are in tune with, the character of their firm. This sensing of company character will help them deal with new problems, interpret policies and instructions, and coordinate their activities. Likewise, materials suppliers, bankers, and others dealing with the company will find it easier to secure desired action if they recognize the character of the firm with which they are working.

The total character of a company, like that of a person, is a complex thing. Moreover, each has an individuality of its own. This complexity and diversity make it difficult to grasp clearly the character of any specific firm.

One very useful way to discover the key features of the character of a company is to concentrate on its basic objectives. These basic objectives will indicate, to a large degree, what the firm wants to be. They tend to override and to permeate the rest of its administration and in this way shape the company character.[1]

For purposes of studying company character and developing a sense of the company as a whole dynamic unit, its basic objectives may be classified under the following headings:

A. What place or niche does the company seek in its industry?
B. Does the firm want to emphasize stability or dynamics; i.e., what is its disposition toward change?
C. What kind of a business citizen does the firm want to be; i.e., what is its social philosophy?
D. What type of administration is desired; i.e., what is its management philosophy?

All too often company objectives in these four areas are not well defined. This leads to confusion in planning and makes it difficult for com-

---

[1] The term "business policies" is often used to cover both the objectives and the general rules of action for an enterprise. In a strict sense, however, an objective is a goal or an end to be sought, whereas a policy is a general rule of action. The objective sets a long-range target; a policy provides guides which will assist the company in reaching this target. When two or more objectives are sought, as is almost always the case, the business administrator must work out a set of policies which provide a practical and balanced way of achieving the diverse aims.

pany executives to work in a consistent manner. It is not necessary that the basic objectives be written up in a company manual, although this practice has been found to be valuable in some companies. What is important is that all key executives of the company develop, by some means, an appreciation of the basic objectives of the enterprise they serve.

THE PLACE A COMPANY SEEKS IN ITS INDUSTRY

The first decision to be made for any company is the industry in which it will operate. The original choice of industry, made by the founders of the company, may be modified if a company adds an entirely new line of products or if it devotes a significant part of its resources to produce its own raw materials. The choice of industry, however, still leaves considerable need for refinement of objectives. The place a company seeks in its industry may be defined in terms of (1) major function to be performed; (2) specialization versus diversification of activities; (3) quality or price level sought; and (4) size of operation.

Major Function to Be Performed

Within any industry there will be found a variety of types of companies. Some serve a particular set of customers; others perform either a basic or a service process; some concentrate on one type of material. In the women's hat industry, for instance, some firms make felt-hat bodies while others specialize in feathers. A great many industries have wholesalers or jobbers who do no manufacturing but give their entire attention to marketing. An early step in defining the objectives, then, is to decide upon the major function or functions which the company will seek to perform.

Specialization versus Diversification

A related issue in defining the particular niche the firm seeks in its industry is the basic question of specialization versus diversification. Many firms achieve distinctiveness by concentrating on some one type of product, such as printing machinery, whereas others will make a widely diversified line of equipment. A book-publishing house may handle a wide variety of books, as does Harper and Brothers or Macmillan Company, or it may concentrate on children's books, business texts for colleges, or some other relatively narrow field. In this industry specialization is much more common than diversification.

The largest companies in the country typically carry on a diversified group of activities. This fact, by itself, suggests that a variety of functions and products is a desirable objective. It should be borne in mind, however, that many of the companies which specialize earn a higher rate of return on invested capital than do the industrial giants. Also, we should not overlook the many firms that tried diversification and failed in the process. This variety of experience clearly indicates that diversification versus specialization is another one of the basic objectives which should be given careful attention.

Quality Level

Most firms seek to become leaders in a particular range of quality in their industry. For example, the manufacturer of occasional tables has a choice of making what are known in the trade as "museum pieces." These include original artistic designs and authentic copies of period furniture. They are typically hand carved and often are individual pieces.

A second quality range is good reproductions. Here, production runs are forty to four hundred tables, and a larger company will often make as many as two hundred to three hundred different kinds. This range of patterns in relatively small production runs permits the company to give each outlet in a given city distinctive patterns. The tables are produced primarily on machinery, but considerable care is exercised in tracing the master-copy, and the tables are usually hand cut.

Still a third possibility for the occasional-table manufacturer is to select a few patterns which have been selling successfully and manufacture them in runs of five to ten thousand. These are almost entirely machine manufactured, and quality is sacrificed so that the tables may be sold at a low price. The production, selling, purchasing, and finance problems of a table manufacturer will be drastically affected by this choice of quality range, and rarely is it practical for a single company to operate at more than one level.

In a great many industries this question of quality range arises: a choice of objectives must be made between Tiffany and the time-payment store, between Marshall Field's and Woolworth's. Often this matter of quality level is an important aspect of the basic objectives.

Size of Operation Desired

Growth has been such a dominant characteristic of the American economy that many people assume that the objective of every company should be to get bigger and bigger. Increase in size may be desirable, but this is not always the case. For example, some of the most successful management consultants and other professional men have found that the need for their personal contact has placed definite limits on the volume of activity they should undertake. Similarly, high transportation costs or other difficulties in reaching distant markets may place sharp restrictions on how large it is profitable for firms to grow in other industries.

This matter of size objective will have a profound influence on sales-promotion activities, financial structure, organization, executive personnel, investment in facilities, operating methods and procedures, and other phases of administration.

The aim of a company regarding size, quality level, specialization versus diversification, and major economic functions will go a long way in defining one set of basic objectives for a company. In a specific industry there may be still other ways to mark off the role or the niche a firm seeks to occupy. However it is defined, a clear understanding of the place a company seeks in its industry is essential to effective administration and will have a marked effect on company character.

EMPHASIS ON STABILITY VERSUS DYNAMICS

The place a company seeks in its industry can be defined in fairly specific terms, whereas its disposition toward change is a much more intangible type of objective. Nevertheless, the emphasis a firm puts on seeking stability as compared with dynamics has a profound influence on its character and administration. This facet of character can be considered in terms of a company's objectives as to (1) *progressiveness*—the seeking of better ways; (2) *aggressiveness*—drive in making changes; (3) willingness to take *risks;* and (4) willingness to share *ownership control*.

Progressiveness

Some companies undertake a continual search for new and, presumably, better ways of performing their activities. The objective of the management of these companies really is to use the most modern facilities, policies, and techniques. One soap manufacturer, for instance, prides itself on being in the forefront, if not the leader, of new personnel practices in regard to selection, training, salary administration, employee services, and the like. This company also is a leader in the adoption of materials-handling equipment and continuous methods of manufacture; its accounting system is highly mechanized; and it employs the latest techniques of market research and analysis. Other companies are progressive leaders in only some of their departments, but usually the desire to be progressive is fairly contagious and will be found to a greater or lesser extent throughout the enterprise.

Progressive management sounds appealing; it is definitely "popular" to be progressive. Nevertheless, some practical managers feel that this idea can be carried too far; they place greater emphasis on stability of operations. New policies and techniques naturally require changes, and there is considerable human energy and financial cost in introducing changes into a going enterprise. If these changes are introduced frequently, a feeling of insecurity and instability is likely to develop among the executives and operating employees.

Moreover, as the executive of a large steel company pointed out, the development of new methods is almost always accompanied by unanticipated difficulties and mistakes. "Our experience indicates that the man who initiates the change often doesn't make the most money out of it. He incurs high costs learning what not to do and may have to discard some projects entirely. As a general rule, we prefer to wait until a new product or new method has been demonstrated to be sound. We may have to pay royalties on patents and may be at a slight disadvantage because of a late start, but, on the whole, we believe we are better off to wait and profit by the other man's mistakes."

There are, of course, other companies such as some financial firms which, because of the nature of business and/or the disposition of their executives, place great stress on stability and prefer to make changes in their operations only when it is essential to do so.

Aggressiveness

Closely associated with progressiveness is the aggressiveness of a company. This refers to the energy, the self-assertiveness, the disposition to attack, with which a company seeks its objectives. One business executive whose aggressiveness has been widely publicized is Henry J. Kaiser. He became a public figure in World War II because of his bold and insistent approach to shipbuilding. He not only employed novel methods but went to great lengths to overcome obstacles in his path. If necessary, he did not hesitate to go directly to the President or to Congress, asking for modifications in existing laws.

Following the war, Mr. Kaiser entered both the aluminum and the automobile industries, in spite of the firmly intrenched positions of the existing producers. Here, again, his attack was bold and determined; for example, when his production of automobiles threatened to be delayed because of a lack of steel, he purchased a small steel company of his own. Not all the Kaiser ventures have been successful, but each has been pursued aggressively. Mr. Kaiser's disposition towards change permeates his entire organization and has become a characteristic way in which his associates do business.

There are fields of business where too much aggressiveness will cause serious trouble. A commercial bank or an exclusive women's dress shop, for example, may well find itself in trouble if it becomes too aggressive in developing its business. An aggressive firm is likely to annoy other members of the industry and its suppliers and, consequently, may find it difficult to secure the cooperation of other firms in troubled times. There are also limits to the aggressiveness which customers will accept. Consequently, in setting the basic objectives of a company, it is well to consider how aggressive a company should be.

Willingness to Take Risks

Change in business operations almost always involves a move from the known to the unknown. Even when the change is based on a thorough investigation, there will be some unknown factors which tend to make the new policy or method more risky than the existing one. Therefore, an important element in a company's disposition toward change is its willingness to take risks.

One moderately successful company, for instance, had operated under a conservative management for over a decade. This management was inclined to play safe and make changes only when they knew that policies or methods had proved to be successful in another company or when the possible gains were so great that there was little room to question the wisdom of the move. The stockholders then installed a new management which took quite a different view toward changes.

This new management quickly abandoned lines of business which had a poor outlook, reorganized the internal administration, and took other steps to make the company a leader in its field. The new program clearly involved more risk, and, when some of the steps taken proved to be unwise, numbers of the "old guard" were quick to point out the losses resulting from the progressive actions of the new management.

The heated discussion which arose at this time was fundamentally a debate on the extent to which the company should take steps which involved a considerable degree of risk. In this particular case the decisions of the new management, when viewed as a whole, appear to have been wise, but there is still doubt in the minds of some whether the objectives of the company should have been centered more around stability than around the more risky, dynamic approach to company problems.

Willingness to Share Ownership Control

Major changes in company operations always require considerable investment of new capital. Some companies are profitable enough, or have sufficient borrowing capacity, to raise the capital needed for any changes they desire to make. Not infrequently, however, a progressive and aggressive company can obtain the necessary capital only by selling more common stock. Whenever the stock is sold to outsiders, it means that the original owners of the business give up a share of the profits and also a share of the ownership control.

There are many stockholders, particularly of small companies, who do not want to dilute their ownership control in this way. In situations like this a willingness or unwillingness to share ownership control has a marked influence on the basic objectives of the company with regard to changes in operation.

A desire to keep ownership control was illustrated recently when a successful manufacturer of plastic toys had an unusual opportunity to enter the manufacture of plastic garden hose. The new line offered the advantages of use of excess plant capacity, better balance of seasonal fluctuation, and easy entry into a rapidly expanding field. However, the plastic-toy manufacturer turned down the deal; it required that he merge with another smaller company, and in the end he would have had only 40 per cent of the outstanding stock instead of his present holding of 60 per cent.

A similar situation existed in a successful crude-oil-producing company which was owned for many years by the three original partners. The business prospered, but it did not become a really significant factor in the petroleum industry until the original stockholders were willing to have their ownership control reduced as a result of mergers and public sale of common stock.

Objectives of a company with regard to stability versus dynamics usually are not stated in writing. Instead, this aspect of company character is likely to be undefined as well as intangible. There can be no doubt of its importance, however. When an executive is sitting back thinking about just what kind of a company or department he wants, one of the aspects he should consider is this disposition toward change. Just how progressive and aggressive should the company be; just how willing is he to take on risks and to share ownership control—should this be necessary?

SOCIAL PHILOSOPHY OF THE COMPANY

A third set of basic objectives which shape the character of a company deal with its social philosophy—what kind of a business citizen does a company want to be? In this connection the company should consider

(1) *community* relations; (2) *government* and economic responsibilities; (3)*customer* service; (4) *supplier* contact; (5) *stockholder* relations; (6) *competitor* contact; and (7) regard for *employees*.

Community Relations

There is a wide difference in the attitudes which companies take toward the community in which they operate. Some firms believe that they have no responsibility other than paying local taxes and obeying local laws. This has been a fairly widespread point of view in the city of Philadelphia, for example, and is aggravated by the fact that the political limits of the city do not include the suburbs where most of the executives live.

In contrast, some firms set a definite goal of being "good neighbors." In communities where they have plants or offices, they try to promote good schools, sound local government, city planning, adequate provision for recreation, and other things which make the community a good place for people to live. They try to accomplish this by encouraging their employees to take an active part in local affairs, by giving financial support, and by cooperating in various community ventures. Such community activities probably cost more money than can be justified, at least in the short run, in terms of direct returns. Nevertheless, the firms feel that it is a part of their responsibility as citizens in a democracy.

For many years, large corporations with absentee management were criticized because of their failure to feel a responsibility for local communities. There has been a marked change in this regard, and many of the larger companies are now taking the lead in building good communities. Several of these large companies definitely state that good community relations is one of their objectives.

Government and Economic Responsibility

In government relations, as in community relations, there is a wide variation in company objectives. One view is a "What can I get out of it?" attitude. Companies with such an attitude seek contracts for government business only if it is to their financial advantage to do so. They often take an active part in lobbying for legislation which will give them tariff subsidy or other protections and against legislation which will interfere in any way with their activities. They seek to influence government officials and regulatory bodies so as to secure favorable treatment.

With the increasing influence of government on business, it behooves any intelligent management to give some attention to the matters just listed. The real question is whether the company objective is solely in terms of reaping short-run benefits regardless of the effects such actions may have on the total economy of the nation.

Another common attitude toward participation in government and economic affairs is indifference. Besides grumbling about taxes and making the conventional remarks about the "damn bureaucrats in Washington," executives with this view take no direct part in shaping governmental policy. Of course, if some governmental action happens to squeeze them directly, they will probably join the first group that is actively trying to influence governmental action for its own immediate benefit.

An increasing number of companies are becoming concerned about the total economic climate in which they must operate. They recognize that governmental activities have become so far-reaching that they have a profound influence on this economic climate. Consequently, when dealing with the government, these companies think in terms of the general economy as well as of their immediate interests. These companies are likely to cooperate with governmental activities by loaning necessary technical personnel and to take on contracts and other assignments which show small prospect of immediate profit. These companies are no more in favor of large-scale governmental operations than are the others, but they accept the governmental work as inevitable and make it their objective to help improve the efficiency of such government action as is taken.

Both community and government relations impinge upon company activities in many ways—materials supply, markets for goods, prices, employee relations, financing, profits after taxes, competition, and plant expansion, to mention only the more obvious ones. Consequently, the basic objectives which control these relationships will permeate and affect the actions of almost every department of a company.

Customer Service

There is considerable difference, for example, in the service rendered by the Parker Pen Company, which sells a "lifetime" pen, and the services of one of the early manufacturers of ballpoint pens who sold as many as he could for over $10.00 each and then, as competition increased rapidly, reduced his price to below $1.00 and finally withdrew from the market altogether.

The company playing for a long pull must give the consumer real benefits and satisfaction, whereas the other firm is interested in a quick sale with an unannounced motto, "caveat emptor." If the company deals with other business concerns rather than with final customers, the contrast is between an objective of helping the customer to prosper versus charging what the traffic will bear.

This facet of company character is important not only to customers but also to everyone in the production, sales, and credit departments who make the product or perform activities directly or indirectly related to customers.

Supplier Contacts

A similar problem arises in deciding the type of relationship to seek with vendors of raw materials, supplies, and equipment. Some firms play one supplier against another in an effort to get the greatest possible concessions in price and services. In fact, a few large companies have been accused of first making their business so important to a small supplier that the supplier gave up his other outlets and then driving such a hard bargain with the supplier that he finally went bankrupt.

In contrast, other companies try to develop relations with suppliers that can continue over a long period of time. They believe that the sound relationship is one that develops wholesome, vigorous suppliers as well as providing them with a continuing and dependable source of materials. Underlying the more specific policy decisions will be the general social philosophy as to the kind of a business citizen the company wants to be.

Stockholder Relations

In those companies where the stockholders are also the key men in its management, there is, of course, no major problem of stockholder relations. When the active management has passed from the hands of the owners to professional executives, quite a different situation arises. Should the stockholders be treated as partners in the venture, or should they be regarded as distant relatives upon whom the executives occasionally bestow dividends in an effort to discourage visits to the family homestead?

General Mills, for example, takes the view that even indifferent stockholders should be encouraged to take an interest in their company. They hold a series of special meetings for stockholders in various parts of the country. On the other hand, the chairman of one of the country's leading banks would not permit a stockholder even to raise a question regarding loans to a foreign country; he stated, categorically, that the stockholders merely elected directors and that it was the exclusive duty of the directors and the officers to consider operating problems. Quite aside from the legal rights of stockholders is the question of whether the bank management conceived of stockholders as active participants in the venture or as impersonal investors.

Contact with Competitors

Another phase of the broad question "What kind of a business citizen does the company want to be?" has to do with contact with competitors. Under a "lone-wolf" objective, a company will have has little as possible to do with competitors and will reject various suggestions for cooperative effort. This point of view has been decreasing in popularity in the United States for several decades; in fact, European visitors remark on the freedom with which all sorts of problems are discussed in industry association meetings.

Many companies actively cooperate with their competitors within certain limited areas. There is often a substantial exchange of operating data. These data may be summarized by some central agency so as not to reveal individual company results, but on a surprisingly large number of matters there will be a frank and direct exchange of "know-how." Companies which engage in this practice believe that they stand to gain substantially more than they will lose.

In some industries the companies join together for united trade promotions or public relations activities. Thus the Wallpaper Institute undertakes to promote the use of wallpaper for the benefit of the entire industry. Another cooperative activity is that of representing the entire industry to the federal and state legislatures. The combined force of an entire industry is often much more effective than the separate individual efforts of the companies. In fact, the pressure of some industry lobbies is so great that Congress has taken steps to control their activities.

Industry cooperation may, of course, slip over into areas prohibited by our antitrust laws. Price agreements, allocation of customers or territories, production quotas, and other restrictions on trade must be avoided. Unfortunately, there are many activities the legality of which is not clear. In the petroleum and other industries there have been certain activities sponsored by government units at one time which are later declared to be illegal. Consequently, in deciding how far to go with industry cooperation, each company must consider the possibility of legal complications.

Regard for Employees

By no means the least important part of the social philosophy of a firm is its regard for its employees. Tangible evidence of this regard will be found in its personnel policies. However, a genuine desire to make a company a "good place to work" affects all activities. It leads to traditions regarding the way personal relationships are handled which become part of the warp and woof of company operations. Many an executive has incurred extra expense simply because "that is the way we treat people here."

In other instances the employment of people may be regarded simply as a necessary step toward some other objective. This is clearly the point of view of a New York manufacturer of air-conditioning equipment. The founders of this company are engineers whose primary interest has always been in the technical side of the business. The personnel policies of this firm are "enlightened" and "reasonably modern." These policies have been adopted, however, because they are regarded as necessary to attract and maintain the skilled work force the company needs. The management of the business would be quite willing to abandon any or all of these policies if their machines could be produced more economically under some other system. This mechanistic view of personnel relations is sensed by the employees, and the company has had to provide employees, services and protection that probably would not have been required of a more friendly management.

In summary, then, a whole range of possible objectives relating to community, government, customers, suppliers, competitors, stockholders, and employees has been suggested in this section on social philosophy of a firm. There are, of course, many other variations which have not been mentioned, but enough has been said to indicate the nature and content of basic objectives in this general field.

One of the disturbing things about such a review of possible social objectives is that a company's aspirations may far exceed its capacity to fulfil them. Is it possible, one may ask, to take an active part in community, industry, and government affairs and maintain good relationships with suppliers, customers, and employees all at the same time?

There are two general answers to this question: (a) At this point we are discussing long-run objectives rather than specific plans of action, and for this purpose it may be all right to set some goals which will be difficult to achieve. To be most useful, however, the objectives should be ranked or given relative weight. These weights will, of course, shift from time to time as circumstances change, but recognition of basic objectives leads to a consistent direction of effort rather than a series of opportunistic actions. (*b*) The objectives do not necessarily conflict with one another; in fact, they may be selected so that one supports the other. For example, the desire to provide good employment conditions is quite compatible with the objective of giving customers dependable merchandise over a long run. An important part of policy-making and programming is planning activities so that the various objectives may be achieved to an optimum degree.

MANAGEMENT PHILOSOPHY OF THE COMPANY

Three broad types of basic objectives have been discussed: the place a company seeks in its industry, its emphasis on stability or dynamics, and the kind of a business citizen it wants to be. There is a fourth type of objective which also has a profound influence on the entire administration of a company. This is concerned with the management philosophy or type of administration desired by the company. It is clearly reflected in (1) *centralization* versus *decentralization* of decision-making; (2) *quality* of key personnel; (3) extent of *advance planning* and research going into such plans; and (4) manner of *supervision*—strictness of control. Again, we are not concerned with the specific management techniques for dealing with each of these topics. The interest here centers on the general character of the enterprise the executive wishes to create.

Centralization versus Decentralization of Decision-Making

Some companies are ruled closely from the top. This is likely to be true of a small company which is still managed by the founder. He knows the customers and watches over sales made to them. He personally approves the selection and pay increases for each of the employees. He negotiates credit with the bank and actively participates in the selection of new equipment or other changes in production methods. In fact, there are few, if any, major decisions which he does not personally make or approve.

Even in some medium-sized and large companies this type of centralization may be found. For instance, while Henry Ford was still active, there was a highly centralized management in the Ford Motor Company. With the growth in size of such a company, there is an increase in the number of special assistants who investigate and recommend; production managers, sales supervisors, and accountants are, of course, authorized to take action, but they must operate within closely prescribed limits. The basic operating plans and all other major decisions are made in the central headquarters.

This method of operation tends to secure uniformity of action; it takes advantage of the special skill and knowledge of the central executives. On the other hand, it tends to make the supervisors and managers "doers" rather than "thinkers." This administration is less adaptable to local conditions, since exception to the standard rule must be made at the central headquarters.

Decentralized administration gives the local managers and supervisors considerable leeway in the direction of their units. Each local manager is expected to figure out for himself the programs and methods best suited to his particular situation. In the American Brakeshoe Company and J. C. Penney & Company, two well-known examples of decentralized management, the managers of local branches or stores have considerable choice in the operation of their particular units. There are a variety of service divisions at the headquarters office which may be called upon for advice and assistance, but it is the local manager who decides whether this advice fits his local needs.

This matter of centralization versus decentralization affects the whole way of doing business. The type and nature of plans needed, the selection of personnel, the building of company morale, the organization structure, the types of controls necessary—all are affected. It is a major aspect of company character for anyone working within the organization.

Quality of Key Personnel

A second vital aspect of the management of any firm is the quality of its key personnel. Over a period of years a company can, if it sets about it, build a corps of executives who, as a group, have a number of distinctive characteristics. A well-known commercial bank, for example, has developed a group of officers who are highly competent and dependable in the performance of their particular tasks. Typically they are conservative and stable men who place a great store in the traditions of the bank and are cautious about making any changes. Consequently, the bank is a stable, respected, conservative institution.

The president of another bank in the same city decided that he wanted to surround himself with executives who were farsighted, energetic, and interested in developing new ways of being of service to the community. It has taken a decade of promotions, transfers, and retirements to develop a corps of key men having these qualities. Now, the whole atmosphere of the second bank is quite different from that in the first.

There are many different qualities which might be set up as objectives for the key personnel of a company. Technical competence, daring, rugged individualism, social attitude, persuasiveness, and many other qualities should be considered in establishing the personnel goals. This is one area, of course, where the objectives will probably never be fully achieved because of great differences between individuals and the changes within a single person over a period of years. Nevertheless, there is real meaning in the expression, "He is our kind of a man."

The personnel objective should be related to several of the other basic objectives. For instance, if a company decides it wishes to emphasize stability rather than dynamics, it would not normally seek highly aggressive men as executives. Likewise, if it is going to emphasize decentralized administration, it will have to get key executives who are resourceful and able to carry responsibility.

Extent of Advance Planning

Some companies make a general practice of "crossing their bridges when they come to them." They rely upon experience and intuition in meeting new problems which arise. This way of managing has the advantage of being flexible and simple.

Such an opportunistic approach to management is in sharp contrast with the modern development of "scientific management." Under the latter, business operations are forecast as far ahead as is practicable, and then considerable analysis and research are done in order to find the best way of dealing with the anticipated problems. On the basis of this research, a plan or blueprint is prepared showing just what is to be done as well as a schedule of when it is to be done. Actual performance, then, consists in carrying out this plan. It should be smooth and efficient (assuming the forecasting and the planning were well done).

For each company there is a real question: How far ahead and in how much detail should such planning be attempted? In a public utility with fairly predictable demand, it may be possible to plan in considerable detail. On the other hand, many department-store executives believe that, in their type of business, detailed advance planning must be confined to accounting and materials handling because of the unpredictability of style changes, competition, and consumer behavior. There is no simple answer as to how much advance planning should be done; it depends partly upon the nature of the activity but is also influenced to a marked degree by the management philosophy of the company.

Strictness of Control

"When my boss says, 'Jump,' he means jump." "We give very few orders around here and rely on guidance and leadership to get things done." These two quotations suggest the differences in the manner of supervision and the strictness of control that may be found in modern business. At one extreme there is prompt, unquestioned obedience to orders which we associate with military management; at the other extreme there is the highly informal relationship between a group of skilled workers who understand their jobs and work through their own volition, with only general guidance and stimulation coming from their supervisors. Most boss-subordinate relationships (including those between the president and the vice-president all the way down to the relations between the first-line supervisor and the unskilled laborer) fall somewhere between these two extremes.

Within any single company, there will, of course, be some difference between the way supervision is exercised in one department as compared with another. Some supervisors will be "strict," while others will be "easy." Nevertheless, taking the company as a whole, there is very likely to be a general pattern or underlying tradition; the way employees are directed and controlled is part of the management philosophy. When an executive is setting objectives as to the kind of company or department he wants to direct, one of the facets to be considered is this nature of supervision.

SUMMARY

Every business firm develops character, an individuality of its own. A sensing of this character is necessary for a member of the company— or an outsider—really to understand the enterprise as a dynamic entity. This character is shaped not only by physical resources and technology but also by the basic objectives of the company. We can learn much about a company as a going concern by asking the following questions.

1. What particular role or niche does the firm seek in its industry? This may be defined in terms of the major function or functions the company will perform, the extent to which the company will specialize or diversify its activities, the quality range it will try to cover, and the size and scale at which it hopes to operate.

2. Does the firm want to emphasize stability or dynamics? This is a more intangible phase of business character, in which the desire to be progressive and aggressive must balance against willingness to assume risks and perhaps to share ownership control with others. This disposition toward change will have a marked effect on how quickly and in what manner the company moves from its present position in the industry to the desired positions, as outlined under the first set of basic objectives.

3. What kind of a business citizen does the company want to be? In working toward its desired position in the industry, a company will have many and continuing relationships with other groups. There will be need for some goals as to the desired relationships with the community, the government, competitors, customers, suppliers, stockholders, and employees.

4. What type of administration is desired? A long-range concept of the company is not complete without some sense of the basic management philosophy which will be employed. Important considerations are the extent to which decision-making will be decentralized, the quality of key personnel, the extent of advance planning, the manner of supervision, and the strictness of control. This set of objectives deals with the internal mechanism of the company, whereas the preceding set is concerned with external relationships.

These basic objectives cut across and permeate other phases of administration. They influence, directly or indirectly, the policies, the organization, the resources, and the operating techniques. Few, if any, companies can achieve all these objectives within a limited period, and consequently the executives have a continuing task of adjusting their more specific plans so as to approach the basic objectives to the greatest practical extent.

The selection of the objectives themselves is an even more subtle process. Some gradually evolve out of long experience; others are influenced by the technology and practice of the industry; and many bear the stamp of dominant individuals who served the company, both past and present.

In so far as objectives are chosen deliberately and rationally, top management should (a) seek something that really needs doing; (b) aim for things the company is qualified to do, in terms of technical skill, temperament, and resources attainable; and (c) strive for internal compatibility among its objectives.

No phase of management calls for more wisdom or a finer sense of values than the setting of basic objectives, and no actions of management have a more profound influence on the character and long-run success of the company.

PATTERNS OF ORGANIZATION FOR APPLIED RESEARCH AND DEVELOPMENT
Herbert A. Shepard*

In this article Herbert Shepard is interested primarily in the best organizational structure for research and development work. In the discussion he explicitly and implicitly points to unique aspects of research and development organizations. Thus, he provides a part of the rationale for classifying them as a species. The following features, then, characterize research organizations: The participating members have greater than normal freedom from hierarchical control; power and prestige are allocated primarily by colleagues; high status and prestige seldom carry the power to command colleagues.†

PROJECT AND FUNCTIONAL FORMS

What organizational structure is most suitable for applied research and development? Every research man has his favorite answer to, or way of disposing of, this question. It is, in fact, one of the most controversial topics in laboratory management.

Very often the issue is drawn over two methods of organizing—by "project" and by "function." The pure project type of organization can be described as follows. When a problem enters the laboratory, a group is formed to solve it. The group is placed together geographically and administratively and contains within it all the resources or skills to be used in solving the problem. When the problem is solved, the group is disbanded.

The pure functional type of organization is one consisting of permanent specialist groups. When a problem enters the laboratory, it is

* Reprinted from The Journal of Business, XXIX, No. 1 (January 1952), 52–58, by permission of The University of Chicago Press. Copyright 1952 by The University of Chicago.

† Cf. James D. Thompson, "Editor's Critique," Administrative Science Quarterly, 1, No. 3 (December 1956), 384. This issue of Administrative Science is devoted to the administration of research and thus points to many other dimensions of research and development as a separate species of organization and management.

routed to the appropriate group. If two or three specialties are required for solution, the problem is broken into parts, and the parts are distributed to the two or three appropriate specialist groups.

In the following two sections information concerning the consequences of the project and functional methods of organizing is presented. These presentations are compiled from interviews with persons experienced in research organization, and the presentation is styled to resemble the arguments given by proponents of each organizational type. The observations they make will sometimes appear to be mutually exclusive, but both are reporting their experiences with care and insight. The remainder of the paper is devoted to an attempt to resolve the arguments and to explore the forces that affect the choice of one or the other organizational type in actual practice.

The data are organized around three questions: First, what are the consequences of each type for the careers and satisfactions of members of the organization? Second, what are the consequences of each type in terms of performance—productivity, creativity, etc.? Third, what are the consequences of each type from the standpoint of administration—which is easier to control?

OBSERVATIONS OF A PROPONENT OF FUNCTIONAL ORGANIZATION

As to the satisfactions of personnel, the short life of a project group means that its members have no secure status in the organization. The man who has gained a good reputation with one project leader may lose it on the next project when confronted with problems on which he is less expert or when judged by a new project leader who is not familiar with the man's field of expertness.

A project member is usually required to spend a good portion of his time on problems which are outside his own specialty. As a result, he tends to become a jack-of-all-trades and to lose touch with the newest developments in his original specialty. Thus he loses the basis for self-respect and recognition as a professional.

In the project type of organization, there are shifting standards of evaluation and no clear path of advancement in the organization. Even the step up to project leader is ambiguous. In the first place, the step is not of a standard size. There is considerable difference in status between the leader of a large project and the leader of a small project. Moreover, the status is not permanent. The leader of a large project may have a small one next time, or not at all.

In a project group the individual may not receive recognition for his contribution, because it is often difficult to determine who made the important contributions. Several people may share credit which rightfully belongs to one person. In particular, the project leader is the person who receives recognition, and he typically has more to do with the project administratively than technically. A highly qualified scientist will find that little recognition is accorded him and little encouragement given to do creative work in his own field.

In a functional organization, on the other hand, judgments of a man are made over a long period by reliable and intelligent standards. The chief of the physics group judges the physicists. Not only is there room for recognition and reward of creative work in the specialty, but the path of promotion is also clear.

As to productivity and creativity, the functional type is better because it prevents misemployment and underemployment. Since all problems of concern to a particular group of specialists are routed to that group, and no others, each man is occupied with tasks on which he is an expert and can pursue efficiently. Moreover, all the expertise in the laboratory is brought to bear on every problem. In the project type, on the other hand, men are occupied in their specialties only a part of the time; most of the time they work on problems for which they are not highly qualified. A man is most productive at what he knows how to do best. As to creativity, the only way a man can work intelligently at the borders of knowledge is to have the knowledge. The members of a specialist group can be creative because they know what the most promising areas for progress in the field are. What passes for creativity in the project group is merely enthusiasm. The members work hard on problems outside their field and end by re-inventing what was already well known to persons in that field, after traveling a number of blind alleys that a specialist in the field would have avoided. The tendency of the project group to think of itself as the problem-solving unit leads the members to avoid consulting the literature, the files, and knowledgeful people in the laboratory who could help. The project form of organization produces more heat than light.

As to ease of administrative control, the members of a project group are likely to prove incompatible; when this happens, the conflict is reflected in poor performance. The greater stability of the functional type provides insurance against this. If, on the other hand, the members of the project work well together, they gain an inflated opinion of the importance of their project, and do their best to short-cut and otherwise interfere with the smooth operation of normal and necessary laboratory procedures. This group unity often seems to be achieved by making a common enemy of the rest of the laboratory. The group may resist turning in reports on time, demand unusual consideration, arguing that all is necessary for the achievement of the project goal. The leader fights for salary increases for members of his group without regard for the effects of his action on other groups in the laboratory. The project group never voluntarily ends its own life, and cutting off a project or breaking up a group may be a very difficult administrative problem. Finally, if the project is large and promises to be successful, the leader may, in fact, have more power of decision in the laboratory than anyone else, to the detriment of morale and the embarrassment of even the director. Thus the project type can produce empires which are destructive of morale and leadership. It is difficult to take action in such cases, because the cost of changing horses in midstream is considerable, so that the project leader achieves near-indispensability for the duration of his project.

In contrast, the functional organization produces no such empires.

Authority is delegated rationally, as it is earned. The stability of the organizational structure makes it possible to achieve adherence to laboratory standards and procedures, to get reports out on time, to keep adequate records, and hence keep the whole operation running smoothly.

OBSERVATIONS OF A PROPONENT OF PROJECT ORGANIZATION

The argument of the proponent of the project type of organization states the matter differently.

As to personnel satisfactions, the "security" of specialists in the functional type is a false security. Members of specialist groups are likely to become insecure because they invest so much in so little. The specialist concerns himself with an ever narrower range of problems, which become of less and less importance to the organization, and even to fellow-members of his specialty, as they become of greater importance to him. If new developments reduce the value of his specialty, the specialist becomes very insecure indeed—in fact, he loses his self-esteem, becomes defensive, is afraid to work on problems which fall outside his specialty. Project groups usually develop and maintain a high level of *esprit de corps* and enthusiasm. The experience is broadening and gives the scientist or engineer a realistic basis for self-confidence and a willingness to meet new and challenging problems. Concern over status in the organization is not a necessary concomitant of the project type; good management and personnel administration can provide the productive scientist with all the assurance he needs.

As to performance, the enthusiasm of project groups should not be underrated as a basis for inventiveness and creativity. Obviously, project members should be selected on the basis that their specialities are needed in the project, but the project member is more than a specialist. The whole point of the project type is that the technical unit—the problem to be solved—is identical with the social unit that is to solve it. The project is a team, and the members are committed to one another and to the project goals. In the functional type, each specialist is committed to the furtherance of his specialty, and thereby his own professional status, but not necessarily to the solution of problems that are important to the laboratory. One trouble with the specialist in the functional type is that knowing what can be done within his specialty leads him to believe that he also knows what cannot be done, and, since he seeks recognition as a specialist, he is wise to spend his time on problems he thinks can be solved. The latter may not be the problems that the laboratory has an interest in solving. In fact, the functional type can be recognized by the anomalies it produces when complex problems are undertaken, for each specialist group exercises its creativity in the areas that are of interest to it rather than the areas that are required for the solution of the laboratory's problem. The specialist in the functional type is evaluated not by a project leader but by the chief of his group of fellow-specialists; hence he feels no obligation to stray outside his field and invent for the sake of achieving research goals.

As to ease of administrative control, what could be more straightforward than the project type? If a project is to be terminated, only one group is involved, and it is a simple matter of transferring the personnel to other groups. In the functional type there is so much red tape and so little commitment to project goals that it is never clear what activities to stop or whether they have actually been terminated. Similarly, progress is very easy to assess in the project type but almost impossible in the complexity of the functional type. In the project type, there is a small number of people responsible for all activities; the activities can be monitored and redirected without long chains of command, memoranda, and so forth. Functional organization simply leads to the slow growth and multiplication of "service groups," who make extra work for the projects and for one another. The maintenance of standards and the creation of systems become ends in themselves, and such important matters as performance and progress are lost in the red tape.

FORCES DETERMINING THE CHOICE BETWEEN PROJECT AND FUNCTIONAL EMPHASES

The foregoing arguments are not exhaustive; they are intended to be representative. There are, however, elements of artificiality in both sides of the debate. One note of artificiality is introduced by the fact that there are no laboratories in existence which are purely the project type or purely the functional type. All laboratories are a combination of the two, although one is usually emphasized at the expense of the other. Another note of artificiality is introduced by the fact that the advantages and disadvantages can be affected by the action or inaction of management. Thus if a director does not believe that the functional type is workable, he is unlikely to try to make it work and may not seek ways of avoiding its undesirable consequences and maintaining its desirable consequences.

It is also worth noting that the definitions themselves refer to states which could exist only under a certain range of conditions. For example, if the technical problems entering the laboratory were small, there would be a series of one-man project groups. In some branches of the chemical industry there is a preponderance of man-size problems. Or if a problem is very large, as often occurs in complex systems laboratories, the project group itself may be a semipermanent functional organization. There is a question not only of the scientific size of a problem but also of its organizational size. That is, a project group may be responsible for research only or for development as well, and conceivably even production and marketing. In the latter event it becomes a company and has all the characteristics of a permanent functional organization. Hence there is a limited universe to which the concept of a project group applies. However, most industrial laboratories are within the bounds of that universe.

There is some evidence that the project type is, in fact, the more primitive type of laboratory organization. A newly established laboratory often resembles a project group in its structure. There are only a few members, so there is no differentiation into groups of specialists. There is one specialist only in some fields and none in others. The group has to work closely together and extend itself into areas where it lacks specialized resources. The members of such a laboratory work as a team. As the laboratory grows larger, however, the drift is usually in the direction of the functional type.

It often happens that the early days of the laboratory seem to the old-timers to have been the best days. They recall the enthusiasm with which members of the original group tackled challenging new problems together, the lack of emphasis on status differences, the apparent irrelevance of matters which later became important problems—authority, responsibility, stealing credit, empire-building, laying blame for mistakes, and so forth. In some cases the *esprit de corps* and sense of achievement characteristic of the early days lead the laboratory director to use a project system in expanding the laboratory.

That the project form is the primitive one is illustrated by the major organizational question which confronts such a director, as compared with the question confronting the director of a functionally organized laboratory. In the project type, the question is: To what extent should inroads on the project organization be permitted? For example, should the draftsmen be put in a drafting room instead of remaining distributed through the project groups? The machine shop is one of the first departments to be thus created, because it involves heavy expensive equipment, though less well-equipped hackshops may continue to be distributed among the projects for some time. Good reasons can usually be found for centralizing a great many such activities, or "services" as they come to be called.

As the services become crystallized, the project groups themselves also begin to assume the character of permanent specialist groups. First, each is stripped to a nucleus, by removal of certain high-status specialists. Commonly, the mathematicians, who are useful to their projects only part of the time, are placed in a permanent mathematics group to service all projects. After such attrition the remainder of each project group, having solved a particular problem or developed a particular device, begins to claim immortality. The problem or device is found to be one example of a class of such problems or devices. The group is now expert on this class and undertakes further investigation.

When this amount of permanence is achieved, the organization resembles the functional type. Since the growth has been Topsy-like, however, new problems may enter the laboratory for which no specialist group exists. But now the question which confronts the laboratory director is not: To what extent should inroads in the project organization be permitted? Instead, it is: How should the laboratory be organized to absorb all the problems it has to solve? That is, should it be divided into functional departments by process and product; by basic research, applied research, and development; by scientific specialties—chemistry, physics, etc.—or by some complex combination of these? At this stage, project groups are tolerated only for "crash" programs or for military contracts with unusual security or accounting requirements. The project group has become the exception instead of the rule.

The natural history of laboratory organization given here is largely descriptive. The forces determining it are difficult to discern, since the preceding arguments pro and con were in fair balance. The interpretation offered here is that there are strong social pressures on the laboratory management toward adopting the functional type, and weak, or even negative, pressures toward adopting the project type.

The pressures favoring the functional type stem both from industrial and scientific organizational traditions and from the requirements of continuous service to other parts of the company. Industrial organization favors specialist groups for several reasons. They insure efficient employment of skilled persons by insuring that they practice their skills rather than learn new skills. They facilitate evaluation and supervision by rendering a supervisor's men mutually comparable. They facilitate the identification and routing of tasks. Similarly, scientific organizational traditions, derived from universities, emphasize specialist groups. One reason for the scientific preference is the belief that a professional can be evaluated only by his colleagues in the profession. Also, his professional identity is established by his membership in the group. Moreover, the growth of the profession is facilitated by grouping colleagues together. Finally, the requirements of production and marketing departments for technical aid and advice and for continuous improvement of established products and processes place a premium on the functional type. A product group in the laboratory corresponding to a production or marketing division facilitates communication. Good personal and group relations with other parts of the company take time to build: this implies long-term specialists and permanent groups.

Pressures favoring the project type come only from such near-whimsical sources as a sudden and unforeseen requirement (e.g., crash programs), the demands of an outside organization (e.g., military security), or a largely unprovable conviction that the project type produces better technical results. Pressures opposing the project type come from service groups concerned with the maintenance of standards or simply with regularizing the provision of their services, avoiding peaks and valleys of demand. They come from professional workers who desire a permanent home base and an opportunity to develop in a specialty for professional security and recognition. The very enthusiasm with which a project group prosecutes its mission may win it enemies in other parts of the company if it is too aggressive in selling its product to marketing or production.

The industrial and scientific organizational traditions are not identical. What they have in common is the principle of specialist groups. A major difference between them is in the way prestige and power are allocated among members. In industrial organization the prestige of an individual is determined by those whose power or authority is greater than his. His prestige, so determined, is a measure of his power over others. In the scientific tradition, the prestige of an individual depends upon his achievement as judged by his colleagues. High prestige carries with it no power of command. Whether a scientist accepts the ideas or suggestions of a colleague depends, traditionally at least, on his own judgment of the worth of the suggestions or ideas.[1] Jointly, the colleagues rule over questions of entry, exit, and discipline.

[1] This difference in the industrial and scientific organizational traditions complicates the industrial research supervisor's job. He is faced with contradictions in

These characteristics of industrial and scientific organizations presumably fit them for the task they perform. Thus the industrial tradition is suitable for organizations whose task is the recognition of known categories of problems and efficient application of known means of solving them. The scientific—more accurately, academic—tradition is suitable for organizations whose task is evaluation, storage, and transmission of information. In the freedom from hierarchical control that it offers the individual, the scientific tradition also makes original, creative effort possible.

The scientific tradition may well provide the most suitable structure for fundamental research. But perhaps neither tradition is well suited for invention and innovation. The requirements for the latter appear to be more nearly met by the project type. It concentrates a complement of specialized resources on a problem and forces commitment to the group and its mission. The group and its members grow and succeed in proportion to the achievement of the mission.

It is not easy to demonstrate in practice that any one of these types should be emphasized in laboratory organization. Organizational structure is only one determinant of productivity and creativity. For creativity, organization structure may matter a good deal less than personnel selection. At the same time, creativity is as much a function of the environment as of the individual. Novel ideas and spirited effort are called forth by novel and spirited surroundings. The creativity and productivity of research and development groups appear to decline rapidly with length of association.[2]

In the face of the pressures noted here, it requires a great deal of administrative determination to maintain an emphasis on project-group organization. There are additional problems which require a large measure of managerial ingenuity. Economically, establishing short-term face-to-face groups is not feasible if heavy equipment must be rearranged for the purpose. Numerous compromises between men and equipment must be made, for both may often have to be shared by more than one project. Formulating distinct, relatively short-term projects is not easy in a company with established products and processes in need of continuous service and improvement. But this could be done much more frequently than it is in many laboratories. Again, frequent movement of personnel involves hidden training costs which may be very burdensome; every transfer must be carefully evaluated. A method for evaluating and rewarding research personnel that provides a justified sense of recognition, professional worth, and autonomy through changes in organizational and specialist status must be developed. This is most difficult to achieve where the laboratory staff has come to believe that advancement in the managerial hierarchy constitutes the only real success. Lastly, the top-management group, incorporating a high level of talent in the scientific specialties represented in the laboratory, must be strong enough to encourage empire-building and to destroy empires.

meeting the requirement that he be senior colleague, boss, disciplinarian, teacher, protector, consultant, representative, servicer, and inspirational leader (from an analysis of the research supervisor's role by Charles Orth, in seminar, M.I.T., 1954).

[2] "Some Social Attributes of Industrial Research and Development Groups" (progress report, M.I.T. School of Industrial Management, February 1955).

ORGANIZATIONAL ADAPTATION AND PRECARIOUS VALUES: A CASE STUDY

Burton R. Clark*

In this article, Burton Clark examines the needs of adult education, and indicates that precarious values determine the manner in which adult-education administrators have adapted their practices and focus. He finds adult education caught between a short-run need for enrollment and a need for educational respectability. In adjusting to this dilemma, it has changed its values and attempted to shift the standards upon which legitimacy of its authority and practices are judged.

With the proliferation of formal organizations in modern bureaucratic society it is apparent that the fate of various social values may be affected by the action of administrative agencies. Organizational analysis has shown that rationally contrived structures may transform their initial values in the process of adjusting to emergent problems.[1] Where a number of organizations undergo a similar value transformation, the change may shape a value system of the larger society. The processes by which organizations shape values, however, are only dimly understood and difficult to discern. It is proposed that such effects can be seen most clearly by studying organizations that are tied to weakly established values. The purpose of this paper is, first, to identify some of the conditions of weakness in social values, and secondly, to present a case study of one type of value modification. The case materials have been taken from research on the adult education movement in California.

PRECARIOUS VALUES

Social values may be defined as conceptions of the desirable that are distinctive of some human group.[2] These conceptions are usually voiced

* From *American Sociological Review*, 21 (June 1956), 327–336. Reprinted with permission.

[1] Chester I. Barnard, *The Functions of the Executive*, Cambridge: Harvard University Press, 1938, Chapters 13 and 14; Herbert A. Simon, Donald W. Smithburg, and Victor A. Thompson, *Public Administration*, New York: Alfred A. Knopf, 1950, Chapters 18 and 19; Philip Selznick, *TVA and the Grass Roots*, Berkeley and Los Angeles: University of California Press, 1949, *passim;* Arthur M. Ross, *Trade Union Wage Policy*, Berkeley and Los Angeles: University of California Press, 1950, Ch. 2; Seymour M. Lipset, "The Political Process in Trade Unions: A Theoretical Statement," in Morroe Berger, Theodore Abel, and Charles H. Page (editors), *Freedom and Control in Modern Society*, New York: Van Nostrand, 1954, pp. 82–124; Sheldon L. Messinger, "Organizational Transformation: A Case Study of a Declining Social Movement," *American Sociological Review*, 20 (February, 1955), pp. 3–10.

[2] Clyde Kluckhohn, "Values and Value-Orientations in the Theory of Action," in Talcott Parsons and Edward A. Shils (editors), *Toward a General Theory of Action*, Cambridge: Harvard University Press, 1952, p. 395 and p. 417.

in goals and standards of action—in relatively specific notions of *what* should be obtained and *how*. The aspect of values that concerns us here is the degree to which they are secure. The degree of security will, of course, be determined by many conditions of the social and cultural context. The following are several general grounds for value insecurity that are identifiable in a wide range of situations.

1. *Social values tend to be precarious when they are undefined.* This concerns the link between general value conceptions and a proximate set of goals and norms. Values are *undefined* when they are not embodied in existing goals and standards of committed groups. They lack specific normative reference and no one knows what various symbols really mean. Democracy becomes a precarious value when, as a symbol, it is emptied of well understood behavior maxims. Then totalitarian as well as democratic practices can be filled in as content and the value traduced. If totalitarianism were to come to America in the *name* of democracy, we would have to say that democratic values had been rendered precarious by the lack of specification of appropriate behavior. A value conception stands to be "lost" as its behavioral meaning becomes diffuse. In this connection it may be noted that many general conceptions, such as "the public welfare," tend to become simply unanalyzed abstractions, with content changed at will. Values may be precarious, then, when there is a strong need for definition of behavioral cues, for identification of what is proper in the name of given symbols. This may be referred to as content weakness, or weakness in the normative system.

2. *Social values tend to be precarious when the position of functionaries[3] is not fully legitimized.*[4] This concerns the grounding of a value in a firm social base. A surrounding population may be so hostile to the value conceptions of a smaller group that the group must struggle even to gain a position within relevant arenas from which to work. In such extreme cases, e.g., the Jehovah Witnesses, the right to act must be won. A search for legitimacy in this sense is a central tactical problem for highly deviant political groups, such as the Communist Party of the United States. The values of the CP are precarious in this country not by virtue of being undefined but, in part, because adherents are unacceptable as legitimate contenders for power.

Legitimation of an operating base is also frequently a basic problem of sub-units of a formal organization, as new programs intrude upon old departments. In such cases, the important groups from whom acceptance

---

[3] A term used by Hertzler in describing those chiefly responsible for the "active implementation" of institutions. Used in this way, functionary refers to activists outside of organizations as well as organizational agents. Joyce O. Hertzler, *Society in Action*, New York: The Dryden Press, 1954, pp. 200–201.

[4] On *legitimacy* as a socio-psychological concept, referring to acceptance by others of one's right to act, see: Max Weber, *The Theory of Social and Economic Organization* [translated by A. M. Henderson and Talcott Parsons], New York: Oxford University Press, 1947, pp. 124–132; Simon, Smithburg, and Thompson, *op. cit.*, pp. 198–201; and Philip Selznick, *The Organizational Weapon*, New York: McGraw-Hill, 1952, pp. 242–252.

must be gained may be other units of the same organization, rather than more remote groups of the larger society. The point is that, in specific organizations or in the general society, values may be precarious because of the weak position of custodians in the social structure.

3. *Social values tend to be precarious when they are unacceptable to a "host" population.* This condition, the most apparent source of weakness, is usually related to the second factor above. Groups supporting a new set of values, for instance, are likely to obtain a legitimate status only as their goals and practices became minimally accepted, i.e., seen as in general accordance with the value systems of the larger society. But to some degree these two conditions are separable. Pluralistic societies "tolerate" minority values. Thus functionaries may have a legitimate status even when their values are somewhat disliked by other groups. Then value weakness stems solely from lack of support by the general membership of the larger social system. Hence, the unacceptability of certain values to a host population can be taken as an analytically distinct factor in the precariousness of those values.

Similarly a value may be precarious within a formal organization because it ranks low relative to immediate competitors in extensiveness of its social support. Other values may be more closely linked to the basic mission of the over-all organization, with resources and recognition granted accordingly.

Secure values, then, are those that are clearly defined in behavior and strongly established in the minds of many. Such values literally take care of themselves. Precarious values, on the other hand, need deliberately intentioned agents, for they must be normatively defined, or socially established, or both. Within a society, values that are precarious are likely to call forth a "movement," e.g., an old age pension movement or a co-operative movement, for adherents must crusade to get their conceptions of the desirable accepted. Within organizations, adherents of a precarious value system must similarly struggle for status and recognition. Secure values may be maintained without strenuous effort, but precarious values are problematic and require implementation.

This poses the general problem of how groups attempt to implement their values when they are precarious, and what changes in meaning and acceptance are incurred. The case in point concerns adult education administrators in a state school system. While adult education has had some acceptance in the American society as a general conception, functionaries have generally found themselves working with a weakly established set of values. As will be seen below, the goals and standards of this field have been somewhat undefined for several decades. In addition, adult education has had a marginal existence within the public schools, with its administrative agencies forced to search diligently for a secure operational base. An organizational adaptation has ensued that involves a transformation in values. This adaptation may be understood by recapitulating the core problems of adult education departments and the general response they have made.

THE CASE OF THE ADULT SCHOOL[5]

Conditions of Administrative Action

Adult education emerged as a movement in the United States in the 1920's with newly acquired organizations and a corps of spokesmen.[6] Within the public schools the movement meant a changed conception of adult participation. Before 1925 "night school" was emphasized, with programs restricted mainly to elementary and high school work, vocational training, and Americanization-Citizenship classes. The schools were heavily "remedial" in orientation, based originally on an extended-day definition. This orientation entailed the following program attributes: first, it was common to have planned, articulated curricula, modeled after the format of regular school levels. The unacculturated were led through a sequence of Americanization courses; those seeking a high school diploma worked through the usual high school curriculum, and so on. Secondly, there was a tendency toward the traditional relationship between school and student, where the school specifies alternative lines of study and student choice is exercised within the predetermined channels. With limited purposes, the schools, in a sense, "knew what they were doing" and student choice was constrained accordingly. For a brief period following World War I the schools had a particularly strong sense of mission in "immigrant education," for here their work was related to a clearly defined national problem.[7] Lastly, the schools were oriented not to the entire adult population, but to those segments that would be involved in these several purposes.

Since 1925 there has been a steady drift away from these characteristics, with a trend toward diversification of effort and broadening of clientele. While a similar tendency is apparent elsewhere in education, adult programs provide an extreme version and the California program has been a prototype, surpassing other states in the size and scope of the

[5] Data for this study were gathered over a fourteen-month period in 1952–53. Field work was carried out principally within the Adult Education Branch of the Los Angeles School System, which embraces twenty-five adult schools. In addition, interview, observation, and documentary analysis were extended to other departments of this school system, several surrounding school systems, the State Department of Education, state associations of adult education personnel, and outside interest groups. Material gathered in informal interviewing or taken from organizational files has been granted anonymity, despite the limitations thus placed upon proof. Documentation has been taken only from sources and records that are available to the public.

[6] The Department of Immigrant Education of the National Education Association became a Department of Adult Education in 1924. The American Association for Adult Education was set up in 1926, under the initiative and support of the Carnegie Corporation. The organizing of the AAAE is generally taken as the beginning of a national "adult education movement." The early development of adult education in the United States is reviewed in: Andrew Hendrickson, *Trends in Public School Adult Education in Cities of the United States, 1929–1939*, New York: Teachers College, Columbia University, 1943, Chapter II; and Morse A. Cartwright, *Ten Years of Adult Education*, New York: Macmillan, 1935, Chapters 1–3.

[7] T. J. Woofter, Jr., "The Status of Racial and Ethnic Groups," in President's Research Committee on Social Trends, *Recent Social Trends in the United States*, New York: McGraw-Hill, 1934, pp. 585–586.

adult activity.[8] The transformation that has occurred in this system, therefore, may highlight consequences of a general trend difficult to discern in other educational contexts. Our interest here lies in several conditions, important in defining the environment of decision for over a quarter of a century, that have propelled a change in values.

1. *The manifest ends of action.* The philosophy that became prevalent in the late 1920's with the emergence of an adult education movement had, in retrospect, two sharply divergent aspects: first, as an outgrowth of the Americanization effort, purpose was frequently voiced in the language of "enlightenment." This connoted a commitment to liberal education and a sense of educational mission. State and national spokesmen were prone to voice this ideology, e.g.:

> It was Plato who said that the best of education should be given to the rulers of the republic after they were thirty. In the American democracy, where all men are rulers of the republic, the process of education must be continuous and lifelong. . . .[9]

But the attempt to tie adult education to the ideals of liberal education did not prove viable. Grass-roots administrators were not in step with this doctrine but increasingly stressed a tenet related to the means of administration—that a proper conception of adult education could be implemented only by breaking away from formal patterns and clientele restrictions. For a quarter of a century this liberation theme has been growing within administrative circles, with the result that administrative units have increasingly worked with diffuse purpose. The evolution toward open-ended intent has reached the following point:

> Adult education embraces the learning achieved by adults during their mature years. . . . The major purposes of adult education are, first, to make adults in the community aware of individual and community needs, and, second, to give such education as will enable them to meet problems that exist now. Adult education stems directly from the people. The curriculum is based on present needs and problems.
>
> Education for the solution of problems in a democratic society includes the total range of human learning, from the learning of the simple means of communication, reading and writing, to the actual solution of the most complicated problems of human realtions.[10]

---

[8] To go back two decades, approximately a million persons were involved in adult education in the public schools in 1935. About one-third (319,000) were in California. See John W. Studebaker (Commissioner of Education, U.S. Office of Education), "Adult Education Under Public School Auspices," in *Handbook of Adult Education in the United States,* New York: American Association for Adult Education, 1936, pp. 169–175.

[9] Assistant Superintendent of Public Instruction in charge of Adult Education, State of California, in *Thirty-First Biennial Report,* Department of Education, State of California, 1924, p. 59.

[10] Formulated by the California Association of Adult Education Administrators and the Bureau of Adult Education, California State Department of Education. *California State Department of Education Bulletin,* 20 (May, 1951), p. 2.

Generality of purpose is apparent, since it now embraces all "adult learning." The program should be extremely diversified in order to meet a host of present individual, group, and societal problems. Such "purposes" hardly constitute directives, however, and officials are under pressure to establish more specific aims. To continue the example, the specific objectives of adult education in California are stated as follows:

1. To make adults aware of their civic responsibilities to one another and to the community
2. To make them economically more efficient
3. To develop an understanding of the attitudes and personal adjustments required for successful home life and family relationships
4. To promote health and physical fitness
5. To provide an opportunity for cultural development
6. To supplement and broaden educational backgrounds
7. To provide for the development of avocational interests through opportunities for self-expression.[11]

Generality of purpose remains, however, with "cultural development," "self-expression," etc., covering a wide range of possibilities. Also, the different objectives do not receive priority or emphasis, since a selective approach would reflect the tendency toward restriction and formalization from which adult education officials have sought to escape. Selective aims have not been forthcoming, and statements about specific objectives merely reaffirm that purpose is to be as broad as possible. Open-ended purpose is a basic characteristic of California adult schools.

The more indefinite purpose becomes, however, the less can ends intervene in administrative choice. For goals to influence decision-making, they must provide cues for what should be done. When the administrator is confronted with the recurrent question of what courses to add to his program, his diffuse aims leave him without criteria. He works within a milieu where there is no *educational* reason for the administrator to favor one subject over another. Thus, stated objectives are likely to become simply a rationale for a program broadly conceived and flexible in administration. The manifest ends of action function to widen administrative discretion.

2. *Organizational marginality.*[12] Since the basic purposes of the public schools center on the training of the young, various levels of education have become legitimized by relevance to this concern. Elementary schools, high schools, and junior colleges form an educational ladder in the public schools, and in California they all come under the doctrine of free public education. It is with these major units, comparatively well established within the school hierarchy and in the public image of education, that adult schools compete for position, budget, and support.

---

[11] *Ibid.*

[12] The "organizations" under analysis are adult schools, units of school systems that have adult education as their only program commitment. Multi-program organizations which may include adult education (e.g., junior colleges) are here excluded.

Within this organizational complex, adult education resides as an activity that is disconnected from the primary endeavor. It is not a part of the sequence of grades, its "students" exist completely outside of the range of compulsory attendance and have other occupations. These attributes leave adult education as a peripheral, non-mandatory effort of the schools, and its officials typically find themselves organizationally marginal. This marginality stems from the program's comparatively low degree of legitimacy as an important school activity and charge on public funds. A school program needs acceptance from various groups—its own personnel, other school units, the state legislature, politically potent interest groups, and the unorganized public. Only in the eyes of its own administrators and some of its teachers has the adult education activity had the level of acceptance that would guarantee its stability. The California Congress of Parents and Teachers, for example, is a strong supporter of adult education and is closely tied to adult schools through co-sponsorship arrangements; but, when pressed, PTA will maintain that the "compulsory education program" should not be jeopardized by "volunteer programs, in which category we place adult education."[13] A common indicator of this marginal status is the strong need, felt by adult administrators, of having to "sell the program" to the public and particularly to other school men. This has been a dominant theme in the adult education literature for several decades,[14] and still today adult education officials in California define their position as "stepchild" in nature:

> ...the adult program should...be accepted...as an equal part-
> ner when it comes to the status of its administrator, the pay of its
> teachers, use of facilities and so on. This equality should be thorough-
> going and sweep away the various forms of second-class treatment of
> adult educators and their students which are still found in many dis-
> tricts. Members of governing boards, superintendents, and day school ad-
> ministrators and teachers...tend to tolerate or show condescension to-
> ward adult programs as though they were step-children in the family of
> public schools, taken in for their subsistence allowances rather than for
> themselves.[15]

The marginality of the program may thus be seen as the *basic source of insecurity for administrative units*. Without a firmly legitimized status, the adult schools have little control over the conditions of their existence. Their position as "low man on the totem pole" is dangerous not only in times of depression, but whenever school finances are under pressure, for they stand to be "cut the first and the most severely when financial support runs low."[16] To win a permanently secure niche, administrative strategy needs to be oriented toward ultimately achieving a "peer" status (the

---

[13] Testimony of PTA representatives in *Partial Report of the Senate Interim Committee on Adult Education*, The Senate, State of California, March, 1953, p. 461.

[14] See Studebaker, *op. cit.*, p. 168; and Paul H. Sheats, Clarence D. Jayne, and Ralph B. Spence, *Adult Education*, New York: The Dryden Press, 1953, pp. 146–147.

[15] Bureau of Adult Education, *Report and Proceedings of the Montecito Workshop in Adult Education*, California State Department of Education, 1952, pp. 80–81.

[16] *Ibid*, pp. 85–86.

ideal), or a fixed partial parity of status that is clearly defined and respected by all. Short-run tactics, however, must be oriented to the problem of justifying a peripheral activity. The schools need "results." Thus
marginality within the larger, host educational systems heightens the effect
of the following conditions.

3. *Operating pressures.* The most important pressures bearing upon
these schools in day-to-day administration arise from *the enrollment economy.* First, school income is largely set by student attendance. Financial
support from the state is figured by the hours of attendance logged the
previous year, producing a direct relation between student turnout and
level of state aid.[17] Unless a school maintains and preferably increases attendance, future support is likely to stagnate, and a major slump in attendance constitutes a serious threat to organizational welfare. The closeness of
this relationship depends upon the degree of *local* support, that is, whether
local authorities will back the program out of their own tax levy if state
aid decreases.[18] The less likely this guarantee, the more budget and support rests on a quantity-of-clientele basis.[19] Since marginality is the common condition, *the appropriations process sets incentives for action in
the direction of building attendance.* There are no dependable sources of
financial support independent of student turnout. Therefore everything is
staked on the search for clientele.

A second important aspect of the enrollment economy is the tenuous
tie of student participants. The student body is part-time, voluntary, and
highly susceptible to casual attendance and easy termination. Participation is sharply affected by outside events beyond the control of the organization, e.g., warm weather, holiday seasons, and community events. Of
all student groups, part-time adult students are surely the most difficult to
maintain, and any adult education agency, public or private, has to solve
the problem of sustaining a non-captive student body. The point is that
the enrollment economy becomes a double-barreled pressure for adaptation
to outside interests. On the one hand, administrators are faced with an
uncommitted clientele; on the other, with the fact that students are the
rationale for existence, and in California their attendance is the basis for
appropriations. These conditions converge to define the prime short-run

---

[17] Five hundred and twenty-five hours of student time are equal to one unit
of "average daily attendance," the basic unit in state apportionments.

[18] State apportionments and local tax levies are the two main sources of school
revenue. Thus there is an inverse relationship between the proportion of costs
covered by one source as compared to the other. Local boards of education and professional administrators tend to view "cost" as the share of total outlay that is shoul-
dered by the local tax levy, for which they are directly responsible.

[19] Some adult education officials are allowed only as much money as their
enrollment brings into the local school system from state aid, i.e., *no* support from
local tax funds. The general picture has been described by a "Strayer Report" in
the following terms: "In practice, it is the exceptional district that uses a substantial
amount of local funds to support classes for adults." [Committee on the Conduct of
the Study of Higher Education in California, *A Report of a Survey of the Needs
of California in Higher Education,* Sacramento, 1948, p. 49.] In addition, some school
systems use the program for its income potential, making a surplus for other activities.
[Partial Report of the Senate Interim Committee on Adult Education, *op. cit.,* pp.
29–33 and 245–265.]

problem to be that of creating and sustaining a clientele base. An adaptation is called for that will reasonably guarantee the attraction, retention, and replacement of students. The needs of the enrollment economy generate persistent pressures to which administrators and teachers must make a number of adaptive responses.

These pressures cannot be ignored, for they are reflected in policies set by school boards and top professional staffs. For example, minimum size requirements for both the introduction and the continuation of classes are widespread throughout the state. Their effect is to make enrollment *the* criterion by which courses are initiated and continued.[20] The enrollment constraint is also reflected in informally derived norms; e.g., it becomes standard wisdom not to experiment with currently unpopular courses. Top administrators naturally take into account the close relationship between attendance, state support, and local costs. Economy and efficiency, as managerial concerns, then become defined in attendance-cost ratios. The result for subordinate adult education officials is an intense need to solve the attendance problem in individual classes, subject-matter areas, and the program at large.

The Organizational Adaptation

These conditions of an organizational system induce the following tendencies. Irrespective of intent, *the enrollment economy* renders the adult school highly sensitive to public likes and dislikes. Since "the public" is quite heterogeneous in both educational background and part-time interest, ready adjustment to it entails a conglomerate, "cafeteria" program. At the same time, the *manifest ends of action* are permissive and allow the school to adapt freely. Stated ends interpose no objection to the tendency that follows from practical pressures; in fact, they favor an effort to do all things for all men. There is an absence of specific missions from which standards and professional authority might flow. In addition, *marginality* deepens the need for administrators to assume an "other-directed" orientation. Insecurity fastens attention on building support by means at hand.

With these conditions lying behind administration, the cumulative effect of decision-making is to adjust the program rapidly to expressed interests of the population. An adaptation to clientele takes place along two dimensions: first, a continual drift toward the pursuits that intrigue a large number of people in the unorganized public—vocational interests on the one hand and hobbies on the other; second, the provision of specific classes for municipal agencies, private firms, and voluntary associations—classes related to in-service training in the case of the public agency or business firm, and membership activities for the service club. Thus there is an adaptation toward both the undifferentiated public and the organized-group structure of the population. In either case, however, organized groups or unorganized aggregates, classes are added and dropped according to the verbalized preferences of clients directly concerned.

[20] E.g., in Los Angeles in 1952–53, class-size policy was a "minimum for class continuation of 14 persons in average attendance per session over a one-month period." [*Board of Education Files, December 11, 1952,* Los Angeles School System.]

The adult education program that has developed in California may therefore be characterized as dominantly *a service enterprise*, for the key feature of this adaptation is the attempt of the schools to service consumers in an immediate way. Here several features of the schools may be adduced as evidence of a normatively unrestricted activity.

(1) The main instruments of program building have become "the sign-up list" and "the group petition."[21] These devices are simply objective ways of gauging demand. If demand is of the magnitude where the survival of a proposed class becomes probable, then its initiation is feasible. If the number of recruits increases, then more classes can be added and that part of the course assortment will grow. Thus the schools have an extreme version of what is known elsewhere in education as the elective system, and the relatively unlimited play of student choice determines the evolution of the collection of courses.[22]

(2) The structure of the teaching force is accommodated to the requirements of a service enterprise. Such a high degree of staff flexibility is needed that full-time work and guaranteed employment become administratively undesirable. Adaptation to a heterogeneous clientele involves considerable specialization in the subject matter and the hiring of the part-time specialist, e.g., a welder, a gardener, a dental technician, a housewife skilled in lampshade-making. In Los Angeles in 1952, for example, over 90 per cent of the adult teachers were part-time, with one-fourth working four hours a week or less.[23] Less than 20 per cent had tenure in adult education and less than 5 per cent possessed tenure at a fulltime level of employment.[24] Tenure requirements are "on the books," but in practice they must give way to the mandates of clientele pressure. This means that the teaching level of the work force remains non-professional, since career patterns are weak and the part-time teachers have their primary occupations elsewhere. Attempts to professionalize the teaching force have been blocked by the needs of a service facility. This is a case where a casual student body means that teachers are casually employed. Thus "service" dictates that the teacher will be dispensable, with his fate decided by the play of the enrollment economy.

(3) An administrative doctrine has emerged wherein officials define themselves to be in a close service relationship with actual and potential clienteles. This point is discussed below.

[21] Los Angeles adult education officials claim that clasess are commonly instituted by three means: petition forms passed out to groups; the accumulation of individual requests; and the recommendations of advisory committees. *Board of Education Files, January 8, 1953, Los Angeles School System.*

In the five largest cities of the state in 1948–49, more than three-fourths of new adult classes were initiated by the first two means—49 per cent of new classes had their origin in "waiting lists," and 27 per cent in "request by organized group." Philip M. Ferguson, *Practices in the Administration of Adult Education in the Public Schools of California,* Ed.D. dissertation, Stanford University, 1951, p. 88.

[22] Such terms as "curriculum" become meaningless in this context, since integrated offerings are very difficult to establish and maintain. A survey made in 1951–52 found some 2,315 different course titles in the state, a rough indication of the tendency toward miscellany. Partial Report of Senate Interim Committee, *op. cit.,* p. 344.

[23] Source: *Adult Education Branch Files, Los Angeles School System.*

[24] Source: *Personnel Division Files, Los Angeles School System.*

Building programs by consumer preference, however, produces an administrative dilemma. Located within school systems, adult education officials find their practices scrutinized by others in the light of school norms that are professional or "inner-directed" in kind, i.e., that educators should plan, initiate, and control changes on the basis of research and the assessment of experts. When laymen challenge school practices, for instance, the administrator ordinarily rests his case on expert opinion. Moreover, the drive for higher professional status on the part of teachers and administrators reinforces these sentiments. Thus there are school values, central to the self-image of the educator, that are against ready adjustment to student demands.

When this professional orientation is brought to bear upon the adult activity, the administrators do not fare well. They are judged to be in a posture of expediency, with much of their work seen as having little relationship to "education."[25] From outside the school system, state legislators and economy-minded interest groups repeatedly challenge the propriety of what is done. Cake decorating, rug making, and square dancing are some of the classes that bring the adult schools under fire. In one recent case of opposition, the entire state program underwent a hostile, sustained scrutiny by an investigating committee of the State Senate.[26] The current program was challenged as one saturated with frills, with 55 per cent of total enrollment placed in the frill category.[27] This investigation resulted in unfavorable publicity and restrictive legislation.

Thus in many ways a service enterprise, uncontrolled by school norms, sorely tries the educational respectability of the agencies involved. But the service tendency cannot be turned off easily since it is impelled by basic pressures of an organizational system. Classes of a questionable nature continually crop up when field administrators work with *ad hoc* demand, under pressure for an enrollment payoff. The crux of the matter is that the adult schools labor under incompatible needs. Their central dilemma is that the short-run need for clientele, set by the enrollment economy, strains against the long-run need for educational respectability as the basis for legitimacy. The adult schools are torn between being a service facility and a school enterprise.

The Ideological Response

With organizational work vigorously questioned, practices of debatable worth have to be justified or withdrawn. In defending their organizations, adult education officials have developed several rationales that reflect an attempt to legitimize a service enterprise.

Adult education is a valuable public relations instrument for the school system. Adult education officials intimate that their schools gather

---

[25] One school superintendent, supportive of adult education, expressed the view to the writer that at best a "by-product" theory of education holds in the adult school; i.e., attract adults on the basis of whatever they want to do and then sneak in some "educating."

[26] See Partial Report of the Senate Interim Committee on Adult Education, *op. cit., passim.*

[27] *Ibid.,* pp. 171–174.

support from "taxpayers and voters" not merely for themselves but for the school system in general.

> Several times in recent years the adult citizens of California have been called upon to vote on measures which provide the legal bases for the financial support of public education in this State. These citizens have consistently supported constructive legislation by popular majorities. It is impossible to measure the extent to which adult education contributed to this result, but it is known to have been substantial. *The best way to interest adults in the public school system is to make them a part of it.*[28]

Such defenses commend a service-oriented program to other educators as a basic public relations tool, one that commits outsiders to the entire system through involvement in adult education. Where this definition of the situation is at least partially accepted, then program costs can be seen in a new light. The adult activity becomes a mechanism by which the schools gain and consolidate public support; figuratively, its expenses can be charged to a good-will account.

Adult education is geared to the people's demands. This is the most important legitimizing principle, since it is widely used outside as well as within school ranks, and helps to fill the vacuum of intent left by open-ended purpose. It is "the public," and not the professional ruling by fiat, that should decide what is to be done. An image of the adult schools as organizations strongly influenced by clients is frequently suggested by a retail business analogy: "These schools and classes are educational service stations for all the people. . . ."[29] Under this rationale, "attendance success" becomes the touchstone of acceptability. Officials claim their practices are legitimized by public demand, defining this as appropriate for a democratic adult education program. In this way, emergent practices are linked to the values of the larger society.

The crucial point is that this two-fold ideology of service shifts the ground upon which the legitimacy of authority and practice is judged. Acceptance is sought on the basis of service rather than on intrinsic educational worth and professional competence.

VALUE DISPERSION: A QUALITATIVE CHANGE

The tendency toward service clearly changes the conception of adult education held by public school officials. In a trend that has continued unabated since the 1920's, general value symbols have become *less* closely linked to a body of educational norms. Instead, specific goals and standards of adult education are "decided" by various schools on a temporary and educationally *ad hoc* basis. What, then, remains as a conception of the desirable? Does adult education now have any universal meaning for its public school officials? At first, diffusion of intent is merely a matter of

---

[28] Remarks by Chief of the Bureau of Adult Education of the California State Department of Education. *California Schools*, 22 (November, 1951), pp. 402–403, emphasis added. See also, Sheats, Jayne, and Spence, *op. cit.*, pp. 151–152; and Jesse B. Sears, *Public School Administration*, New York: Ronald Press, 1947, p. 229.

[29] *Self Realization thru Adult Education* (brochure), Los Angeles School System, 1952.

degree; some schools have more ambiguous purpose than others. But a point is reached in the diffusion process where a different type of school must be said to have emerged. Where the service tendency is strong, the universal meaning of adult education for its officials is a particular mode of administration that is innocent of an educational mission. Schools become related to their students in a student-dominance pattern. To use a stimulus-response analogy: potential students stimulate action by indicating their desires, and the schools respond by adjusting courses and personnel. The S–R pattern is relatively unmediated by stable program norms, with tradition and professional choice intervening minimally between the stimuli and the organizational responses. As intervening structure, the organization is relatively *neutral*. This pattern, it may be noted, is characteristic of an adult community center, where educational purpose is essentially irrelevant. It is a pattern likely to emerge within schools whenever goal-directed action gives way to the pressures of adaptation to clientele.

In general, diffusion of intent means that purpose may be replaced by response. This is a general process by which organizations may shape values.[30] Within education, the most ready evidence of this transformation lies in *curriculum relativity*, when nearly all course alternatives become equal in educational value and their organizational worth is decided by demand. When this relativity obtains, we may say that there has been a qualitative shift in values, with "leadership" understood as the administering of a service facility.[31]

This type of change will occur frequently in democratic societies, as fields of effort that were once selective in orientation become responsive to a heterogeneous public. The tendency seems apparent throughout American education at the present time—in the university as well as in the public schools—but at levels other than adult education it is likely to be controlled to a greater degree by tradition and professionalism. Central school units are also under less pressure to cater to the interests of customers and are in a position to exercise some control over adaptations. And even in adult education this modification of values must be seen as only a *tendency*, since its extent will be determined by the specific conditions of organizational systems. The foregoing case study suggests why this adaptation is likely to occur frequently and in an extreme form in adult education. Weak normative definition and insecure operational base have rendered adult education a relatively precarious value in most organizational contexts,

---

[30] This process is a variant of the general phenomenon of "goal displacement." Merton has stressed the substitution of means for ends in bureaucratic routinization. [Robert K. Merton, *Social Theory and Social Structure*, Glencoe: Free Press, 1949, pp. 154–155.] A valuing of means to the exclusion of ends may also be a common result of organizational adaptation to environmental pressures. For a general statement of "retreat to technology" as a response to administrative anxiety, see Philip Selznick, *The Executive as Statesman*, Evanston: Row, Peterson and Company, 1956 (forthcoming). Several interesting cases of goal displacement may be found in Messinger, *op. cit.;* and Warren Breed, "Social Control in the Newsroom: A Functional Analysis," *Social Forces*, 33 (May, 1955), pp. 326–335.

[31] Cf. Mannheim's discussion of *laissez-faire* adult education. Karl Mannheim, *Freedom, Power, and Democratic Planning*, London: Routledge and Kegan Paul, 1951, pp. 254–255.

e.g., the university, the trade union, the public school. Unless there is special protection granted by the larger organization, the marginal agency will adjust purpose to pressures more than is usually the case. But the move toward pure service may be affected by many factors in the internal and external environment of organizations, such as state and regional traditions, the degree of professionalism in the administrative staff, and particularly the bases for financial support.

We may expect that this value adaptation, where purpose is reduced to service, will be pronounced when (a) organizations attached to a precarious value (b) continue to find themselves without a dependable clientele, or more broadly, with no *specific* outside social forces to sustain them. Then organizational needs of survival and security are likely to propel an adaptation to a diffuse social base, and purpose will be adjusted accordingly. The organization adaptation will achieve broader acceptance of given value symbols and secure a stronger operational base for functionaries, but goals and standards will be attenuated. The paradox is that value weakness may be reduced on one ground and increased on another. Value symbols become more firmly grounded in a social base, but less defined in a proximate system of goals and standards.

TECHNOLOGY, ORGANIZATION AND ADMINISTRATION

James D. Thompson and Frederick L. Bates*

This article compares administration in the factory, the mine, the hospital, and the university. The central theme of the article is that differences in organizations' goals lead to differences in technology and consequently to differences in administration. The following specific areas are compared: (1) determination of objectives; (2) management of resources (manpower, the authority structure, materials, and money); (3) effects of change on resource management; and (4) execution, or the problem of coordination and integrating.

Large-scale organizations have evolved to achieve goals which are beyond the capacities of the individual or the small group. They make possible the application of many and diverse skills and resources to complex systems of producing goods and services. Large-scale organizations, therefore, are particularly adapted to complicated *technologies*, that is, to those

* From *Administrative Science Quarterly*, 2, No. 3 (December 1957), 325–343. Reprinted with permission.

sets of man-machine activities which together produce a desired good or service.[1]

As scientific knowledge has led to increasingly complicated technologies, large-scale organizations have multiplied; they have become necessary in new fields, and they have changed their characteristics. Medical care affords a striking illustration, for in this area the technology has been revolutionized within a generation. From reliance on a few simple home remedies, passed from generation to generation, and ultimate resource to a general practitioner with standard prescriptions for standard systems, health-care practice in Western cultures has moved to a much more specialized, more highly divided technology. The diagnostic equipment and procedures used by the physician are no longer simply constructed and exercised, and prescriptions are no longer blended from a small list of basic powders and essences easily stocked by any local pharmacist. The "simple" treatment of a virus infection, for example, now relies on a whole series of large-scale organizations which perform research, produce pharmaceuticals, and ship, store, and prepare medications. Certain conditions which once required confinement of the patient to the home with nursing by other (amateur) members of the family now call for confinement in the hospital, where a battery of technical specialists, nurses, and dieticians can contribute specialized skills toward therapy.

The list of examples is endless, illustrating the point that the elaboration of technology usually means that activities which formerly were considered single units of effort are dissected and split into multiple units of effort, each of them specialized and highly developed. With this "elongation" of the technology comes increasing complexity of the social organization designed to operate it.

In the following paragraphs we will explore some of the ways in which technology, as a variable, may impinge on organization and on administration. We will develop the general proposition that the type of technology available and suitable to particular types of goals sets limits on the types of structures appropriate for organizations and that the functional emphases, the problems of greatest concern, and the processes of administration will vary as a result. For this exploratory effort, we will focus on four types of organizations: the mining enterprise, the manufacturing organization, the hospital, and the university. While these clearly do not exhaust the major types of organizations, they have sufficiently different goals and technologies to serve as illuminating examples.[2] The discussion necessarily will be general; we are seeking

---

[1] We are thus using the term *technology* in its broad sense as a system of techniques. Similar usage is made by E. D. Chapple and C. S. Coon, who say: "Our present purpose is to show how different peoples combine their various techniques into total adjustments (to their environments), which we shall call technologies" (*Principles of Anthropology* [New York, 1942], p. 223).

[2] A number of valuable studies throw light on these four kinds of organizations. While our gross examination here is highly simplified and is not necessarily an accurate reflection of any of these studies, we are indebted to the following: On mining: J. F. Scott and R. P. Linton, *Three Studies in Management* (London, 1952); A. W. Gouldner, *Patterns of Industrial Bureaucracy* (Glencoe, Ill., 1954). On the factory: E. Jaques, *The Changing Culture of a Factory* (London, 1951); H. Ronken and P. R. Lawrence, *Administering Changes* (Boston, 1954); and Scott and Linton, cited

central tendencies. Each class of organization displays variations. This is particularly true in the field of manufacturing, and to make the discussion manageable we will conceive of a factory mass-producing a single line of products widely distributed to consumers. Moreover, references to technology will be based on present technology.

We will compare these types of organizations with respect to three broad functional areas of administration: the setting of objectives, or policy formulation; the management of resources (including people, authority structure, money, and materials); and execution.[3]

DETERMINATION OF OBJECTIVES

Whatever the motives of its members—accumulating wealth, achieving fame, exercising power, and so on—an enterprise must in the long run produce something useful or acceptable to others in order to merit support. The determination of what the enterprise will seek to produce we will refer to as the determination of objectives or goals or, alternatively, as policy formulation.

The manufacturing enterprise may have difficulty in determining what particular demands of what potential customers it will attempt to satisfy, and this is especially true in dynamic and highly competitive markets. Unless the product is extremely costly, however, or costs vary greatly with variations in volume, the manufacturing enterprise may test its decision through pilot operations. In any event the acceptance of the product is rather quickly and accurately reflected in sales figures or ultimately in profit figures, and reappraisal of decisions regarding objectives can therefore be rapid. If reappraisal leads to a redefinition of objectives, capital goods including machinery and raw materials can often be adapted to the new purpose or be sold, so that the manufacturing enterprise may be able to convert effectively from one objective to another; the technology may be relatively flexible. Finally, policy determination in the manufacturing enterprise is largely a matter for top administrators.

The mine is less flexible. It possesses highly specialized equipment and property rights which for the most part cannot be converted to other major objectives. The objectives of the mine may be adjusted to the extent that it may offer new sizes, grades, packaging, or delivery arrangements and hence may cater to a new market, but those responsible for the mining enterprise would find it difficult to get it out of mining and into a different industry—or even to shift from the mining of coal to the mining of a different mineral. The scope of alternative objectives thus appears to be less for those enterprises with heavy, specialized capital investments.

---

above. On the hospital: A. H. Stanton and M. S. Schwartz, *The Mental Hospital* (New York, 1954); T. Burling, E. M. Lentz, and R. N. Wilson, *The Give and Take in Hospitals* (New York, 1956). On the university: L. Wilson, *The Academic Man* (New York, 1942); F. Znaniecki, *The Social Role of the Man of Knowledge* (New York, 1940).

[3] This framework is taken from E. H. Litchfield, Notes on a General Theory of Administration, *Administrative Science Quarterly*, 1 (1956), 3–29.

In both the university and the hospital the general or abstract purpose of the enterprise is relatively fixed. But in both cases there is wide latitude for interpretation of the general into more specific objectives. Because knowledge is so specialized the members of the university must decide what it will teach, and as new areas of knowledge develop or split off, they must decide anew. Here the product is intangible, and reappraisal of the policy decision is difficult and drawn out. Furthermore, because of the heterogeneity of university objectives and departments, top administrative officers can reappraise decisions only in gross or general terms; professional members specialized in the particular subject can claim greater qualification to judge. The university president is also highly dependent on that professional staff to interpret and implement a new educational policy. Hence, in a real sense, power to determine or veto objectives in the university is widely diffused.

The hospital, likewise, is highly dependent in the matter of objectives on the decisions of its professional medical members, who are the obvious authorities on health matters and who in the final analysis must implement the policy they believe in. Any shift in emphasis, for example, from treatment of the ill to maintenance of health can become effective only through the persuasion and conviction of professional members.

Thus in both the university and the hospital the general goal of the organization specifies an area of activity instead of a specific activity and therefore is subject to wide differences in specific interpretations. Since the technology employed by both types of organizations is relatively flexible as compared to that of the factory or the mine, goals may be revised or adjusted more easily to the technological resources available.

It appears, therefore, that the following variables are of particular importance as conditions affecting policy formulation:

(1) *Degree of concreteness of the goal*, as expressed in the product. This is a matter of tangibility and is verbally expressed by such questions as the precision with which the product can be described, the specificity with which it can be identified, and the extent to which it can be measured and evaluated.

(2) *Adaptability of the technology* associated with the goal. Here the question is the extent to which the appropriate machines, knowledge, skills, and raw materials can be used for other products.

While these definitions have not been operationalized, they seem to be adequate for our exploratory purposes, and we can advance the following hypotheses regarding these two variables and their relationships to policy formulation:

(1) If the product is concrete, such as mined material, and the technology unadaptable, the major concerns over policy will be the possibility that the environment may reject or dispense with the product. This is happening now in the case of the tuberculosis hospital, for example.

(2) If the product is concrete or tangible and the technology adaptable, the major concerns over policy will be when to shift to new products and which of the possible alternative uses of the technology present the most favorable opportunities. For example, should the watch

manufacturer shift to cosmetic jewelry, to armament mechanisms, or to still another product calling for the machinery and skills at his disposal?

(3) If the product is abstract and the technology adaptable, the organization again has great adaptability to its environment, and the major policy-formulation problem will be achieving agreement on goals and on the appropriate application of technologies in pursuit of them. The modern university, for example, seems torn between emphasis on applied and on traditional studies; the National Foundation for Infantile Paralysis is seeking new causes to support, having all but achieved its original purpose.

(4) If the product is abstract but the technology unadaptable, environmental redefinition of goals presents a serious threat to the organization, since the technology can be adapted to redefined goals only within limits. The administrative problem here is to "educate" or influence relevant parts of the environment to accept those products which are possible with existing technology. Political parties and fundamentalist churches seem to be facing this problem in modern America.

MANAGEMENT OF RESOURCES

Every enterprise has problems of acquiring and employing people, finances, materials, and authority. The difficulties of management are not necessarily equal in each of these four resource areas, however, and the amount of attention given to each probably varies from enterprise to enterprise as well as within one enterprise at different stages of its development. Likewise, the content of those activities which serve to manage any one resource varies, as the following paragraphs will illustrate.

Management of Manpower

The factory and the mine, as enterprises operating on physical objectives, have relatively few problems of personnel selection below the management level, since the operational activities are either standardized or are settled by experience, and the training of operators is not overly difficult. There may be a high degree of functional differentiation in the factory, but this differentiation tends to be based on the machine rather than on the operator; operation of a complicated machine may be so simplified and repetitive that individuals are relatively interchangeable. Hierarchical distinctions tend to be shaded or gradual, with normal skill and experience qualifying the operator for advancement. Vacancies, therefore, can be filled from below. Since machinery is so important, a major personnel-management problem is to ensure safety in its operation.

Because many members of the general population are potentially qualified as members of the factory or the mine and because training to entrance-level standards is quick, expansion of activities may be undertaken on relatively short notice. Long-range forecasting of personnel needs may be an important factor in factory location, but "personnel-development" or training programs can be confined largely to preparation for future executive or supervisory positions. The large percentage of operative personnel, coupled with an open hierarchy, provides the factory enterprise with opportunity to screen members on the job and hence to locate future supervisory or executive talents. This is less likely in the mine, where the division between those working above and below ground is rather sharp, and mobility between these categories is low. In the mine, moreover, flexibility of daily operations is necessary because of the lack of control over the natural environment from which the material is taken. This front-line flexibility requires the exercise of judgment, and hence experience is a major basis for functional and hierarchical differentiation.

Both the hospital and the university must rely heavily on professionally trained people. In the case of the hospital, moreover, the situation is complicated by the fact that some of the key professionals are not employees of the hospital, in the sense of being on the pay roll. They are not, therefore, recruited as employees. This is true also for many supporting activities which are performed by a voluntary "staff." Functional differentiation is extreme in both the hospital and the university, and the intensity of training required for each special area is so great that interchangeability is virtually unknown. There is sharp differentiation between student, clerical, and professional ranks in the university, as well as little opportunity within a given university for a member to move from one level to another. Similar distinctions exist between patient, nurse, and doctor levels in the hospital. The length and cost of medical training mean that for practical purposes members cannot move from one category to a higher category; experience and seniority have nothing to do with a nurse's becoming a doctor.

The long periods of training required for professional competence in universities and hospitals mean that recruitment of professionals is not easy. On-the-job training may enhance the member's value within his specialty, but it is not a major means of obtaining replacements for vacancies in upper-level jobs. Moreover, while professional recognition or licensing presumably guarantees a minimum level of competence, there are many shades of ability above that minimum which are not easily judged until the individual member has already been established in the enterprise.

Thus in the modern factory and mine the technology relies largely on mechanical facilities supported by "know-how" which grows out of familiarity with the mechanical operation. But in the hospital and university, even complicated mechanical devices play second fiddle to professional expertise which is wrapped up in the human being and which grows out of long exposure to academic and abstract systems of thought. These differences are reflected in recruitment, allocation, and training of personnel.

Management of Authority Structure

In the factory, authority may be highly centralized or, conversely, the discretion of individual operators may be severely circumscribed, since activities are relatively routine and engineering standards such as quality controls can be used extensively. Particularly where various sub-assembly products feed into a final assembly line, central direction of the speed of operations and of the size, quality, or color mix is essential. The factory also has problems in maintaining a recognized position of authority for the supervisor, since experience tends to be a major basis for supervisory selection and the "boss" was formerly "one of us."

The mine, too, is predominantly staffed by "blue-collar" members, but the lack of standardization of the environment, together with distance and communication difficulties, requires a more decentralized day-to-day operation, with greater discretion lodged in the mine team and the supervisor. Constant danger, coupled with discomfort and darkness, makes members of the mining team somewhat reluctant to accept authoritative communications from executives above ground, and the mining enterprise probably would run into severe resistance if it attempted to set up and enforce rigid, disciplinary communications. Instead, authority or the exercise of discretion tends to be based on familiarity with the problem, and hence it is lodged in the most experienced member of the work team.

In the university, traditionally dominated by professional persons, authority on educational matters must be highly decentralized, since knowledge rather than title or seniority is recognized as the basis for authority—as reflected in "academic freedom"—and knowledge is highly specialized. Discretion in academic activities is controlled less by university executives than by professional peers of the faculty member. Student members of the university are more subject to centralized authority, but this is limited by a tradition that faculty members determine academic or educational policies, and anything which affects the student can be construed as an educational matter.

The authority structure of the modern hospital is an even more complicated matter. Since treatment of patients is not easily standardized, judgment must be exercised frequently by those with greatest knowledge of the case. The professional physician has the greatest knowledge about the ailment or disease, but on the other hand the nurse who is with the patient much more often may believe she has more knowledge of the patient. The social distance between physician and nurse is great, however, and the exercise of authority by the physician tends to be resented by the nurse (or vice versa) unless a strong informal organization bridges the two ranks. The bridging of this gap may be helped by the fact that both the nurse and the doctor know that the nurse cannot really threaten the doctor's position either in the hospital or in the larger community.

Thus it appears that in the mine and the factory, which rely heavily on mechanical aspects of the technology, authority is allocated primarily as control over the mechanical operation and takes the form of authority over people to the extent that behavior must be disciplined to the requirements of the mechanical operation. In the hospital and university, however, the heavy reliance on human (professional) abilities means that authority is exercised primarily with reference to people. Lacking the mechanical referent to bolster authoritative behavior, the university and hospital must depend to a much greater extent upon agreement or consensus, backed up by professional ethics and standards.

Materials Management

The factory is concerned with acquiring and changing things, and there is emphasis, therefore, on moving inventory and on plant and machinery. Achieving volume and quality at low cost usually requires routinization of operations, and this in turn requires standardization of raw materials. Because a steady flow of standardized raw materials is so important to the factory and often constitutes a rather high portion of costs, purchasing, inventory, and transportation procedures attract a large amount of attention in day-to-day operations. The emphasis on precision scheduling and on predictability of production means that equipment failure may seriously cripple an entire operation, and preventive maintenance receives much time and thought. Control over use of materials can be approached in the factory through measurement of spoilage or waste. Since standardization is high, deviation can be measured readily. Hence responsibility for materials management can be widely diffused in the factory.

In the mining enterprise, rights to deposits replace plant as a major concern, and preventive maintenance and steps to control the sources of the mineral against flooding, cave-ins, and so on are particularly important. These can be standardized only in a rough way, and therefore judgment must be exercised frequently. Furthermore, maximum "winning" of the material must be balanced against risk to personnel and to the remaining deposits. Machinery is cumbersome and difficult to move; hence effective placement is important. Purchasing is not the major matter in the mine that it is in the factory, but shipping is extremely important, since storage facilities can be depleted rapidly by the bulky product, and breakdown of transportation facilities can lead to shutdown of operations. Materials management in the mine is by and large a matter for supervisory and executive personnel rather than for operators.

Both the hospital and the university have important interests in plant, since both deal with people (who are "bulky") and both must provide space and facilities for a variety of human needs, including sleeping, eating, and recreation. Management frequently involves decisions as to the allocation of activities to various parts of the physical plant as shifts occur in technological procedures or in work loads.

Since in the university symbolic materials are major aids to the student and instructor, the collection, storage, and issuance of books require constant attention. These materials, moreover, are far from standardized and are highly specialized, so that judgment regarding new materials must be exercised constantly and must be made frequently by the instructor concerned. Again, because symbolic materials are easily lost, stolen, or damaged, rigorous procedures must be established to maintain inventories.

The hospital has additional complications, since many of its expendable materials are highly specialized, easily confused, and perishable and since the hospital must be prepared for any of a variety of possible emergencies. Improper storage or errors in labeling medicines can be extremely costly, and the hospital often must rely on the health team to exercise care and discretion in these matters. Professional standards, reinforced by dread of being the cause of human suffering or loss of life, facilitate this decentralization of responsibility. Nevertheless the hospital provides a number of security routines, including the keeping of complete accounts of the disposal of certain materials and restriction on the identity of persons who can withdraw or use them.

Management of Money

During periods of economic stability at least, the manufacturing firm may be able to estimate its money needs rather accurately. Since its inventories and other assets are largely tangible, it can obtain needed money by frank exchange of the product for cash, by pledging assets as collateral, or by sale of an interest in the firm. Hence frequently the question of acquisition of money becomes one of seeking the most favorable terms, and large errors in such decisions can be detected relatively rapidly. During growth periods, however, investment matters may become more complicated, involving broader and less easily established alternatives and considerable risk. Expenditure of available money can be allocated within the manufacturing enterprise on the basis of expected return on yield and can be controlled by budgetary and accounting procedures, since standardization and predictability are relatively great. While neither allocation nor control are foolproof, such procedures are effective in the factory, and operating members can be held responsible for costs.

The mining enterprise can estimate its needs for money less precisely, since the cost of winning coal or ore is never perfectly known in advance, and disaster or geological fault may abruptly increase costs. Acquisition of money is again more difficult; reserves are less easily pledged as collateral than are the easily accessible inventories of the manufacturing firm. Allocation of available money may be budgeted on the basis of periodic estimates, but the technological requirements for flexibility may require frequent change of these programs. Formal control over the expenditure of money remains rather centralized, since the miner tends to be more safety conscious than cost conscious; and because mining operations call for judgment by the mining team, economic use of costly resources is not easily ensured.

For the university the determination of need is not difficult on the face of it, since enrollments and other costs can be fairly well forecast. But the intangibility of the product means that whether enough money has been raised is always a moot question. Acquisition, especially for the privately financed university, is a constant problem because those who most directly benefit from university activities usually are not able to pay the total costs for their training, and it is difficult to demonstrate graphically to potential contributors the indirect benefits they receive from the university's activities. Financial support rests largely on appeal, not trade.

Allocation of money is a time-consuming activity in the university. It cannot be accomplished by a few central officers because the various departments of a university are so specialized that there are few standards for evaluating the strength of their claims to scarce money. Control of expenditures through budgeting and accounting practices is relatively easy, although it tends to be accomplished only through administrative policing, since professional members of the university tend to place knowledge values above cost values.

Monetary needs of the hospital can be determined reasonably well; although work loads may vary widely from day to day or week to week, general trends can be predicted and irregularities averaged out. Acquisition of needed funds, however, presents another and more important problem, for the hospital in our culture is expected to render service on the basis of health needs rather than on ability to pay, and recovery of expenses often has been a drawn-out procedure. As far as operating costs are concerned, hospitalization insurance is relieving this problem, but capital funds still are difficult to acquire.[4] Allocation of funds may depend partly on budget procedures, but changes in work loads or new technological developments may require frequent revision. Control over the use of funds is accomplished largely by centralized handling of purchasing, but professional norms of service sometimes conflict with cost-reduction norms, and professional personnel tend to feel that cost drives interfere with their activities. Control over expenditure of items which eventually are translated into monetary terms is therefore somewhat difficult. Waste and spoilage are not easily checked.

IMPLICATIONS OF CHANGE FOR RESOURCE MANAGEMENT

From the foregoing section, it appears that an important variable distinguishing various types of organizations is the extent to which the technology is lodged in human as contrasted with nonhuman resources. For the sake of simplicity we will refer to this variable as the *ratio of mechanization to professionalization*. Reflecting this variable against the *adaptability of the technology*, discussed earlier, it is possible to hypothesize the following:

(1) If the technology of an organization has a high ratio of mechanization and is readily adaptable, the major resource problem involved in a change of product is likely to center around properly standardized raw materials.

(2) If the technology of an organization has a high ratio of mechanization but is not adaptable, the problem will be to avoid technological obsolescence; major resource concerns will involve materials and money and the maintenance of fluidity by amassing financial reserves.

(3) If the technology has a low ratio of mechanization but the human abilities are easily refocused on new products, the major problems are likely to be those involved in execution, to be discussed below.

(4) If the technology has a low ratio of mechanization and at the

---

[4] This is evidenced by the fact that fund-raising organizations have grown up to provide money-gathering services primarily for hospitals, churches, and colleges.

same time is not easily adapted to other goals, personnel-management problems are likely to come to the fore, with emphasis on replacing and retraining members of the organization.

EXECUTION

The problem of welding an enterprise into an integrated whole varies with the amount and kinds of differentiation of its parts and with the kinds of relationships which the technological process requires; that is, different kinds of heterogeneity call for different ways of homogenizing. The technology appropriate to a particular purpose not only determines in an important way the extent and type of differentiation but also determines the amount of coordination and cooperation required and the locus of responsibility for these.

The manufacturing enterprise, for example, may have major need for sequential interdependence, with each work team or section depending on others only for the timely and satisfactory completion of certain prior operations. Coordination required by this type of interdependence can be achieved largely by work scheduling and controls over the flow of materials and the quality of operations. In the factory, then, coordination between individual members of the work team may be the responsibility of an on-the-spot supervisor, but the linking together of various functional activities can be achieved largely by executives at relatively centralized points in the enterprise.

Mining involves separation or removal of minerals from their environment, and mining operations are therefore subject to unpredictable environmental changes—water seepage, geological faults, cave-ins, gas pockets, and so forth. Routinization is not easily achieved, and even with mechanized equipment environmental changes may make schedules inapplicable. The judgment of the miner is therefore indispensable, and the communication difficulties introduced by the above-ground and below-ground dichotomy increase the importance of the miner's reliability. Because day-to-day activities are somewhat unpredictable, relationships among members of the mining team can be specified only abstractly; specific relationships must be worked out on the spot, spatial requirements present close constant supervision, and coordination therefore is highly dependent on the informal organization.

Routinization of many aspects of hospital activity is essential, both to prevent dangerous omissions or oversights and to provide some predictability as the basis for carrying on when crises occur. On the other hand, each medical case is considered unique, and hence considerable flexibility (based on professional judgment) is required. To a much greater extent than in the factory, the hospital has need for collateral coordination, with the nurse, doctor, laboratory technician, dietician, and so on, integrating their activities simultaneously around the needs of the patient. In these cases central executives may act to facilitate coordination, but in the final analysis it must come largely through the cooperative efforts of operating individuals. Moreover, while there is ordinarily a certain rhythm in the amount and type of attention required during each twenty-four-hour period, the patient is an around-the-clock charge and requires periodic attention. Hence communication between shifts is vital, and there is considerable attention given to accurate posting of elaborate records. Nevertheless the specialized and complicated nature of medical technology means that records and charts cannot convey everything of importance, and informal organization of the therapy team is essential.

In the university, routinization of a superficial sort is easily achieved. Hours of class meetings, systems of examinations and grading, and so forth, usually are standardized. But in teaching matters routinization is not easily achieved because the imparting of knowledge remains a matter of judgment. The ability of the instructor to inspire and motivate the student cannot be centralized, and the integration of extracurricular activities can be centralized only partially. The instructor is free to maintain that he and only he can determine what his students should know and how they should proceed to acquire that knowledge about his special area of competence. Routinization tends, therefore, to be by discipline or topic rather than university-wide, and standardization is accomplished more by professional codes and standards than by administrative directive. Traditionally there is little interdependence between faculty members; although it is recognized that each deals with only "part" of the student, the integration of these part activities has been up to the student or is accomplished through informal interaction among faculty members and students. Faculty members typically are "not interested" in administrative matters except to escape interference by administrators, but the faculty may involve itself in many matters outside the classroom under the guise of "educational policy," since the development of the "whole" student is believed to result from his total experience in the university setting.

Under the more standardized conditions of the manufacturing firm, and to a lesser extent the mine, coordination can be planned and controlled relatively effectively from the center. In the less standardized, more professional fields, this is less likely to be the case—but at the same time more types of supporting activities usually are required. In the hospital and university these include feeding, housing, providing recreation, and providing opportunities for spiritual or religious expression, and so on.

Thus while responsibility for the integration of primary operations is relatively diffuse in professional-type enterprises, central executives tend to have a greater variety of activities and departments to integrate. Generally, it would seem, the greater the differentiation of an enterprise into identifiable parts, the greater is the need for fitting those parts together. Add to this the fact that human beings set themselves apart from one another on bases other than those officially arranged by administrators—on such bases as sex, age, ethnic origin, religion, style of living, political views, professional or union affiliations, and so on, and one perceives that the heterogeneity of the modern enterprise can be amazing.

Every criterion for differentiation of functions or hierarchy presents a possible or potential basis for cleavage and conflict—for the withholding of cooperation. Hence the more functional or hierarchical distinctions there are within the enterprise, the greater the problems of integration. Since systems low in mechanization of the technology and high in professionalization tend to be more clearly differentiated in this respect, it is in this kind of system that coordination problems are greatest.

Furthermore, it is in the enterprises where human differentiation is greatest that collateral types of coordination are most required, and hence interaction between people of various categories is the more intense. This interaction among people who are different or who have been led to believe they are different means that interpersonal frictions or tensions are to be expected. And yet it is in these same enterprises that interpersonal interaction must carry much of the burden for necessary coordination. In the hospital and the university, then, leadership in the form of emphasizing objectives and of stressing such factors as common devotion to a cause loom more important than they do in the manufacturing enterprise or the mine. And while resource management is important in the hospital and the university, the problems this presents are less demanding on the administrator than are those of executing.

The following hypotheses can now be advanced, based on the variable *ratio of mechanization* as it is related to the executing function of administration:

(1) If the technology has a high ratio of mechanization, executing problems are likely to be of an engineering nature since specialization is largely in the machine, the bases for human differentiation are small, and the human "zones of indifference" are great.

(2) If the technology has a low ratio of mechanization, however, the coordination and integration of human activities will be a major administrative concern. Members of the organization differentiate among themselves as specialists, a distinction leading to problems of status and authority relationships. Any change in technology is likely to upset established relationships among members. Furthermore, if the goal is abstract, there is likely to be disagreement over the interpretation of the goal in terms of products; the human "zones of indifference" are small.[5]

CONCLUSIONS

The foregoing paragraphs have attempted to illustrate some of the differences that various goals—and appropriate technologies—can make for organization and administration. At one level of analysis, all large organizations have similar problems, but at a more detailed level of analysis, these problems become variables.

We have attempted to show that the following three variables are important enough to deserve extended research: (1) abstractness of the goal, as expressed in the product, (2) adaptability of the technology, and (3) ratio of mechanization to professionalization of the technology. We may perhaps underscore our argument that the general relationships between technology, organization, and administration provide important areas for study by advancing a final set of more general propositions:

[5] The concept "zone of indifference" was advanced by Chester I. Barnard, *The Functions of the Executive* (Cambridge, Mass., 1938), pp. 167 ff. See also Herbert A. Simon, *Administrative Behavior* (New York, 1955), pp. 11 ff. Simon prefers the term "zone of acceptance."

(1) An organization overly identified with a particular technology may lose its opportunity to produce a particular product as more effective technologies are adopted by other organizations pursuing the same goal. This proposition simply applies the concept of "trained incapacity" to the organizational level rather than the personal level.[6]

(2) As a technology becomes more specialized, it appears that the organization's flexibility in shifting from one goal to another is curtailed. The corporation desiring to withdraw from a given industry, for example, no longer rearranges its resources once applied to that industry, but rather sells a division or subsidiary as a unit to another corporation.

(3) As a technology becomes more complicated, entry of a new organization into a field becomes more difficult. Entrance seems to occur usually in the case of (a) an existing organization with tremendous resources, shifting part of those into a new field, or (b) the formation of a new enterprise at a time when a new technology is appearing; by avoiding problems of relearning and reequipping itself, the new organization may be able to exploit a new technology more advantageously than an established organization.

(4) As a technology becomes elongated, any particular organization will tend to have less control over the total technological process, to be more dependent on other organizations for prior or subsequent operations in the total process (for resources and so on). This, again, tends to reduce flexibility in deciding goals and managing resources. The increased dependence on specialists, for example, means greater reliance on pretraining of personnel by organizations specializing in that training, such as universities and institutes.

(5) The organization adapting to new technology—as most are doing constantly—will be faced with "new" resource-management problems which established procedures and strategies will not always handle satisfactorily. Hence improvisation and constant learning will be characteristic of such organizations.

(6) Technological development, by requiring more specialization of personnel and equipment, adds to the heterogeneity of an organization. Related skills and knowledge formerly lodged in one person or one group are split. While such divisive developments undoubtedly allow for greater precision within an area of activity, they also intensify the need for, and concern over, integration of the several activities.

(7) Increasing technological complication is accompanied by the proliferation of professional and technical societies and associations, each with its unique values and code of ethics. Hence there is more likelihood for organizational members to owe loyalty or allegiance to a profession as well as to the organization, greater opportunity for the demands of the organization to conflict with those of the profession, and at the same time a greater opportunity for the individual employee to enforce de-

---

[6] This a restatement of Thorstein Veblen's concept. For a penetrating discussion of this and similar concepts at the personal level, see R. K. Merton, "Bureaucratic Structure and Personality," in his *Social Theory and Social Structure* (Glencoe, Ill., 1949), pp. 151–160.

mands on the organization by invoking sanctions from the profession.[7] Finally, the proliferation of specialization provides additional bases for organizational members to differentiate among themselves and hence for cleavage to develop.

[7] The organization may also resort to the reverse of this procedure.

JOB DESIGN RESEARCH
Louis E. Davis and Ralph R. Canter*

This article points to the kind of impact the design of jobs can have upon the functioning of an organization. As such, it represents what has become identified as the "job-enlargement" approach to job design. From the point of view of this book, the significance of the article is that it shows the manner in which the design of work per se may determine the character of an organization.

In two previous articles[1] the subject of Job Design, i.e., the process of designing job content (as distinguished from methods design), was introduced, and current practices and the need for research on this important problem were indicated. Following a brief review of the previous material, a recent research study specifically designed to test the effects of modifications in job content on productivity, quality, and job satisfaction will be presented. In addition, two other studies are reviewed to help indicate the scope and complexity of the problem area.

TRENDS IN JOB DESIGN

Very recently a number of organizations have begun to experiment with changing the content of jobs in the direction of specifying job content having greater complexity, containing a longer sequence of tasks, requiring greater skills, permitting rotation between tasks, and having greater responsibility for inspection, for setting up and maintaining equipment, and for controlling production rates. This development, known as job enlargement, has been received with great enthusiasm by the public, press, and business community.[2]

* From The Journal of Industrial Engineering, 7, No. 6 (November–December 1956), 275–282. Reprinted with permission.
[1] L. E. Davis and R. R. Canter, "Job Design," Journal of Industrial Engineering, VI, No. 1 (January 1955), 3; L. E. Davis, R. R. Canter, and J. F. Hoffman, "Current Job Design Criteria," Journal of Industrial Engineering, VI, No. 2 (March 1955), 5.
[2] "Broadening the Job," Time, 63 (April 12, 1954), 100; D. R. Wright, "Job Enlargement," Wall Street Journal, March 11, 1954, p. 1; D. Wharton, "Removing Monotony from Factory Jobs," American Mercury, October 1954, p. 91; J. K. Lagemann, "Job Enlargement Boosts Production," Nation's Business, 42, No. 12 (December 1954), 34.

The results flowing from job enlargement programs that have been undertaken are not those that could have been anticipated when the bases of prediction are the classic methods of job specification through job fractionation. The results reported indicate apparent gains in productivity, quality, morale, job satisfaction, and so on. The gains may be explained—although this has not been done—by a resolution or lessening of conflict existing between the individual's motivational forces and his assigned work. Such a conflict has been observed to exist in many instances. When present, this conflict may have a deleterious effect upon productivity, costs, morale, and social organization.

The implications of job enlargement are of great importance because of the indicated challenge to the heretofore inviolate principles of specialization and functionalization. Currently, however, serious students of management, production, and human relations may feel that it is much too premature to consider job enlargement as an antidote for the ills of highly specialized jobs, typified by the assembly line. Still needed are theories of job design carefully evaluated by experimentation to produce principles to guide job designers in specifying the content of jobs and to predict accurately the consequences of their designs.

Considerable study has been undertaken and a large body of knowledge exists concerning the design of job methods; so much so that a specialized professional branch of industrial engineering, called methods engineering, has become devoted to it.[3] On the other hand, relatively little information has been available concerning the design of job content.

Two years ago a survey[4] was undertaken to obtain information regarding the manner in which American industry designs jobs as to their content. The study sought to determine:

1. The decisions made in the process of designing jobs.
2. The precepts, principles, intuitions, and other guides used in making these decisions.
3. Where in the production planning process these decisions were made.
4. Who was responsible for making decisions concerned with the design of job content.

As to the question of who is responsible for the design of jobs, the survey indicated that line foremen or supervisors always had the responsibility for job design in about one quarter of the cases, and the engineering department always had the responsibility in about one quarter of the cases. The foreman sometimes had the responsibility in about 30% of the cases, and the engineering department sometimes had the responsibility in about half the cases. The personnel department sometimes had the responsibility in about one quarter of the cases, and in about 70% of the cases never had the responsibility.

[3] L. E. Davis, "Work Methods Design and Work Simplification," in *Progress in Food Research*, ed. E. M. Mark and G. F. Stewart (New York: Academie Press, 1953), IV, 37.

[4] L. E. Davis, R. R. Canter, and J. F. Hoffman, "Current Job Design Criteria" (see note 1 above).

As to precepts or principles used in job design and where in the production planning procedure jobs are designed, the survey revealed the following information:

1. The job design process is centered around the phase of manufacturing planning concerned with the planning of separate operations in the production sequence.
2. No systematic methods of job design can be said to exist.
3. No methods for evaluating the effectiveness of job design can be said to exist.
4. Of overwhelming influence in the design of industrial jobs is the criterion of minimizing immediate cost of producing, i.e., the immediate costs of performing the required operations. The usual indicator of satisfying the criterion is minimum unit operation time.

Designers of jobs see the criterion of minimum cost (or immediate cost) of producing as being satisfied by the application of the following precepts or guides for specifying job content:

1. The content of individual tasks comprising a job is specified so as to:
   a. Achieve specialization of skills.
   b. Minimize skill requirements.
   c. Minimize learning time or worker training time.
   d. Equalize and permit the assignment of a full workload.
   e. Provide for worker satisfaction (no specific criteria for job satisfaction are known to be in use).
   f. Conform to the requirements of layout of equipment or facilities and, where they exist, of union restrictions on work assignment.
2. Individual tasks are combined into specific jobs so that:
   a. Specialization of work is achieved whenever possible by limiting the number of tasks in a job and limiting the variations in tasks or jobs.
   b. Content of a job is as repetitive as possible.
   c. Training time is minimized.

Engineers and industrial managers have been the doers concerning job design. As such, they have determined the nature of jobs for large segments of business and industry. The concepts of job design held by them, and the concepts advocated by economists, have exerted an exceedingly strong influence. These concepts are centered around specialization of labor, minimizing skills, and minimizing immediate production time. They are based upon limited criteria of minimizing immediate cost or maximizing immediate productivity. Thus, job design is based upon the principles of specialization, repetitiveness, low skill content, and minimum impact of the worker on the production process.

Social philosophers have long pointed out the consequences of current job design concepts. They have decried the dehumanizing aspects of repetition without mental activity, of absolute conformity to job descriptions, of methods and standards lacking challenge, without intellectual activity, and without expression of needs and aspirations except through other channels. They would like to know the consequences, for democratic society, of rigidly imposed jobs, completely described, requiring absolute conformity, prohibiting challenge of the status quo, and resulting in utter dependence for satisfaction of needs and aspirations on superiors in the hierarchy. Many serious social scholars see the consequences to be anti-democratic in their effects. Perhaps it is too early in the history of our industrial society to be able to predict whether the worker subjected to such a life experience can also be an effective and responsible citizen of a free democratic society.

Serious students of management and organization are not completely wed to the traditional concepts of job design. They have questioned the application of specialization that requires the human being to function as a single-purpose machine tool. They ask whether or not this may lead to inefficiency in the form of fatigue, stresses, and strains. Concern is expressed over the design of jobs that have little inherent interest, challenge, or meaning (except monetary).[5] It has been said that the division of labor has been overdone, resulting in specialization far beyond the degree necessary for efficient production. While there is some evidence to support this,[6] little or no experimentation with the variables that underlie effective job design has been undertaken in the half century since the rationalization of production.

According to Drucker,[7] there is concrete but fragmentary evidence that the use of the worker as a single-purpose tool is wasteful, unproductive, and an inefficient use of man in the production process. It is poor engineering. It leads to tension, frustration, and dissatisfaction. Drucker summarizes this as follows:

> The principle of specialization is productive and efficient. But it is very dubious, indeed, whether we yet know how to apply it except to machinery. There is first the question of whether "specialization" as it is understood and practiced today is a socially and individually satisfying way of using human energy and production—a major question of the social order of industrial society.

Some of the current concepts which are characterized by conflicting precepts and goals are summarized by Drucker.[8]

> The industrial engineer sees in the human being a tool and that means that, to him, the human being is the more productive, the more

---

[5] J. C. Worthy, "Organization Structure and Employee Morale," *American Sociological Review*, 15, No. 2 (April 1950), 169; C. R. Walker and R. H. Guest, "The Man on the Assembly Line," *Harvard Business Review*, 30, No. 3 (May 1952), 71.

[6] F. L. Richardson and C. R. Walker, *Human Relations in an Expanding Company* (New Haven: Labor Management Center, Yale University, 1948); R. H. Guest, "Men and Machines: An Assembly Line Worker Looks at His Job," *Personnel*, 21, No. 6 (May 1955), 496.

[7] P. F. Drucker, *The New Society* (New York, Harper & Brothers, 1950), p. 171.

[8] P. F. Drucker "The Human Being in Industrial Production," *Proceedings of Fifth Annual Time Study and Methods Conference*, Society for Advancement of Management, April 1950, p. 71.

thoroughly his work has been set up and laid out *for* him. The social scientist lays stress on man's need to participate. He, therefore, concludes that the human being is the more productive and the more efficient, the more *he himself* designs and lays out his own work.

RESEARCH RESULTS–WALKER

Walker[9] has indicated that he believes "we are only at the threshold of a scientific understanding of man's relation to work and especially his relation to the new technological environments within which much of the work of the modern world is being performed."

Aside from the early work under the British Medical Research Council, there has been relatively little research on the relationship between job content and productivity (quality and quantity of work produced), morale, job satisfaction, and long-term economic cost. A great deal of research has been, and is, going on which is concerned with the effect of surrounding variables and conditions on productivity, satisfaction, etc. Omitted from consideration here are the various trial and error attempts, popularly known as job enlargement, that have been undertaken by a number of companies[10] in their efforts to overcome the consequences of completely "engineered" job designs. While we do not question the good intentions underlying these efforts, we would like to address ourselves to investigations carried out under controlled conditions.

Three significant research projects on job design are presented here to illustrate the complexity of the problem area, the variety of research interests, the variety of investigational methods that are being brought into use, and the different concern shown for the variables that are operating. Each project is concerned with job content and job design, and in its own way is a pioneering effort that provides needed research data.

The work of Walker and Guest at the Institute of Human Relations, Yale University, has had a major impact on the problem area by proving interest and impetus for examining the effects of job design on boredom, motivation, and job satisfaction. It is one of the first thoroughly organized and systematic investigations into the consequences of job specialization. The detailed research findings have been reported extensively.[11]

The study took the form of surveys of jobs in automobile assembly plants and was devoted to an examination of the effects of mass production technology on job satisfaction and human relations of workers on the assembly line. It was an exploration of workers' experiences, as gath-

---

[9] C. R. Walker, "Work Methods, Working Conditions and Morale," in *Industrial Conflict*, ed. A. Kornhauser, R. Dubin, and A. M. Ross (New York, McGraw-Hill, 1954), Chap. 26, p. 358.

[10] J. D. Elliott, *Increasing Office Productivity through Job Enlargement* (New York: American Management Association, 1954), Office Management Series, No. 134, p. 3.

[11] "The Man on the Assembly Line" (see note 5); "Men and Machines" (see note 6).

ered through depth interviews. The highlights of this study are summarized in the following material.

Mass production technology has evolved the following principles which have been characteristics of the method wherever it is applied:

1. Standardization.
2. Interchangeability of parts.
3. Orderly progression of the product through the plant in a series of planned operations at specific work stations.
4. Mechanical delivery of parts to work stations at the right time, and mechanical removal of assemblies.
5. Breakdown of operations into their simple constituent motions.

To apply these principles, the engineer translates them into job designs for individual workers. The individual job designs flow from the establishment of job cycles which specify the work methods, tools, and the prescribed number of operations to be performed by a worker in a given time period or, in the case of those working on moving conveyors, within a given distance on the belt. The result of such specification results in jobs that, on the average, have the following characteristics:

1. Mechanical pacing of work (particularly on the main assembly line).
2. Repetitiveness.
3. Minimum skill requirement.
4. Predetermined specification of tools and methods.
5. Minute subdivision of product worked on.
6. Severe limitation on social interaction.
7. Surface mental attention.

With these characteristics identified, the study proposes to examine the consequences of such job designs in terms of the effects on individual workers, and the gains and costs to the company. The consequences can be divided into both social and economic gains and costs. Looking first at the gains, the "engineered" job has yielded high levels of output per man-hour at low costs, providing profits for the company and giving the public a relatively low-cost product. In view of these contributions, the engineer and manager feel that they may rightfully ask, "Should not this be sufficient justification for any social costs that may be incurred?" Unfortunately, once we attempt to answer this question, we are ensnared; for this is not the question with which we are concerned. We accept the concept that low unit cost production is perhaps the fundamental requirement for the progress made by our industrial society. However, what we are concerned with is the method of achieving low unit cost production. So our question should be: "Is the method of designing jobs chosen by the engineer the optimum one for achieving low unit cost production or minimum total economic cost, which by definition includes social costs?"

An examination of the social costs indicates some significant and disturbing effects. All of the effects add up to the simple fact that workers on mass production jobs despise their jobs. This dissatisfaction with the job is not due primarily to what is usually considered important to a job; for the pay, security, working conditions, pension plan, supervision, etc., are seen to be good. What, then, are the consequences of these job designs that lead to this dismal result? These may be grouped into two categories as follows:

1. Those leading to the anonymity of the individual worker, which we have previously called minimizing the impact of the worker on the organization. The anonymity results from designing out of the job virtually everything that might be of real personal value to the worker.
   a. The worker has no control over his *work pace* and rate of production.
   b. His job is highly *repetitive*, having been broken down into the simplest motions possible.
   c. There is little or no need for *skill*, because of the simple movements required.
   d. His job is completely specified as to methods and tools. He has *no control* over these or any changes introduced.
   e. Because he never works on more than a small fraction of the product, he has *no identity* with the product and does not see the final results of his work.
   f. He has *no identity* with the process and cannot estimate his contribution to it in terms of quality.
   g. The demands of the job require *only surface attention* on his part. Some attention is required but not enough to allow him to become really absorbed in his work.
   h. The geographic arrangement of the production line severely limits his social interactions. Men on the line work as individuals, having no identification as a work group. The *lack of group awareness* appears to reinforce the sense of anonymity.
2. Those leading to the depersonalization of the job, in that there are no means for job progression vertically through a series of distinct steps. Simplified tasks have all but eliminated skill differences from one job to the next. Very few workers in the study had experienced any substantial change in job classification during a period of 12 to 15 years.

The effects on the individual resulted in strong dissatisfaction with the job and frustration of aspirations because of the lack of progress or advancement. As a consequence, there were some serious economic costs for the company. Turnover was high. Quality performance was not maximized because of inherent lack of interest in the job. Labor-management relations were in a state of constant tension.

RESEARCH RESULTS—MARKS

The second research project to be examined represents one of the first controlled experiments on job design in an industrial plant. An experimental investigation of the effects on some measures of economic productivity stemming from alteration of the design of jobs was conducted by A. R. N. Marks[12] for his doctoral dissertation under the primary direction of the authors.

The specific purpose of the study was to explore the conditions under which improvement in productivity could be expected from change in the content of a job. A set of hypotheses was derived which is paraphrased below.

Higher economic productivity will result from modifying work content of a job in the direction of:

a. Increasing the number of tasks in a job.
b. Putting together tasks that are similar in technological content and skill demands.
c. Putting together tasks that are sequentially related in the technical process (process = complete systematic sequence of events or operations required to produce an item, part, or complete product).
d. Putting together tasks that include final activities in the process or sub-process.
e. Putting together tasks that increase worker responsibility, e.g., that enlarge the area of decision-making in regard to work rate, methods, set-up, etc., and the area of autonomy in regard to quality, material supply, etc.
f. Putting together tasks that increase the opportunity for the worker to perceive the relationship of his contribution to the completion of the work process.

These hypotheses were used broadly in the experiment as guides for modifying jobs. Because of the nature of the industrial situation, their individual effects upon selected dependent variables could not be analyzed separately.

With all the attempts to avoid it, we still seem to have developed a special language, and it may be helpful if we define some terms as follows:

1. *Economic productivity* may be defined as direct productivity modified by the addition of appropriate "overhead" or hidden charges, e.g., those relating to costs stemming from absenteeism, labor turnover, quality requirements, scrap, etc.

2. *Job* is defined as the structure of the tasks and work methods and the setting in which they take place. The content of a job may be considered to be the sum of the work content, methods content, organizational content, and personal content, plus their interaction.

3. *Work content* is the assigned series of tasks which grow from the requirements of the technical process.

4. *Methods content* is the design of the ways in which the work activities are to be performed. It is often referred to as methods design.

5. *Organizational content* is the organizational setting of the work situa-

12 A. R. N. Marks, "An Investigation of Modifications of Job Design in an Industrial Situation and Their Effects on Some Measures of Economic Productivity," Ph.D. Dissertation, unpublished. Berkeley, University of California, 1954.

tion in which the assigned tasks are to be carried out, e.g., the location of the job in a work group, hierarchical relations, etc.

6. *Job design* is the process of specifying the content of a job in terms of the definition of a job. The design of a job involves the specification of work methods, organizational, and personal contents.

Two major criteria were chosen for analyzing the effectiveness of the job design modifications: quantity of production per man-hour, and quality of work. In addition, some measures of attitude and satisfaction were also used.

The experimental setting was a manufacturing department of a West Coast company which was unionized. The department was devoted to the manufacture of a line of similar products and had been the subject of careful and detailed engineering study over the years. The activities of the department were organized according to the latest manufacturing engineering practices. At the start of the experiment, the product was made on an assembly line, using carefully specified, minutely subdivided operations at which twenty-nine of the department's thirty-five members worked. The rest of the people were concerned with preparing and removing material for the line, inspection and supply. The department was under a manager and two supervisors. A similar department in the company was used as a control group to permit monitoring of the presence of plant-wide changes which might affect employee attitudes, practices, and performance.

The investigation centered around the jobs on the assembly line, and modifications were introduced through the department manager. The assembly line workers were unskilled women having an average of four and a half years' experience on the line, ranging approximately from one to seven years. The work content of the original jobs (called Line Job Design) involved performing one of the nine operations, spaced at stations along the conveyor line, required to assemble a hospital appliance. Inspection, in the form of rejecting defective parts going into the assembly, was part of each operation. Job rotation from hard to easy stations and vice versa took place every two hours. The operations were similar in skill requirements and technological content. Pacing eliminated responsibility for productivity, and job rotation with the grouping of work stations for identical operations practically eliminated individual responsibility for quality of work performed.

The experiment was divided into four phases as indicated in Table 1.

Results

To provide anonymity for company production records, indexes are used. The average hourly conveyor line rate obtained over a period of the consecutive days and divided by the number of persons working on the line is taken as a productivity index of 100. Because individual data are unavailable except for individual job designs, a daily productivity index is used which is the average of individual indexes. The changes in productivity can be seen in Figures 1 and 2. In the Group Job Design which

TABLE 1
Experimental Conditions

	Purpose	Criteria	Locations	Workers	Total Number of Days	Number Days Worker Assigned	Production Method
A. Line Job Design	Obtain reference base of job design where separate tasks performed on rotated basis by workers	Quantity, quality, some measures of attitude and satisfaction	Main department	29	26	26	Workers rotate among nine stations on belt conveyor, performing specified minute operations at pace of conveyor
B. Group Job Design	Eliminate conveyor pacing effects; other conditions primarily the same	Quantity, quality	Adjacent room	29	14	2	Workers rotate among nine individual stations using batch method
C. Individual Job Design #1	Give workers experience on experimental job design where assembly tasks are performed by worker	Quantity, quality	Adjacent room	29	16	2	Workers perform all nine operations at own stations, plus inspection and getting own supplies
D. Individual Job Design #2	Obtain measure on experimental job design	Quantity, quality, some measures of attitude and satisfaction	Main department	21	27	6	Same as C above

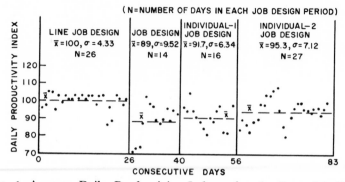

FIG. 1. Average Daily Productivity Indexes for the Four Job Designs (From A. R. N. Marks, "An Investigation of Modifications of Job Design in an Industrial Situation and Their Effects on Some Measures of Economic Productivity," Ph.D. Dissertation, unpublished, University of California, Berkeley, Nov. 1954, p. 82).

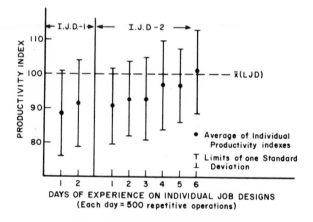

FIG. 2. Average Individual Productivity Indexes (From A. R. N. Marks, p. 83).

eliminates conveyor pacing, productivity falls markedly below the Line Job Design, indicating the influence of conveyor pacing on maintaining output. Introduction of the Individual Job Design in which workers performed all the operations, controlled the sequence of assembly, secured materials, and inspected their own work brought about increases in productivity above the Group Job Design. It should be noted that after six days on the Individual Job Design, the average productivity of the work group exceeded the Line average on which workers had an average of four and a half years of experience.

Measures of quality are based upon results of sampling inspection for attributes both before and after sterilization of the product, and upon the number of kinked assemblies produced. The latter provided a positive direct measure of quality of workmanship since the quality of parts and sub-assemblies were not involved. The changes in quality are given in Tables 2 and 3, and in Figure 3. It is to be noted that beginning with a

TABLE 2

Composite Quality Indexes (AQL Weighted Defects) for the Four Job Designs

Inspection	Statistic	Line Job Design	Group Job Design	Individual Job Design–1	Individual Job Design–2
Before sterilization	$\overline{X}$	4.17	3.52	2.14	1.55
	σ	3.91	4.40	2.63	2.22
	N = Lots	60	16	14	26
After sterilization	$\overline{X}$	2.42	3.11	2.27	1.35
	σ	3.23	4.63	2.39	1.45
	N	60	10	8	13

TABLE 3

Summarized Data of Sampling Inspection on the Four Job Designs

p = estimated process average (fraction defective in per cent)
R = probability of lot being rejected $\times 10^4$
R_{aql} = R for process average equal to AQL value

Inspection	Type of Defect	AQL Value	Measure	Line Job Design	Group Job Design	Individual Job Design–1	Individual Job Design–2
Before sterilization	Major	0.65	p	0.173	0.262	0.087	0.090
			R	0.10	7.80	0.00	0.00
			R_{aql}	167.6	174.9	148.2	148.2
	Minor A	2.5	p	0.626	0.393	0.304	0.231
			R	0.00	0.00	0.00	0.00
			R_{aql}	128.0	148.1	102.6	102.6
	Minor B	6.5	p	0.609	0.044	0.435	0.051
			R	0.00	0.00	0.00	0.00
			R_{aql}	82.2	113.6	22.3	22.3
After sterilization	Major	0.65	p	0.124	0.061	0.048	0.026
			R	0.10	0.00	0.00	0.00
			R_{aql}	167.6	174.9	148.2	148.2
	Minor A	2.5	p	0.224	0.121	0.191	0.103
			R	0.00	0.00	0.00	0.00
			R_{aql}	128.0	148.1	102.6	102.6
	Minor B	6.5	p	0.704	1.090	0.905	0.077
			R	0.00	0.00	0.00	0.00
			R_{aql}	82.2	113.6	22.3	22.3

high level of quality, quality levels rose with the removal of conveyor pacing. When responsibility for quality was placed in the hands of the workers, quality levels rose still higher, for kinked assemblies dropped to one fourth of the original value.

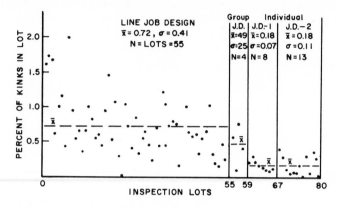

Fig. 3. Percentage of Kinked Assemblies in Consecutive Lots for Four Job Designs (From A. R. N. Marks, p. 87).

Conclusions

The Individual Job Design:

1. Brought about an improvement in quality, although quality levels were very high originally.

2. Increased the flexibility of the production process.

3. Permitted identification of individuals having deficiencies in productivity and quality.

4. Reduced service functions of the department, e.g., material delivery, inspection.

5. Developed a more favorable attitude toward individual responsibility, individual work rate, effort expenditure, distribution of work load, and making whole units as compared with *lack* of personal responsibility on conveyor line type work. After experience with the Individual Job Design, workers disliked the lack of personal responsibility characteristic of the Line Job Design.

RESEARCH RESULTS—RICE

The third piece of research indicates the importance of productivity of the organizational component of job design. A study conducted in an Indian textile mill[13] indicates the impact of job designs which center only about worker-machine allocations and inhibit interaction of workers. The mill had recently been intensively studied by engineers for the purpose of laying out equipment and assigning work loads based on careful work studies of all the job components. After the installation, the mill still failed to produce at satisfactory productivity levels. The job designs provided can be seen by reviewing the assignments of workers in one room

[13] A. K. Rice, "Productivity and Social Organization in an Indian Weaving Shed," *Human Relations*, 6, No. 4 (1953), 297.

containing two hundred and forty looms. Twelve specialist activities were used to run the equipment as follows:

1. A weaver tended approximately thirty looms.
2. A "battery filler" served about fifty looms.
3. A "smash-hand" tended about seventy looms.
4. A "gater," "cloth carrier," "jobber," and "assistant jobber" were each assigned to 112 looms.
5. A "bobbin carrier," "feeler motion fitter," oiler, sweeper, and "humidification fitter" were each assigned to 224 looms.

The occupational tasks were all highly interdependent, and the utmost coordination was required to maintain continuity of production. However, the worker-machine assignments and consequent organizational grouping produced an interaction pattern which mitigated continuity of production. The interaction resulting from work assignment brought each weaver into contact with five-eighths of a "battery filler," three-eighths of a "smash-hand," one-quarter of a "gater" and one-eighth of a "bobbin carrier."

After study of travel patterns and communication patterns, job designs were reorganized so that all of the workers who were interdependent were made part of the same work group. Work groups were organized so that a single group was responsible for the operation and maintenance of a specific bank of looms. The geographic division rather than functional division of the weaving room produced interaction patterns which made for regularity of relationships among individuals whose jobs were interrelated and could be held responsible for their production. The results of these changes brought about the following changes in efficiency and damage. Efficiency rose from an average of eighty per cent to an average of ninety-five per cent after sixty working days. For the part of the weaving shed that was not reorganized, efficiency dropped to seventy and finally rose to eighty per cent. The mean per cent of damage dropped from thirty-two per cent to twenty per cent after sixty days. Where the job design changes were not installed, damage continued at thirty-two per cent.

The studies presented here are intended to indicate the multidimensionality of the job design problem and the pervasiveness of its influence on quantity and quality of output, job satisfaction, etc.

FUTURE NEEDS

By relying on very narrow criteria, jobs have been designed which have a host of disturbing secondary effects in terms of dissatisfaction, monotony, resistance, and obstruction. In addition, designs of jobs have frequently failed to yield predicted results. Such failures to achieve anticipated results frequently have been laid to the "contrariness of human nature." This may be taken as another way of stating that, given the current state of knowledge, the effects of job designs cannot be estimated. In view of the engineering, economic, psychological, and social consequences of job designs, the inability to predict effectiveness of a particular design indicates two fundamental needs:

1. What factors should guide the design of jobs?
2. What criteria should be used to evaluate the effectiveness of job designs?

Where the content of jobs has been manipulated or redesigned, within a given state of technology, in the direction of enlarging job size or responsibility, gains in productivity and morale as well as reduced costs have been reported. These results serve to illustrate the inability, from the standpoint of the classical method of job fractionation, to predict the consequences of job designs. It is hypothesized that many current personal and productivity problems in industry stem directly from existing job designs.

Some fundamental questions must be raised concerning the design of jobs and the effectiveness of performance on jobs of given design. It is difficult if not impossible at present to provide definitive answers for these. The questions can be divided into three groups, as follows:

1. What influence does job design have on effectiveness of an individual's performance as measured by productivity, quality, long-term costs, satisfaction, morale, etc.?

2. What are the most effective methods of achieving optimum performance? This requires a consideration of the methods of design and specification of jobs, as compared with the methods of palliating the effects of given designs by various means internal and external to the content of one job itself. The effectiveness of job design methods must be compared with the alteration of factors external to the physical job, such as human relations programs, supervision and leadership, incentives, etc.

3. Can a theory of job design be developed and, if so, can it be expressed in the form of guides and principles that can be used by engineers, personnel people, supervisors, and managers? Satisfying this need will require a comprehensive research program, concerned with:

   a. The nature of job content as related to job performance, to aspiration, to perception of the individual's role in the organization.
   b. The interrelationships between the technical, organizational, and personal requirements of each job.
   c. An evaluation of organization design theories and methods as related to technical and personal requirements for effective performance on jobs.
   d. An evaluation of technical production theories and methods as related to organizational and personal requirements for effective performance on jobs.
   e. An evaluation of the effectiveness of manipulating factors internal and external to job content and the boundary limitations of each.

A good many of the difficulties, the inconsistencies of results, and the opinions held concerning the design of jobs can be traced to the lack of fundamental or true criteria. Before much progress can be made beyond the current status, adequate criteria and sub-criteria will need to be developed. The lack of criteria has led to job designs based upon the satisfaction of apparent economic criteria. The term "apparent" is used because total costs are seldom considered, for there is little data available to provide yardsticks for total cost analysis of a given job design.

Needed is the development of a total economic cost criterion which is concerned with the total cost of achieving productivity, and therefore includes relevant long-term charges in the form of money, time, growth, and psychological, social, and cultural stress costs. One of the serious research problems here is to determine how total economic cost is to be measured in terms of economic, engineering, organizational, social, psychological, physiological, material, and human resource cost criteria.

The nature of job design research and experimentation should reflect the multi-dimensional character of the problem. The problem area is amenable to attack from many quarters, under certain requirements. Paramount among the requirements is that job content must be a central theme of all experimentation, with other variables included in various experimental designs. In addition, multi-dimensionality and interaction among variables calls for a problem-centered, research-team approach. Some of the dangers and defects of a compartmentalized approach have been indicated previously.

The types of data that will be required will call for research and field studies that may need to be conducted by industrial engineers, industrial psychologists, sociologists, anthropologists, economists, and researchers in personnel administration and industrial relations. Obtaining the data needed will require that studies be conducted that will range from determining and measuring "meaningfulness" as applied to operations, work methods, work groups, and jobs, through the determination of long-term total economic cost criteria, to the determination of the means of designing processes, systems, methods, and product components in terms of job needs.

Industry's need to be involved in the development of effective job designs is acute at present and will continue to be so as our economy moves into the era of automation. Where automation is not applicable, determining optimum job designs will be one of the major needs to be met by industry and business in order to maintain, and meet competitively, increasing levels of productivity. In addition, effective introduction and use of automation places a very strong demand on job design, theory and principles. These will be needed to help ascertain what processes should be automated with reference to what workers can and cannot do better. They will also aid in the effective design of automation systems regarding the human links, particularly where essential data for making judgments cannot be furnished.

The payoff value that may be estimated for job design research will be extensive for the management sciences, engineering sciences, and social sciences. Concerning management, the availability of job design theories will have a strong bearing on organizational theories and organizational designs, on the design of reward systems, on the design of control systems, communication systems, and the operation of a large part of the personnel administration function. In terms of engineering science, the availability of job design theories will have a strong bearing on the development of theories and methods for the design of product, process, equipment, plant conditions, control systems, operations, methods, jobs, etc. Concerning the social sciences in the industrial setting, the availability of job design theories will have a strong bearing upon the formulation of human relations programs and methods, employee relations programs and methods, organizational methods, supervisory methods (embracing leadership methods), selection and placement of personnel, design of communication networks and reward systems, etc.

THE FACTORY IN THE COMMUNITY
W. Lloyd Warner and J. O. Low*

In this section, Warner and Low describe the interdependence of the factory and the community; they point out that changes in ownership and control of a community industry provided the seeds of change in labor-management relations. In developing their case, the authors help focus attention on the types of problems caused by factory organization, the tie between community and factory, and the relationship of local cultural patterns to labor-management relations.

The American social system has been drastically changed by the development of our industrial institutions; on the other hand, our industrial organization has become what it is by virtue of being a part of the larger American social system. The two are interdependent and mutually influence each other, yet we know almost nothing about the nature of the relations that exist between the two. Much is known about the factory as a production and economic unit, but little is known about the influence of the factory on the community and the community on the factory. We shall attack the problem in the present chapter. To do so we shall concentrate our attention on one city where the factory and social system of the community were carefully studied over a period of years by a group of social anthropologists.

The relations of this factory and the community were studied when they were in equilibrium and the various parts of the factory and the city were well integrated and formed a functioning unit. They were also examined when industrial strife and social conflict had disrupted this equilibrium. Social anthropologists study periods of social disruption to

* From *Industry and Society*, edited by William Foote Whyte (New York: McGraw-Hill Book Co., Inc., 1946). Copyright, 1946, McGraw-Hill Book Company, Inc. Used by permission.

gain deeper insight into what normally takes place in a social system because crisis periods reveal and dramatize the important and significant factors that often lie hidden during times of peace and quiet.

We are going to examine a strike in the shoe industry of an American community to learn what we can about the place of the factory in contemporary American life.[1]

In the worst year of the depression all the workers in all the factories of the principal industry of a New England community walked out. They struck at management with little or no warning; they struck with such impact that all the factories closed and no worker remained at his bench. Management had said they would never strike, for the workers of Yankee City were sensible, dependable, and, by a long peaceful history, had proved that they would always stay on the job. Union men outside the city agreed that Yankee City could not be organized and held that the local shoe workers were obstinate and "always stupid enough to play management's game." Many of the workers had told us that there would be no strike. Most of the townspeople, from the autocrats of Hill Street to the people on city welfare in the clam flats, said Yankee City workers would never strike. But they did—the foreigners and the Yankees of ten generations—the men and the women, the very old and the very young, Jews and Gentiles, Catholics and Protestants, the whole heterogeneous mass of workers left their benches and in a few hours wiped out most of the basic productive system from which Yankee City earned its living. Not only did they strike and soundly defeat management, but they organized themselves, joined an industrial union, and became strong union members.

The industrial battle was fought between the owners of seven factories and 1,500 workers. Four of the factories, "the larger ones," employed the vast majority of the workers and accounted for most of the "34,000-dollar weekly pay roll." This industrial war lasted a month. It began on a bleak and snowy day in early March and lasted well into April. There were three clearly marked periods, each with different objectives and strategy, and in each the industrial workers and the managers were dominated by different feelings.

In the first period, when management and the union fought desperately to gain control over the workers, the union was successful in organizing the workers and management was prevented from regaining control over them. The second period began when all the workers requested the union to represent them in the struggle with management, and the union, secure with the workers organized behind them, began frontal attacks on management. During this time each continued its intense efforts to influence and dominate public opinion in Yankee City. The union also won this fight since the public identified the union with the workers and most of Yankee City sided with the shoe operators. The final phase, that of mediation and peace negotiations, began when a gov-

[1] We cannot deal with the whole problem here because of the limitations of space. All aspects of the problem are treated in detail in Warner and Low, *The Social System of the Modern Factory*, Vol. IV, *Yankee City Series*, Yale University Press, New Haven. Most of the material in this chapter has been taken from that volume.

ernment labor board entered and started a series of negotiations that terminated the strike. Other efforts had been made from the beginning but none was successful.

The ultimate objective of each side, to which each fashioned its strategy, was, of course, to make the other side capitulate and accept its demands; for management this meant the workers would return to their benches under approximately the same working conditions and wages as they had left; for the workers it meant that the management would agree to their demands and increase wages and improve working conditions; and for the union officials it meant that the union would maintain its control over the workers and keep them members of their organization, and management would be forced to deal directly with the union and not with the unorganized workers.

Each side organized itself and developed its strategies of offense and defense. The workers' defense tactics were centered around maintaining their unity and defeating management's offensive strategy of breaking up the workers' group and of destroying their morale. Accordingly, the workers used ritual and ceremonial procedures, where recognized symbols of solidarity such as the flag, patriotic hymns, and the American Legion band played prominent parts. They achieved a defensive organization by means of meetings, speeches, entertainments, and the formation of a large number of committees that gave the mass of the workers opportunities to participate and to become and feel a part of a powerful and aggressive group. They took offensive action against management by making a series of demands for better wages and working conditions, by picketing, by making attacks against management in the newspaper, and by using the platform to influence public opinion. Management's defense was always to take the offense. The tactics tried included sending foremen to talk to the workers individually and thereby separating them from the group, spreading discouraging rumors, advertising in the paper, insisting on secret balloting by the workers when they voted on the issue of returning to work, and, above all, threatening to move their factories elsewhere should the workers continue with their demands and join the union. Of course, it must be remembered that each side, throughout the strike, was being deprived of its income, labor of its wages and management of its profits.

The strike occurred almost to the very year of the three hundredth anniversary of the founding of Yankee City and the beginning of the shoe industry. Shoemaking was always important there, but it was not until near the end of the nineteenth century that it achieved its place of supreme importance in the economy of the town. From the beginning, shipping, shipbuilding, fishing, and the other trades of the sea had dominated Yankee City's economic existence and set their mark on the community. When the New England shipping industries disappeared, Yankee City turned from the sea and sent its many drummers, salesmen, and manufactured goods westward to make the profits necessary for the establishment and continuance of its factory system. It was then that the textile manufacturers moved into the lead, but throughout the whole period shoemaking contributed significantly to the economic life of the city and, by the end of the century, had risen to a commanding place. Yankee City's shoe workers and owners throughout this time were known everywhere in the country for the excellence of their products.

Although the economy of the city went through revolutionary changes, the social superstructure that guided and maintained the lives of its citizens remained very much what it had been at the end of the War of 1812. The physical city stretches in a thin rectangle two miles inland along the bank of a large river from the harbor. Here, when the field study was made, lived 17,000 people. They were distributed from the river bottoms and clam flats back to the high ground on which Hill Street is located. The people of high status, some of them the descendants of those who made their fortunes in the sea trade, lived on this broad, elm-lined avenue. The people of lowest status, many of whom could trace their ancestry through long lines of fishermen to the city's founding, lived in Riverbrook on the clam flats. Between the two were the "Side-streeters" who, appropriately enough, occupied a middle-class status.[2]

The upper class of Hill Street was composed of two levels: the "Old Families," who could trace their aristocratic position through an ancestry of many generations; and the "New Families," who had but recently achieved high status. In the latter group were several families who "got their money out of shoes." The upper middle and lower middle classes were very much like such people wherever they are found in the United States or, for that matter, in all English-speaking countries. They were the conservatives, who, dominated by a "Protestant ethic," maintained, and often controlled, the moral order of the city. Below them was the upper lower class composed of the "poor but honest workmen" who ran the factories. At the bottom were the "broken-down Yankees," often called the "Riverbrookers," who also worked in the factories and who did a moderate amount of clamming and fishing for a living.

Scattered throughout the status system from the lower upper class ("New Family" level) to the lower lower class ("Riverbrookers") were the descendants of the Irish and, at somewhat lower levels, the French-Canadians, Jews, Poles, Greeks, and other ethnic groups, who began settling in Yankee City in the 1840's and continued until 1924. They had their own social system that preserved an increasingly small stock of the ancestral culture while relating their populations to the larger world of Yankee City. The Yankees were dominant and the most powerful group in the city, but the ethnics each year increased their power and prestige while they shed their variant mores and accepted those of the dominant Yankees.[3]

All these people were involved in the strike; the bread of most of them was directly or indirectly earned in the shoe factories. Men everywhere in the city asked themselves, when the strike occurred, why such a

[2] The status and social structure of Yankee City are described in Warner and Lunt, *The Social System of a Modern Community* and *The Status System of a Modern Community*, Vols. I and II, *Yankee City Series*, Yale University Press, New Haven, 1941, 1942.

[3] The social systems of eight ethnic groups are analyzed and the processes of assimilation described in Warner and Srole, *The Social System of American Ethnic Groups*, Vol. III, *Yankee City Series*, Yale University Press, New Haven, 1945.

thing should have happened to the people of Yankee City. Each man had his own answer. The answer of each tended to reveal more about the life and status of the man who talked than about the cause or causes of the strike. More often than not the explanations were economic. These townspeople forgot that there had been serious depressions before and that there had been no strikes. Each of them forgot that there had been low wages before and that there had been no unions. Each forgot, too, that there had been strikes when wages were high and times were said to be good. Although these economic arguments supplied important and necessary reasons for the strike and the unionization of the workers, they were insufficient explanations.

It seems to us the secrets of industrial strife in Yankee City and elsewhere lie beyond the words and deeds of the strike. They can only be found in the whole life of the community in which the workers and owners are but a part. The answers of the economic determinists or of the historians, while important, are not sufficient.

If social science is to be of any worth to us, it must be capable of adding significance and meaning to human behavior that will give us deeper insight into human life and explain more fully than common-sense knowledge why human beings act the way they do. Science necessarily solves problems. To solve them it must know what questions need to be answered. Let us reexamine the questions implied in the statements of the Yankee City townsmen in a more explicit and pointed manner to determine if we can learn what happened in this industrial crisis and to see if such knowledge about the strike can tell us about other similar crises in American life.

The immediate questions are basic to the whole problem, but, of even greater importance, they lead us into more fundamental ones about the nature of our industrial society. We will endeavor to give at least partial answers to some of these larger questions.

The first questions we must answer about the strike are

1. In a community where there had been very few strikes and *no* successful ones, why did the workers in *all* the factories of the largest industry of the community strike, win all their demands and, after a severe struggle, soundly defeat management?

2. In a community where unions had previously tried and failed to gain even a foothold and where there had never been a union, why was a union successful in separating the workers from management?

3. Why was the union successful in organizing *all* the workers in *all* the shoe factories in the community?

4. Why was the union successful in maintaining the organization despite the intense and prolonged efforts of management to prevent unionization and break up the shoe union?

5. Why did Yankee City change from a nonunion to a union town?

Perhaps the best way to gain an understanding of the strike and of the relations of the contemporary factory and the community is to view the present in the light of the past. The history of Yankee City's shoe factories may be conveniently divided into four periods ranging from the earliest times when the family was the productive unit through the periods of early and late small-city capitalism to the present stage when mass production and the machine dominate the industry, and control has shifted to New York. Included were revolutionary technological developments, increases in the division of labor, radical modifications of ownership and control, and rearrangements of the relations of producer and consumer and of workers among themselves.

During the technological development of Yankee City's shoe industry, the tools changed from a few basic ones, entirely hand-used, to machines in an assembly line; and their product changed from a single pair of shoes to tens of thousands in mass production. In the beginning, the family made its own shoes, or a highly skilled artisan, the cobbler, made shoes for the family. In time, several families divided the highly skilled jobs among themselves and their families. Ultimately a central factory developed and the jobs were divided into a large number of systematized low-skilled jobs. The history of ownership and control is correlated with the changes in the division of labor. In early days, tools, skills, and materials were possessed by the family. Eventually the materials were supplied by the owner-manager and soon he also owned the tools and machines. The sequence of development of producer-consumer relations tells a similar pointed story. The family produced and consumed its shoes all within the circle of its simple unit. Then the local community was the consumer-producer unit, and ultimately the market became national and even world-wide. Workers' relations changed from those of kinship and family ties to those of occupation, where apprenticeships and craftsmanship relations were superseded, and the industrial union became dominant in organizing the affairs of the workers. The structure of economic relations changed from the immediate family into a local hierarchy, and the locally owned factory changed into a vast, complex system owned, managed, and dominated by New York City.

With these several histories in mind, let us ask ourselves what would have happened if the strike had taken place in each of the several periods. In period one, with a family consuming and producing economy, such a conflict would have been impossible. The social system had not evolved to sufficient complexity; the forces had not been born that were to oppose each other in civil strife. In the second phase, several families in a neighborhood might have quarreled but it is only in one's imagination that one could conceive of civil strife among the shoemakers.

In the third phase, however, there appears a new social personality, and an older one begins to take on a new form and assume a new place in the community. The capitalist is born and during the following periods he develops into full maturity. Meanwhile the worker loses control and management of his time and skills and becomes a subordinate in a hierarchy. There are, thus, distinct and opposing forces set up in the shoemaking system. What is good for one is not necessarily good for the other, but the interdependence of the two opposing groups is still very intimate, powerful, and highly necessary. The tools, the skills, and the places of manufacture belong to the worker, but the materials, the place of assembly, and the market are now possessed by the manager. Striking is possible but extremely difficult and unlikely.

In the fourth period, full capitalism has been achieved; the manufacturer is now the owner of the tools, the machines, and the industrial plant; he controls the market. The workers have become sufficiently self-conscious and antagonistic to machines to organize into craft unions. Industrial warfare might prove difficult to start, although it did occur, because in a small city where most people know each other, the owner and manager more often than not knows "his help" and they know him. The close relation between the two often implies greater compatibility and understanding that cut down the likelihood of conflict. But when strikes do occur, the resulting civil strife is likely to be bitter because it is in the confines of the community.

In the last period, the capitalist has become the super-capitalist and the workers have forgotten their pride in their separate jobs, have dismissed the small differences among them, and have united in one industrial union with tens and hundreds of thousands of workers throughout the country combining their strength to assert their interests against management. In such a social setting strikes are inevitable and certain.[4]

An examination of the status of the worker in the factory and in the community reveals another important factor contributing to industrial strife. During the early periods of the factory in Yankee City a skill hierarchy dominated the lives of the workers and helped establish

CHART I

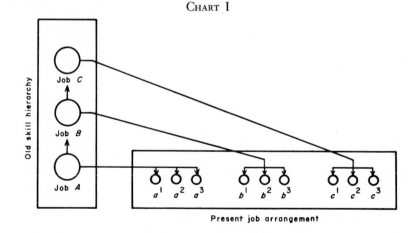

Present job arrangement

their place in the community. The introduction of the machine into all parts of the production processes of the factory largely destroyed the skill hierarchy.

Chart I illustrates what has happened to craft and skill in the modern factory. The vertical hierarchy of skilled jobs has become a horizontal layer of low-skilled ones. Each of the skilled jobs has been divided

[4] See Chap. II of Vol. IV of the *Yankee City Series* for the details of this whole industrial development.

into a number of simple, low-skilled ones and machines are performing most of the actions necessary for each job. Jobs formerly at the top and bottom of the hierarchy, that were separated by higher and lower prestige and paid accordingly, are now in the same category of prestige and pay. We believe that the breakup of the skill hierarchy contributed importantly to the outbreak of the strike, to the course it took, and, in particular, to the coming of the union. The hierarchy of crafts that once organized the relations of the workers and provided a way of life for the shoe workers was really an age-grade system. Youngsters served their hard apprenticeship and, as neophytes, learned their task and, even more importantly, were taught to respect the skills they had learned and those they looked forward to learning. Above all, they acquired respect and admiration for the older men above them who had acquired the skills and who occupied the proud positions of journeymen and master craftsmen. These youngsters aspired to achieve for themselves a similar high position and to be the objects of a similar respect of their fellow craftsmen and fellow townsmen. Each young man, in direct face-to-face interaction with those above, imitated and learned a way of life while being highly motivated by the strong desire to escape the irksome limitations of his present low position and to attain the higher place where he would have the satisfaction of making his own decisions and possess the prestige and pay consequent to such great eminence. By the time he had learned how to do the things needed to equip himself for advancement, enough time had passed to mature him sufficiently to act the part of a man. There can be little doubt that age factors as well as those of skill determined the time for advancement. During this preliminary period he learned that he was a craftsman and that he had a particular place in the whole system, with responsibilities and obligations that, once acquired, gave him rights and privileges. Thus, while he internalized this behavior and all its values and their many subtleties and learned what he was as a man, he became an inextricable member of the honorable fraternity of those who made, and who knew how to make, shoes. In this system, workers and managers were indissolubly interwoven into a common enterprise with a common set of values. In this system the internal personal structure of each was made up of very much the same apparatus, and their personalities were reinforced by the social system of shoemaking.

In learning to respect the skill of the master craftsman, the apprentice learned to respect himself. He had security in his job, but he had even greater personal security because he had learned how to respect it. And because he was a member of an age-graded male fraternity made up of other men like himself who had the knowledge and necessary skills to make shoes, he possessed that feeling of freedom and independence and of being autonomous that comes from leading a disciplined life. He spent his life acquiring virtue, prestige, and respect, learning as he aged and climbed upward and at the same time teaching those who were younger than he and who aspired to be like him.

Slowly this way of life degenerated and the machine took the virtue and respect from the workers, and at the same time broke the skill hierarchy that dominated their occupation. There was no longer a period for young men to learn to respect those in the age grade above them and in so doing to become self-respecting workers. The "ladder to the stars" was gone and with it much of the fabric of the "American dream."

When the age-grade structure that organized the male aborigines of Melanesia and North America into a hierarchy of prestige and achievement was broken under the impact of white civilization in many of these societies, the frustrations suffered by those who had once known self-respect crystallized into aggressive movements or into attempts to abolish the new ways and to retreat into the old and cherished ways of the past. There are, thus, some resemblances to developments in non-European societies.

The parallel between Yankee City's age-grade structure and theirs cannot be pushed too far but certainly the two share obvious characteristics. In the earlier days of the machine, the Knights of St. Crispin organized themselves and attempted to stop the further introduction of machinery, and most of them longed for the good old days when there were no machines, when a trained hand and eye did the job. These attempts failed and their organization collapsed, for they were not adaptive and could not stop the inevitable advance of our industrial technology.

When the whole age-grade structure of craftsmanship had almost entirely collapsed and the American shoe worker was thereby denied his share of the American dream, he and his kind were ready for any mass movement that would strike at those whom they charged, in their own minds, with responsibility for their unhappy condition. Much of this behavior was not conscious. Much of it was feeling rather than thought, as indeed were the feelings and thoughts that composed the mass movements of the aboriginal Melanesians and North American Indians. It seems certain, however, that American workers, taught from childhood that those who work and apply themselves and practice the ethics of the middle class would be rewarded by achievement and success, would rebel and strike back out of sheer frustration when they found out that the American dream no longer was true and that the hard facts belied the beautiful words they had been taught. It seems even more likely that the effects of the break in the skill hierarchy were potent forces that contributed their full share to the workers' striking and accepting the union as their champion.

Two other important causes of the strike must now be dealt with. The first is the expansion of the hierarchy upward, out of Yankee City, through the expansion of individual enterprises and the establishment by them of central offices in distant large cities. The second is the expansion of the structure outward from Yankee City through the growth of manufacturers' associations and labor unions, also with headquarters outside Yankee City and with units in many other shoemaking communities in New England and elsewhere. Both of these developments have gone on concurrently, each reacting upon the other. And both decrease Yankee City's control over its shoe factories by subjecting the factories, or segments of them, to more and more control exerted from outside Yankee City.

In the early days of the shoe industry, the owners and managerial staffs of the factories, as well as the operatives, were residents of Yankee City; there was no extension of the factory social structures outside the local community. The factories were then entirely under the control of the community—not only the formal control of city ordinances and laws, but also the more pervasive informal controls of community traditions and attitudes. There were feelings of neighborliness and friendship between manager and worker and of mutual responsibilities to each other and to the community that went beyond the formal employer-employee agreement.

In the days of local capitalism, the shoe manufacturers were accepted by all social strata as leaders of the total community. Shortly after the death of the most powerful of these business leaders, a number of prominent Yankee City men published a memorial volume that contained the usual words of high praise for great men. Since these same words, unlike those of many memorial volumes, were said about him by ordinary men of the street and were used during the strike, it is important to examine them. A member of one of the oldest families of Yankee City wrote:

> He (the manufacturer) was one of the most remarkable men ever connected with Yankee City; a businessman of liberal culture, of fine literary taste, gifted as an orator, in music and theatricals. . . . He was an acquisition to any society. He honored any public station, however high. . . . He achieved more in his fifty years of life than most men can point to after marking a very old age. . . .
>
> He was identified with the public health of this city and was a conspicuous figure in all its great social functions as long as his health permitted it. He was a leading financier and a man who at once took and ever afterwards occupied a prominent position in this community. For years, by common consent, he was the leading man of the city. . . . Forcefulness of character made him the commanding spirit in every undertaking in which he shared and in every circle in which he moved.

Our analysis of the manufacturer's participation in the community provides the crucial evidence to show why he became the powerful collective symbol that was used against the contemporary managers during the strike.

In the business and financial sphere he was

1. Owner and head of his million-dollar shoe company.
2. President of one of the most powerful banks in the city.
3. Member of the Board of Trustees of the Financial Institute, a firm of the utmost prestige and power in the community.
4. Director of the Security Trust Company, another powerful financial institution.
5. Director of the Yankee City Gas and Electric Company.

He was involved in a large number of civic enterprises and was a member of many civic institutions. He was

6. Director and one of the founders of the city's most important hospital.

7. Director of the public library.
8. Member of the school committee.
9. Trustee of the Revere Free School.
10. President of the City Improvement Society.

He also took an important part in politics. He was

11. Chairman of the Republican City Committee.
12. Member of the City Council.
13. Delegate to the National Republican Convention.
14. Mayor of the city.

He was also prominent in church and religious affairs. He was

15. President of the Yankee County Unitarian Club.
16. President of the Yankee County Unitarian Conference.

He was a leader in fraternal affairs and was

17. Past Master of St. John's Lodge.
18. Member of several important fraternal orders.

He was an active member of some of the most exclusive clubs of the city including

19. The Drama Club.
20. The Thursday Night Club.
21. The Friday Evening Club.
22. The February Club.
23. The Revere Club.
24. The Country Club.

The evidence demonstrates that in all these organizations he was active and powerful. This brief survey of some of his participation in the community demonstrates that his activities ramified throughout the city and that much of the life of the city was centered in him. It also demonstrates that he accepted responsibility for the larger affairs of the community and helped integrate its activities, for he provided responsible leadership for the whole life of the community. "He was a man you could depend on."

Very much the same could be said about his two successors. They, too, were responsible elders of the city. They not only provided jobs and wages through their factories, but they were citizens of the town and men who felt obligated to it. Their membership in local institutions compares very favorably with that of their predecessor.

In the days before big-city capitalism took control, the local enterpriser was financed by Yankee City banks. These banks and other investment houses possessed more autonomy and prestige then than they do now. In the development of the local shoe industry, local financiers played important and necessary roles and, at least part of the time, were silent partners in the business. Much of the wealth they derived from their investments was reinvested in Yankee City. The money was put into new enterprises, their own living, or civic activities. Their white Georgian houses on Hill Street, whose gardens bordered those of the manufacturers, were majestic symbols of their power and prestige and forever reminded and often reassured everyone of the visible presence of these powerful and protecting men in Yankee City.

The Yankee City financiers, too, were men of responsibility, dominated by sentiments of local pride. They did well for themselves, but they also did well for the city. Perhaps the price was high, but the product bought by the rest of the community was substantial and of high quality. Their philanthropies, combined with their power and leadership, contributed enormously to the city's development and provided a firm foundation for the larger civic life of the community. Parks, libraries, hospitals, societies to help the unfortunate and aged, foundations to send young men to college, endowments of schools, churches, and many other worthy civic enterprises were granted and maintained by the money and leadership of the local financiers and manager owners.

The essential point to remember for these leaders of industry and finance is that they were subject to local control (1) because they were dominated by local sentiments which motivated them "to take care of their own people," and (2) they were under the powerful influence of the numerous organizations to which they belonged and of their personal contacts with local citizens, which directly related them to influence from every part of the city.

The advent of big-city capitalism shattered this closely woven network of personal relations, loyalties, and obligations. Yankee City shoe factories are no longer owned exclusively by local citizens. More and more of them have been absorbed by larger enterprises whose executive offices are in New York City. At the time of our study, the largest shoe factory in Yankee City was owned by a company which operated several other factories in New England and which also owned the nationwide *ABC* chain of retail shoe stores, all of which were controlled from a central office in New York. Even some of the smaller Yankee City shoe factories, although still locally owned and managed, sold most of their shoes to chain-store organizations.

Yankee City has become a pin point upon the map of industrial empire for these large investment houses. The flow of wealth from Yankee City's banks and factories, once a great local arterial system giving life and strength to the town, now has shrunk to an infinitesimal part of big-city, world-wide capitalism and is of no vital significance in the life of this great system.

The extent of this change may be seen from the following account of the finances of the *ABC* company, which appeared in a June 1945 issue of a large New York newspaper:

> A group headed by Oppenheimer and Co. and Brandeis and Son, and including the Stultz Co., has concluded an agreement for purchase of the majority of Lion Shoe Corp. stock, it was announced today.
>
> Lion Shoe will be merged into its wholly owned retail subsidiary,

the *ABC* Shoe Corp., with subsequent public issue of securities of the latter company.

Abraham Cohen, associated with the companies in an executive capacity for more than 20 years, will be elected president and general manager. Frederick Stultz, president of the Stultz Co., will be made chairman of the board.

The *ABC* Shoe Corp. owns a number of factories equipped to manufacture 20,000 pairs of shoes daily and operates a chain of 110 stores in 56 cities.

Decisions on these high levels of national and international finance are being made without regard for the needs and vital interests of Yankee City. The old ties between top management and the community have completely broken down.

As the vertical hierarchy of the factory system extended to executive offices in New York, even the local factory managers came to be, for the most part, "outsiders" and members of ethnic minorities. They had their factories in the town and some of them drove down to work in the morning and left at night. The workers knew or felt that the forces that controlled local men would not control these outsiders. The vast network of relations and memberships that made the former owners local leaders, as well as local manufacturers, had been reduced to a purely economic one of employer and employee. It was that and nothing more. It is small wonder that the workers during this strike "gave the horse laugh to the managers when they talked about being good fellows."

At the time of the strike the few local men who were managers, although born and reared in Yankee City, were little more than the factory managers for big-city capitalists, for they occupied inferior positions in this vastly extended vertical structure. They were not in a position to take leadership. They were not in a position of great power where they were free to make the decisions that always characterized the lives of the owners of the previous period.

Each of these local men felt what had happened very deeply and some of them were explicit enough about it to say so. We knew some of them well. They were not the weak or unscrupulous men that their opponents made them out to be. Personally, they were men of good reputations in the business world. Some of them had been trained by their own fathers to be community leaders but their place in the new socioeconomic structure of Yankee City prevented them from playing this role and each in his own way contributed directly to the defeat of the managerial group. Part of their ineptness was due to their inability to measure up in their own minds to the great men of the past. This was a dead past, glorious and safe, when men knew themselves to be free men and Yankee City was "the hub of the universe." This whole period was symbolized in the memories of the workers and management by the names and reputations of the former owners. The lives of these men epitomized the period for all those who remembered. They symbolized the longing of everyone to return to those days when it was possible for one of them, with all his power and prestige, to stop and gently chide Sam Taylor, the cutter, for not calling him by his first name, and he and Sam could talk about "the trouble in the cutting room." Power was under control and security was present then; manager and worker were part of a self-contained system in which each knew his part in the total system.

In these days of big-city capitalism, when Yankee City had lost control of its own destinies, few workers would go up to the "big boss" to tell him "what's wrong in the cutting room," and those who did were not considered the respected friends of the workers but "stool pigeons who were getting theirs from management."

During the strike the local men cut poor figures as fighters for management's side. Two of them openly lined up with the strikers. Local sentiment and the feeling against "the foreigners" was too much for them. They materially contributed to the workers' victory.

One of them damaged the cause of management when he tried to fight the head of the union during a peace conference. Everyone said he blustered and acted badly when he used such tactics. He was under the control of higher management and occupied an inferior managerial position where he had little freedom to assume command and take leadership. Yet he had learned from "one of the grand old men" of the last period, when he worked for him, how his kind of man should act and he knew that an owner and manager should assume control. It seems a reasonable hypothesis that the conflict between his beliefs on how a manager should act and what he was permitted to do by his status greatly contributed to causing his unfortunate act, an act which materially aided the union. He tried to take command in a situation where it was impossible to do so, and instead of commanding he could only "bluster."

His antagonist, on the other hand, was "top manager" of the union. He did have power and he could make decisions. His beliefs about what should be done and his status were commensurate and he used them to the greatest effect for the cause of the union.

All these local men knew somehow they were not the men their "fathers" were and these dead men, symbolizing the glorious past, overawed and helped defeat them. While the men of yesterday are dead, "their souls go marching on" in the memories of the living. They have become collective symbols of that lost age when the prestige and power of local financiers and local producers "took care of our own people." These symbols were powerful influences upon the sentiments of workers as well as managers during the strike crisis. Sapping the confidence of the local managers, they gave strength to the strikers who dramatized their cause in terms of a struggle of Yankee City against big-city capitalism.

From this analysis of today's and yesterday's owners several important propositions can be offered that contribute to our understanding of the strike. The vertical extension of the corporate structure of the shoe-manufacturing enterprises had pushed the top of the hierarchy into the great metropolises and, in so doing, had brought in outsiders who were foreigners in culture, had no local prestige, and were lacking in understanding and feeling for the local workers and the town itself. This extension of the industrial hierarchy reduced the local men to inferior positions in the hierarchy, where they were incapable of making decisions and could not initiate actions that would give them the power of leadership for the workers and for the rest of the town.

The local managers, reduced to inferior statuses in the industrial hierarchy, also occupied lower social class ranking in the community than their predecessors. This greatly reduced their strength as leaders who could form community opinion in times of crisis when the position of management was threatened. They could no longer lead the workers or the community. Because of this inferior position of the managers, those men in the community who would once have been their natural allies and who enjoyed top social class position were now above them and shared none of their interests, were hostile to them and friendly to the workers.

In "the good old days," the people of Yankee City felt that they all shared in a common way of life, in which business and industry was closely integrated into the community. This way of life had its frictions and conflicts, but it provided all the people with a set of common symbols to guide their behavior, and it also provided effective leadership from the top of the social order. Furthermore, these personal ties made it possible for workers to redress their grievances through going right up to members of management.

When New York financiers assumed control of the industrial hierarchy, the social and civic leaders of Yankee City were no longer active in local management. The management of industry was no longer directly tied in with the wider life of the community. This split between management and the community made it possible to mobilize the workers into an organization to fight management.

In the same period, the solidarity of the workers was strengthened by the breakup of the old skill hierarchy. No longer could the workers start at the bottom as apprentices and progress upward step by step as they grew older and acquired the skills and learned the way of life of the skilled craftsman. This age-graded skill hierarchy served to differentiate the workers from one another and to provide increasing security, prestige, and freedom with every step up from the bottom of the ladder. Now the rewards and satisfactions of this way of life are gone forever. Mechanization of the shoe industry has leveled the skills so that there is little room for such differentiation. When workers become interchangeable cogs in a machine, they come to feel that the only security for the individual lies in belonging to an organization of fellow workers.

What happened in Yankee City appears to have been happening throughout the country. With advances in technology and the development of big-city capitalism, the social distance between workers and management has been increasing, and we seem to be witnessing the emergence of an industrial working class.

The status of the worker has steadily deteriorated, and he has lost his chance to work his way up the craft ladder onto higher rungs of skill or into management. He has also lost the personal ties with management that might enable him to settle his grievances on an individual basis. Since the workers are now sufficiently alike to have had common experiences and anxieties, it is no longer difficult for the industrial union to organize them into a group for collective bargaining. Besides exerting economic pressure, the union gives the workers a new sense of strength and becomes a powerful weapon to force management to recognize their worth as men. To compensate for their loss of status and for their anxieties in a changing industrial civilization, workers have been trying to find status and security in union organization.

American industry has been undergoing far-reaching changes in technology and human relations. It is only through an understanding of the nature of these changes in our way of life that it is possible to explain the labor strife that spreads through the cities and towns of America.

PART 3

AN APPROACH TO THE
THEORY OF MANAGEMENT

5

REFLECTIONS ON THE
THEORY OF MANAGEMENT

In this chapter we draw together a number of inferences derived from the articles in this book. In doing so, we frame an introduction to the theory of management.

The purpose of this section is to develop the concept of management and organization which is implied in the first two parts of this book. Following are the basic ideas that contribute to a theory of management. The presentation is preliminary; and additional research effort, focused on the concepts presented, is still needed.

Before discussing the broader theory of management, we should first discuss the concept of organization upon which it is based.

ORGANIZATION AND MANAGEMENT

Each organization is a dynamic cooperative system. It may be viewed as a model of bureaucracy, as a social movement, or in numerous other ways. Each of these approaches provides useful insights, but each is incomplete. An organization is a system of relationships: parts related to the whole, and parts related to one another. It is also the interaction of these forces and parts. Probably most important, the actions and interactions that constitute organization have a *continuity in time*. Thus, any attempt to understand a specific organization immediately broadens into a study of its history and environment. The organization cannot be isolated from the broader society of which it is a part.

Within this approach, management is an organ (similar to the heart, lungs, or other organs found in human anatomy) functioning in the total system. Its activities are organization, direction, and control. An organization cannot live without management, and management is identified by the functions it performs. However, the manner in which management carries out its functions is, to a considerable degree, determined by the *unique character* of the organization in which it is functioning. Thus, a theory of management which has general applicability must clearly accommodate the differential aspects of organizations.

PARTS VERSUS THE WHOLE

The study of organizations *should deal with functioning wholes*. However, the complexity of organizations poses special problems, so that we are caught in the "parts-versus-the-whole" dilemma. To study the parts in isolation fails to give knowledge of the whole; and knowledge of specific techniques by themselves will not necessarily lead to effective utilization. What is absolutely essential is the ability to relate techniques to a specific functioning organization.

In a sense, students of management are like the blind men in the old Buddhist parable. A rajah brought these men into his courtyard and put in their midst an elephant. He asked each of the men to describe the animal. One blind man felt a leg, another an ear, another a tusk, another the trunk, and so forth. When asked to describe the animal, one man said it was like a tree trunk, another that it was a winnowing fan, another that it was like a stone, and another that it was similar to a snake. Each attempted to describe the whole elephant as the part which he had personally touched. None of them described the elephant accurately. By dealing with the parts in isolation, they failed to comprehend the whole. They failed to see the interrelationship of the parts, and hence could not understand the elephant as a functioning organism. Similarly, students find it easier to concentrate on individual aspects of organizations and thus often fail to comprehend an organization as a functioning entity.

ORGANIZATION CHARACTER

The dilemma stated above led me to the concept of "organization character" as a methodological tool for developing a general theory of management. In general, the conceptual scheme employed is as follows:

There is both an integral and a differential aspect to organization and management. The integral or common aspect involves what we have covered in Part I of this book. Common aspects of organizations may be summarized as follows:

1. An organization is a formal grouping of people to attain certain established goals or purposes.

2. The mechanistic aspects of organizations include division of labor, specialization, a formal hierarchy, rules and regulations (see Weber's model of bureaucracy, pp. 33–38).

3. Formal organization inevitably leads to informal organization. Individuals bring their whole selves to the organization and, to satisfy their needs as individuals, establish informal organizations; these organizations later become institutionalized. (See the selections by Selznick, Roy, Dalton.)

4. Within any organization managers perform the functions of organization, direction, and control.

5. Common to all organizations are the processes of decision making, leadership, communication, authority, influence, change, and delegation.

6. Every relatively permanent organization develops a body of doctrines and techniques and has an internal life of its own, which tends toward a closed system. The organization develops needs of its own (the need for continuity in policy and leadership; the need to maintain continuous consent of the individuals who make up the organization as a whole); these needs are separate and distinct from the organization's overall goals.

7. An organization is dynamic rather than static. Hence, its present is always related to its past; and its immediate environment is related to the broader environment of which it is a part.

Each relatively permanent organization is, in a sense, unique. It has its own character or distinctive competence and way of doing things. In short, a type of differential analysis should be applied to organizations. The differential analysis of organizations has been illustrated by research reports of different industries. Thus, from the readings in Part Two we can tentatively identify several "species" of organizations: hospital administration, banking, research and development, adult education, and restaurant administration:

1. Effective management involves adjustment to local forces—i.e., to *the character of the specific organization*—because managers deal with specific organizations, established traditions, and given personnel. To a large degree, then, the successful manager adapts his practices and procedures to fit the situation.

2. *Organization character* is a concept similar to that of individual character as used by psychologists. Although a somewhat fuzzy concept, it is a useful tool for analysis and action. Almost all practical men of affairs are either implicitly or explicitly aware of organization character, for it is manifested as distinctive competence in achieving goals, a style in carrying out functions, commonly held values of members, and a body of tra-

ditions. Other aspects of organization character are seen in the types of persons who fit into the organization, the kind of leadership that is dominant, the attitudes of the members, and the "public image" presented by advertising and public relations.

Some aspects of organization character are consciously and explicitly planned; others are intuitively arrived at and unplanned. Moreover, organization character is usually "felt" rather than scientifically measured: "For a long time executives have sensed that organizations tend to select and fashion a certain type, and while they cannot put their finger on it, they know that, say, a Union Carbide man is somehow different from a W. R. Grace man."[1] Similarly, the selections in Part Two alert us to differences in the "right type" of employee and value systems of employees in different organizations. (For example, McMurry, pp. 205–219, points out that the "right type" of banking employee is commonly a passive, dependent individual. Shepard, pp. 245–252, indicates that scientific personnel in research and development organizations are more interested in professional recognition than in supervisory approval, identify with the professions rather than the firm, and manifest other distinctive values.)

3. Some of the major processes by which an organization's character develops can be identified:

(a)   One fundamental aspect of organization character is the organization's *aims and purposes*. These purposes, or sets of goals, constitute the "charter" of the organization.[2] The charter is strategic in the development of organization character, for it influences the behavior of the managers in the organization as well as the reaction of the broader society to the specific enterprise. Thus, in the banking industry the charter leads to a particular public image: banks represent status, stability, and security. As a result, individuals who put a high premium on these values are attracted to banking. Moreover, the leadership patterns in an organization as well as the technical skills required of the leaders are defined by the charter. For example, some organizations require leadership with a heavy sales orientation, and such organizations tend to get the kind of leader they need.

(b)   Another aspect of organization character is its particular type of *leadership*. The leadership casts its shadow by implicitly or explicitly clarifying and defining the value system in the organization. The leadership, in a position of formal authority, approves the major decisions. If they are good decisions, they usually are in tune with the organization (perpetuating the integrity of the organization). *In fact, it is in the decision-making process that one finds a central core of organization character.* And, as in the

[1] William H. Whyte, Jr., *The Organization Man* (New York: Doubleday, Anchor Books edition, 1957), p. 138.

[2] The term "charter" was used by the eminent anthropologist Bronislaw Malinowski in *The Scientific Theory of Culture* (New York: Galaxy Books, 1960). Malinowski defines the charter as "the idea of the institution as entertained by its members and defined by the community" (p. 42).

development of human character, organization character is influenced by a system of feedback, where decisions and actions having favorable consequences become built into the system. Policies, rules, and regulations serve to perpetuate them. As a result, the organization becomes unified and homogeneous.

(c) *The selection process* contributes to organization character by screening out those individuals who do not appear to "fit in." If a "square peg" does successfully get through the screening process, he is soon discovered in day-to-day relations. He is discouraged from staying, or encouraged to change his values so that they are in closer conformity with those generally held by the members of the organization.[3]

(d) Indoctrination, training, and education as carried out within organizations provide still additional evidence that there is a tendency to build a common identity with the organization and a system of generalized responses.

In summary, we see that organization character is dynamic and evolving. However, once formed, it tends to persevere. It resists change because leadership perpetuates itself through formal policies and regulations, and because new members are selected on the basis of how well they "fit in." Moreover, deviant personalities generally leave or are forced out. Despite this tendency toward rigidity, however, environmental forces do compel changes; and clinical analysis of the history of organizations clearly indicates the process of evolving character. Usually, the change is forced upon the organization from outside (e.g., by competition, technology, unions). But it may be generated internally (e.g., by a rapid rate of growth or a change in leadership). From our point of view, the important thing is that each organization does develop a distinctive flavor, competence, style, type of employee, and value system.

Approach for Diagnosis of Organization Character

In diagnosing the evolving character of a specific organization, we proceed on three basic propositions regarding the study of organizations.

1. Organizations are creatures of the broader environment; hence, their character is influenced by environmental features such as climate, culture, politics, and the economic organization of society. The organization exists by cooperating with this broader environment. The environment provides resources such as tools, capital, land, labor, fuel. It has established rules and customs of trade, as well as legal, religious, and moral customs, which influence specialization, delegation, authority, communication, and incentives. In short, to understand any specific organization, one must relate its activities to its environment.

2. An organization's character is related to its own distinctive history, tradition, rules, ethics, status systems, and knowledge. Thus, to

---

[3] Although this process seldom works with precision, the readings in this book substantiate this tendency (see Dalton, Pfiffner and Sherwood, Gross).

understand an organization, we need to become acquainted with the rules and customs that coordinate the activities of its members.

3. To understand a specific organization, we need to know its history (to study it institutionally); in addition, we have to analyze its strategic aspects: size, leadership, technology, labor market, "charter." An analysis of each such aspect assumes significance and is meaningful only if we relate it to that organization's history, social setting, and each of the other important aspects. What we have to do is relate each of the significant dimensions of the organization to each other and to the organization as a whole.

These three key concepts—(1) the relationship of an organization to the broader environment, (2) the tendency for each organization to have a continuity in time and to develop its own character, and (3) the systematic analysis of strategic factors to relate them to each other, to the organization's environment, and to the emerging totality (i.e., that organization's character)—are the essentials of a general theory of management. Such analysis, coupled with a broad knowledge of general managerial processes, can give sound guidance to those who manage.

Strategic Factors in Diagnosing Organization Character

As pointed out above, we are caught in the parts-versus-whole dilemma. Organizations are too complex to be studied as totalities. Yet, to study only their specific parts is unsatisfactory; for if we are really to understand the parts, we must see them in relation to the whole of which they are part, and in relation to one another.

One compromise that is a useful way of mitigating this dilemma is to study the strategic factors (that is, those that are of major importance in determining or revealing organization character). For example, we might analyze the strategic factor *style of supervision* as an independent variable, such as was done by Lewin and his associates.[4] We would then discover certain patterns associated with different styles: for example, under autocratic supervision, a tendency for subordinates to manifest low morale, repressed hostility, increased tension, and accident proneness. Similarly, we could define settings in which specific leadership styles are most effective; for example, autocratic leadership tends to fit certain situations where specialized technical knowledge is essential to the carrying out of a task.

Thus, our procedure is to consider strategic factors as independent variables, and then to reason through the impact that each may have if other aspects of the organization are held constant. Thus, we do study the individual parts of an organization—but in such a manner that we also gain an awareness of the important dimensions of the whole.

The procedure is to examine strategic parts one at a time. For each part, we make the following assumptions:

1. There is an explanation for the condition or dimension of that part as it exists in the organization; that is, we assume causality. Every as-

---

[4] Ronald O. Lippett, "An Experimental Study of the Effect of Democratic and Authoritarian Group Atmospheres," *University of Iowa Studies in Child Welfare*, 16, No. 3 (1940), 43–195.

pect of an organization can be explained and its purpose or *raison d'être* discovered—provided we have adequate knowledge.

2. There exists a functional relationship between each strategic factor and various dimensions of the organization; consequently, given a strategic factor with specified dimensions, we can derive tentative but reasonably sound hypotheses about other dimensions of that organization.

3. The inferences drawn from an analysis of any one specific strategic factor may be reinforced or contradicted by analysis of other strategic factors. Where constellations of reinforcing or consistent inferences are drawn, one may tentatively assume that the inference is sound.

4. By analyzing a number of strategic factors and noting reinforcing as well as contradictory inferences, one can develop a perspective of the organization as a whole.

The readings in Part Two of this book serve to illustrate dimensions of some of the strategic factors found in organizations and their environments. Edith Lentz points out that the social role of an organization, as well as the organization's place in the cultural environment, influences administration. Similarly, McMurry suggests the importance of these factors in determining the character of banks. And close analysis of the readings in Part Two of the collection suggests a number of other strategic factors. Many of these factors, external to the organization, are aspects of the broader environment—e.g., social role of the institution, economics of raw-material markets, economics of consumer's markets. Some of the factors are internal to the organization—e.g., layout, technology used, formal organization structure. However, these internal and external forces are closely related; moreover, external forces tend to dominate and shape many of the internal ones.

Probably the easiest way to bring together the concepts presented here is to give a short illustration. First, we will list a number of facts about a company; then we will relate them to the manner in which that company is managed:

1. The company manufactures briefcases, wallets, and men's travel kits for toilet articles.
2. The business experiences large seasonal variations in demand for its products.
3. All of the company's products are made of leather.
4. The policy of the company is to compete on the basis of quality rather than price.
5. Raw materials used constitute approximately 38 per cent of manufacturing costs.
6. The demand for the products varies widely from season to season on the bases of style factors such as colors, shapes, decorative stitching.
7. The company has only one manufacturing plant, and for its industry it does a volume business.

From facts such as these, we can draw a number of inferences about the management of the firm: the organization is (or should be) sales oriented; it has difficulty maintaining a steady flow of production; it doesn't use many mass-production techniques. The logic underlying these inferences would run as follows: This company manufactures leather products. Raw-material costs are a significant part of total cost. Because the company produces a "quality" line, and because each leather hide has to be selectively cut to get maximum utilization, it is unlikely that highly automated procedures are used. Furthermore, if the company is to be successful, it will have to have a strong sales organization: in a business such as this, with low fixed-capital requirements, it is easy for new producers to go into business; moreover, since there are few cost advantages to be gained by volume production, the key to a competitive advantage is aggressive sales and distribution.

The seasonal nature of the business, the variations in styles, and the high cost of raw materials indicate problems in maintaining a stable work force in the manufacturing plant, although ways of dealing with this problem (through subcontracting work or development of compensatory lines) may be utilized.

Several additional facts—(a) that the management of the firm is profit motivated and doesn't identify closely with its labor force; (b) that the manufacturing facilities are located in a neighborhood with a large reservoir of marginal labor; (c) that workers on the payroll ninety days or more become permanent employees and have collective-bargaining rights to recall after layoff, as well as to pensions, vacation pay, and other fringe benefits—all lead to the inference that management would tend to dilute job skills, discourage workers from becoming permanent employees, and otherwise keep labor costs low by varying the size of the labor force to meet seasonal needs. One way to cope with wide seasonal variations in a manufacturing business is to simplify jobs and dilute skill requirements, so that a marginal worker may be brought up to a peak performance in a short period of time. The fact that this company located its plant in a labor market where many unskilled people from minority groups are available would reinforce this inference.

The soundness of the inference that the company tries to discourage workers from becoming permanent employees would be determined by analyzing other aspects of the organization. Supporting evidence would be a tendency to minimize personnel service activities—personnel picnics, bowling teams, etc.—as well as designing jobs to discourage worker interaction.

In contrast, we might postulate that management wants the manufacturing plant to be a "big happy family." If this were so, jobs would probably be set up to encourage interaction among employees, personnel techniques would be used to increase the camaraderie in the organization, and seasonal variations in production would be met by varying the hours of work, and/or calling back to work people who have left the organization for good reasons (such as pregnancy or family responsibilities). Moreover, the manufacturing plant would probably be located near a stable labor market.

The above illustrates the type of analysis suggested for building a theory of management. At this stage in our knowledge of management, we are quite limited. We lack a formalized body of knowledge of the various strategic factors and the implications to the total organization of each variation in a strategic factor. Thus, there are a number of tasks to be done. First, we need a systematic analysis of each strategic factor. Here we need to ask what kinds of variations in that factor may be encountered. Second, we need to build a body of illustrative materials demonstrating the manner in which the impact of different strategic factors gives character to the organization as a whole.

The problems of building such an analytical structure are great. We can illustrate the approach by taking the factor of formal organization structure (specialized departments and their relationships) and examining its dimensions and its effect on the total organization.

How do formal structures vary? We can perceive variations in terms of:

1. Number of interdependent units established within the total organization.
2. Number of levels of formal authority designated in the hierarchy.
3. Size of each formally designated unit within the organization.
4. Kind of authority formally delegated to the various units.
5. Kind of work done by the formally designated units.
6. Location of work.
7. Degree of autonomy granted to each unit.

There is reason to believe that the *span of control* of supervisors (the number of subordinates reporting to one supervisor) influences the nature of supervision, the types of subordinates who "fit in," morale, and efficiency. Where a supervisor has only a few subordinates, and where his superior also has relatively few men reporting to him, one is apt to find close supervision. Such a structure encourages subordinates to adhere closely to established rules and regulations. This and related tendencies are reported in the studies conducted by Sears, Roebuck and Company. Sears studied its class-B retail stores and, on the basis of a thorough analysis, concluded that formal organization structure was a significant factor in determining the character of a store.[5] They found that retail stores with many layers of authority (numerous levels of supervision) were more rigid, less adaptive, and less satisfactory to employees than retail stores of comparable size but with few levels of supervision. These "flat" organizations tended to keep formal controls at a minimum, whereas in the organizations with many levels of supervision the employees felt restricted, controlled, and policed. The "flat" organizations exhibited greater creativity and flexibility and were more profitable. Moreover, Sears found that deep hierarchical organizations tended to weed out employees with self-reliance and initiative.[6]

[5] The Sears studies isolate the impact of a flat organization structure with an extended span of control. It should be recognized, however, that retail selling is a separate species of organization, and Sears is a special case in this species. It is unlikely that a flat organization would be more efficient in an organization where there is a close interdependency between departments, or where morale is less directly related to profitability, such as in mail-order sales.

[6] James C. Worthy, "Factors Influencing Employee Morale," *Harvard Business Review*, 28, No. 1 (January 1950), 61–73. See also "Democratic Principles in Business

Another dimension of formal structure is seen in the relations between line and staff units. As our reading by Melville Dalton (pp. 144–156) points out, friction may develop between the line and the staff; and this apparently stems from forces inherent in such a structure.[7]

Similarly, where interdependent departments come under different supervisors, one often encounters frictions between those departments.[8]

Similarly, the specific location of work enters into the broad character of organizations. For example, if a department is placed near the central headquarters of a firm, that department's functions very probably carry status or are otherwise considered important within the total system.

Where work is divided between a central headquarters and regional units, one encounters what appear to be common patterns in the problems of managing. For example, the sub-unit tends to develop a character all its own and tries to preserve its own integrity. The central office, feeling a need to maintain formal control, specifies procedures and policies. The local unit, in turn, interprets these policies as it sees fit. Thus, suspicion frequently develops between the leadership in the central office and that in the local unit. One device used to remedy this problem is to have a local manager report directly to the top manager in his unit and also to a staff officer at central headquarters. However, the manager who must report to two bosses is in the precarious position of violating the confidence of one of his superiors. Of course, the outcome of such an organization structure is intimately tied to the interpersonal relations of the men involved. Yet, the fact is that the basic nature of the structure releases tendencies toward such a conflict.

The location of a supervisor's work station relative to his subordinates also relates to the character of the organization. For example, if the supervisor's work station automatically gives him a full view of his subordinates, an accepted part of the work climate is to have the boss make visual inspections of what is going on. However, if the boss's office is located in an isolated corner or at a distance from the workers he supervises, then workers may interpret inspection trips of the boss as "snoopervising."

Before leaving this illustration, it is important to point to the fundamental problem encountered in this type of analysis; namely, that our knowledge is incomplete, so that we are dealing with tendencies or trends rather than precise facts. Hence, only as we note reinforcing tendencies released by other strategic factors should we give weight to what we have inferred.

Numerous other "strategic" factors should be considered in any given situation. The following are some of the more commonly en-

---

Management," address given at the Industrial Management Institute, Lake Forest College, May 27, 1948; and "Organizational Structure and Employee Morale," *American Sociological Review*, Vol. 15, No. 2 (April 1950), pp. 169–179.

[7] See also Douglas McGregor, "The Staff Function in Human Relations," *The Journal of Social Issues*, IV (Summer 1948), 5–22.

[8] Cf. F. J. Jasinski, "Foremen Relations outside the Work Group," *Personnel*, 33 (September 1956), 130–136; C. R. Walker et al., *The Foreman on the Assembly Line* (Cambridge, Mass.: Harvard University Press, 1956).

countered ones. However, the significance of any one factor is a function of the field in which it occurs; thus, what is considered "strategic" in one setting may not be so in another.

Strategic Factors

1. Charter
2. Location
3. Physical facilities
4. Size
5. Ownership and control
6. Labor force
7. History of organization—age, rate of growth, changes in character
8. Competing organizations
9. Leadership
10. Labor market
11. Economics of markets for supplies
12. Public image of the organization—its social role or place in the cultural environment
13. Technology[9]
14. Formal organization structure
15. Status systems
16. Cliques and interpersonal interactions
17. Communications systems
18. Finances
19. Formal systems of controls
20. Supervisors
21. Job design
22. Strategic policies

ORGANIZATION HEALTH

Implicit in this discussion is a concept or point of view toward organizations that needs to be made explicit; namely, that we are viewing organizations from the point of view of executives (those who manage). Our criterion of organizational effectiveness is survival. We view organizations as dynamic cooperative systems. Their survival involves change and adaptation, as well as economic performance and the distribution of incentives to members.

The presentation is organized to help the executive understand the dimensions of his job in contributing to organizational survival. As mentioned elsewhere, we hold that the manager should have awareness of how

[9] One of the possible criticisms of this volume is that it doesn't give adequate attention to computers and other aspects of the automation revolution. In the framework presented here, computers are an aspect of technology. There is no doubt that they are having a far-reaching effect upon management. Thus, "computerization" of an organization changes the knowledge and skills requirements of managerial jobs, reduces the number of middle-management jobs (i.e. flattens the organization structure), allows new variations in organization structure, and encourages more centralized control.

organizations in general function, as well as an understanding of the character of his specific organization. In short, the organization is seen as a *system* with needs for its own security, stability, and continuity. Managers perform the functions of organizing, directing, and controlling within the system.

The criteria for judging managers (i.e. organizational health or effectiveness) are not measures such as performance, morale, lack of conflict, or profit per se. These are important but insufficient criteria. Rather, we have to evaluate managers in terms of the total dynamic system represented by the organization. In this framework, it is more important to judge managerial effectiveness upon the basis of how the organization handles its problems (i.e., adapts and changes to pressures), rather than whether or not it has problems.

CONCLUSION

What is present here is a rudimentary theory of management. It is a theory in the sense that it is a conceptualization that provides a way of ordering and understanding the multitude of facts related to managerial actions. The theory is not new or startling. A similar approach is now used in all sciences dealing with complex organisms: abandonment of the traditional mechanistic or atomistic approach and, in its place, emphasis on the organism as a whole. This orientation is clearly discernible in Gestalt psychology, field theory in physics, systems theory, and organismic theories of personality.

This approach is not without weaknesses. Perhaps a major problem inherent in it is that one must accept a concept of relativity that is tremendously complex and, when followed through logically, leaves one with little firm ground upon which to stand. Absolutes vanish, and events and happenings have to be explained in relation to other aspects of the situation. With respect to this, Chester I. Barnard's comment is worth noting:

> It seems to me quite in order to cease encouraging the expectation that human behavior in society can be anything less than the most complex study to which our minds may be applied. However desirable clarity and simplicity of statement, it is not desirable to underestimate either the difficulties of observation and experiment or those of constructing hypotheses that may prove helpful.[10]

[10] Chester I. Barnard, *The Functions of the Executive* (Cambridge, Mass.: Harvard University Press, 1938), pp. xii–xiii.

INDEX